Rick Steves'

VENICE

Rick Steves & Gene Openshaw

2011

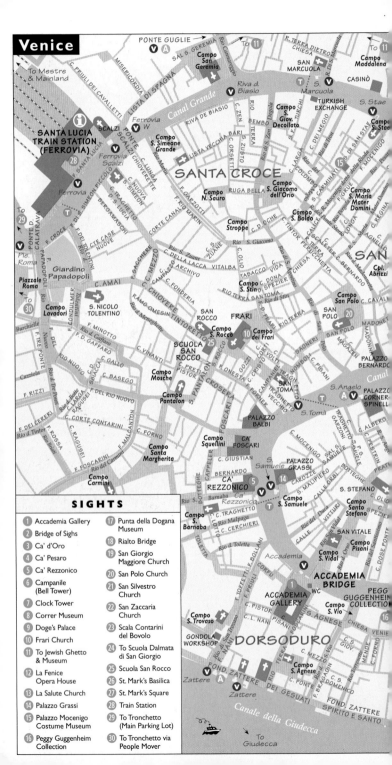

Venice

PONTE GUGLIE

To Mestre & Mainland

SANTA LUCIA TRAIN STATION (FERROVIA)

Canal Grande

SAN MARCUOLA

TURKISH EXCHANGE

SANTA CROCE

SAN

Piazzale Roma

Giardino Papadopoli

S. NICOLO TOLENTINO

FRARI

SCUOLA SAN ROCCO

SAN POLO

PALAZZO BERNARDO

Campo Santa Margherita

CA' FOSCARI

PALAZZO GRASSI

CA' REZZONICO

Campo Santo Stefano

ACCADEMIA BRIDGE

PEGGY GUGGENHEIM COLLECTION

ACCADEMIA GALLERY

DORSODURO

Zattere

Canale della Giudecca

To Giudecca

SIGHTS

1. Accademia Gallery
2. Bridge of Sighs
3. Ca' d'Oro
4. Ca' Pesaro
5. Ca' Rezzonico
6. Campanile (Bell Tower)
7. Clock Tower
8. Correr Museum
9. Doge's Palace
10. Frari Church
11. To Jewish Ghetto & Museum
12. La Fenice Opera House
13. La Salute Church
14. Palazzo Grassi
15. Palazzo Mocenigo Costume Museum
16. Peggy Guggenheim Collection
17. Punta della Dogana Museum
18. Rialto Bridge
19. San Giorgio Maggiore Church
20. San Polo Church
21. San Silvestro Church
22. San Zaccaria Church
23. Scala Contarini del Bovolo
24. To Scuola Dalmata di San Giorgio
25. Scuola San Rocco
26. St. Mark's Basilica
27. St. Mark's Square
28. Train Station
29. To Tronchetto (Main Parking Lot)
30. To Tronchetto via People Mover

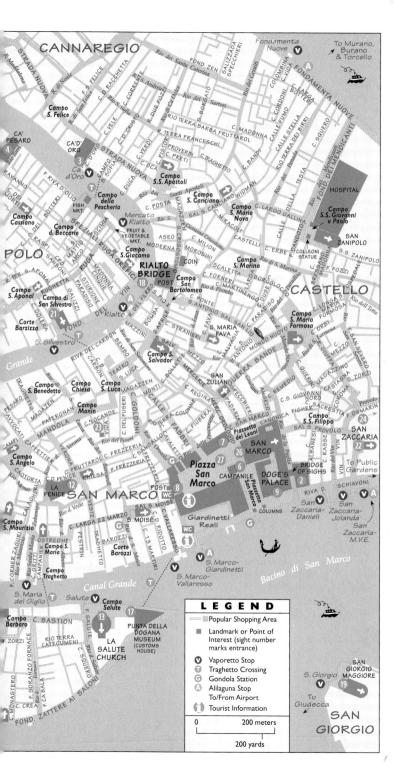

Rick Steves' ®

VENICE

2011

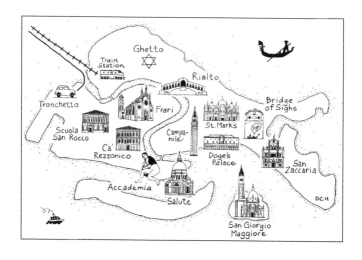

AVALON
TRAVEL

CONTENTS

Venice Overview

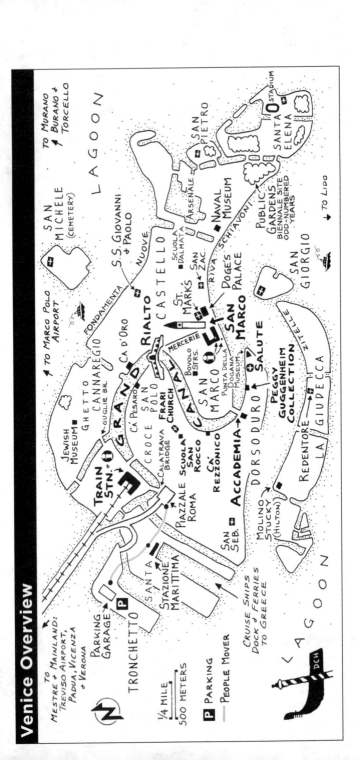

INTRODUCTION

Engineers love Venice—a completely man-made environment rising from the sea, with no visible means of support. Romantics revel in its atmosphere of elegant decay, seeing the peeling plaster and seaweed-covered stairs as a metaphor for beauty in decline. And first-time visitors are often stirred deeply, awaking from their ordinary lives to a fantasy world unlike anything they've ever seen before.

Those are strong reactions, considering that Venice today, frankly, can also be an overcrowded, prepackaged, tacky tourist trap. But Venice is unique. Built on a hundred islands with wealth from trade with the East, its exotic-looking palaces are laced together by sun-speckled canals. The car-free streets suddenly make walkers feel big, important, and liberated.

By day, it's a city of museums and churches, packed with great art. Everything's within a half-hour walk. Cruise the canals on a vaporetto water bus. Climb towers for stunning seascape views. Shop for Venetian crafts (such as glass and lace), high fashions, or tacky souvenirs for your Uncle Eric. Linger over lunch, trying to crack a crustacean with weird legs and antennae. Sip a *spritz* at a café on St. Mark's Square while the orchestra plays "New York, New York."

At night, when the hordes of day-trippers have gone, another Venice appears. Dance across a floodlit square. Glide in a gondola through quiet canals while music echoes across the water. Pretend it's Carnevale time, don a mask—or just a clean shirt—and become someone else for a night.

About This Book

Rick Steves' Venice 2011 is a personal tour guide in your pocket. Better yet, it's actually two tour guides in your pocket: The co-author of this book is Gene Openshaw. Since our first "Europe through the gutter" trip together as high school buddies in the 1970s, Gene and I have been exploring the wonders of the Old World. An inquisitive historian and lover of European culture, Gene wrote most of this book's self-guided museum tours and neighborhood walks. Together, Gene and I keep this book current (though for simplicity, from this point "we" will shed our respective egos and become "I").

In this book, you'll find the following chapters:

Orientation includes specifics on public transportation, helpful hints, local tour options, easy-to-read maps, and tourist information. The "Planning Your Time" section offers a suggested schedule for how to best use your limited time.

Sights in Venice describes the top attractions and includes cost, hours, location, and contact information.

The **Self-Guided Tours** lead you through Venice's most important sights, with tours of the Grand Canal, St. Mark's Square, St. Mark's Basilica, Doge's Palace, Correr Museum, Accademia, Frari Church, Scuola San Rocco, Ca' Rezzonico (Museum of 18th-Century Venice), Peggy Guggenheim Collection, La Salute Church, San Giorgio Maggiore, and the islands in Venice's lagoon (including San Michele, Murano, Burano, and Torcello).

The **Self-Guided Walks** take you through Venice's back streets. The walk from St. Mark's to Rialto follows a less touristy route between these two major landmarks than the one most tourists travel. The walk from Rialto to Frari Church (and its exquisite art) takes you through the bustling markets and by a mask-making shop. The walk from St. Mark's to San Zaccaria explores the area behind the basilica, featuring a historic church and a seldom-seen view of the famous Bridge of Sighs.

Sleeping in Venice describes my favorite hotels, from good-value deals to cushy splurges. I've focused on hotels conveniently located near St. Mark's Square, the Rialto Bridge, and the Accademia—all handy to the sights in this compact city.

Eating in Venice serves up a range of options, from inexpensive eateries to fancy restaurants.

Venice with Children includes my top recommendations for keeping your kids (and you) happy in Venice.

Shopping in Venice gives you tips for shopping painlessly and enjoyably, without letting it overwhelm your vacation or ruin your budget.

Nightlife in Venice is your guide to after-dark Venice, including gondola rides, concerts, theaters, pubs, and clubs.

Venice Connections lays the groundwork for your smooth arrival and departure, covering transportation by train, bus, car, plane, and cruise ship. It provides detailed information on Venice's

Key to This Book

Updates

This book is updated every year—but once you pin down Italy, it wiggles. For the latest, visit www.ricksteves.com/update. For a valuable list of reports and experiences—good and bad—from fellow travelers, check www.ricksteves.com/feedback.

Abbreviations and Times

I use the following symbols and abbreviations in this book:
Sights are rated:

▲▲▲	**Don't miss**
▲▲	**Try hard to see**
▲	**Worthwhile if you can make it**
No rating	**Worth knowing about**

When you see a ✪ in a sight listing, it means that the sight is covered in much more detail in one of the tour chapters.

Tourist information offices are abbreviated as **TI,** and bathrooms are **WC**s. To categorize accommodations, I use a **Sleep Code** (described on page 237).

Like Europe, this book uses the **24-hour clock.** It's the same through 12:00 noon, then keep going: 13:00, 14:00, and so on. For anything over 12, subtract 12 and add p.m. (14:00 is 2:00 p.m.).

When giving **opening times,** I include both peak season and off-season hours if they differ. So, if a museum is listed as "May-Oct daily 9:00-16:00," it should be open from 9 a.m. until 4 p.m. from the first day of May until the last day of October (but expect exceptions).

For **transit** or **tour departures,** I first list the frequency, then the duration. So, a train connection listed as "2/hour, 1.5 hours" departs twice each hour and the journey lasts an hour and a half.

two airports (Marco Polo and Treviso), train station (Santa Lucia), and cruise port (Stazione Marittima).

Day Trips include art-filled Padua and romantic Verona.

Venetian History fills you in on the background of this fascinating city.

The **appendix** is a traveler's tool kit, with telephone tips, useful phone numbers, the basics on transportation in Italy, recommended books and films, a festival list, a climate chart, a handy packing checklist, a hotel reservation form, and Italian survival phrases.

Browse through this book and choose your favorite sights. Then have a *buono* trip! Traveling like a temporary local, you'll get the absolute most out of every mile, minute, and euro. As you visit

Major Holidays and Weekends

Popular places are even busier on weekends...and inundated on three-day weekends. Holidays bring many businesses to a grinding halt. Plan ahead and reserve your accommodations and transportation well in advance.

In Venice, hotels get booked up for Carnevale (Feb 26–March 8 in 2011), Easter and Easter Monday (April 24–25 in 2011), St. Mark's Day (April 25), Labor Day (May 1), Feast of the Ascension Day (June 2 in 2011), Feast and Regatta of the Redeemer (July 16–17 in 2011), Historical Regatta (Sept 3–4 in 2011), All Saints' Day (Nov 1), Feast of Our Lady of Good Health (Nov 21), Christmas (Dec 25–26), New Year's, and on Fridays and Saturdays year-round.

For more information, check "Holidays and Festivals" in the appendix. A myriad of religious and neighborhood celebrations can catch you by surprise anywhere in Italy.

places I know and love, I'm happy you'll be meeting my favorite Venetians.

Planning

This section will help you get started on planning your trip—with advice on trip costs, when to go, and what you should know before you take off.

Travel Smart

Many people travel through Italy thinking it's a chaotic mess. They feel any attempt at efficient travel is futile. This is dead wrong—and expensive. Italy, which seems as orderly as spilled spaghetti, actually functions well. Only those who understand this and travel smart can enjoy Italy on a budget.

This book can save you lots of time and money. But to have an "A" trip, you need to be an "A" student. Read it all before your trip, noting holidays, specific advice on sights, and days when sights are closed. If you save St. Mark's Basilica for Sunday morning (when it's closed), you've missed the gondola. You can sweat in line at the Doge's Palace, or you can buy your San Marco Museum Plus Pass at the nearby Correr Museum and zip right through the palace turnstile. Day-tripping to Verona on Monday, when the major sights are closed, is bad news. A smart trip is a puzzle—a fun, doable, and worthwhile challenge.

Be sure to mix intense and relaxed periods in your itinerary. Every trip—and every traveler—needs at least a few slack days (for picnics, laundry, people-watching, and so on). Pace yourself.

Assume you will return.

As you travel, take advantage of the Internet and phones to make your trip run smoothly. Get online at Internet cafés or your hotel, and buy a phone card or carry a mobile phone. You can get tourist information, learn the latest on sights (special events, English tour schedule, etc.), book tickets and tours, make reservations, reconfirm hotels, research transportation connections, and keep in touch with your loved ones.

Enjoy the friendliness of the Venetian people. Connect with the culture. Set up your own quest for the best piazza, vaporetto ride, or gelato. Slow down and be open to unexpected experiences. Ask questions—most locals are eager to point you in their idea of the right direction. Keep a notepad in your pocket for organizing your thoughts. Wear your money belt, learn the currency, and figure out how to estimate prices in dollars. Those who expect to travel smart, do.

Trip Costs

Six components make up your trip costs: airfare, surface transportation, room and board, sightseeing/entertainment, shopping/miscellany, and gelato.

Airfare: A basic, round-trip US–to-Venice (or even cheaper, Milan) flight should cost $980–$1,600, depending on where you fly from and when (cheapest in winter). If your trip covers a wide area, consider saving time and money in Europe by flying "open jaw" (flying into one city and out of another—e.g., into Venice and out of Paris).

Surface Transportation: Venice's sights are within walking distance of each other, but vaporetto boat rides, while expensive ($8), are fun and save time. For a one-way trip between Venice's airport and the city, allow about $4 by bus, $16 by Alilaguna water bus, or $125 by water taxi (can be shared by up to 4 people).

The cost of round-trip, second-class train transportation to day-trip destinations is affordable and depends on the speed of the train (about $20–40 to Padua and about $25–50 to Verona).

Room and Board: You can easily manage in Venice in 2011 on an overall average of $130 a day per person for room and board. This allows $15 for lunch, $25 for dinner, and $90 for lodging (based on two people splitting the cost of a $180 double room that includes breakfast). If you've got more money, I've listed great ways to spend it. Students and tightwads can enjoy Venice for as little as $65 a day ($35 for a hostel bed, $30 for meals and snacks).

Sightseeing and Entertainment: Figure about $10–20 per major sight (Accademia, Doge's Palace, Guggenheim), $5–10 for smaller ones (museums, climbing church towers), and $25–30 or more for splurge experiences (e.g., tours and concerts). A gondola ride costs $100 (by day) or $125 (at night); split the cost by going with a pal. An overall average of $35 a day works for most people. Don't skimp here. After all, this category is the driving force behind your trip—you came to sightsee, enjoy, and experience Venice.

Shopping and Miscellany: Figure $2 per postcard and $5 per coffee, soft drink, or gelato. Shopping can vary in cost from nearly nothing to a small fortune. Good budget travelers find that this category has little to do with assembling a trip full of lifelong, wonderful memories.

When to Go

Venice's best travel months (also its busiest and most expensive) are May, June, September, and October. These months combine the convenience of peak season with pleasant weather.

Between November and April you can usually expect mild winter weather, some flooding (particularly March and Nov), shorter lines, and generally none of the sweat and stress of the tourist season (except during the Carnevale festival).

Summer in Venice is more temperate than in Italy's scorching inland cities. Venetian temperatures hit the high 70s and 80s in summer and drop to the 30s and 40s in winter (see the climate chart in the appendix). Most mid-range hotels come with air-conditioning—a worthwhile splurge in the summer—but usually available only from May (at the earliest) through September. Spring and fall can be cool, and many hotels do not turn on their heat until winter.

Venice has two main weather patterns: Wind from the southeast (Bulgaria) brings cold and dry weather, while the sirocco wind from the south (Egypt) brings warm and wet weather, pushing more water into the lagoon and causing flooding *(acqua alta)*. This shouldn't greatly affect your sightseeing plans. Tobacco shops and some souvenir shops sell boots to keep your feet dry. Elevated wooden walkways are sometimes set up in the busier, more flooded squares to keep you above the water. And it's worth a trip to St. Mark's Square to see waiters in fancy tuxes and rubber boots.

Off-Season Travel Tips: Off-season has none of the sweat and stress of the tourist season, but sights may have shorter hours, lunchtime breaks, and fewer activities. Here are several things to keep in mind if you visit Venice off-season, roughly November through March.

• Certain sights close early, often at 17:00 (Correr Museum, Campanile, San Giorgio Maggiore, Ca' Rezzonico, and Ca' Pesaro). Many sights stop selling tickets an hour before closing. The glassmaking demonstrations on Murano close early in winter, as do the sights on Torcello.

- The orchestras in St. Mark's Square may stop playing at 18:00 (and may not play at all in bad weather or during their annual vacations, usually in March).
- Vaporetto #2 (the Grand Canal fast boat) may have limited off-season hours (approximately 9:15–20:30).
- Expect occasional flooding, particularly at St. Mark's Square and along Zattere (southern edge of Venice, opposite Giudecca Island).
- Room prices should be about 25 percent less than those quoted in this book.

Know Before You Go

Your trip is more likely to go smoothly if you plan ahead. Check this list of things to arrange while you're still at home.

You need a **passport**—but no visa or shots—to travel in Italy. You may be denied entry into certain European countries if your passport is due to expire within three to six months of your ticketed date of return. Get it renewed if you'll be cutting it close. It can take up to six weeks to get or renew a passport (for more on passports, see www.travel.state.gov). Pack a photocopy of your passport in your luggage in case the original is lost or stolen.

Book rooms in advance, particularly during peak season (roughly May–Sept). Check to see if you'll be visiting Venice during any **holidays or festivals** (such as Carnevale), when rooms can cost more and get booked up quickly. (See "Major Holidays and Weekends" sidebar, earlier).

In Padua, reservations are mandatory to visit the **Scrovegni Chapel,** known for its frescoes by Giotto, so book well in advance (easily done online; see page 318).

Call your **debit and credit card companies** to let them know the countries you'll be visiting, to ask about fees, and more (see page 10).

Do your homework if you want to buy **travel insurance.** Compare the cost of the insurance to the likelihood of your using it and your potential loss if something goes wrong. For more information, see www.ricksteves.com/insurance.

If you're bringing an MP3 player, you can download free information from **Rick Steves Audio Europe,** featuring hours of travel interviews on Italy, audio tours of major sights, and more (at www.ricksteves.com and on iTunes; for details, see page 391). If you're going to Padua, you can download their free—and good—audio tour at www.turismopadova.it.

Bring your driver's license if you're planning on **renting a car** in Italy, and consider getting an International Driving Permit from AAA (see page 386).

If you're taking an **overnight train** and need a couchette (cuccetta) or sleeper—and you must leave on a certain day—consider booking it in advance through a US agent (such as www.raileurope.com), even though it may cost more than buying it in Italy. Other Italian trains, like the high-speed ES trains, require a seat reservation, but for these it's usually possible to make arrangements in Italy just a few days ahead. (For more on train travel, see the appendix.)

Because **airline carry-on restrictions** are always changing, visit the Transportation Security Administration's website (www.tsa.gov/travelers) for an up-to-date list of what you can bring on the plane with you...and what you have to check.

Practicalities

Emergency and Medical Help: In Italy, dial 113 for English-speaking police help. To summon an ambulance, call 118.

If you get sick, do as the Venetians do and go to a pharmacist for advice. Or ask at your hotel for help; they'll know the nearest medical and emergency services. For the hospital, see page 26.

Time Zones: Italy, like most of continental Europe, is generally six/nine hours ahead of the East/West Coasts of the US. The exceptions are the beginning and end of Daylight Saving Time: Europe "springs forward" the last Sunday in March (two weeks after most of the US), and "falls back" the last Sunday in October (one week before US). For a handy online converter, try www.timeanddate.com/worldclock.

Business Hours: Traditionally, Venice uses the siesta plan, though many businesses have adopted the government's recommended 8:00 to 14:00 workday. In tourist areas, shops are open longer. People usually work from about 9:00 to 13:00 and from 15:30 to 19:00. Some stores and restaurants close on Sunday. Banking hours are generally Monday through Friday 8:30 to 13:30 and 15:30 to 16:30, but they can vary wildly.

Saturdays are virtually weekdays, with earlier closing hours. Sundays have the same pros and cons as they do for travelers in the US: Sightseeing attractions are generally open, while shops and banks are closed. Rowdy evenings are rare on Sundays.

Watt's Up? Europe's electrical system is different from North America's in two ways: the shape of the plug (two round prongs) and the voltage of the current (220 volts instead of 110 volts). For your North American plug to work in Europe, you'll need an adapter, sold inexpensively at travel stores in the US. As for the voltage, most newer electronics or travel appliances (such as hair dryers, laptops, and battery chargers) automatically convert the voltage—if you see a range of voltages printed on the item or its plug (such as "110–220"), it'll work in Europe. Otherwise, you can buy a converter separately in the US (about $20).

Discounts: Venice's city museums offer youth and senior discounts to Americans and other non-EU citizens (bring ID). These museums include the Doge's Palace, Correr Museum, Clock Tower on St. Mark's Square, Ca' Rezzonico, Ca' Pesaro, Palazzo Mocenigo Costume Museum, Murano's Glass Museum, and Burano's Lace Museum.

News: Americans keep in touch via the *International Herald Tribune* (published almost daily throughout Europe and online at www.iht.com). Other newsy sites are http://news.bbc.co.uk and www.europeantimes.com. Every Tuesday, the European editions of *Time* and *Newsweek* hit the stands with articles of particular interest to travelers in Europe. Sports addicts can get their daily fix online or from *USA Today.* Many hotels have CNN and BBC News television channels.

Money

This section offers advice on how to pay for purchases on your trip (including getting cash from ATMs and paying with plastic), dealing with lost or stolen cards, VAT (sales tax) refunds, and tipping.

What to Bring

Bring both a credit card and a debit card. You'll use the debit card at cash machines (ATMs) to withdraw local cash for most purchases, and the credit card to pay for larger items. Some travelers carry a third card as a backup, in case one gets demagnetized or eaten by a temperamental machine.

I also carry a few hundred dollars in hard cash as an emergency backup (in $20 bills rather than hard-to-exchange $100 bills). Don't bother changing cash before you leave home—European ATMs are easy to find and easy to use. And skip traveler's checks—they're a waste of time (long waits at slow banks) and a waste of money in fees.

Cash

Cash is just as desirable in Europe as it is at home. Small European businesses (hotels, restaurants, shops, etc.) prefer that you pay your bills with cash. Some vendors will charge you extra for using a credit card, and some won't take credit cards at all.

Throughout Europe, ATMs offer the best and simplest way to get local currency. To use an ATM (called a *bancomat*) to withdraw money from your account, you'll need a debit card—ideally with a Visa or MasterCard logo for maximum usability—plus a PIN code. Know your PIN code in numbers; there are only numbers—no

INTRODUCTION

Exchange Rate

1 euro (€) = about $1.25

To convert prices in euros to dollars, add about 40 percent: €20 = about $25, €50 = about $65. (Check www.oanda.com for the latest exchange rates.) Just like the dollar, one euro is broken down into 100 cents. You'll find coins ranging from €0.01 to €2, and bills ranging from €5 to €500.

Look carefully at any €2 coin you get in change. Some unscrupulous merchants give out similar-looking, gold-rimmed old 500-lire coins (worth $0) instead of €2 coins (worth $2.80). You are now warned!

letters—on European keypads. You could use a credit card for ATM transactions, but it's generally more expensive (because it's considered a "cash advance" rather than a "withdrawal").

When using an ATM, taking out large sums of money can reduce your per-transaction bank fees. If the machine refuses your request, try again and select a smaller amount (some cash machines limit the amount you can withdraw—don't take it personally). If that doesn't work, try a different machine. It's easier to pay for purchases with smaller bills; if the ATM gives you big bills, try to break them at a bank or larger store.

To keep your cash safe, use a money belt—a pouch with a strap that you buckle around your waist like a belt, and wear under your clothes. Pickpockets target tourists. A money belt provides peace of mind, allowing you to carry lots of cash safely. Don't waste time every few days tracking down a cash machine—withdraw a week's worth of money, stuff it in your money belt, and travel!

Credit and Debit Cards

For purchases, Visa and MasterCard are more commonly accepted than American Express. While you can use either a credit card or a debit card for most transactions, credit cards offer a greater degree of fraud protection (since debit cards draw funds directly from your account).

Just like at home, credit or debit cards work easily at larger hotels, restaurants, and shops. I typically use my credit card only in a few specific situations: to book hotel reservations by phone, to make major purchases (such as car rentals, plane tickets, and long hotel stays), and to pay for things near the end of my trip (to avoid another visit to the ATM).

Ask Your Credit- or Debit-Card Company: Before your trip, contact the company that issued your debit or credit cards.

• Confirm your card will work overseas, and alert them that you'll be using it in Europe; otherwise, they may deny transactions if they perceive unusual spending patterns.

• Ask for the specifics on transaction **fees.** When you use your credit or debit card—either for purchases or ATM withdrawals—you'll often be charged additional "international transaction" fees of up to 3 percent plus $5 per transaction. If your card's fees are too high, consider getting a card just for your trip: Capital One (www.capitalone.com) and most credit unions have low-to-no international fees.

• If you plan to withdraw cash from ATMs, confirm your daily **withdrawal limit.** Some travelers prefer a high limit that allows them to take out more cash at each ATM stop, while others prefer to set a lower limit in case their card is stolen.

• Ask for your credit card's **PIN** in case you encounter Europe's "chip and PIN" system.

Chip and PIN: If your card is declined for a purchase in Europe, it may be because of chip and PIN, which requires card-holders to punch in a PIN instead of signing a receipt. While chip and PIN is not yet common in Italy, much of Europe is adopting it. Chip and PIN is used by some merchants, and also at automated payment machines—such as those at train and subway stations, toll roads, parking garages, luggage lockers, bike-rental kiosks, and self-serve pumps at gas stations. If you're prompted to enter your PIN (but don't know it), ask if the cashier can print a receipt for you to sign instead, or just pay cash. If you're dealing with an automated machine that won't take your card, look for a cashier nearby who can make your card work. But if the place is unstaffed and you don't have cash, you might simply be out of luck.

Dynamic Currency Conversion: If merchants offer to convert your purchase price into dollars (called dynamic currency conversion, or DCC), refuse this "service." You'll pay even more in fees for the expensive convenience of seeing your charge in dollars.

Damage Control for Lost Cards

If you lose your credit, debit, or ATM card, you can stop people from using your card by reporting the loss immediately to the respective global customer-assistance centers. Call these 24-hour US numbers collect: Visa (410/581-9994), MasterCard (636/722-7111), and American Express (623/492-8427).

At a minimum, you'll need to know the name of the financial institution that issued you the card, along with the type of card (classic, platinum, or whatever). Providing the following information allows for a quicker cancellation of your missing card: full card number, whether you are the primary or secondary cardholder, the cardholder's name exactly as printed on the card, billing address, home phone number, details of the loss or theft, and identification verification (your birth date, your mother's maiden name, or your Social Security number—memorize this, don't carry a copy). If you are the secondary cardholder, you'll also need to provide the primary cardholder's identification-verification details. You can generally receive a temporary card within two or three business days in Europe (see www.ricksteves.com/help for more).

If you promptly report your card lost or stolen, you typically won't be responsible for any unauthorized transactions on your account, although many banks charge a liability fee of $50.

Tipping

Tipping in Italy isn't as automatic and generous as it is in the US, but for special service, tips are appreciated, if not expected. As in the US, the proper amount depends on your resources, tipping philosophy, and the circumstances, but some general guidelines apply.

Restaurants: The service charge *(servizio)* is usually already included in your bill. If you're pleased with the service, you can round up the bill by a euro or two (though Italians rarely add this additional tip). For more on tipping in restaurants, see page 260.

Traghetti, **Gondolas, and Water Taxis:** There's no need to tip on a cheap *traghetto* ride (a stand-up ride in a gondola across the Grand Canal); it'd be a little like tipping for a city bus ride. You also don't need to tip for a romantic gondola ride; you're already paying plenty. If you ride in a water taxi, round up your fare a bit (e.g., if the fare is €37, pay €40). If the driver hauls your bags and zips you to the airport to help you catch your flight, you might want to toss in a little more. But if you feel like you got on the slow boat to nowhere fast, skip the tip.

Special Services: Tour guides at public sights sometimes hold out their hands for tips after they give their spiel. If I've already paid for the tour, I don't tip extra, unless they've really impressed me. At hotels, if you let the porter carry your luggage, it's polite to give them a euro for each bag. I don't tip the maid, but if you do, you can leave a euro per overnight at the end of your stay.

In general, if someone in the service industry does a super job for you, a small tip (the equivalent of a euro or two) is appropriate...but not required.

When in doubt, ask. If you're not sure whether (or how much) to tip for a service, ask your hotelier or the tourist information office; they'll fill you in on how it's done on their turf.

Getting a VAT Refund

Wrapped into the purchase price of your Italian souvenirs is a Value-Added Tax (VAT) of about 20 percent. You're entitled to get most of that tax back if you purchase more than €155 (about

$195) worth of goods at a store that participates in the VAT-refund scheme. Getting your refund is usually straightforward and, if you buy a substantial amount of souvenirs, well worth the hassle. If you're lucky, the merchant will subtract the tax when you make your purchase. (This is more likely to occur if the store ships the goods to your home.) Otherwise, you'll need to:

Get the paperwork. Have the merchant completely fill out the necessary refund document, called a "cheque." You'll have to present your passport.

Get your stamp at the border or airport. Process your cheque(s) at your last stop in the EU with the customs agent who deals with VAT refunds. It's best to keep your purchases in your carry-on for viewing, but if they're too large or dangerous (such as knives) to carry on, track down the proper customs agent to inspect them before you check your bag. You're not supposed to use your purchased goods before you leave. If you show up at customs wearing your new gondolier outfit, officials might look the other way— or deny you a refund.

Collect your refund. You'll need to return your stamped document to the retailer or its representative. Many merchants work with a service, such as Global Refund (www.globalrefund .com) or Premier Tax Free (www.premiertaxfree.com), which have offices at major airports, ports, or border crossings. These services, which extract a 4 percent fee, can refund your money immediately in your currency of choice or credit your card (within two billing cycles). If the retailer handles VAT refunds directly, it's up to you to contact the merchant for your refund. You can mail the documents from home, or quicker, from your point of departure (using a stamped, self-addressed envelope or one that's been provided by the merchant). You'll then have to wait—it can take months.

Customs for American Shoppers

You are allowed to take home $800 worth of items per person duty-free, once every 30 days. The next $1,000 is taxed at a flat 3 percent. After that, you pay the individual item's duty rate. You can also bring in duty-free a liter of alcohol (slightly more than a standard-size bottle of wine, packed carefully in checked luggage; you must be at least 21), 200 cigarettes, and up to 100 non-Cuban cigars.

As for food, you can take home vacuum-packed cheeses; dried herbs, spices, or mushrooms; and canned fruits or vegetables, including jams and vegetable spreads. Baked goods, candy, chocolate, oil, vinegar, mustard, and honey are OK. Fresh fruits and vegetables (even that banana from your airplane breakfast) are not permitted. Meats are generally not allowed, though canned pâtés from some countries are usually permitted if made from goose, duck, or pork. Just because a duty-free shop in an airport sells a food product, that doesn't mean it will automatically pass US customs. Be prepared to lose your investment.

Note that you'll need to carefully pack any bottles of wine, jam, honey, oil, and other liquid-containing items in your checked luggage, due to the three-ounce limit on liquids in carry-on baggage. To check customs rules and duty rates, visit www.cbp.gov, and click on "Travel," then "Know Before You Go."

Sightseeing

Sightseeing can be hard work. Use these tips to make your visits to Venice's finest sights meaningful, fun, fast, and painless.

Plan Ahead

Set up an itinerary that allows you to fit in all your must-see sights. For a one-stop look at opening hours, see "Venice at a Glance" (page 42; also see "Daily Reminder" on page 22). Most sights keep stable hours, but you can easily confirm the latest by checking their website or asking at the TI.

Don't put off visiting a must-see sight—you never know when a place will close unexpectedly for a holiday, strike, or restoration. On holidays (see list on page 396), expect shorter hours or closures. In summer, some sights stay open late, allowing easy viewing without crowds. Many museums have shorter hours October through March. If you want to visit Padua's Scrovegni Chapel, make reservations in advance (see page 318).

When possible, visit the major sights in the morning (when your energy is best) and save other activities for the afternoon. Hit the highlights first, then go back to other things if you have the stamina and time.

Depending on the sight, there are ways to avoid crowds. This book offers tips on doing this at specific sights. Try visiting the sight very early, at lunch, or very late. Evening visits are usually peaceful with fewer crowds.

Study up. To get the most out of the self-guided tours and sight descriptions in this book, read them before you visit.

At Sights

Here's what you can typically expect:

Some important sights have metal detectors or conduct bag searches that will slow your entry, while others require you to check daypacks and coats. They'll be kept safely. If you have something you can't bear to part with, stash it in a pocket or purse. To avoid checking a small backpack, carry it under your arm like a purse as you enter. From a guard's point of view, a backpack is generally a problem while a purse is not.

Photography is normally allowed, but flashes or tripods usually are not. Look for signs or ask. Flashes damage oil paintings and distract others in the room. Even without a flash, a handheld camera will take a decent picture (or just buy postcards or posters at the museum bookstore). If photos are permitted, video cameras generally are okay too.

You'll likely have to pay cash for the admission fee; few sights take credit cards. Museums may have special exhibits in addition to their permanent collection. Some exhibits are included in the entry price, while others come at an extra cost (which you may have to pay even if you don't want to see the exhibit).

Expect changes—artwork can be on tour, on loan, out sick, or shifted at the whim of the curator. To adapt, pick up any available free floor plans as you enter, and ask the museum staff if you can't find a particular item. Say the title or artist's name, or point to the photograph in this book and ask, *"Dov'è?"* (doh-VEH, meaning "Where is?").

Many sights rent audioguides, which generally offer excellent recorded descriptions in English (about €4–7). If you bring along your own pair of headphones and a Y-jack, you can sometimes share one audioguide with your travel partner and save money. I have produced free audio tours for the major sights in the book (see page 391). Guided tours in English are most likely to be available during peak season (usually €5–15 and widely ranging in quality). Some sights also run short films about the attraction. These are generally well worth your time. I make it standard operating procedure to ask when I arrive at a sight if there is a film in English.

Important sights may have an on-site café or cafeteria (usually a good place to rest and have a snack or light meal). The WCs at many sights are free and generally clean.

Many sights sell postcards and guidebooks that highlight their attractions. Before you leave, scan the postcards and thumb through the biggest guidebook (or skim its index) to be sure you haven't overlooked something that you'd like to see.

Most sights stop admitting people 30–60 minutes before closing time, and some rooms close early (generally about 45 minutes before the actual closing time). Guards usher people out, so don't save the best for last.

Every sight or museum offers more than what is covered in this book. Use the information in this book as an introduction—not the final word.

Find Religion

Churches offer some amazing art (usually free), a cool respite from heat, and a welcome seat.

How Was Your Trip?

Were your travels fun, smooth, and meaningful? If you'd like to share your tips, concerns, and discoveries, please fill out the survey at www.ricksteves.com/feedback. I value your feedback. Thanks in advance—it helps a lot.

A modest dress code (no bare shoulders or shorts for anyone, even kids) is enforced at larger churches, such as St. Mark's Basilica and the Frari Church, but is often overlooked elsewhere. If you are caught by surprise, you can improvise, using maps to cover your shoulders and a jacket for your knees. (I wear a super-lightweight pair of long pants rather than shorts for my hot and muggy big-city Italian sightseeing.)

Some churches have coin-operated audioboxes that describe the art and history; just set the dial on English, put in your coins, and listen. Coin boxes near a piece of art illuminate the art (and present a better photo opportunity). I pop in a coin whenever I can. It improves my experience, is a favor to other visitors trying to appreciate a great piece of art in the dark, and is a little contribution to that church and its work. Whenever possible, let there be light.

Traveling as a Temporary Local

We travel all the way to Italy to enjoy differences—to become temporary locals. You'll experience frustrations. Certain truths that we find "God-given" or "self-evident," such as cold beer, ice in drinks, bottomless cups of coffee, hot showers, and bigger being better, are suddenly not so true. One of the benefits of travel is the eye-opening realization that there are logical, civil, and even better alternatives. A willingness to go local ensures that you'll enjoy a full dose of Italian hospitality.

Europeans generally like Americans. But if there is a negative aspect to Italians' image of Americans (apart from our foreign policy), it's that we are big, loud, aggressive, impolite, rich, and a bit naive. Think about the rationale behind "crazy" Italian decisions. For instance, many hoteliers turn off the heat in spring and can't turn on air-conditioning until summer. The point is to conserve energy, and it's mandated by the Italian government. You could complain about being cold or hot...or bring a sweater in winter, and in summer, be prepared to sweat a little like everyone else.

While Italians, flabbergasted by our Yankee excesses, say in disbelief, *"Mi sono cadute le braccia!"* ("I throw my arms down!"), they nearly always afford us individual travelers all the warmth we deserve.

Judging from all the happy feedback I receive from travelers who have used this book, it's safe to assume you'll enjoy a great, affordable vacation—with the finesse of an independent, experienced traveler.

Thanks, and *buon viaggio!*

Back Door Travel Philosophy
From *Rick Steves' Europe Through the Back Door*

Travel is intensified living—maximum thrills per minute and one of the last great sources of legal adventure. Travel is freedom. It's recess, and we need it.

Experiencing the real Europe requires catching it by surprise, going casual..."Through the Back Door."

Affording travel is a matter of priorities. (Make do with the old car.) You can eat and sleep—simply, safely, and enjoyably—anywhere in Europe for $120 a day plus transportation costs. In many ways, spending more money only builds a thicker wall between you and what you traveled so far to see. Europe is a cultural carnival, and time after time, you'll find that its best acts are free and the best seats are the cheap ones.

A tight budget forces you to travel close to the ground, meeting and communicating with the people. Never sacrifice sleep, nutrition, safety, or cleanliness to save money. Simply enjoy the local-style alternatives to expensive hotels and restaurants.

Connecting with people carbonates your experience. Extroverts have more fun. If your trip is low on magic moments, kick yourself and make things happen. If you don't enjoy a place, maybe you don't know enough about it. Seek the truth. Recognize tourist traps. Give a culture the benefit of your open mind. See things as different, but not better or worse. Any culture has plenty to share.

Of course, travel, like the world, is a series of hills and valleys. Be fanatically positive and militantly optimistic. If something's not to your liking, change your liking.

Travel can make you a happier American, as well as a citizen of the world. Our earth is home to six and a half billion equally precious people. It's humbling to travel and find that other people don't have the "American Dream"—they have their own dreams. Europeans like us, but with all due respect, they wouldn't trade passports.

Thoughtful travel engages us with the world. In tough economic times, it reminds us what is truly important. By broadening perspectives, travel teaches new ways to measure quality of life.

Globetrotting destroys ethnocentricity, helping us understand and appreciate other cultures. Rather than fear the diversity on this planet, celebrate it. Among your most prized souvenirs will be the strands of different cultures you choose to knit into your own character. The world is a cultural yarn shop, and Back Door travelers are weaving the ultimate tapestry. Join in!

ORIENTATION

The island city of Venice is shaped like a fish. Its major thoroughfares are canals. The Grand Canal winds through the middle of the fish, starting at the mouth where all the people and food enter, passing under the Rialto Bridge, and ending at St. Mark's Square (Piazza San Marco). Park your 21st-century perspective at the mouth and let Venice swallow you whole.

Venice is a car-less kaleidoscope of people, bridges, and odorless canals. The city has no major streets, and addresses are

hopelessly confusing. There are six districts (shown on map on page 21): San Marco (most touristy), Castello (behind San Marco), Cannaregio (from the train station to the Rialto), San Polo (other side of the Rialto), Santa Croce (the "eye" of the fish, east of the train station), and Dorsoduro (the belly of the fish and southernmost district of the city). Each district has about 6,000 address numbers.

To find your way, navigate by landmarks, not streets. Many street corners have a sign pointing you to *(per)* the nearest major landmark, such as San Marco, Accademia, Rialto, and Ferrovia (train station). Obedient visitors stick to the main thoroughfares as directed by these signs...and miss the charm of back-street Venice.

Beyond the city's core lie several other islands, including San Giorgio (with great views of Venice), Giudecca (more views), San Michele (old cemetery), Murano (famous for glass), Burano (lace-making), Torcello (old church), and the skinny Lido beach.

Planning Your Time

Venice is remarkably small. You can walk across it, from head to tail, in about an hour. Nearly all of your sightseeing is within a 20-minute walk of the Rialto Bridge or St. Mark's Square. Remember that Venice itself is its greatest sight. Make time to wander, explore, shop, and simply be.

Key considerations: Maximize your evening magic, and avoid the midday crowds around St. Mark's Basilica and the Doge's Palace. If you arrive in Venice at the end of the day, try taking the Grand Canal Cruise and St. Mark's Square Tour. These sights are more romantic and much less crowded after dark—and they provide a wonderful welcome to the city. (Also see "Crowd Control" tips in the "Daily Reminder" sidebar.)

Take advantage of the free, self-guided **Rick Steves audio tours** based on the tours in this book (download them from www.ricksteves.com or search for "Rick Steves Audio Tours" in iTunes); these are available for St. Mark's Basilica, St. Mark's Square, Frari Church, and the Grand Canal Cruise.

Depending on when you visit, you may have to juggle the itineraries below, as sights' visiting hours will vary by season and day of the week.

Venice in One Busy Day

9:00	Take the Grand Canal Cruise, hopping off two times—first at the Mercato Rialto stop to enjoy the market action, and then at the San Tomà stop to tour the Frari Church.
12:00	Lunch near the Frari.
13:00	Catch the vaporetto (boat) to St. Mark's Square to explore.
14:30	Correr Museum (ticket bought here includes Doge's Palace).
15:30	St. Mark's Basilica (closes at 17:00).
17:00	Doge's Palace (closes at 19:00).
18:00	Tour St. Mark's Square.
19:00	Dinner—pub crawl or restaurant.
21:00	Gondola ride.
22:00	Enjoy the dueling orchestras with a drink on St. Mark's Square.

Venice in Two or More Days
Day 1

9:00	Walk to the train station and over the Calatrava Bridge to Piazzale Roma. Then catch the slow boat vaporetto (line #1) to take my self-guided Grand Canal Cruise.

ORIENTATION

Venice's Districts

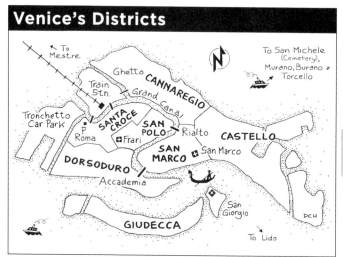

10:30   Interrupt the tour, hopping off at Mercato Rialto to explore the market. Eat an early lunch of *cicchetti* (Venetian tapas) at the bars recommended on page 274.

13:00   Continue the Grand Canal Cruise, ending at St. Mark's Square.

13:30   Tour St. Mark's Square.

14:30   Correr Museum (ticket here includes Doge's Palace).

15:30   St. Mark's Basilica (closes at 17:00).

17:00   Doge's Palace (closes at 19:00).

19:00   Go up the Campanile for city view (July–Sept only, when it's open until 21:00; in other months, squeeze it in on the afternoon of Day 2).

20:00   Dinner (make a reservation).

22:00   Enjoy the dueling orchestras with a drink on St. Mark's Square.

Day 2

9:00   Shopping or exploring.

10:00   Visit the Frari Church.

11:30   Tour Ca' Rezzonico (Museum of 18th-Century Venice).

13:00   Lunch (pizza near Accademia Bridge?).

ORIENTATION

Daily Reminder

Sunday: While anyone is welcome to worship, most churches are closed to sightseers during Mass on Sunday morning. The Church of San Giorgio Maggiore (on an island across from St. Mark's Square) hosts a Gregorian Mass at 11:00. The Church of San Polo is closed today, and these sights are open only in the afternoon: St. Mark's Basilica (14:00–17:00, until 16:00 Nov–March), Frari Church (13:00–18:00), and the Church of San Zaccaria (16:00–18:00). Today, the Rialto open-air market consists mainly of souvenir stalls (fish and produce sections closed). It's a bad day for a pub crawl, as most pubs are closed.

Monday: All sights are open except the Rialto produce market, Ca' Pesaro, and Torcello Museum (on Torcello Island). The Accademia and Ca' d'Oro close at 14:00. Don't side-trip to Verona today, as most sights there are closed.

Tuesday: All sights are open except the Peggy Guggenheim Collection, Ca' Rezzonico (Museum of 18th-Century Venice), and Punta della Dogana.

Wednesday/Thursday/Friday: All sights are open.

Saturday: All sights are open except the Jewish Museum.

Notes: The Accademia is open earlier (daily at 8:15) and closes later (19:15 Tue–Sun) than most sights in Venice. Some sights close earlier off-season (such as the Correr Museum, Campanile bell tower, and St. Mark's Basilica).

14:00 Your choice: Tour Accademia, explore Dorsoduro neighborhood (wander back lanes to the Zattere promenade), or visit La Salute Church or Peggy Guggenheim Collection.

18:00 Commence pub crawl (perhaps on a pub tour with Alessandro—see page 33), eating dinner along the way.

20:00 Concert and/or gondola ride.

Day 3—Lagoon Tour

10:00 Catch boat at Fondamenta Nuove to San Michele (old cemetery), then continue to Murano.

11:00 Tour Murano, see glassworks.

13:00 Boat to Burano for lunch and browsing.

15:00 Shuttle boat to Torcello, tour church, back to Burano.

18:00 Take the long way back by boat via the Lido (but don't stop there—just enjoy a cruise on the lagoon).

20:00 Dinner and/or concert in Venice.

Churches: Modest dress is recommended at churches and required at St. Mark's Basilica—no bare shoulders, shorts, or short skirts. Some churches are closed to sightseers on Sunday morning (including St. Mark's Basilica, Frari Church, Church of San Zaccaria, and after 11:00 at San Giorgio Maggiore), and many are closed from roughly 12:00 to 14:30 or 15:30 Monday through Saturday (this includes La Salute and San Giorgio Maggiore).

Crowd Control: The city is inundated with cruise-ship crowds and tours from mainland hotels daily from 10:00 to about 17:00. Crowds can be a serious problem at **St. Mark's Basilica.** Try going early or late, or even better, you can bypass the line if you have a bag to check (see page 82).

At the **Doge's Palace,** avoid the long line by purchasing your ticket at the less-crowded Correr Museum. You can also visit late in the day, buy your ticket online, or book a tour (see Doge's Palace Tour chapter).

For the **Campanile,** ascend late (it's open until 21:00 July–Sept), or skip it entirely if you're going to the similar San Giorgio Maggiore bell tower.

For the **Accademia,** go early or late—or you can reserve a ticket in advance by phone or online (see Accademia Tour chapter).

The sights that have crowd problems get even more crowded when it rains.

Day 4 and Beyond

Take a Venicescapes tour or other tour.
Visit the Church of San Giorgio Maggiore.
Follow additional self-guided neighborhood walks in this book.
Side-trip to Padua (30 minutes away by train).

Overview

Tourist Information

With this book, a free city map from your hotel, and *Un Ospite di Venezia* entertainment guide (described below), there's little need to visit a tourist office in Venice. That's fortunate, because the city's TIs are crowded and clunky. If you need to check or confirm something, there are four offices: **train station** (daily 8:00–21:00), **St. Mark's Square** (daily 9:00–15:30, opposite end from church), nearby at the **San Marco-Vallaresso vaporetto stop** (daily 10:00–18:00), and at the **airport** (daily 9:00–21:00). You can save time by phoning 041-529-8711 or visiting www.turismovenezia.it.

At the TI—or at many hotels—pick up two free pamphlets:

Shows and Events and *Un Ospite di Venezia*. Besides upcoming events and nightlife, they also list museum hours, train and vaporetto schedules, emergency telephone numbers, and so on (www.aguestinvenice.com, info@aguestinvenice.com).

For a creative travel guide written by young Venetians, consider *My Local Guide Venice*, for its neighborhood histories, self-guided walking tours, and recommendations on sights and activities (sold at TIs for €9.90).

Maps: Of all places, you need a good map in Venice. Hotels give away freebies (no better than the small color one at the front of this book). The TI sells a decent €2.50 map and miniguide—but you can find a wider range at bookshops, newsstands, and postcard stands. The cheap maps are pretty bad, but if you spend €5, you'll get a map that shows you everything. Investing in a good map can be the best €5 you'll spend in Venice. Don't take street names too seriously—spellings change with the dialect. Also, keep in mind that many street names change midway.

Arrival in Venice

For a rundown on Venice's train station and airport, and tips for drivers, see the Venice Connections chapter.

Passes for Venice

The sights you probably care the most about (Accademia, Peggy Guggenheim Collection, Scuola San Rocco, Campanile, and the three sights within St. Mark's Basilica that charge admission) are not covered on any pass. To see the Doge's Palace, you must also pay for the less-visited Correr Museum (both on St. Mark's Square). While this €13 ticket is called a "pass" (described next), think of it as just a combo-ticket. Venice offers various other cards and passes that cover multiple sights few visitors want to see; these are generally not worth the trouble. Here are the specifics per pass.

Doge's Palace/Correr Museum Tickets: The **San Marco Museum Plus Pass** (€13) covers admission to the Doge's Palace and Correr Museum (including two other museums within the Correr—the National Archaeological Museum and the Monumental Rooms of Marciana National Library), plus your choice of **one** of these seven museums: Ca' Rezzonico (Museum of 18th-Century Venice); Palazzo Mocenigo Costume Museum; Casa Goldoni (home of the Italian playwright); Ca' Pesaro (modern art); Museum of Natural History in the Santa Croce district; Murano's Glass Museum; or Burano's Lace Museum (www.museiciviciveneziani.it). To bypass the long line at the Doge's Palace, purchase this pass at the less-crowded Correr Museum (or any other included museum).

The San Marco Museum Plus Pass is available only from

April through October. Off-season (Nov-March), it's replaced by the **Museum Card of the Museums of St. Mark's Square** (€12), which covers only the Doge's Palace and Correr Museum (includes the two museums inside the Correr).

Museum Pass: Busy sightseers may prefer the more expensive Museum Pass. This pass covers the Doge's Palace and Correr Museum, plus entry to **all** of the museums listed above for the San Marco Museum Plus Pass (€18, www.museicivicivenezieni .it). In general, this pass saves you money only if you visit five or more sights; before you buy, make sure they're sights you really want to see.

Chorus Pass: Church-lovers can get admission to 16 of Venice's churches and their art (generally €3 each)—including the Frari—for €9 (€18 for Family Pass, www.chorusvenezia.org).

Transportation Passes: Venice also sells transit-only passes covering *vaporetti* and buses that arrive on the edge of town. For a rundown on these, see "Getting Around Venice," later.

Helpful Hints

Get Lost: Accept the fact that Venice was a tourist town 400 years ago. It was, is, and always will be crowded. While 80 percent of Venice is, in fact, not touristy, 80 percent of the tourists never notice. Hit the back streets. Venice is the ideal town to explore on foot. Walk and walk to the far reaches of the town. Don't worry about getting lost. In fact, get as lost as possible. Keep reminding yourself, "I'm on an island, and I can't get off." When it comes time to find your way, just follow the directional arrows on building corners or simply ask a local, *"Dov'è San Marco?"* ("Where is St. Mark's?") People in the tourist business (that's most Venetians) speak some English. If they don't,  listen politely, watch where their hands point, say *"Grazie,"* and head off in that direction. If you're lost, refer to your map, or pop into a hotel and ask for their business card—it comes with a map and a prominent "You are here."

Be Prepared to Splurge: Venice is expensive for residents as well as tourists. Demand is huge, supply is limited, and running a business is costly. Things just cost more here; everything must be shipped in and hand-trucked to its destination. Perhaps the best way to enjoy Venice is just to succumb to its charms and blow a lot of money.

Warning: The dark, late-night streets of Venice are safe. Even so, pickpockets (often elegantly dressed) work the crowded main streets, docks, and *vaporetti* (wear your money belt, zip up your valuables, and watch your purse or day bag). Your biggest risk of pickpockets is inside St. Mark's Basilica.

A handy Polizia station is on the right side of St. Mark's Square (near Caffè Florian). A service called Counter of Tourist Mediation at the Venice Complaint Office handles complaints about local crooks—including gondolier, restaurant, or hotel rip-offs (tel. 041-529-8710, fax 041-523-0399, complaint.apt@turismovenezia.it).

Immigrants selling items such as knock-off handbags on the streets are doing so illegally—if you buy goods from them, you'll risk getting a big fine.

Medical Help: Venice's S.S. Giovanni e Paolo hospital (tel. 118) is a 10-minute walk from both the Rialto and San Marco neighborhoods, located on Fondamenta dei Mendicanti toward Fondamenta Nuove. You can take vaporetto #41 from San Zaccaria-Jolanda to the Ospedale stop.

Take Breaks: Venice's endless pavement, crowds, and tight spaces are hard on the tourist. Schedule breaks in your sightseeing. Grab a cool place to sit down, relax, and recoup—meditate on a pew in an uncrowded church, or stop in a café.

Etiquette: Walk on the right and don't loiter on bridges. On St. Mark's Square, a "decorum patrol" admonishes snackers and sunbathers. Picnicking is forbidden (keep a low profile). The only place for a legal picnic is in Giardinetti Reali, the small park along the waterfront west of the Piazzetta near St. Mark's Square.

Dress Modestly: Men should keep their shirts on. When visiting St. Mark's Basilica or other major churches, men, women, and even children must cover their shoulders and knees (or risk being turned away). Remove hats when entering a church.

Public Toilets: Handy public WCs (€1.50) are near major landmarks, including: St. Mark's Square (one is behind the Correr Museum, to the left of the post office; another is at the waterfront park, Giardinetti Reali), Rialto, and at the Accademia Bridge. Use free toilets whenever you can—in a museum you're visiting or a café you're eating in. Like Mom always said, "Just try."

Best Views: While the best views of Venice may be from water level, there are several upper-altitude viewing spots: On St. Mark's Square, try the soaring Campanile, St. Mark's Basilica (specifically the balcony of the San Marco Museum, requires admission), or the St. Mark's Square clock tower (requires tour). The Rialto and Accademia bridges provide free, expansive views of the Grand Canal, along with a cooling breeze. Or get off the main island for a view of the Venetian skyline: Ascend the Church of San Giorgio Maggiore's bell tower, or venture to La Giudecca island to visit the swanky bar of the Molino Stucky Hilton Hotel (free shuttle boat from San Zaccaria-M.V.E. vaporetto stop).

Pigeon Poop: If your head is bombed by a pigeon, resist the initial response to wipe it off immediately—it'll just smear into your hair. Wait until it dries, and it should flake off cleanly. But if the poop splatters on your clothes, wipe it off immediately to avoid a stain.

Water: I carry a water bottle to refill at public fountains. Venetians pride themselves on having pure, safe, and tasty tap water piped in from the foothills of the Alps. You can actually see the mountains from Venice's bell towers on crisp, clear winter days.

Street Lingo: *Campo* means square, *campiello* is a small square, *calle* is street, *fondamenta* is the road running along a canal, *rio* is a small canal, *rio terra* is a street that was once a canal and has been filled in, and *ponte* is a bridge.

Services

Internet Access: You'll find handy, if pricey (up to €8/hour), little Internet places all over town. They are usually on back streets: Ask your hotelier for the nearest place. Most hotels provide both free Internet access and Wi-Fi for guests.

Post Office: The main P.O. is near the Rialto Bridge (on the St. Mark's side, Mon–Sat 8:30–13:00, closed Sun). Use post offices only as a last resort, as simple transactions can take 45 minutes if you get in the wrong line. You can buy stamps from tobacco shops and mail postcards at any of the red postboxes around town.

Bookstores: In keeping with its literary heritage, Venice has classy and inviting bookstores. The following have great English-language travel sections (and stock my guidebooks): **Libreria Mondadori** is a block behind St. Mark's Square (daily May–Oct 10:00–23:00, Nov–April 10:00–20:00, 1345 Complesso del Ridotto—see map on page 72, tel. 041-522-2193); **Libreria Studium** is a block behind St. Mark's Basilica (Mon–Sat 9:00–19:30, Sun 9:30–13:30, Calle de la Canonica—see map on page 72, tel. 041-522-2382). **Acqua Alta** ("high water") is a funky secondhand bookstore

with bargain books in English and reproduction prints of Venice. Quirky Luigi has prepared for the next "high water" by displaying his wares in a selection of vessels, including bathtubs and a gondola (daily 9:00–21:00, just beyond Campo Santa Maria Formosa at Calle Longa Santa Maria Formosa 5176, tel. 041-296-0841, mobile 340-680-0704).

Laundry: I've listed launderettes near some of my recommended hotels (see listings in the Sleeping in Venice chapter). For more options, ask your hotelier to direct you to one nearby.

Travel Agencies: If you need to get train tickets, make seat reservations, or arrange a *cuccetta* (koo-CHET-tah—a berth on a night train) avoid a time-consuming trip to the crowded train station by using a downtown travel agency. Most trains between Venice, Florence, and Rome require reservations, even for railpass-holders. A travel agency can also give advice on cheap flights (book at least a week in advance for the best fares).

Near St. Mark's Square, **Oltrex Change and Travel** sells train and plane tickets and books train reservations for a €3.50 fee (tickets sold daily May–Oct 9:00–18:00, Nov–April 9:00–16:30, one bridge past the Bridge of Sighs, Riva degli Schiavoni 4192—see map on page 72, tel. 041-524-2828, Luca and Beatrice).

Near Rialto, **Kele & Teo Travel** sells train tickets for about a 10 percent service charge (Mon–Fri 9:00–18:00, Sat 9:00–12:00, closed Sun; leaving the Rialto Bridge heading for St. Mark's, it's half a block away, tucked down a side street on the right; tel. 041-520-8722).

English Church Services: The **San Zulian Church**—the only church in Venice that you can actually walk around—offers a Mass in English (generally May–Sept Mon–Fri at 9:30 and Sun at 11:30, Sun only Oct–April, 2 blocks toward Rialto off St. Mark's Square). **St. George's Anglican Church** welcomes all Christians to its English-speaking Eucharist (Sun at 10:30, located in Dorsoduro, midway between Accademia and Peggy Guggenheim Collection).

Haircuts: I've been getting my hair cut at **Coiffeur Benito** for nearly two decades. Benito has been keeping local men and women trim for 27 years. He's an artist—actually a "hair sculptor"—and a cut here is a fun diversion from the tourist grind (about €20 for women, €18 for men, Tue–Fri 8:30–13:00 &

15:30–19:30, Sat 8:30–13:00 only, closed Sun–Mon, behind San Zulian Church near St. Mark's Square, Calle S. Zulian Già del Strazzariol 592a, tel. 041-528-6221).

Getting Around Venice
On Foot

Navigate by major landmarks. There are signs on street corners all over town pointing to *San Marco, Accademia, Ferrovia* (train station), and *Piazzale Roma* (the bus stop behind the train station). Determine whether your destination is in the direction of a major signposted landmark, then follow the signs through the maze of squares, lanes, and bridges.

By Vaporetto

The public-transit system is a fleet of motorized bus-boats called *vaporetti*. They work like city buses except that they never get a flat, the stops are docks, and if you get off between stops, you might drown.

For most travelers, only two *vaporetti* lines matter: Line #1 and line #2. These lines leave every 10 minutes (less frequently off-season) and go up and down the Grand Canal, between the "mouth of the fish" at one end and San Marco at the other. Line #1 is the slow boat, taking 45 minutes and making every stop along the way. Line #2 is the fast boat that zips down the Grand Canal in 25 minutes, stopping only at Tronchetto (parking lot), Piazzale Roma (bus station), Ferrovia (train station), San Marcuola, Rialto Bridge, San Tomà (Frari Church), Accademia Bridge, San Marco (west end of St. Mark's Square), and San Zaccaria (east end of St. Mark's Square).

Catching a vaporetto is very much like a catching a city bus.

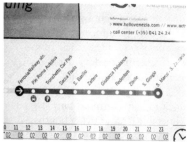

Helpful charts at the docks show a map of the lines and stops. At one end of the Grand Canal are Tronchetto, Piazzale Roma (Ple. Roma), and Ferrovia. At the other end is San Marco. The sign on the dock lists the line number that stops there and which direction the boat is headed, for example: "#2—Direction San

ORIENTATION

Handy *Vaporetti* from San Zaccaria, near St. Mark's Square

Several *vaporetti* leave from the San Zaccaria docks, located 150 yards east of St. Mark's Square. There are four separate San Zaccaria docks spaced about 70 yards apart: Danieli, Jolanda, M.V.E., and Pietà. (Note: Although I list which specific dock these lines leave from, they often change from season to season—be prepared.)

- Line #1 goes up the Grand Canal, making all the stops, including San Marco-Vallaresso, Rialto, Ferrovia (train station), and Piazzale Roma (but it does not go as far as Tronchetto). In the other direction, it goes to the Lido. Line #1 departs from the San Zaccaria-Danieli dock.
- Line #2 zips over to San Giorgio Maggiore, the island church across from St. Mark's Square (5 minutes, €2 ride). From there, it continues on to the parking lot at Tronchetto (departs from San Zaccaria-M.V.E.).
- Line #41 goes to San Michele and Murano in 45 minutes (departs from San Zaccaria-Jolanda).
- The "LN" heads to Burano (70 minutes, from San Zaccaria-Pietà dock).
- The Molino Stucky shuttle boat takes even non-guests to the Hilton Hotel, with its popular view bar (free, 20-minute ride, leaves at 0:20 past the hour from near the San Zaccaria-M.V.E. dock).
- Lines #51 and #52 are the *circulare* (cheer-koo-LAH-ray), making a loop around the perimeter of the island, with a stop at the Lido—perfect if you just like riding boats. Line #51 goes counterclockwise (departs from San Zaccaria-Danieli), and #52 goes clockwise (departs from San Zaccaria-Jolanda).
- The Alilaguna airport shuttle to and from the airport stops at the San Zaccaria-Jolanda dock.

Marco." Nearby is the sign for line #2 going in the other direction, for example: "#2—Direction Tronchetto."

It's simple, but there are a few quirks. Some stops have just one dock for boats going in both directions, so make sure the boat you get on is pointing in the direction you want to go. Larger stops might have two separate docks side-by-side (one for each direction), while some smaller stops have docks across the canal from each other (one for each direction). Electronic reader boards on busy docks display which boats are coming next, and when.

To clear up any confusion, ask a ticket-seller or conductor (there's often one stationed on the dock to help confused tourists), or pick up the most current ACTV timetable (free at ticket booths,

ORIENTATION

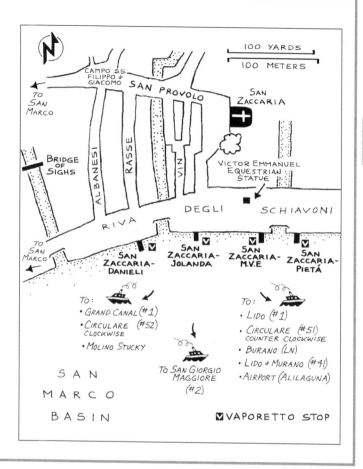

in English and Italian, tel. 041-2424, www.hellovenezia.com or www.actv.it).

These are your ticket and pass options:

Individual Vaporetto Tickets: A single ticket costs a whopping €6.50. (Don't worry—much cheaper passes are described below.) Tickets are good for 60 minutes in one direction; you can hop on and off at stops during that time. Technically, you're not allowed a round-trip (though in practice, a round-trip is allowed if you can complete it within a 60-minute span). Note that you'll pay only €2 for a few shorter runs, including the route from San Marco to La Salute or from San Zaccaria-Jolanda to San Giorgio Maggiore.

ORIENTATION

Vaporetto Passes: You can buy a pass for unlimited use of *vaporetti* and ACTV buses: €16/12 hours, €18/24 hours, €23/36 hours, €28/48 hours, €33/72 hours, €50/7-day pass). Because single tickets cost a hefty €6.50 a pop, these passes can pay for themselves in a hurry. Think through your Venice itinerary before you step up to the ticket booth to pay for your first vaporetto trip. It makes sense to get a pass if you'll be taking four rides or more (e.g., to your hotel, on a Grand Canal joyride, into the lagoon and back, to the train station). And it's fun to be able to hop on and off spontaneously, and avoid long ticket lines. On the other hand, many tourists just walk and rarely use a boat.

Those settling in can ride like a local by buying the **CartaVenezia** ID card (€40, which lets you ride for about €1 per trip; see www.actv.it for details).

Buying and Validating Tickets and Passes: Buy vaporetto tickets or passes at ticket booths at main stops (such as Ferrovia, Rialto, Accademia, and San

Marco-Vallaresso). You can buy individual tickets on board from a conductor (do it immediately upon boarding or you risk a €50 fine). Plan your travel so you'll have tickets or a pass handy when you need them— not all stops have ticket booths. Passes are validated and start with your first swipe. The pass system (called iMob) is electronic—just touch your card to the electronic reader on the dock to validate it.

Vaporetto Tips: For fun, take the Grand Canal Cruise (see that chapter). Boats can be literally packed during the tourist rush hour. Morning rush hour (8:00–10:00) is headed in the direction of St. Mark's Square, as tourists and commuters arrive. Afternoon rush hour (about 17:00) is when they're headed in the other direction for the train station. Riding at night, with nearly empty boats and chandelier-lit palace interiors viewable from the Grand Canal, is an entirely different experience.

By *Traghetto*

Only four bridges cross the Grand Canal, but *traghetti* (gondolas) shuttle locals and in-the-know tourists across the Grand Canal at eight handy locations (marked on the color map of Venice at the

front of this book). Venetians stand while riding, but you shouldn't (€0.50, don't tip—literally). Note that *traghetti* generally don't run in the evening.

By Water Taxi

Venetian taxis, like speedboat limos, hang out at busy points along the Grand Canal. Prices, which average €65, are soft (about €70 to train station or €110 to airport for up to four people, extra fees for very early or late runs). Negotiate and settle on the price before stepping in. For travelers with lots of luggage or small groups who can split the cost, taxi boat rides can be a worthwhile and time-saving convenience—and skipping across the lagoon in a classic wooden motorboat is a cool indulgence. For €90 an hour, you can have a private, unguided taxi-boat tour.

By Gondola

To hire a gondolier for your own private cruise, see the Nightlife in Venice chapter.

Tours in Venice

Avventure Bellissime Venice Tours—This company offers a selection of two-hour walks, including a basic St. Mark's Square introduction called the "Original Venice Walking Tour" (€21, includes church entry, most days at 11:00, Sun at 14:00; 45 minutes on the square, 15 minutes in the church, 60 minutes along back streets). Other walks include Cannaregio/Jewish Ghetto, San Polo/Dorsoduro, and

ghost stories and legends (€20, group size 8–22, English-language only, tel. 041-520-8616, see www.tours-italy.com for details, info @tours-italy.com, Monica or Jonathan). Their 70-minute Grand Canal boat tour is timed for good late-afternoon light (€40, daily at 16:30, limited to eight people). To get a 10 percent discount on any tour, say "Rick sent me."

Classic Venice Bars Tour—Debonair guide Alessandro Schezzini is a connoisseur of Venetian *bacari*—classic old bars serving wine and traditional *cicchetti* snacks. He organizes two-hour Venetian pub tours (€30, any night on request at 18:00, depart from the top of the Rialto Bridge, reserve by phone or email, mobile 335-530-9024, www.schezzini.it, alessandro@schezzini.it).

Is Venice Sinking?

Venice has been battling rising water levels since the fifth century. But today, the water is winning. Due to many factors, including global warming, Venice now floods about 100 times a year—usually from October until late winter— a phenomenon called the *acqua alta*.

Simply put, Venice is sinking and the water is rising. Venice sits atop sediments deposited at the ancient mouth of the Po River, which are still compacting and settling. Twentieth-century industry worsened things by pumping out massive amounts of ground-water from the aquifer beneath the lagoon for nearly 50 years before the government stopped it in the 1970s.

Meanwhile, as the ground sinks beneath this sea-level city, the waters around Venice are rising, especially during the winter. The notorious *acqua alta* happens when a high tide combines with strong sirocco winds and a storm. Although tides are miniscule in the Mediterranean, the narrow, shallow Adriatic Sea has about a three-foot tidal range. When a storm, which is an area of low pressure, travels over a body of water, it pulls the surface of the water up into a dome. As strong sirocco winds from Africa blow storms north up the Adriatic, they push this high water ahead of the front, caus-ing a storm tide, or storm surge. Add to that the effects of climate change—rising sea level from melting polar ice caps, thermal expansion of the water itself as temperatures rise (remember high-school chemistry), and storms that are more frequent and more powerful—and it makes a high sea that much higher.

So what is Venice doing about the flooding? Since the 1966 flood, officials knew something had to be done, but it took about four decades to come up with a solution that some are still unhappy about. In 2003, a consortium of engi-neering firms began construction on the MOSE or Moses Project, which is expected to be operational by 2014. Named for the acronym of its Italian name, *Modulo Sperimentale Elettromeccanico*, it's also a nod to Moses and his (albeit tem-porary) mastery over the sea.

Underwater "mobile" gates are being built on the floor of the sea that will lie flat at the entrances of the three inlets that lead into Venice's lagoon. When the seawater rises above a certain level, air will be pumped into the gates, causing them to rise, and shutting out the Adriatic.

Will it work? Time...and tides...will tell.

Alessandro's tours include sampling *cicchetti* with wines at three different *bacari*, plus he'll answer all of your questions about Venice. (If you think of this tour as a light dinner with a local friend, you can consider it part of your eating budget.)

Venicescapes—Michael Broderick's private theme tours of Venice are intellectually demanding and beyond the attention span of most mortal tourists. But those with a keen interest in learning and a desire to gain a solid understanding of Venice find him passionate and engaging. Rather than a "sightseeing tour," your time with Michael is more like a rolling, graduate-level lecture. For a description of his various itineraries, see his website (book well in advance, tours last 4–6 hours: $275 for 2 people, $50/person after that, pay in dollars or the current euro equivalent, admissions and transportation are extra, tel. 041-520-6361, www.venicescapes.org, info@venicescapes.org).

Artviva: The Original and Best Walking Tours—This company offers a number of tours, including a Venice in One Glorious Day Special and four themed tours (Grand Canal, Venice Walk, Doge's Palace, Gondola Tour). The two-hour "Learn to Be a Gondolier" tour teaches the ancient craft of rowing Venetian-style (€80, 4 people maximum). See the tour details and Rick Steves readers' discounts on their website (book in advance, tours run March–Nov, tel. 055-264-5033, www.italy.artviva.com, staff@artviva.com).

Local Guides—Licensed guides are carefully trained and love explaining Venice to visitors. If you organize a small group from your hotel at breakfast to split the cost (figure on roughly €70/hour with a 2-hour minimum), the fee becomes more reasonable. The following companies and guides give excellent tours to individuals, families, and small groups.

Elisabetta Morelli (€65/hour with this book in 2011, 2-hour minimum, tel. 041-526-7816, mobile 328-753-5220, bettamorelli @inwind.it).

Walks Inside Venice is a group of three women enthusiastic about teaching (€70/hour per group, 3-hour minimum; Roberta: mobile 347-253-0560; Cristina: mobile 348-341-5421; Sara: mobile 335-522-9714; www.walksinsidevenice.com, info@walksinsidevenice .com).

Venice with a Guide is a co-op of 10 equally good guides (www.venicewithaguide.com).

Alessandro Schezzini, mentioned earlier for his Classic Venice Bars Tour, isn't a licensed Italian guide and therefore can't take you into sights. But his relaxed, two-hour, back-streets "Rick Steves" tour does a great job of getting you beyond the clichés and into offbeat Venice (€15/person, book by email—alessandro @schezzini.it, mobile 335-530-9024, www.schezzini.it).

ORIENTATION

Treviso Car Service, run by Igor, offers tours beyond Venice to 16th-century villas, wine-and-cheese tastings, and the Dolomites, in addition to airport transfers (see listing on page 304, mobile 348-900-0700, www.trevisocarservice.com, tvcarservice@gmail.com).

ORIENTATION

SIGHTS IN VENICE

Venice's greatest sight is the city itself. As well as seeing world-class museums and buildings, make time to wander narrow lanes, linger over a meal, or enjoy evening magic on St. Mark's Square. One of Venice's most delightful experiences—a gondola ride, worth ▲▲▲—is covered in the Nightlife in Venice chapter.

In this chapter, don't judge a listing by its length. Some of Venice's most important sights have the shortest listings and are marked with a ✪. These sights are covered in much greater detail in the individual tour chapters later in this book.

For information on sightseeing passes, see page 24. Remember that Venice's city museums offer youth and senior discounts to Americans and other non-EU citizens; see page 9.

San Marco District

▲▲▲**St. Mark's Square (Piazza San Marco)**—This grand square is surrounded by splashy, historic buildings and sights: St. Mark's Basilica, the Doge's Palace, the Campanile bell tower, and the Correr Museum. The square is filled with music, lovers, pigeons, and tourists by day, and is your private rendezvous with the Venetian past late at night, when Europe's most magnificent dance floor is *the* romantic place to be.

For a slow and pricey evening thrill, invest about €12–20 (including the cover charge for the music) in a glass of wine or coffee at one of the elegant cafés with the dueling orchestras (see "Cafés on St. Mark's Square," page 75). For an unmatched experience that offers the best people-watching, it's worth the small splurge.

The **Clock Tower** (Torre dell'Orologio), built during the Renaissance in 1496, marks the entry to the main shopping drag, called the Mercerie, which connects St. Mark's Square with the

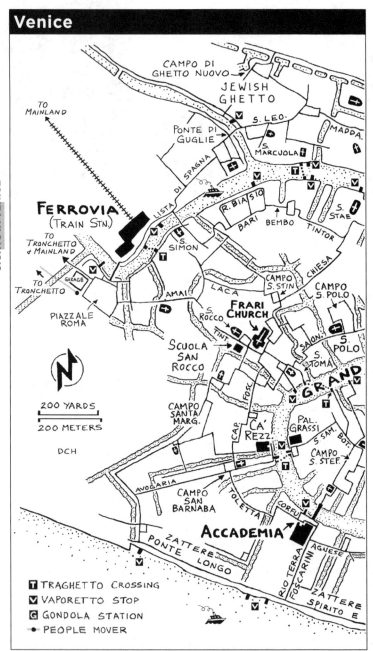

Venice

CAMPO DI GHETTO NUOVO

JEWISH GHETTO

TO MAINLAND

PONTE DI GUGLIE

S. LEO.

S. MARCUOLA

MAPDA

LISTA DI SPAGNA

R. BIASIO

BARI   BEMBO   TINTOR

S. STAE

FERROVIA
(TRAIN STN.)

TO TRONCHETTO & MAINLAND

TO TRONCHETTO

GARAGE

S. SIMON

AMAI

LACA

CAMPO S. STIN

CHIESA

CAMPO S. POLO

PIAZZALE ROMA

S. ROCCO

FRARI CHURCH

SALON.

S. POLO

TINT.

S. TOMA

SCUOLA SAN ROCCO

GRAND

200 YARDS

200 METERS

DCH

CAMPO SANTA MARG.

FOSC

CAP

CA' REZZ.

PAL. GRASSI

S. SAM. BOT.

CAMPO S. STEF.

AVOGARIA

CAMPO SAN BARNABA

TOLETTA

CORFU

S. AGNESE

ACCADEMIA

ZATTERE PONTE LONGO

RIO TERRA FOSCARINI

ZATTERE SPIRITO E

T TRAGHETTO CROSSING

V VAPORETTO STOP

G GONDOLA STATION

• PEOPLE MOVER

SIGHTS IN VENICE

Rialto. From the piazza, you can see the bronze men (Moors) swing their huge clappers at the top of each hour. In the 17th century, one of them knocked an unsuspecting worker off the top and to his death—probably the first-ever killing by a robot. Notice one of the world's first "digital" clocks on the tower facing the square (with dramatic flips every five minutes). You can go inside the Clock Tower only with a pre-booked guided tour that takes you close to the clock's innards and out to a terrace with good views over the square and city rooftops. Reserve in person at the Correr Museum, by calling 848-082-000, or online at www.museicivicieneziani.it (€12 combo-ticket includes Correr Museum; tours in English Mon–Wed at 10:00 and 11:00, plus 13:00 in peak season; also Thu–Sun at 13:00, 14:00, and 15:00, plus 17:00 in peak season). Book a day in advance or show up at the Correr Museum prior to a scheduled tour to see if space is available.

A good **TI** is on the square (with your back to the basilica, it's in the far-left, southwest corner of the square; daily 9:00–15:30), and a €1.50 WC is 30 yards beyond St. Mark's Square (see *Albergo Diorno* sign marked on pavement, WC open daily 9:00–17:30). Another TI is on the lagoon (daily 10:00–18:00, walk toward the water by the Doge's Palace and go right, €1.50 WCs nearby).

For more about the square, ✪ see the St. Mark's Square Tour chapter.

▲▲▲**St. Mark's Basilica (Basilica di San Marco)**—Built in the 11th century to replace an earlier church, this basilica's distinctly Eastern-style architecture underlines Venice's connection with Byzantium (which protected it from the ambition of Charlemagne and his Holy Roman Empire). It's decorated with booty from returning sea captains—a kind of architectural Venetian trophy chest. The interior glows mysteriously with gold

mosaics and colored marble. Since about A.D. 830, the saint's bones have been housed on this site.

Cost and Hours: Basilica entry is free, open Mon–Sat 9:45–17:00, Sun 14:00–17:00 (Sun until 16:00 Nov–March), St. Mark's Square, vaporetto stops: San Marco or San Zaccaria, tel. 041-270-8311, www.basilicasanmarco.it. The dress code is strictly enforced

Billboards

As part of Venice's ongoing renovation, you may see not only scaffolding covering major monuments, but also advertising covering the scaffold-

ing. Cash-strapped Venice is seeking funding from corporations in exchange for advertising space. Might there be Coca Cola ads covering St. Mark's Square? The mayor of Venice said of the possibility of more billboards: "It's not beautiful. It's not ugly. It's necessary."

for everyone (no bare shoulders or bare knees). Lines can be long, and bag check is mandatory, free, and can save you time in line; for details, see the "Orientation" section in the St. Mark's Basilica Tour chapter. No photos are allowed inside.

Three separate exhibits within the church charge admission: the **Treasury** (€3, includes free audioguide), **Golden Altarpiece** (€2), and **San Marco Museum** (€4). The San Marco Museum has the original bronze horses (copies of these overlook the square), a balcony offering a remarkable view over St. Mark's Square, and various works related to the church.

○ See the St. Mark's Basilica Tour chapter.

▲▲▲**Doge's Palace (Palazzo Ducale)**—The seat of the Venetian government and home of its ruling duke, or doge, this

was the most powerful half-acre in Europe for 400 years. The Doge's Palace was built to show off the power and wealth of the Republic. The doge lived with his family on the first floor, near the halls of power. From his once-lavish (now sparse) quarters, you'll follow the one-way tour through the public rooms of the top floor, finishing with the Bridge of Sighs and the prison. The place is wallpapered with masterpieces by Veronese and Tintoretto. Don't worry much about the great art. Enjoy the building.

Cost and Hours: Covered by €13 San Marco Museum Plus Pass, which also includes admission to the Correr Museum (both sights also covered by €18 Museum Pass); no individual tickets

Venice at a Glance

▲▲▲**St. Mark's Square** Venice's grand main square. **Hours:** Always open. See page 37.

▲▲▲**St. Mark's Basilica** Cathedral with mosaics, saint's bones, treasury, museum, and viewpoint of square. **Hours:** Basilica—Mon–Sat 9:45–17:00, Sun 14:00–17:00 (until 16:00 Nov–March); Treasury, Golden Altarpiece, and San Marco Museum close 15 minutes before church (shorter hours in winter). See page 40.

▲▲▲**Doge's Palace** Art-splashed palace of former rulers, with prison accessible through Bridge of Sighs. **Hours:** Daily April–Oct 8:30–18:30, Nov–March 9:00–18:00. See page 41.

▲▲▲**Rialto Bridge** Distinctive bridge spanning the Grand Canal, with a market nearby. **Hours:** Bridge—always open; market—souvenir stalls open daily, produce market closed Sun–Mon, fish market closed Sun. See page 49.

▲▲**Correr Museum** Venetian history and art. **Hours:** Daily April–Oct 9:00–19:00, Nov–March 9:00–17:00. See page 44.

▲▲**Accademia** Venice's top art museum. **Hours:** Mon 8:15–14:00, Tue–Sun 8:15–19:15. See page 47.

▲▲**Peggy Guggenheim Collection** Popular display of 20th-century art. **Hours:** Wed–Mon 10:00–18:00, closed Tue. See page 47.

▲▲**Frari Church** Franciscan church featuring Renaissance masters. **Hours:** Mon–Sat 9:00–18:00, Sun 13:00–18:00. See page 50.

▲▲**Scuola San Rocco** "Tintoretto's Sistine Chapel." **Hours:** Daily 9:30–17:30. See page 50.

▲**Campanile** Dramatic bell tower on St. Mark's Square with elevator to the top. **Hours:** Daily April–June and Oct 9:00–19:00, July–Sept 9:00–21:00, Nov–March 9:30–15:45, closed from Christmas to mid-Jan. See page 44.

▲**Bridge of Sighs** Famous enclosed bridge, part of Doge's Palace, near St. Mark's Square. **Hours:** Generally viewable, but covered with scaffolding during renovation. See page 45.

▲**La Salute Church** Striking church dedicated to the Virgin Mary. **Hours:** Daily 9:00–12:00 & 15:00–17:30. See page 47.

▲**Ca' Rezzonico** Posh Grand Canal palazzo with 18th-century Venetian art. **Hours:** April–Oct Wed–Mon 10:00–18:00, Nov–March Wed–Mon 10:00–17:00, closed Tue. See page 48.

▲**Punta della Dogana** Museum of contemporary art. **Hours:** Wed–Mon 10:00–19:00, closed Tue. See page 48.

▲**Ca' Pesaro International Gallery of Modern Art** in a canalside palazzo. **Hours:** Tue–Sun 10:00–17:00, closed Mon. See page 49.

▲**Scuola Dalmata di San Giorgio** Exquisite Renaissance meeting house. **Hours:** Mon 14:45–18:00, Tue–Sat 9:15–13:00 & 14:45–18:00, Sun 9:15–13:00. See page 55.

Church of San Zaccaria Final resting place of St. Zechariah (San Zaccaria), plus a Bellini altarpiece and an eerie crypt. **Hours:** Mon–Sat 10:00–12:00 & 16:00–18:00, Sun 16:00–18:00 only. See page 54.

Church of San Polo Ninth-century church with works by Tintoretto, Veronese, and Tiepolo. **Hours:** Mon–Sat 10:00–17:00, closed Sun. See page 51.

Nearby Islands
▲**San Giorgio Maggiore** Island across the lagoon featuring church with Palladio architecture, Tintoretto paintings, and fine views back on Venice. **Hours:** May–Sept Mon–Sat 9:30–12:30 & 14:30–18:00, Sun 8:30–11:00 & 14:30–18:00; Oct–April until 16:30. See page 46.

San Michele Cemetery island on the lagoon. **Hours:** Daily April–Sept 7:30–18:00, Oct–March 7:30–16:30. See page 56.

Murano Island famous for glass factories and glassmaking museum. **Hours:** Glass museum open daily April–Oct 10:00–18:00, Nov–March 10:00–17:00. See page 56.

Burano Sleepy lacemaking island. **Hours:** Always open. See page 57.

Torcello Near-deserted island with old church, bell tower, and museum. **Hours:** Most sights open daily March–Oct 10:30–17:30, Nov–Feb 10:00–17:00, museum closed Mon. See page 57.

are sold to this sight. If the line is long at the Doge's Palace, buy your pass at the Correr Museum across the square; then you can go directly through the Doge's turnstile without waiting in line. Open daily April–Oct 8:30–18:30, Nov–March 9:00–18:00, last entry one hour before closing.

Location: Next to St. Mark's Basilica, just off St. Mark's Square. Vaporetto stops: San Marco or San Zaccaria.

Tours: The audioguide costs €5. For a live guided tour, consider the Secret Itineraries Tour, which takes you into palace rooms otherwise not open to the public (€18, or €12 with San Marco Museum Plus Pass; two or three English-language tours each morning). Reserve ahead for this tour in peak season—it can fill up as much as a month in advance. Book online at www.museicivicivenetiani.it, reserve by phone (tel. 848-082-000, or from the US dial 011-39-041-4273-0892), or ask at the info desk.

○ See the Doge's Palace Tour chapter.

▲▲**Correr Museum (Museo Civico Correr)**—This uncrowded museum gives you a good overview of Venetian history and art. The doge memorabilia, armor, banners, statues (by Canova), and paintings (by the Bellini family and others) re-create the festive days of the Venetian Republic. There are English descriptions and breathtaking views of St. Mark's Square throughout the museum.

Cost and Hours: Covered by €13 San Marco Museum Plus Pass, which also includes the Doge's Palace (both are also covered by €18 Museum Pass). Open daily April–Oct 9:00–19:00, Nov–March 9:00–17:00, last entry one hour before closing, enter at far end of square directly opposite basilica, tel. 041-240-5211, www.museicivicivenetiani.it.

○ See the Correr Museum Tour chapter.

▲**Campanile (Campanile di San Marco)**—This dramatic bell tower replaced a shorter lighthouse, once part of the original for-

tress that guarded the entry of the Grand Canal. The lighthouse crumbled into a pile of bricks in 1902, a thousand years after it was built. For the next few years, you'll see construction work being done to strengthen the base of the tower. Ride the elevator 300 feet to the top of the bell tower for the best view in Venice (especially at sunset). For an ear-shattering experience, be on top when the bells ring. The golden archangel Gabriel at the top always faces into the wind. Lines are longest at midday; beat the crowds and enjoy the crisp morning air at 9:00 or the cool evening breeze at 18:00.

Cost and Hours: €8, daily April–June and Oct 9:00–19:00, July–Sept 9:00–21:00, Nov–March 9:30–15:45, closed from Christmas to mid-Jan, tel. 041-522-4064.

For more on the Campanile, ✪ see the St. Mark's Square Tour chapter.

La Fenice Opera House (Gran Teatro alla Fenice)—During Venice's glorious decline in the 18th century, this was one of

seven opera houses in the city, and one of the most famous in Europe. For 200 years, great operas and famous divas debuted here, applauded by ladies and gentlemen in their finery. Then in 1996, an arson fire completely gutted the theater. But La Fenice ("The Phoenix") has risen from the ashes, thanks to an eight-year effort to rebuild the historic landmark according to photographic archives of the interior. To see the results at their most glorious, attend an evening performance.

You can also tour the opera house during the day. All you really see is the theater itself; there's no "backstage" tour of dressing rooms, or an opera museum. The auditorium, ringed with box seats, is impressive: pastel blue with sparkling gold filigree, muses depicted on the ceiling, and a star-burst chandelier. It's also a bit saccharine and brings sadness to Venetians who remember the place before the fire. Other than a minor exhibit of opera scores and Maria Callas memorabilia, there's little to see from the world of opera. The dry audioguide recounts two centuries of construction. Opening hours vary wildly, depending on the performance schedule—from none at all, to an hour or two, to being open all day—so confirm in advance.

Cost and Hours: €7 entry fee includes 45-minute audioguide, generally open daily 10:00–19:30, closed for rehearsals or performances, concert box office open daily 9:30–18:30, call-center open daily 7:30–20:00, on Campo San Fantin between St. Mark's Square and Accademia Bridge, vaporetto stop: Santa Maria del Giglio, tel. 041-2424, www.teatrolafenice.it.

Behind St. Mark's Basilica

▲**Bridge of Sighs**—Connecting two wings of the Doge's Palace high over a canal, this enclosed bridge will be surrounded by scaffolding for the next few years for restoration.

Travelers popularized this bridge in the Romantic 19th century. Supposedly, a condemned man would be led over this bridge on his way to the prison, take one last look at the glory of Venice, and sigh. Though overhyped, when it's uncovered the bridge is undeniably tingle-worthy—especially after dark, when the crowds have dispersed and it's just you and floodlit Venice. A local legend

says that lovers will be assured eternal love if they kiss on a gondola at sunset under the bridge.

The bridge is around the corner from the Doge's Palace: Walk toward the waterfront, turn left along the water, and look up the first canal on your left. You can walk across the bridge (from the inside) by visiting the Doge's Palace.

✪ See the St. Mark's to San Zaccaria Walk chapter; also see the Doge's Palace Tour chapter.

Church of San Zaccaria—This historic church is home to a sometimes-waterlogged crypt, a Bellini altarpiece, a Tintoretto painting, and the final resting place of St. Zechariah, the father of John the Baptist (free, €1 to enter crypt, €0.50 coin to light up Bellini's altarpiece, Mon–Sat 10:00–12:00 & 16:00–18:00, Sun 16:00–18:00 only, 2 canals behind St. Mark's Basilica).

✪ See the St. Mark's to San Zaccaria Walk chapter.

Across the Lagoon from St. Mark's Square

▲**San Giorgio Maggiore**—This is the dreamy church-topped island you can see from the waterfront by St. Mark's Square. The striking church, designed by Palladio, features art by Tintoretto, a daily Gregorian Mass, a bell tower, and good views of Venice.

Cost and Hours: Free entry to church; May–Sept Mon–Sat 9:30–12:30 & 14:30–18:00, Sun 8:30–11:00 & 14:30–18:00; Oct–April until 16:30.

Gregorian Mass is sung Mon–Sat at 8:00 and on Sun at 11:00. The bell tower costs €3 and is accessible by elevator (runs from 30 min after the church opens until 30 minutes before the church closes).

Getting There: To reach the island from St. Mark's Square, take the five-minute ride on vaporetto #2 (€2, 6/hour, ticket valid for one hour; leaves from San Zaccaria-M.V.E. stop located east of Bridge of Sighs by equestrian statue; catch boat in direction: Tronchetto).

● See the San Giorgio Maggiore Tour chapter.

Dorsoduro District

▲▲**Accademia (Galleria dell'Accademia)**—Venice's top art museum, packed with highlights of the Venetian Renaissance, features paintings by the Bellini family, Titian, Tintoretto, Veronese, Tiepolo, Giorgione, Canaletto, and Testosterone. It's just over the wooden Accademia Bridge from the San Marco action.

Cost and Hours: €6.50, Mon 8:15–14:00, Tue–Sun 8:15–19:15, last entry 45 minutes before closing, no photos allowed. The dull audioguide costs €5 (€7/2 people). One-hour guided tours in English are €5 (€7/2 people, Sat–Sun at 11:00). At Accademia Bridge, vaporetto stop: Accademia. Tel. 041-522-2247, www.gallerie accademia.org.

Avoiding Crowds: Expect long lines in the late morning, because they allow only 300 visitors in at a time; visit early or late to miss the crowds, or make a reservation at least a day in advance (€1 fee; calling 041-520-0345 is easier than reserving online at their clunky website).

● See the Accademia Tour chapter.

▲▲**Peggy Guggenheim Collection**—The popular museum of far-out art, housed in the American heiress' former retirement palazzo, offers one of Europe's best reviews of the art of the first half of the 20th century. Stroll through styles represented by artists whom Peggy knew personally—Cubism (Picasso, Braque), Surrealism (Dalí, Ernst), Futurism (Boccioni), American Abstract Expressionism (Pollock), and a sprinkling of Klee, Calder, and Chagall. The place is staffed by international interns working on art-related degrees.

Cost and Hours: €12, generally includes temporary exhibits, Wed–Mon 10:00–18:00, closed Tue, last entry 15 minutes before closing, audioguide–€7, mini-guidebook–€6, free and mandatory baggage check for anything bigger than a small purse, pricey café, photos allowed only in garden and terrace—a fine and relaxing perch overlooking Grand Canal. It's at Dorsoduro 704, a five-minute walk from the Accademia Bridge (vaporetto: Accademia) or from La Salute Church (vaporetto: Salute). Tel. 041-240-5411, www.guggenheim-venice.it.

● See the Peggy Guggenheim Collection Tour chapter.

▲**La Salute Church (Santa Maria della Salute)**—This impressive church with a crown-shaped dome was built and dedicated to the Virgin Mary by grateful survivors of the 1630 plague.

Cost and Hours: Free entry to church, daily 9:00–12:00 & 15:00–17:30. Sacristy—€2, may have shorter hours than church. It's a 10-minute walk from the Accademia Bridge; the Salute vaporetto stop is at its doorstep (the San Marco-Vallaresso to

Water, Water Everywhere, but...

As you explore Venice, notice the wells that grace nearly every square. Well water in the middle of the sea? Venice, surrounded by water, originally had no natural source of drinking water. For centuries, residents collected water from the mainland with much effort and risk. Eventually, in the ninth century, they devised a way to collect rainwater by using town squares as catchment systems. The rain falls into the square, flows down through the slightly sloped pavement, drains through the lime-  stone grates, and filters through sand into a large clay tub under the pavement. Citizens could drop their buckets down the "well" to draw up fresh rainwater. With a safe local source of drinking water, Venice's population began to grow. Several thousand of these cisterns provided lagoon communities with drinking water right up until 1886, when an aqueduct was built (paralleling the railroad tracks across the lagoon) to bring in water from nearby mountains. Since then, the clay tubs have rotted out and the wells have been capped. Now, with a high tide, the floods show first on these limestone grates, which mark the low point of each town square.

Salute vaporetto #1 hop is €2). Tel. 041-274-3928.

○ See the La Salute Church Tour chapter.

▲**Ca' Rezzonico (Museum of 18th-Century Venice)**—This grand Grand Canal palazzo offers the best look in town at the life of Venice's rich and famous in the 1700s. Wander under ceilings by Tiepolo, among furnishings from that most decadent century, enjoying views of the canal and paintings by Guardi, Canaletto, and Longhi.

Cost and Hours: €7, covered by passes—see page 24, April–Oct Wed–Mon 10:00–18:00, Nov–March Wed–Mon 10:00–17:00, closed Tue, last entry one hour before closing, audioguide-€4 or €6/2 people, free and mandatory baggage check, at Ca' Rezzonico vaporetto stop, tel. 041-241-0100, www.museicivicivenezianiani.it.

○ See the Ca' Rezzonico Tour chapter.

▲**Punta della Dogana**—This new museum of contemporary art makes the Dorsoduro a major destination for art-lovers. Housed in the former Customs House at the end of the Grand Canal, it features cutting-edge 21st-century art in spacious rooms. This isn't Picasso and Matisse, or even Pollock and Warhol—those guys are

ancient history. But if you're into the likes of Jeff Koons, Cy Twombly, Rachel Whiteread, and a host of newer artists, the museum is world-class. The displays change completely about every year, drawn from the museum's large collection. In fact, the art spreads over two locations—the triangular Customs House and Palazzo Grassi.

Cost and Hours: €15 for one locale, €20 for both. Wed–Mon 10:00–19:00, closed Tue, last entry one hour before closing, audioguide-€5 (€8/2 people), small café. The Customs House is near La Salute Church (Dogana *traghetto* or vaporetto: Salute).

Palazzo Grassi is a bit upstream, on the east side of the Grand Canal (vaporetto: San Samuele). Tel. 199-139-139, www.palazzo grassi.it.

Santa Croce District

▲▲▲**Rialto Bridge**—One of the world's most famous bridges, this distinctive and dramatic stone structure crosses the Grand Canal with a single confident span. The arcades along the top of the bridge help reinforce the structure...and offer some enjoyable shopping diver-
sions, as does the **market** surrounding the bridge (souvenir stalls open daily,

produce market closed Sun–Mon, fish market closed Sun).

○ See the St. Mark's to Rialto Walk chapter.

▲**Ca' Pesaro International Gallery of Modern Art**—This museum features 19th- and early 20th-century art in a 17th-century canalside palazzo. The collection is strongest on Italian (especially Venetian) artists, but also presents a broad array of other well-known artists. The highlights are in one large room: Klimt's beautiful/creepy *Judith II,* with eagle-talon fingers; Kandinsky's *White Zig Zags* (plus other recognizable shapes); the colorful *Nude in the Mirror* by Bonnard that flattens the 3-D scene into a 2-D pattern of rectangles; and Chagall's surprisingly realistic portrait of his hometown rabbi, *The Rabbi of Vitebsk.* The adjoining Room VII features small-scale works by Matisse, Max Ernst, Mark Tobey, and a Calder mobile. Admission also includes an Oriental Art wing.

Cost and Hours: €5.50, covered by passes—see page 24, Tue–Sun 10:00–17:00, closed Mon, last entry one hour before closing, 2-minute walk from San Stae vaporetto stop, tel. 041-524-0662.

Palazzo Mocenigo Costume Museum—The Museo di Palazzo Mocenigo offers a walk through six rooms of a fine 17th-century mansion with period furnishings, family portraits, ceilings painted (c. 1790) with family triumphs (the Mocenigos produced seven doges), Murano glass chandeliers in situ, and a paltry collection of costumes with sparse descriptions (€6, covered by passes, Tue–Sun 10:00–16:00, closed Mon, a block in from San Stae vaporetto stop, tel. 041-721-798).

San Polo District

If you'll be walking from the Rialto Bridge to the following sights, note that they're all stops on the Rialto to Frari Church Walk (see that chapter).

▲▲**Frari Church (Chiesa dei Frari)**—My favorite art experience in Venice is seeing art in the setting for which it was designed—as it is at the Frari Church. The Franciscan "Church of the Brothers" and the art that decorates it is warmed by the spirit of St. Francis. It features the work of three great Renaissance masters: Donatello, Giovanni Bellini, and Titian—each showing worshippers the glory of God in human terms.

Cost and Hours: €3, Mon–Sat 9:00–18:00, Sun 13:00–18:00, last entry 15 minutes before closing, no visits during services, audioguide-€2 or €3/2 people, modest dress recommended. On Campo dei Frari, near San Tomà vaporetto and *traghetto* stops.

Concerts: The church occasionally hosts evening concerts (€15, buy ticket at church). For concert details, look for fliers, check www.basilicadeifrari.it, or call the church at 041-272-8611.

○ See the Frari Church Tour chapter.

▲▲**Scuola San Rocco**—Sometimes called "Tintoretto's Sistine Chapel," this lavish meeting hall (next to the Frari Church) has some 50 large, colorful Tintoretto paintings plastered to the walls and ceilings. The best paintings are upstairs, especially the *Crucifixion* in the smaller room. View the neck-breaking splendor

A Dying City?

Venice's population (about 60,000) is half what it was just 30 years ago, and people are leaving at a rate of a thousand a year. Of those who stay, 25 percent are 65 or older.

Sad, yes, but imagine raising a family here: Apartments are small, high up, and expensive. Humidity and occasional flooding make basic maintenance a pain. Home-improvement projects require navigating miles of red tape, and you must follow regulations intended to preserve the historical ambience. Everything is expensive because it has to be shipped in from the mainland. You can easily get glass and tourist trinkets, but it's hard to find groceries or get your shoes fixed. Running basic errands involves lots of walking and stairs—imagine crossing over arched bridges while pushing a child in a stroller and carrying a day's worth of groceries.

With over 12 million visitors a year (150,000 a day at peak times), on any given day Venetians are likely outnumbered by tourists. Despite government efforts to subsidize rents and build cheap housing, the city is losing its residents. The economy itself is thriving, thanks to tourist dollars and rich foreigners buying second homes. But the culture is dying. Even the most hopeful city planners worry that in a few decades, Venice will not be a city at all, but a museum, a cultural theme park, a decaying Disneyland for adults.

with one of the mirrors available at the entrance.

Cost and Hours: €7, audioguide-€1, daily 9:30–17:30, last entry 30 minutes before closing, tel. 041-523-4864, www.scuola grandesanrocco.it.

○ See the Scuola San Rocco Tour chapter.

Church of San Polo—This nearby church, which pales in comparison to the two sights just listed, is only worth a visit for artlovers. One of Venice's oldest churches (from the ninth century), San Polo features works by Tintoretto, Veronese, and Tiepolo and son (€3, Mon–Sat 10:00–17:00, closed Sun, last entry 15 minutes before closing).

Cannaregio District

Jewish Ghetto—Tucked away in the Cannaregio District is the "original" ghetto, where Venice's Jewish population once lived

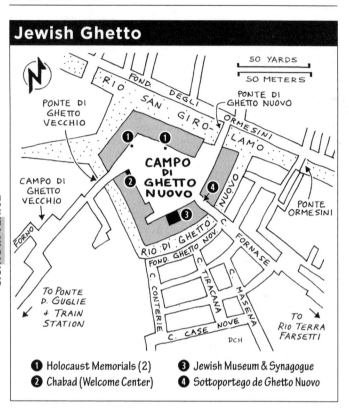

Jewish Ghetto

50 YARDS
50 METERS

PONTE DI GHETTO NUOVO

PONTE DI GHETTO VECCHIO

RIO FOND. SAN GIRO-LAMO DEGLI ORMESINI

CAMPO DI GHETTO NUOVO

CAMPO DI GHETTO VECCHIO

PONTE ORMESINI

C. VOLTO

C. FORNASE

RIO DI GHETTO NOV.

FOND. GHETTO NOV.

FORNO

C. CONTERIE

C. TIRACANA

C. MASENA

C. CASE NOVE

DCH

TO PONTE D. GUGLIE + TRAIN STATION

TO RIO TERRA FARSETTI

- ❶ Holocaust Memorials (2)
- ❷ Chabad (Welcome Center)
- ❸ Jewish Museum & Synagogue
- ❹ Sottoportego de Ghetto Nuovo

segregated from their non-Jewish neighbors. While today's Jewish population is dwindling, the neighborhood still has centuries of history, not to mention Jewish-themed sights and eateries.

Getting There: From either the San Marcuola vaporetto stop or the train station, walk five minutes to the Pont di Guglie bridge that crosses the Cannaregio Canal. About 50 yards north of the bridge, a small covered alleyway (Sottoportego del Ghetto) leads between the *farmacia* and the Gam-Gam Kosher Restaurant and through a newer Jewish section, across a bridge, and into the historic core of the Ghetto at Campo di Ghetto Nuovo.

◐ **Self-Guided Tour: Campo di Ghetto Nuovo** must have been quite a scene in the past, ringed by 70 shops and with all of Venice's Jewish commerce compressed onto this one spot. As late as the 1930s, 12,000 Jews called Venice home, but today there are only 500—and only a few dozen

Jews in Venice's Ghetto

In medieval times, Jews were grudgingly allowed to do business in Venice, but they weren't permitted to live there until 1385 (subject to strict laws and special taxes). Anti-Semitic forces tried to oust them from the city, but in 1516, the doge compromised by restricting Jews to a special (undesirable) neighborhood. It was located on an easy-to-isolate island near the former foundry (geto), coining the word "ghetto" for a segregated neighborhood.

The population swelled with immigrants from elsewhere in Europe, reaching 5,000 in the 1600s, the Golden Age of Venice's Jews. Restricted within their tiny neighborhood (the Ghetto Nuovo, or "New Ghetto"), they expanded upward, building six-story "skyscrapers" that still stand today. The community's five synagogues were built atop the high-rise tenements. (As space was very tight and you couldn't live above a house of worship, this was the most practical use of precious land.) Only two synagogues are still active. You can spot them (with their five windows) from the square, but to visit them you have to book a tour through the Jewish Museum (described later).

Relations with the non-Jewish community were complex: While the Jewish moneylenders were treated harshly, Jewish merchants were more valued and treated with more respect. The island's two bridges were locked at night, when only Jewish doctors—coming to the aid of Venetians—were allowed to come and go. Eventually the ghetto community was given more land and spread to adjacent blocks.

---

live in the actual Ghetto. The square is still surrounded by the six-story "skyscrapers" that once made this a densely packed neighborhood.

Today the square, with its three cistern wells, is quiet. The Jewish people you may see here are likely tourists. Look for the large Jewish senior center/community center (Casa Israelitica di Riposo), flanked by two different Holocaust memorials by the Lithuanian artist Arbit Blatas. The barbed wire and bronze plaques remind us that it was on this spot that the Nazis rounded up 200 Jews for deportation (only eight returned). At #2884A is the Chabad, a welcome center that helps visiting Hasidic Jews find places to pray, get kosher food, and so on. The Locanda del Ghetto is the city's only kosher hotel.

The **Jewish Museum** (Museo Ebraico) consists of two parts: a museum and a synagogue. The humble two-room museum has silver menorahs, cloth covers for the Torah scrolls, various religious objects, artifacts from the old community, and scant English explanations (€3, June–Sept Sun–Fri 10:00–17:00, Oct–May

Sun–Fri 10:00–16:30, closed Sat and Jewish holidays, Campo di Ghetto Nuovo, vaporetto stop: San Marcuola, tel. 041-715-359, small café and bookstore). To see the **synagogue,** you must sign up for a half-hour English tour (€8.50, tours run hourly on the half-hour June–Sept Sun–Fri 10:00–19:00, Oct–May Sun–Fri 10:00–17:30, closed Sat and Jewish holidays). Group sizes are limited (the 11:30 tour is often booked full), so show up 20 minutes early to be sure you get in.

Exit the square through Sottoportego de Ghetto Nuovo for the best view of the "fortress ghetto," with tall tenement buildings rising from the canal and an easy-to-lock-up little bridge and gateway.

Calatrava Bridge (a.k.a. Ponte della Costituzione)—This controversial bridge, officially called "Constitution Bridge," is just upstream and around the bend from the train station. Only the fourth bridge to cross the Grand Canal, it carries foot traffic between the train station and Piazzale Roma. A modern structure of glass, steel, and stone, the bridge finally opened in 2008 after

delays, cost overruns, and questions about its stability.

The bridge was designed by Spanish architect Santiago Calatrava, whose other projects include a museum in his hometown of Valencia, Spain; the twisting torso skyscraper in Malmö, Sweden; and the Olympic Sports complex in Athens, Greece.

The bridge draws snorts from Venetians. With an original price tag of €4 million, the cost rose to around €11 million. The modern design of the bridge is also a sore point for a city with such rich medieval and Renaissance architecture. And, to add practical insult to aesthetic injury, the heavy bridge is crushing the centuries-old foundations at either end, threatening nearby buildings.

Interestingly, Calatrava's modern structure harkens back to the past, employing the same low-arch design of many older Venetian bridges. Pedestrians walk over similar shallow stair steps, and the bridge uses local Istrian stone.

Ca' d'Oro—This "House of Gold" palace, fronting the Grand Canal, is quintessential Venetian Gothic (Gothic seasoned with Byzantine and Islamic accents—see page 63). Inside, the permanent collection includes a few big names in Renaissance painting—Ghirlandaio, Signorelli, and Mantegna; a glimpse at a lush courtyard; and a grand view of the Grand Canal (€5, slow and dry audioguide-€4, Mon 8:15–14:00, Tue–Sun 8:15–19:15, free peek through hole in door of courtyard, vaporetto stop: Ca' d'Oro, Calle Ca' d'Oro 3932).

Castello District

▲Scuola Dalmata di San Giorgio—This little-visited "school" (which means "meeting place") features an exquisite wood-paneled chapel decorated with the world's best collection of paintings by Vittorio Carpaccio (1465–1526).

The Scuola, a reminder that cosmopolitan Venice was once Europe's melting-pot, was one of a hundred such community centers for various ethnic, religious, and economic groups, supported by the government partly to keep an eye on foreigners. It was here that the Dalmatians (from the southern coast of present-day Croatia) worshiped in their own way, held neighborhood meetings, and preserved their culture.

Cost and Hours: €3, Mon 14:45–18:00, Tue–Sat 9:15–13:00 & 14:45–18:00, Sun 9:15–13:00, on Calle dei Furlani, tel. 041-522-8828.

Getting There: The Scuola is located midway between St. Mark's Square and the Arsenale. Go north from Campo San Provolo (by Church of San Zaccaria), following the street as it changes names from L'Osmarin to St. George to Greci. At the second bridge, turn left on Fondamenta dei Furlani.

❂ Self-Guided Tour: The chapel on the ground floor is one of the best-preserved Renaissance interiors in Venice. Ringing the room is the cycle of paintings that Carpaccio was hired to paint (1502–1507). Pick up the English explanation from the ticket booth.

The scenes tell the story of St. George (the Dalmatians' patron saint), who slew a dragon and metaphorically conquered paganism. Carpaccio cuts right to the climax. In the first panel on the far left, George meets the dragon on the barren plain, charges forward, and jams his spear through the dragon's skull, to the relief of the damsel in distress (in red). George gets there just in time—notice half a damsel on the ground. This painting is one of Carpaccio's masterpieces. He places George and the dragon directly facing each other. Meanwhile, the center of the composition—where George meets dragon—is also the "vanishing point" that draws your eye to the distant horizon. Very clever.

The story of St. George continues in the next panel, as George leads the bedraggled dragon (spear still in his head) before the thankful, wealthy pagan king and queen. Next, they kneel before George (now in red, far right) as he holds a pan of water, baptizing them.

The rest of the panels (about St. Jerome and St. Tryphone) are also by Carpaccio. In the last panel on the right, St. Augustine pauses while writing. He hears something. The dog hears it, too. It's the encouraging voice of St. Jerome, echoing mysteriously through the spacious room. Carpaccio sweated small details like the scattered books and the shadow cast by the statue of Christ.

In the adjoining room, see the cross and censers (incense burners) used by the community in religious processions. Upstairs, there's another paneled room with more depictions of St. George (but not by Carpaccio).

Santa Elena—For a pleasant peek into a completely non-touristy, residential side of Venice, walk or catch vaporetto #1 from St. Mark's Square to the neighborhood of Santa Elena (at the fish's tail). This 100-year-old suburb lives as if there were no tourism. You'll find a kid-friendly park, a few lazy restaurants, and beautiful sunsets over San Marco.

La Biennale—Every odd year (including 2011), Venice hosts a world's fair of contemporary art. Countries around the world send their best and most outrageous art to be displayed in buildings and pavilions scattered over the Giardini park and the Arsenale. Some artists convert entire buildings into a single installation, creating a weird wonderland of colors, video images, stage fog, laser lights, and piped-in sound. The festival is an excuse for temporary art exhibitions, concerts, and other cultural events around the city (roughly Feb–Nov, take vaporetto #1 or #2 to Giardini-Biennale stop, www.labiennale.org).

Venice's Lagoon

With more time, venture to some nearby islands in Venice's lagoon. While still somewhat touristy, they offer an escape from the crowds, a chance to get out on a boat, and some enjoyable museums for fans of glassmaking and lace.

The islands are listed in order of proximity to Venice, from nearest to farthest. For more information, ✪ see the Venice's Lagoon Tour chapter.

San Michele (a.k.a. Cimitero)—This island is the final resting place of Venetians and a few foreign VIPs, from poet Ezra Pound to composer Igor Stravinsky. Many visitors find this island (expectedly) pretty dead.

Murano—Famous for its glassmaking, this island is home to several glass factories and the **Glass Museum** (Museo Vetrario), which traces the history of this delicate art (€5.50, covered by passes—see page 24, daily April–Oct 10:00–18:00, Nov–March 10:00–17:00, tel. 041-739-586, www .museiciviciveneziani.it).

Burano—This island's claim to fame is lacemaking, and (along with countless lace shops) it offers a delightful pastel village alternative to big, bustling Venice.

Torcello—This sparsely populated island features what's claimed to be Venice's oldest church. With impressive mosaics, a climbable bell tower, and a modest museum of Roman sculpture and medieval sculpture and manuscripts, the church is worth a wander (€3 for any one sight or €10 for all sights plus an audioguide; most sights open daily March–Oct 10:30–17:30, Nov–Feb 10:00–17:00, museum closed Mon; museum tel. 041-730-761, church/bell tower tel. 041-730-119).

GRAND CANAL CRUISE

Canal Grande

Take a joyride and introduce yourself to Venice by boat. Cruise the Canal Grande all the way to San Marco, starting at Ferrovia (the train station).

If it's your first trip down the Grand Canal, you might want to stow this book and just take it all in—Venice is a barrage on the senses that hardly needs narration. But these notes give the cruise a little meaning and help orient you to this great city.

This tour is designed to be done on the slow boat #1 (which takes about 45 minutes). The express boat #2 travels the same route, but it skips many stops and takes only 25 minutes, making it hard to sightsee on.

To help you enjoy the visual parade of canal wonders, I've organized this tour by boat stop. I'll point out both what you can see from the current stop, and what to look forward to as you cruise to the next stop.

Orientation

Cost: €6.50 for a 60-minute vaporetto ticket (or covered by a pass). For more on riding the vaporetto, see page 29.

When to Go: Boats run every 10 minutes. Enjoy the best light and the fewest crowds by riding late in the day. Avoid the morning rush hour (8:00–10:00), when local workers and tourists commute into town (from Ferrovia to San Marco—in the same direction as this tour). In the evening, the crowds head the opposite way, and boats to San Marco are less crowded. Sunset bathes the buildings in gold. After dark, chandeliers light up building interiors.

Getting There: This tour starts at the Ferrovia vaporetto stop (at Santa Lucia train station). It also works if you board upstream from Ferrovia, either at Tronchetto (where cars arrive) or Piazzale Roma (where airport buses and the People Mover monorail from Tronchetto arrive). Just start the tour when your vaporetto reaches Ferrovia.

Tips: You're more likely to find an empty seat if you catch the vaporetto at Piazzale Roma, which is just a short walk from Ferrovia over the Calatrava Bridge. If you start at Tronchetto, your only choice is boat #2—which really rushes this tour. Wherever you catch your vaporetto, confirm that you're on a boat that goes all the way to San Marco, by way of Rialto *("San Marco via Rialto")*. If the conductor announces *"Solo Rialto!"*, the boat only goes as far as Rialto.

Stops to Consider: You can break up the tour by hopping on and off at various sights that are described in greater depth elsewhere in this book (but remember, a single-fare vaporetto ticket is good for just 60 minutes). Note that only boat #1 docks at all the stops we list; the faster boat #2 skips some stops.

These are all worth considering as hop-off spots: San Marcuola (near the Jewish Ghetto), Mercato Rialto (fish market and famous bridge), Ca' Rezzonico (Museum of 18th-Century Venice), Accademia (art museum and the nearby Guggenheim Collection), and Salute (huge and interesting church).

Information: Some city maps (on sale at postcard racks) have a handy Grand Canal map on the back.

Audioguide Tours: Those traveling with an iPod or other MP3 player can download a free audio tour of this chapter at www.ricksteves .com (or search for "Rick Steves Audio Tours" in iTunes).

Sightseeing Tips: As you board the vaporetto, make a beeline for an open-air seat in the front of the boat, which has the best seats for this tour. From the front, you can easily look left, right, and forward. If you find yourself stuck on the side or in the cabin, do your best. Avoid sitting in the back, only because you'll miss the wonderful forward views.

Some readers do this cruise twice—once in either direction—because it's hard to see it all while trying to read along aboard a moving boat.

Length of This Tour: Allow 45 minutes on vaporetto #1, or 25 minutes on vaporetto #2.

Starring: Palaces, markets, boats, bridges—Venice.

The Tour Begins

While you wait for your boat, here's some background on Venice's "Main Street."

At more than two miles long, nearly 150 feet wide, and nearly

Grand Canal

GRAND CANAL CRUISE

CANNAREGIO CANAL

JEWISH GHETTO

🚏 TRAGHETTO CROSSING

PONTE GUGLIE

SANTA LUCIA TRAIN STATION

SCALZI CHURCH

CASINÒ

FADED FRESCOES

CALATRAVA BRIDGE

SCALZI BRIDGE

Turkish "Fondaco" Exchange

CA' D'ORO

TRAGHETTO

SAN STAE

CA' PESARO

SAN SIMEONE PICCOLO

FISH & PRODUCE MARKET

FORMER GERMAN EXCHANGE (POST)

← TO PIAZZALE ROMA & TRONCHETTO

RIALTO BRIDGE

MERCHANTS' PALACES

PALAZZO BALBI

FIRE STATION

CA' FOSCARI

CA' REZZONICO

PALAZZO GRASSI

TWO PALACES

CAMPANILE

BRIDGE OF SIGHS

SAN MARCO

GRITTI PALACE HOTEL

HARRY'S BAR

DOGE'S PALACE

RIVA

ACCADEMIA GALLERY & BRIDGE

PEGGY GUGGENHEIM COLLECTION

LA SALUTE

CUSTOMS HOUSE (PUNTA DELLA DOGANA MUSEUM)

TO LIDO →

PALAZZO DARIO & SALVIATI BUILDING

DCH

200 YARDS
200 METERS

TO SAN GIORGIO MAGGIORE & GIUDECCA →

Vaporetto Stops

1 Ferrovia
2 Riva di Biasio
3 San Marcuola
4 San Stae
5 Ca' d'Oro
6 Mercato Rialto
7 Rialto
8 San Silvestro
9 Sant'Angelo
10 San Tomà
11 Ca' Rezzonico
12 Accademia
13 Santa Maria del Giglio
14 Salute
15 San Marco
16 San Zaccaria

15 feet deep, the Grand Canal is the city's largest, lined with its most impressive palaces. It's the remnant of a river that once spilled from the mainland into the Adriatic. The sediment it carried formed barrier islands that cut Venice off from the sea, forming a lagoon.

Venice was built on the marshy islands of the former delta, sitting on wood pilings driven nearly 15 feet into the clay (alder was the preferred wood). About 25 miles of canals drain the city, dumping like streams into the Grand Canal. Technically, Venice has only three canals: Grand, Giudecca, and Cannaregio. The 45 small waterways that dump into the Grand Canal are referred to as rivers (e.g., Rio Nuovo).

Venice is a city of palaces, dating from the days when the city was the world's richest. The most lavish palaces formed a grand

chorus line along the Grand Canal. Once frescoed in reds and blues, with black-and-white borders and gold-leaf trim, they made Venice a city of dazzling color. This cruise is the only way to truly appreciate the palaces, approaching them at water level, where their main entrances were located. Today, strict laws prohibit any changes in these buildings, so while landowners gnash their teeth, we can enjoy Europe's best-preserved medieval city—slowly rotting. Many of the grand buildings are now vacant. Others harbor chandeliered elegance above mossy, empty (often flooded) ground floors.

❶ Ferrovia

The **Santa Lucia train station,** one of the few modern buildings in town, was built in 1954. It's been the gateway into Venice since 1860, when the first station was built. "F.S." stands for "Ferrovie dello Stato," the Italian state railway system.

More than 20,000 people a day commute in

from the mainland, making this the busiest part of Venice during rush hour. The **Calatrava Bridge,** spanning the Grand Canal between the train station and Piazzale Roma upstream, was built in 2008 to alleviate some of the congestion and make the commute easier (for more about the new bridge, see page 54).

Opposite the train station, atop the green dome of **San Simeone Piccolo** church, St. Simeon waves *ciao* to whoever enters or leaves the "old" city. The pink church with the white Carrara-marble facade, just beyond the train station, is the **Church of the Scalzi** (Church of the Barefoot, named after the shoeless Carmelite monks), where the last doge (Venetian ruler) rests. It looks relatively new because it was partially rebuilt after being bombed in 1915 by Austrians aiming (poorly) at the train station.

❷ Riva de Biasio

Venice's main thoroughfare is busy with all kinds of **boats:** taxis, police boats, garbage boats, ambulances, construction cranes, and even brown-and-white UPS boats. Somehow they all manage to share the canal in relative peace.

About 25 yards past the Riva de Biasio stop, you'll look left down the broad **Cannaregio Canal** to see what was the **Jewish Ghetto** (see page 51). The twin, pale-pink, six-story "skyscrapers"—the tallest buildings you'll see at this end of the canal—are reminders of how densely populated the world's original ghetto was. Set aside as the local Jewish quarter in 1516, this area became extremely crowded. This urban island developed into one of the most closely knit business and cultural quarters of all the Jewish communities in Italy, and gave us our word "ghetto" (from *geto*, the copper foundry located here).

❸ San Marcuola

At this stop, facing a tiny square just ahead, stands the unfinished church of San Marcuola, one of only five churches fronting the

Grand Canal. Centuries ago, this canal was a commercial drag of expensive real estate in high demand by wealthy merchants. About 20 yards ahead on the right stands the stately gray **Turkish "Fondaco" Exchange,** one of the oldest houses in Venice. Its horseshoe arches and roofline of triangles and dingleballs are reminders of its Byzantine heritage. Turkish traders in turbans docked here, unloaded their goods into the warehouse on the bottom story, then went upstairs for a home-style meal and a place to sleep. Venice in the 1500s was very cosmopolitan, welcoming every religion and ethnicity, so long as they carried cash. (Today the building contains the city's newly reopened Museum of Natural History—and Venice's only dinosaur skeleton.)

Just 100 yards ahead on the left, Venice's **Casinò** is housed in the palace where German composer Richard *(The Ring)* Wagner died in 1883. See his distinct, strong-jawed profile in the white plaque on the brick wall. In the 1700s, Venice was Europe's Vegas, with casinos and prostitutes everywhere. Casinòs ("little houses") have long provided Italians with a handy escape from daily life. Today they're run by the state to keep Mafia influence at bay. Notice the fancy front porch, rolling out the red carpet for high rollers arriving by taxi or hotel boat.

❹ San Stae

The San Stae Church sports a delightful Baroque facade. Opposite the San Stae stop, look for the peeling plaster that once made up **frescoes** (scant remains on the lower floors). Imagine the facades of the Grand Canal at their finest. As colorful as the city is today, it's still only a faded, sepia-toned remnant of a long-gone era, a time of lavishly decorated, brilliantly colored palaces.

Just ahead, jutting out a bit on the right, is the ornate white facade of **Ca' Pesaro.** *"Ca'"* is short for *casa* (house). Because only the house of the doge (Venetian ruler) could be called a palace *(palazzo),* all other Venetian palaces are technically *"Ca'."*

In this city of masks, notice how the rich marble facades along the Grand Canal mask what are generally just simple, no-nonsense brick buildings. Most merchants enjoyed showing off. However, being smart businessmen, they only decorated the side of the buildings that would be seen and appreciated. But look back as you pass Ca' Pesaro (which houses the International Gallery of Modern Art—see page 49). It's the only building you'll see with a fine side facade. Ahead, on the left, with its glorious triple-decker medieval arcade (just before the next stop) is Ca' d'Oro.

❺ Ca' d'Oro

The lacy **Ca' d'Oro** (House of Gold) is the best example of Venetian Gothic architecture on the canal. Its three stories offer different variations on balcony design, topped with a

spiny white roofline. Venetian Gothic mixes traditional Gothic (pointed arches and round medallions stamped with a four-leaf clover) with Byzantine styles (tall, narrow arches atop thin columns), filled in with Islamic frills. Like all the palaces, this was originally painted and gilded to make it even more glorious than it is now. Today the Ca' d'Oro is an art gallery (see page 54).

Look at the Venetian chorus line of palaces in front of the boat doing an architectural cancan. On the right is the arcade of the covered **fish market,** with the open-air **produce market** just beyond. It bustles in the morning but is quiet the rest of the day. This is a great scene to wander through—even though European Union hygiene standards have made it cleaner, but less colorful

than it once was. Find the *traghetto* gondola ferrying shoppers—standing like Washington crossing the Delaware—back and forth. There are eight *traghetto* crossings along the Grand Canal, each one marked by a classy low-key green-and-black sign. Make a point to use them. At €0.50 a ride, they are one of the best deals in Venice.

❻ Mercato Rialto

This stop was opened in 2007 to serve the busy market (boats only stop here from 8:00 to 20:00). The long and officious-looking building is at this stop is the Venice courthouse. Straight ahead in the distance, rising above the huge post office, is the tip of the Campanile (bell tower) crowned by its golden angel at St. Mark's Square, where this tour will end. The former post office (100 yards directly ahead, on left side, soon to be a shopping center) used to be the German Exchange, the trading center

for German metal merchants in the early 1500s.

You'll cruise by some trendy and beautifully situated wine bars on the right, but look ahead as you round the corner and see the impressive Rialto Bridge come into view.

A major landmark of Venice, the **Rialto Bridge** is lined with shops and tourists. Constructed in 1588, it's the third bridge built on this spot. Until the 1850s, this was the only bridge crossing the

Grand Canal. With a span of 160 feet and foundations stretching 650 feet on either side, the Rialto was an impressive engineering feat in its day. Earlier Rialto Bridges could open to let big ships in, but not this one. When this new bridge was completed, much of the Grand Canal was closed to shipping and became a canal of palaces.

When gondoliers pass under the fat arch of the Rialto Bridge, they take full advantage of its acoustics: *"Volare, oh, oh..."*

❼ Rialto

Rialto, a separate town in the early days of Venice, has always been the commercial district, while San Marco was the religious and governmental center. Today, a winding street called the Mercerie connects the two, providing travelers with human traffic jams and a mesmerizing gauntlet of shopping temptations. This is the only stretch of the historic Grand Canal with landings upon which you can walk. They unloaded the city's basic necessities here: oil, wine, charcoal, iron. Today, the quay is lined with tourist-trap restaurants.

Venice's sleek, black, graceful **gondolas** are a symbol of the city (for more on gondolas, see page 294). With about 500 gondoliers joyriding amid the churning *vaporetti*, there's a lot of congestion on the Grand Canal. Pay attention—this is where most of the gondola and vaporetto accidents take place. While the Rialto is the highlight of many gondola rides, gondoliers understandably prefer the quieter small canals. Watch your vaporetto driver curse the better-paid gondoliers.

Ahead 100 yards on the left, two gray-colored **palaces** stand side by side (the City Hall and the mayor's office). Their horseshoe-shaped, arched windows are similar and their stories are the same height, lining up to create the effect of one long balcony.

❽ San Silvestro

We now enter a long stretch of important **merchants' palaces,** each with proud and different facades. Because ships couldn't navigate beyond the Rialto Bridge, the biggest palaces—with the major shipping needs—line this last stretch of the navigable Grand Canal.

Palaces like these were multi-functional: ground floor for the warehouse, offices and showrooms upstairs, and the living quarters above the offices on the "noble floors" (with big windows designed to allow in maximum light). Servants lived and worked on the top floors (with the smallest windows). For fire safety reasons, the kitchens were also located on the top floors. Peek into the noble floors to catch a glimpse of their still-glorious chandeliers of Murano glass.

❾ Sant'Angelo

Notice how many buildings have a foundation of waterproof white stone *(pietra d'Istria)* upon which the bricks sit high and dry. Many canal-level floors are abandoned as the rising water level takes its toll.

The **posts**—historically painted gaily with the equivalent of family coats of arms—don't rot under water. But the wood at the water-line, where it's exposed to oxygen, does. On the smallest canals, little blue gondola signs indicate that these docks are for gondolas only (no taxis or motor boats).

❿ San Tomà

Fifty yards ahead, on the right side (with twin obelisks on the rooftop) stands **Palazzo Balbi,** the palace of an early–17th-century captain general of the sea. These Venetian equivalents of five-star admirals were honored with twin obelisks decorating their palaces. This palace, like so many in the city, flies three flags: Italy (green-white-red), the European Union (blue with ring of stars), and Venice (a lion on a field of red and gold). Today it houses the administrative headquarters of the regional government.

Just past the admiral's palace, look immediately to the right, down a side canal. On the right side of that canal, before the bridge, see the traffic light and the **fire station** (with four arches hiding fireboats parked and ready to go).

The impressive **Ca' Foscari,** with a classic Venetian facade (on the corner, across from the fire station), dominates the bend in the canal. This is the main building of the University of Venice, which has about 25,000 students. Notice the elegant lamp on the corner.

The grand, heavy, white **Ca' Rezzonico,** just before the Ca' Rezzonico stop, houses the Museum of 18th-Century Venice (✪

see the Ca' Rezzonico Tour chapter). Across the canal is the cleaner and leaner **Palazzo Grassi,** the last major palace built on the canal, erected in the late 1700s. It was recently purchased by a French tycoon and now displays his contemporary art collection.

⓫ Ca' Rezzonico

Up ahead, the Accademia Bridge leads over the Grand Canal to the **Accademia Gallery** (right side), filled with the best Venetian paintings (✪ see the Accademia Tour chapter). The bridge was put up in 1934 as a temporary structure. Locals liked it, so it stayed.

⓬ Accademia

From here, look through the graceful bridge and way ahead to enjoy a classic view of **La Salute Church,** topped by a crown-shaped dome supported by scrolls (✪ see the La Salute Church Tour chapter). This Church of Saint Mary of Good Health was built to thank God for delivering Venetians from the devastating plague of 1630 (which had killed about a third of the city's population).

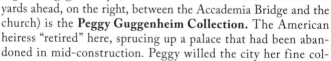

The low, white building among greenery (100 yards ahead, on the right, between the Accademia Bridge and the church) is the **Peggy Guggenheim Collection.** The American heiress "retired" here, sprucing up a palace that had been abandoned in mid-construction. Peggy willed the city her fine collection of modern art (✪ see the Peggy Guggenheim Collection Tour chapter).

As you approach the next stop, notice on the right how the fine line of higgledy-piggledy palaces evokes old-time Venice. Two doors past the Guggenheim, Palazzo Dario has a great set of characteristic **funnel-shaped chimneys.** These forced embers through a loop-the-loop channel until they were dead—required in the days when stone palaces were surrounded by humble, wooden buildings, and a live spark could make a merchant's workforce homeless. Notice this early Renaissance building's flat-feeling facade with "pasted-on" Renaissance motifs. Three doors later is the **Salviati building** (with the fine mosaics), which was once a glassworks.

⓭ Santa Maria del Giglio

Back on the left stands the fancy Gritti Palace hotel. Hemingway and Woody Allen both stayed here (but not together).

Take a deep whiff of Venice. What's all this nonsense about stinky canals? All I smell is my shirt. By the way, how's your captain? Smooth dockings? To get to know him, stand up in the bow and block his view.

⓮ Salute

The huge La Salute Church towers overhead as if squirted from a can of Catholic Reddi-wip. Like Venice itself, the church rests upon pilings. To build the foundation for the city, more than a million trees were piled together, reaching beneath the mud to the solid clay. Much of the surrounding countryside was deforested by Venice. Trees were exported and consumed locally to fuel the furnaces of Venice's booming glass industry, to build Europe's biggest

merchant marine, and to prop up this city in the mud.

As the Grand Canal opens up into the lagoon, the last building on the right with the golden ball is the 17th-century **Customs House,** which now houses the Punta della Dogana Museum of Contemporary Art (see page 48). Its two bronze Atlases hold a statue of Fortune riding the ball. Arriving ships stopped here to pay their tolls.

⓯ San Marco

Up ahead on the left, the green pointed tip of the Campanile marks **St. Mark's Square,** the political and religious center of

Venice...and the final destination of this tour. You could get off at the San Marco stop and go straight to St. Mark's Square. But I'm staying on the boat for one more stop, just past St. Mark's Square (it's a quick walk back).

Survey the lagoon. Opposite St. Mark's Square, across the water, the ghostly white church with the pointy bell tower is **San Giorgio Maggiore,** with great views of Venice (✪ see the San Giorgio Maggiore Tour chapter). Next to it is the residential island Giudecca, stretching from close to San Giorgio Maggiore past the Venice youth hostel (with a nice view, directly across) to the Hilton Hotel (good nighttime view, far right end of island).

Still on board? If you are, as we leave the San Marco stop, prepare for a drive-by view of St. Mark's Square. First comes the bold white facade of the old mint (where Venice's golden ducat, the "dollar" of the Venetian Republic, was made) and the library facade. Then the twin columns, topped by St. Theodore and St. Mark, who've welcomed visitors since the 15th century. Between the columns, catch a glimpse of two giant figures atop the **Clock Tower**—they've been whacking their clappers every hour since 1499. The domes of **St. Mark's Basilica** are soon eclipsed by the lacy facade of the **Doge's Palace.** Next you'll see the **Bridge of Sighs** (currently under scaffolding), and then the grand harborside promenade—the **Riva.**

Follow the Riva with your eye, past elegant hotels to the green area in the distance. This is the largest of Venice's few **parks,** which hosts the Biennale art show every odd year, including in 2011. Much farther in the distance is the **Lido,** the island with Venice's beach. Its sand and casinos are tempting, but its car traffic disrupts the medieval charm of Venice.

⑯ San Zaccaria

OK, you're at your last stop. Quick—muscle your way off this boat! (If you don't, you'll eventually end up at the Lido.)

At San Zaccaria, you're right in the thick of the action. A number of other *vaporetti* depart from here (see page 30). Otherwise, it's a short walk back along the Riva to St. Mark's Square. Ahoy!

ST. MARK'S SQUARE TOUR

Piazza San Marco

Venice was once Europe's richest city, and Piazza San Marco was its center. As middleman in the trade between Asia and Europe, wealthy Venice profited from both sides. In 1450, Venice had 180,000 citizens (far more than London) and a gross "national" product that exceeded that of entire countries.

The rich Venetians taught the rest of Europe about the good life—silks, spices, and jewels from the East, crafts from northern Europe, good food and wine, fine architecture, music, theater, and laughter. Venice was a vibrant city full of painted palaces, glittering canals, and impressed visitors. Five centuries after its power began to decline, Venice is all of these still, with the added charm of romantic decay. In this tour, we'll spend an hour in the heart of this Old World superpower.

Orientation

Getting There: Signs all over town point to *San Marco*—meaning both the square and the basilica—located where the Grand Canal spills out into the lagoon. Vaporetto stops: San Marco or San Zaccaria.

Campanile: If you ascend the bell tower, it'll cost you €8 (daily April–June and Oct 9:00–19:00, July–Sept 9:00–21:00, Nov–March 9:30–15:45, closed from Christmas to mid-Jan, tel. 041-522-4064).

Clock Tower: To see the interior, you need to reserve a spot on a tour (tours offered Mon–Wed mornings plus 13:00 in peak season and Thu–Sun afternoons—see page 37 for specifics).

Information: There are two TIs. One is in the southwest corner of the square; the other is along the waterfront at the San Marco-Vallaresso vaporetto stop.

Audioguide Tours: Those traveling with an iPod or other MP3 player can download a free audio tour of this chapter at www.ricksteves .com (or search for "Rick Steves Audio Tours" in iTunes).

WCs: Handy public WCs (€1.50) are behind the Correr Museum and at Giardinetti Reali park.

Cuisine Art: Cafés with live music provide an engaging sound-track for St. Mark's Square (see "Cafés on St. Mark's Square" sidebar, later). The Correr Museum (at the end of the square opposite the basilica) has a quiet coffee shop overlooking the crowded square. For a list of restaurants in the area, see page 275.

Necessary Eyesores: Expect scaffolding and advertising billboards to cover parts of the square and its monuments when you visit. The Campanile's foundation is being fortified, an effort that will take years. The nearby Bridge of Sighs is also covered with scaffolding during restoration.

Cardinal Points: The square is aligned (roughly) east–west. So, facing the basilica, north is to your left.

Starring: Byzantine domes, Gothic arches, Renaissance arches... and the wonderful, musical space they enclose.

The Tour Begins

• *For an overview of this grand square and the buildings that sur-round it, view it from the west end of the square (away from St. Mark's Basilica).*

The Piazza

St. Mark's Basilica dominates the square with its Byzantine-style onion domes and glowing mosaics. Mark Twain said it looked like

"a vast warty bug taking a medita-tive walk." (I say it looks like tiara-wearing ladybugs copulating.) To the right of the basilica is its 300-foot-tall Campanile. Between the basilica and the Campanile, you can catch a glimpse of the pale-pink Doge's Palace. Lining the square are the former govern-ment offices *(procuratie)* that administered the Venetian empire's vast network of trading outposts, which stretched all the way to Turkey.

The square is big, but it feels intimate with its cafés and dueling orchestras. By day, it's great for people-watching and pigeon-chasing. By night, under lantern light, it transports you to another century, complete with its own romantic soundtrack.

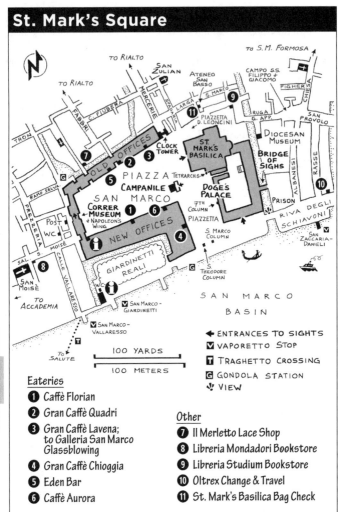

St. Mark's Square

Eateries
1. Caffè Florian
2. Gran Caffè Quadri
3. Gran Caffè Lavena; to Galleria San Marco Glassblowing
4. Gran Caffè Chioggia
5. Eden Bar
6. Caffè Aurora

Other
7. Il Merletto Lace Shop
8. Libreria Mondadori Bookstore
9. Libreria Studium Bookstore
10. Oltrex Change & Travel
11. St. Mark's Basilica Bag Check

The piazza draws Indians in saris, English nobles in blue blazers, and Nebraskans in shorts. Napoleon called the piazza "the most beautiful drawing room in Europe." Napoleon himself added to the intimacy by building the final wing, opposite the basilica, that encloses the square.

For architecture buffs, here are three centuries of styles, bam, side by side, *uno-due-tre*, for easy comparison:

1. On the left side (as you face the basilica) are the "Old" offices, built in about 1500 in solid, column-and-arch Renaissance style.

2. The "New" offices (on the right), in a High Renaissance style from a century later (c. 1600), are a little heavier and more ornate. This wing mixes arches, the three orders of columns from bottom to top—Doric, Ionic, and Corinthian—and statues in the Baroque style.

3. Napoleon's wing, at the opposite end from the basilica, is Neoclassical (c. 1800)—a return to simpler, more austere classical

columns and arches. Napoleon's architects tried to make his wing bridge the styles of the other two. But it turned out a little too high for one side and not high enough for the other. Nice try.

Imagine this square full of water, with gondolas floating where people now sip cappuccinos. That happens every so often at very high tides *(acqua alta)*, a reminder that Venice and the sea are intertwined. (Now that one is sinking and the other is rising, they are more intertwined than ever.)

Venice became Europe's richest city from its trade with northern Europeans, Ottoman Muslims, and Byzantine Christians. Here in St. Mark's Square, the exact center of this East–West axis, we see both the luxury and the mix of Eastern and Western influences.

Watch out for pigeon speckle. The pigeons are not indigenous to Venice (they were imported by the Habsburgs) nor loved by residents. In fact, Venetians love seagulls because they eat pigeons. In 2008, Venice outlawed the feeding of pigeons, so their days may be numbered. There are now fewer pigeons, but they're still there. Vermin are a problem on this small island, where it's said that each Venetian has two pigeons and four rats. (The rats stay hidden, except when high tides flood their homes.)

• *The TI is nearby, in the corner of Napoleon's wing. It's wise to confirm your sightseeing plans here and pick up the latest list of opening hours. Behind you (southwest of the piazza), you'll find the public WC (€1.50) and a post office with a helpful stamps-only line (usually closes at 14:00).*

Now approach the basilica. If it's hot and you're tired, grab a shady spot at the foot of the Campanile.

St. Mark's Basilica—Exterior

The facade is a crazy mix of East and West. There are round, Roman-style arches over the doorways, golden Byzantine mosaics, a roofline ringed with pointed French Gothic pinnacles, and Muslim-shaped onion domes (wood, covered with lead) on the

roof. The brick-structure building is blanketed in marble that came from everywhere—columns from Alexandria, capitals from Sicily, and carvings from Constantinople. The columns flanking the door-ways show the facade's variety—purple, green, gray, white, yellow, some speckled, some striped horizontally, some vertically, some fluted, all topped with a variety of different capitals.

What's amazing isn't so much the variety as the fact that the whole thing comes together in a bizarre sort of harmony. St. Mark's remains simply the most interesting church in Europe, a church that (paraphrasing Goethe) "can only be compared with itself."

For more on the basilica, inside and out, see the ✪ St. Mark's Basilica Tour chapter.

• *Facing the basilica, turn 90 degrees to the left to see...*

The Clock Tower (Torre dell'Orologio)

Two bronze "Moors" (African Muslims) stand atop the Clock

Tower (built originally to be giants, they only gained their ethnicity when the metal darkened over the centuries). At the top of each hour they swing their giant clappers. The clock dial shows the 24 hours, the signs of the zodiac, and, in the blue center, the phases of the moon. Above the dial is the world's first digital clock, which changes every five minutes. The Clock Tower retains some of its original coloring of blue and gold, a reminder that, in centuries past, this city glowed with bright color.

An alert winged lion, the symbol of St. Mark and the city, looks down on the crowded square. He opens a book that reads *"Pax Tibi Marce,"* or "Peace to you, Mark." As legend goes, these were the comforting words that an angel spoke to the stressed evangelist, assuring him he would find serenity during a stormy night that the saint spent here on the island. Eventually, St. Mark's body found its final resting place

Cafés on St. Mark's Square

Cafés line the square. Those with live music feature similar food, prices, and a three- to five-piece combo playing a selection of classical and pop hits, from Brahms to "Bésame Mucho." If you sit outside and get just a drink, expect to pay €12–20, including a €6 cover charge when the orchestra is playing. A coffee—your cheapest option—costs about €6 if you sit at an outside table, plus the €6 cover charge when the music plays, bringing it to €12 total. It's perfectly acceptable to nurse a cappuccino for an hour—you're paying for the music with the cover charge.

Caffè Florian (on the right as you face the church—see

map earlier in this chapter) is the most famous Venetian café and one of the first places in Europe to serve coffee. It's been a popular spot for a discreet rendezvous in Venice since 1720. The orchestra plays a more classical repertoire than at the other cafés. The outside tables are the main action, but do walk inside through the richly decorated, old-time rooms where Casanova, Lord Byron, Charles Dickens, and Woody Allen have all paid too much for a drink (reasonable prices at bar in back).

Gran Caffè Quadri, opposite the Florian, has an equally illustrious history of famous clientele, including the writers Stendhal and Dumas, and composer Richard Wagner. **Gran Caffè Lavena,** near the Clock Tower, is newer and less prestigious.

Gran Caffè Chioggia, on the Piazzetta facing the Doge's Palace, charges slightly less, with one or two musicians, usually a pianist, playing cocktail jazz.

The following less-expensive options don't have live music, but you can enjoy overhearing music from nearby cafés: **Eden Bar,** next to Gran Caffè Quadri, is touristy, but that doesn't matter when you're enjoying your hot dog and Coke while sitting out on the piazza. **Caffè Aurora,** in the shadow of the Campanile, features nearly all the ambience of the orchestra cafés at half the price.

ST. MARK'S SQUARE

inside the basilica, and now his winged-lion symbol is everywhere. (Find four in 20 seconds. Go.)

Venice's many lions express the city's various mood swings through history—triumphant after a naval victory, sad when a favorite son has died, hollow-eyed after a plague, and smiling when the soccer team wins. The pair of lions squatting between the Clock Tower and basilica have probably been photographed being ridden by every Venetian child born since the dawn of cameras.

The Campanile

The original Campanile (cam-pah-NEE-lay), or bell tower, was a lighthouse and a marvel of 10th-century architecture until the 20th century (1902), when it toppled into the center of the piazza. It had groaned ominously the night before, sending people scurrying from the cafés. The next morning...crash! The golden angel on top landed right at the basilica's front door, standing up.

The Campanile was rebuilt 10 years later complete with its golden archangel Gabriel, who always faces the breeze. You can ride a lift to the top for the best view of Venice. It's crowded at peak times, but well worth it.

In 2011, you may see construction work around the Campanile's base. Hoping to prevent a repeat of the 1902 collapse, they've wrapped the underground foundations with a titanium girdle to shore up a crack that appeared in 1939.

Because St. Mark's Square is the first place in town to start flooding, there are tide gauges at the outside base of the Campanile (near the exit, facing St. Mark's Square) that show the current sea level *(livello marea)*. Find the stone plaque (near the exit door) that commemorates the high-water 77-inch level from the disastrous floods of 1966. In December of 2008, Venice suffered another terrible high tide, cresting at 61 inches.

If the tide is mild (around 20 inches), the water merely seeps up through the drains. But when there's a strong tide (around 40 inches), it looks like someone's turned on a faucet down below. The water bubbles upward and flows like a river to the lowest points in the square, which can be covered with a few inches of water in an hour or so. When the water level rises one meter above mean sea level, a warning siren sounds, and it repeats if a serious flood is imminent.

Many doorways have three-foot-high wooden or metal barriers to block the high water *(acqua alta)*, but the seawater still seeps in through floors and drains, rendering the barriers nearly useless. (To learn the reasons for the flooding, see the sidebar on page 34.)

You might see stacked wooden benches in the square; during floods, the benches are placed end-to-end to create elevated sidewalks. If you think the square is crowded now, when it's flooded it turns into total gridlock, as all the people normally sharing the whole square jostle for space on the narrow wooden walkways.

In 2006, the pavement around St. Mark's Square was taken up, and the entire height of the square was raised by adding a layer of sand, and then replacing the stones. If the columns along the ground floor of the Doge's Palace look stubby, it's because this process has been carried out many times over the centuries.

• *The small square between the basilica and the water is...*

The Piazzetta

This "Little Square" is framed by the Doge's Palace on the left, the library on the right, and the waterfront of the lagoon. In former

days, the Piazzetta was closed to the public for a few hours a day so that government officials and bigwigs could gather in the sun to strike shady deals.

The pale-pink Doge's Palace is the epitome of the style known as Venetian Gothic. Columns support traditional, pointed Gothic arches, but with a Venetian flair—they're curved to a point, ornamented with a trefoil (three-leaf clover), and topped with a round

medallion of a quatrefoil (four-leaf clover). The pattern is found on buildings all over Venice and on the formerly Venetian-controlled Croatian coast, but nowhere else in the world (except Las Vegas).

The two large 12th-century columns near the water were looted from Constantinople. Mark's winged lion sits on top of one. The lion's body (nearly 15 feet long) predates the wings and is more than 2,000 years old. The

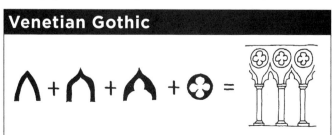

Venetian Gothic

$$\bigwedge + \bigcap + \bigwedge + \clubsuit =$$

ST. MARK'S SQUARE

other column holds St. Theodore (battling a crocodile), the former patron saint who was replaced by Mark. I guess stabbing crocs in the back isn't classy enough for an upwardly mobile world power. Criminals were executed by being hung from these columns in the hopes that the public could learn its lessons vicariously.

Venice was the "Bride of the Sea" because she depended on sea trading for her livelihood. This "marriage" was celebrated annually by the people. The doge, in full regalia, boarded a ritual boat (his Air Force One equivalent) here at the edge of the Piazzetta and sailed out into the lagoon. There a vow was made, and he dropped a jeweled ring into the water to seal the marriage.

In the distance, on an island across the lagoon, is one of the grandest views in the city, of the Church of San Giorgio Maggiore. With its four tall columns as the entryway, the church, designed by the late-Renaissance architect Andrea Palladio, influenced future government and bank buildings around the world.

Speaking of architects, I will: Sansovino. Around 1530, Jacopo Sansovino designed the library (here in the Piazzetta) and the delicate Loggetta at the base of the Campanile (pictured at the top of page 76; it was destroyed by the collapse of the tower in 1902 and was pieced back together as much as possible).

The Tetrarchs and the Doge's Palace's Seventh Column

Where the basilica meets the Doge's Palace is the traditional entrance to the palace, decorated with four small Roman statues—

the Tetrarchs. No one knows for sure who they are, but I like the legend that says they're the scared leaders of a divided Rome during its fall, holding their swords and each other as all hell breaks loose around them. Whatever the legend, these statues—made of precious purple porphyry stone—are symbols of power. They were looted from Constantinople and then placed here proudly as spoils of war. How old are they? They've guarded the palace entrance since the city first rose from the mud.

The Doge's Palace's seventh column (the seventh from the water) tells a story of love, romance, and tragedy in its carved capital: 1) In the first scene (the carving facing

ST. MARK'S SQUARE

Escape from St. Mark's Square

Crowds getting to you? Here are some relatively quiet areas near St. Mark's Square.

Correr Museum: Sip a cappuccino in the café of this uncrowded history museum in a building that overlooks St. Mark's Square (enter at the far end of the piazza). ✪ See the Correr Museum Tour chapter.

Giardinetti Reali: The small park is along the waterfront, west of the Piazzetta (facing the water, turn right—it's next to the TI and the only place for a legal picnic).

San Giorgio Maggiore: This is the fairy-tale island you see from the Piazzetta (catch vaporetto #2 from the San Zaccaria-M.V.E. stop, past the Bridge of Sighs). ✪ See the San Giorgio Maggiore Tour chapter.

Il Merletto: This lace shop is in a small chapel (daily 9:30–17:00, 10:00–17:00 in winter, near the northwest corner of St. Mark's Square, on Sotoportego del Cavalletto). The history of Venetian lace is explained in an English brochure.

La Salute Church: This cool church in a quiet neighborhood is a short €2 hop on vaporetto #1 from the San Marco-Vallaresso stop, or ride the nearby *traghetto*. ✪ See the La Salute Church Tour chapter.

Caffè Florian: The plush interior of this luxurious 18th-century café, located on St. Mark's Square, is generally quiet and nearly empty. An expensive coffee here can be a wonderful break (see "Cafés on St. Mark's Square," earlier).

the Piazzetta), a woman on a balcony is wooed by her lover, who says, "Babe, I want *you!*" 2) She responds, "Why, little ol' *me?*" 3)

They get married. 4) Kiss. 5) Hit the sack—pretty racy for 14th-century art. 6) Nine months later, guess what? 7) The baby takes its first steps. 8) And as was all too common in the 1300s...the child dies.

The pillars along the Doge's Palace look short—a result of the square being built up over the centuries. It's happening again today. The stones are taken up, sand is added, and the stones are replaced, buying a little more time as the sea slowly swallows the city.

• *At the waterfront in the Piazzetta, turn left and walk (east) along the water. At the top of the first bridge, look inland at...*

The Bridge of Sighs

In the Doge's Palace (on your left), the government doled out justice. On your right are the prisons. (Don't let the palatial facade fool you—see the bars on the windows?) Prisoners sentenced in the palace crossed to the prisons by way of the covered bridge in front of you. This was called the Prisons' Bridge until the Romantic poet Lord Byron renamed it in the 19th century. From this bridge, the convicted got their

final view of sunny, joyous Venice before entering the black and dank prisons. According to the Romantic legend, they sighed. As you will, too, when you see the scaffolding.

Venice has been a major tourist center for four centuries. Anyone who's ever come here has stood on this very spot, looking at the Bridge of Sighs. Lean on the railing leaned on by everyone from Casanova to Byron to Hemingway.

> *I stood in Venice, on the Bridge of Sighs,*
> *a palace and a prison on each hand.*
> *I saw, from out the wave, her structures rise,*
> *as from the stroke of the enchanter's wand.*
> *A thousand years their cloudy wings expand*
> *around me, and a dying glory smiles*
> *o'er the far times, when many a subject land*
> *looked to the Winged Lion's marble piles,*
> *where Venice sat in state, throned on her hundred isles!*

—from Lord Byron's *Childe Harold's Pilgrimage*

ST. MARK'S SQUARE

ST. MARK'S BASILICA TOUR

Basilica di San Marco

Among Europe's churches, St. Mark's is peerless. From the outside, it's a riot of domes, columns, and statues, completely unlike the towering Gothic churches of northern Europe or the heavy Baroque of much of the rest of Italy. Inside, the decor of mosaics, colored marbles, and oriental treasures is rarely seen elsewhere. The Christian symbolism is unfamiliar to Western eyes, done in the style of Byzantine icons and even Islamic designs. Older than most of Europe's churches, it feels like a remnant of a lost world.

This is your best chance in Italy (outside of Ravenna) to glimpse a forgotten and somewhat mysterious part of the human story—Byzantium.

Orientation

Cost: Though entering the church is free, there are three separate, optional sights requiring paid admission inside: the Treasury (€3, includes audioguide—free for the asking), Golden Altarpiece (€2), and San Marco Museum (€4, enter museum from atrium either before or after you tour the church, skip the €3.50 audioguide). The San Marco Museum is the one most worth its entry fee.

Hours: The church is open Mon–Sat 9:45–17:00, Sun 14:00–17:00 (Sun until 16:00 Nov–March). The three sights inside close 15 minutes earlier; in winter, the Treasury and Golden Altarpiece close an hour earlier.

Dress Code: Modest dress (no shorts or bare shoulders) is strictly enforced, even for kids.

Getting There: Signs throughout Venice point to *San Marco,* meaning the square and the church. Vaporetto stops: San Marco or San Zaccaria.

Lines: There's almost always a long line to get into St. Mark's. Once inside, it's usually crowded, and you just have to shuffle through on a one-way system. It's best to read this chapter before you go...or while standing in line. Those checking a bag can skip to the front of the line—see "Bag Check," next.

Bag Check (and Skipping the Line): Small purses and shoulder-slung bags may be allowed inside the church, but larger bags and backpacks are not. Check them for free for up to one hour at the nearby Ateneo San Basso, 30 yards to the left of the basilica, down narrow Calle San Basso (see map on page 84 for location; open Mon–Sat 9:30–17:30, Sun 14:00–16:30).

Those with a bag to check actually get to skip the line. Leave your bag at Ateneo San Basso and pick up your claim tag. Two people per tag are allowed to enter the basilica. Take your tag to the basilica's tourist entrance. Keep to the left of the railing where the line forms and show your tag to the gatekeeper. He'll let you in, ahead of the line. After touring the church, come back and pick up your bag. (Note: Ateneo San Basso may not let you check small bags that would be allowed inside.)

Theft Alert: St. Mark's Basilica is the most dangerous place in Venice for pickpocketing—inside, it's always a crowded jostle.

Information: Guidebooks are sold in the bookstand in the basilica's atrium. Tel. 041-270-8311, www.basilicasanmarco.it.

Tours: Free, hour-long English **tours** (heavy on the mosaics' religious symbolism) are generally offered daily at 11:00; meet in the atrium. But the schedule varies, so see the schedule board in the atrium. Those traveling with an iPod or other MP3 player can download a free **Rick Steves audio tour** at www.ricksteves.com (or search for "Rick Steves Audio Tours" in iTunes).

WCs: A free WC is inside the San Marco Museum. Public WCs (€1.50) are nearby (one behind the Correr Museum, another at Giardinetti Reali park).

Mass: Experience the church in its uncrowded glory at any Mass outside of visiting hours (e.g., 8:00 or 18:45; see website for full schedule). Enter through the door around the left side of the basilica.

Length of This Tour: Allow one hour.

Cuisine Art: No food is allowed inside the church. For suggestions nearby, see page 275.

Photography: Although forbidden inside the church, it is allowed on the balcony of the San Marco Museum, with great views overlooking the square.

Starring: St. Mark, Byzantium, mosaics, and ancient bronze horses.

ST. MARK'S BASILICA

The Tour Begins

Start outside in the square, far enough back to take in the whole facade. Then zero in on the details. As you tour the interior, do your best to follow this tour. At busy times, your actual itinerary and pace may be determined by the sheer flow of the masses.

❶ Exterior—Mosaic of Mark's Relics

St. Mark's Basilica is a treasure chest of booty that was looted during Venice's glory days. That's most appropriate for a church built on the stolen bones of a saint.

The **mosaic over the far left door** shows the theft that put Venice on the pilgrimage map. Two men (in the center, with crooked staffs) enter the church bearing a coffin with the body of St. Mark, who looks somewhat grumpy from the long voyage.

St. Mark was the author of one of the Gospels, the four Bible books telling the story of Jesus' life (Matthew, Mark, Luke, and John). Seven centuries after his death, his holy body was in Muslim-occupied Alexandria, Egypt. In 828, two visiting merchants of Venice "rescued" the body from the "infidels," hid it in a pork barrel (which was unclean to Muslims), and spirited it away to Venice.

The merchants presented the body—not to a pope or bishop—but to the doge (with white ermine collar, on the right) and his wife, the dogaressa (with entourage, on the left), giving instant status to Venice's budding secular state. They built a church here over Mark's bones and made him the patron saint of the city. You'll see his symbol, the winged lion, all over Venice.

The original church burned down in 976. Today's structure was begun in 1063. The mosaic, from 1260, shows that the church hasn't changed much since then—you can see the onion domes and famous bronze horses on the balcony.

The St. Mark's you see today, mostly from the 11th century, was modeled after a sixth-century church in Constantinople. Venice needed roots. By building a retro church, the city could imply that it had been around for longer than it actually had been. (Throughout European history, upstarts loved to fake deep roots

St. Mark's Basilica

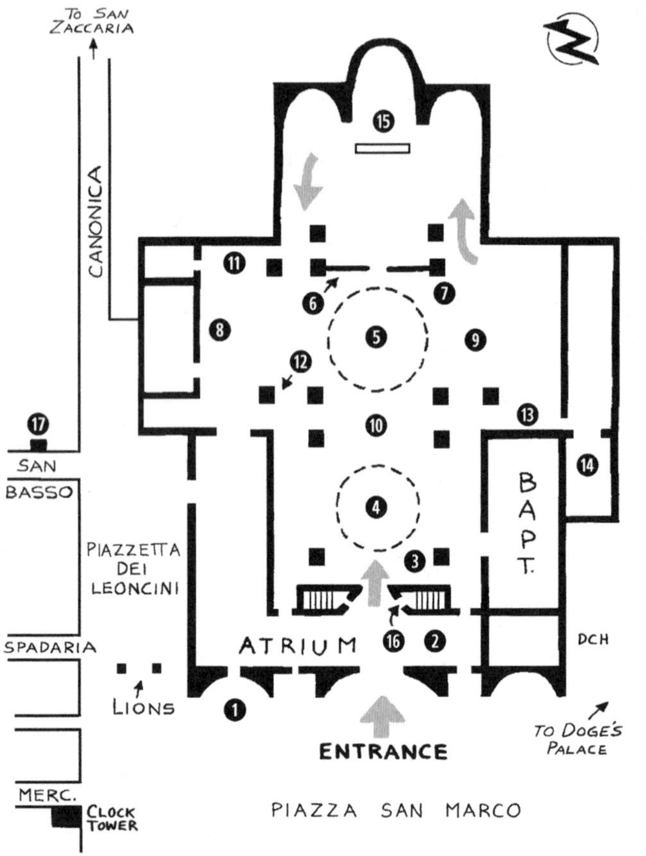

1 Exterior – Mosaic of Mark's Relics

2 Atrium – Mosaic of Noah's Ark and the Great Flood

3 Nave – Mosaics and Greek-Cross Floor Plan

4 Pentecost Mosaic

5 Central Dome – Ascension Mosaic

6 Rood Screen

7 Doge's Pulpit

8 Tree of Jesse Mosaic

9 Last Supper Mosaic

10 Crucifixion Mosaic

11 Nicopeia Icon

12 Rifle on Pillar

13 Discovery of Mark Mosaic

14 Treasury

15 Golden Altarpiece

16 Stairs up to San Marco Museum, Loggia & Bronze Horses

17 Ateneo San Basso Bag Check

St. Mark's...Cathedral, Church, or Basilica?

All three are correct. The church is also a cathedral, because it's the home church of the local bishop. It's a basilica,

because it's the home of a patriarch and because the meaning of "basilica" evolved into an honorary title conferred on select churches by the pope. Coincidentally, it's also a basilica in the architectural sense. Its floor plan (if you ignore the transepts) has a central nave with flanking side aisles, a layout patterned after the ancient Roman public buildings called "basilicas." The transepts turn the basilica plan into a cross—in this case, a Greek cross, as it has four equal arms.

this way. Germany embraced mystic, medieval lore as it emerged as a modern nation in the 19th century, England cooked up the King Arthur legend, and so on.)

In subsequent centuries, the church was encrusted with materials looted from buildings throughout the Venetian empire. Their prize booty was the four bronze horses that adorn the balcony, stolen from Constantinople during the Fourth Crusade (these are copies, as the originals are housed inside the church museum). The architectural style of St. Mark's has been called "Early Ransack."

• *Enter the atrium (entrance hall) of the basilica, through a sixth-century, bronze-paneled Byzantine door.*

Immediately after being admitted by the dress-code guard, look up and to the right into an archway decorated with fine mosaics.

❷ Atrium—Mosaic of Noah's Ark and the Great Flood

St. Mark's famous mosaics, with their picture symbols, were easily understood in medieval times, even by illiterate masses. Today's literate masses have trouble reading them, so let's practice on these, some of the oldest (13th century), finest, and most accessible mosaics in the church.

Noah and sons are sawing logs to build a boat. Venetians— who were great ship builders—related to the Ark. At its peak,

Venice's Arsenale warship-building plant employed several thousand.

Below that are three scenes of Noah putting all species of animals into the Ark, two by two. (Who's at the head of the line? Lions.) Another scene shows the Flood in full force, drowning the wicked. Noah sends out a dove twice to see whether there's any dry land where he can dock. He finds it, leaves the Ark with a gorgeous rainbow overhead, and offers a sacrifice of thanks to God. Easy, huh?

• *Now that our medieval literacy rate has risen, rejoin the slow flow of people. Notice the entrance to the San Marco Museum (Loggia dei Cavalli), which you can visit later. Now climb seven steps, pass through the doorway, and enter the nave. Loiter somewhere just inside the door (crowd flow permitting) and let your eyes adjust.*

❸ The Nave—Mosaics and Greek-Cross Floor Plan

The initial effect is dark and unimpressive (unless they've got the floodlights on). But as your pupils slowly unclench, you'll

notice that the entire upper part is decorated in mosaic—4,750 square yards (imagine paving a football field with contact lenses). These golden mosaics are in the Byzantine style, though many were designed by artists from the Italian Renaissance and later. The often-overlooked lower walls are covered with green-, yellow-,

purple-, and rose-colored marble slabs, cut to expose the grain, and laid out in geometric patterns. Even the floor is mosaic, mostly geometrical designs. It rolls like the sea. Venice is sinking and shifting, creating these cresting waves of stone.

The church is laid out with four equal arms, topped with domes, radiating out from the center to form a Greek cross (+). Those familiar with Eastern Orthodox churches will find familiar elements in St. Mark's: a central floor plan, domes, mosaics, and iconic images of Mary and Christ as Pantocrator—ruler of all things. As your eyes adjust, the mosaics start to give off a "mystical, golden luminosity," the atmosphere of the Byzantine heaven.

ST. MARK'S BASILICA

Christ as Pantocrator

Most Eastern Orthodox churches have at least one mosaic or painting of Christ in a standard pose—as "Pantocrator," a Greek word meaning "Ruler of All." St. Mark's features several Pantocrators, including the central dome, over the altar, and over the entrance door. The image, so familiar to Orthodox Christians, is a bit foreign to Protestants, Catholics, and secularists.

As King of the Universe, Christ sits (usually on a throne) facing directly out, with penetrating eyes. He wears a halo divided with a cross, worn only by the Trinity. In his left hand is a Bible, while his right hand blesses, with the fingers forming the Greek letters chi and rho, the first two letters of "Christos." The thumb touches the fingers, symbolizing how Christ unites both his divinity and his humanity. On either side of Christ's head are the Greek letters "IC XC," short for "IesuC XristoC."

The air itself seems almost visible, like a cloud of incense. It's a subtle effect, one that grows on you as the filtered light changes. There are more beautiful, bigger, more overwhelming, and even holier churches, but none is as stately.

• *Find the chandelier near the entrance doorway (in the shape of a Greek cross cathedral space station), and run your eyes up the support chain to the dome above.*

❹ Pentecost Mosaic

In a golden heaven, the dove of the Holy Spirit shoots out a pin-

wheel of spiritual lasers, igniting tongues of fire on the heads of the 12 apostles below, giving them the ability to speak other languages without a Rick Steves phrase book. You'd think they'd be amazed, but their expressions are as solemn as...icons. One of the oldest mosaics in the church (c. 1125), it has distinct "Byzantine" features: a gold background and apostles with halos, solemn faces,

Mosaics

St. Mark's mosaics are designs or pictures made with small cubes of colored stone or glass pressed into wet plaster. Ancient Romans paved floors, walls, and ceilings with them. When Rome "fell," the art form died out in the West but was carried on by Byzantine craftsmen. They perfected the gold background effect by baking gold leaf into tiny cubes of glass called *tesserae* (tiles). The surfaces of the tiles are purposely cut unevenly to capture light and give off a shimmering effect. The reflecting gold mosaics helped to light thick-walled, small-windowed, lantern-lit Byzantine churches, creating a golden glow that symbolized the divine light of heaven.

St. Mark's mosaics tell the entire Christian history from end to beginning. Entering the church, you're greeted with scenes from the end of the world (Apocalypse) and the Pentecost. As you approach the altar, you walk backward in time to the source, experiencing Jesus' Passion and Crucifixion, his miraculous life, and continuing back to his birth and Old Testament predecessors. Over the altar at the far end of the church  (and over the entrance door at the near end) are images of Christ—the beginning and the end, the Alpha and Omega of the Christian universe.

almond eyes, delicate blessing hands, and rumpled robes, all facing forward.

This is art from a society still touchy about the Bible's commandment against making "graven images" of holy things. Byzantium had recently emerged from two centuries of Iconoclasm, in which statues and paintings were broken and burned as sinful "false gods." The Byzantine style emphasizes otherworldliness rather than literal human detail. The poet W. B. Yeats stood here and described what he saw: "O sages standing in God's holy fire as in the gold mosaic of a wall, come from the holy fire...and be the singing-masters of my soul."

• *Shuffle along with the crowds up to the central dome.*

❺ Central Dome—Ascension Mosaic

Gape upward to the very heart of the church. Christ—having lived his miraculous life and having been crucified for man's sins—ascends into the starry sky on a rainbow. He raises his right hand and blesses the universe. This isn't the dead, crucified, mortal Jesus featured in most churches, but a powerful, resurrected god, the ruler of all.

Christ's blessing radiates, rippling down to the ring of white-robed apostles below. They stand amid the trees of the Mount of Olives, waving good-bye as Christ ascends. Mary is with them, wearing blue with golden Greek crosses on each shoulder and looking ready to play patty-cake. From these saints, goodness descends, creating the Virtues that ring the base of the dome between the windows. In Byzantine churches, the window-lit dome represented heaven, while the dark church below represented earth—a microcosm of the hierarchical universe.

Beneath the dome at the four corners, the four Gospel writers ("Matev," "Marc," "Luca," and "Ioh") thoughtfully scribble down the heavenly events. This wisdom flows down like water from the symbolic Four Rivers below them, spreading through the church's four equal arms (the "four corners" of the world), and baptizing the congregation with God's love. The church building is a series of perfect circles within perfect squares—the cosmic order—with Christ in the center solemnly blessing us. God's in his heaven, saints are on earth, and all's right with the world.

Under the Ascension Dome— The Church as Theater

Look around at the church's furniture and imagine a service here. The **rood screen** ❻, topped with 14 saints, separates the congregation from the high altar, heightening the "mystery" of the Mass. The **pulpit on the right** was reserved for the doge, who led prayers and made important announcements ❼. Mosaics were visual aids for the priest, telling the whole story of Jesus. It starts with his ancestors perched in the **Tree of Jesse** ❽ (in the north transept,

to the left as you face the altar). The story continues through Jesus' life, to the **Last Supper** ❾ (in the arch leading to the south transept), and culminates in the **Crucifixion** ❿ (in the west arch).

The Crucifixion mosaic features a stick-figure Christ, emphasizing the symbolic solemnity of the moment, not its Mel Gibson–style gruesomeness. In fact, there aren't very many crucifixes at all in the church, giving it an Eastern Orthodox flavor. While Western Christianity focuses on the death of Jesus, to Orthodox believers, Christ's death is just the tragic Act I. Other scenes in the arch show the rest of the story, Christ's triumphant Resurrection and post-death miracles, leading to the climax, his Ascension (in the central dome).

Byzantium

The Byzantine Empire was the eastern half of the ancient Roman Empire that *didn't* "fall" in A.D. 476. It remained Christian, Greek-speaking, and enlightened for another thousand years.

In A.D. 330, Constantine, the first Christian emperor, moved the Roman Empire's capital to the newly expanded city of Byzantium, which he humbly renamed Constantinople (modern Istanbul). With him went Rome's best and brightest. When the city of Rome decayed and fell, plunging Western Europe into its "Dark Ages," Constantinople lived on as the greatest city in Europe.

Venice had strong ties with Byzantium from its earliest days. In the sixth century, Byzantine Emperor Justinian invaded northern Italy, briefly reuniting East and West, and making Ravenna his regional capital. In 800, Venetians asked the emperor in Constantinople to protect them from Charlemagne's marauding Franks.

Soon Venetian merchants were granted trading rights to Byzantine ports in the Adriatic and eastern Mediterranean. They traded raw materials from Western Europe for luxury goods from the East.

When Muslim Ottoman Turks threatened the Christian Byzantine Empire, the Venetians joined the Crusades, the series of military expeditions that were designed to "save" Jerusalem and Constantinople. Venetians grew rich renting ships to the Crusaders in exchange for money, favors, and booty.

During the Fourth Crusade (1202–1204), which went horribly awry, the Crusaders—led by the Venetian doge

ST. MARK'S BASILICA

The Venetian church service is a theatrical multimedia spectacle, combining words (prayers, biblical passages, Latin and Greek phrases), music (chants, a choir, organ, horns, strings), costumes and props (priests' robes, golden reliquaries, candles, incense), set design (the mosaics, rood screen, Golden Altarpiece), and even stage direction (processionals through the crowd, priests' motions, standing, sitting, kneeling, crossing yourself). The symmetrical church is itself part of the set design. The Greek-cross floor plan symbolizes perfection, rather than the more common Latin cross of the crucifixion (emphasizing man's sinfulness). Coincidentally or not, the first modern opera—also a multimedia theatrical experience—was written by St. Mark's *maestro di cappella*, Claudio Monteverdi (1567–1643).

North Transept

In the north transept (the arm of the church to the left of the altar), today's Venetians pray to a painted wooden icon of Mary and baby Jesus known as **Nicopeia**, or "Our Lady of Victory" (on the east

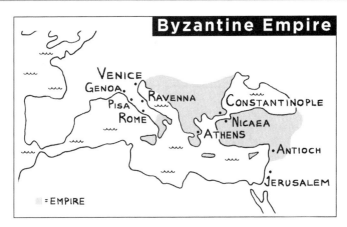

Byzantine Empire

VENICE
GENOA
PISA — RAVENNA
ROME
CONSTANTINOPLE
NICAEA
ATHENS
ANTIOCH
JERUSALEM

= EMPIRE

Dandolo—sacked Constantinople, a fellow Christian city. This was, perhaps, the lowest point in Christian history, at least until the advent of TV evangelism. The Venetians carried home the bronze horses, the Pala d'Oro enamels, the Treasury's treasures, the Nicopeia icon, and much of the marble that now covers the (brick) church.

Venice rose while the Byzantine Empire faded. Then both civilizations nose-dived when Constantinople finally fell to the Ottomans in 1453.

Today, we find hints of the Byzantine Empire in the Eastern Orthodox Church, in mosaics and icons, and in the looted treasures shipped back to Venice.

wall of the north transept, it's a small painting crusted over with a big stone canopy) **⓫**. Supposedly painted by the evangelist Luke, it was once enameled with bright paint and precious stones, and Mary was adorned with a crown and necklace of gold and jewels (now on display in the Treasury). This Madonna has helped Venice persevere through plagues, wars, and crucial soccer games. When Mary answers a prayer, grateful Venetians give her offerings, like the old **rifle** that hangs next to a Madonna-and-child on a pillar (as you approach the north transept) **⓬**. A wife prayed to the Madonna for her husband's safe return from war with Austria in 1848. When he came home alive, she gave his rifle to the Virgin in thanks.

• *In the south transept (to right of main altar), find the dim mosaic high up on the west wall.*

⓭ Discovery of Mark Mosaic

Not a biblical scene, this mosaic depicts the miraculous event that capped the construction of the present church.

It's 1094, the church is nearly complete (see the domes shown in cutaway fashion), and they're all set to re-inter Mark's bones under the new altar. There's just one problem: During the decades of construction, they forgot where they'd stored his body!

So (in the left half of the mosaic), all of Venice gathers inside the church to bow down and pray for help finding the bones. The doge (from the Latin *dux*, meaning leader) leads them. Soon after (the right half), the patriarch (far right) is inspired to look inside a hollow column where he finds the relics. Everyone turns and applauds, including the womenfolk (left side of scene), who stream in from the upper-floor galleries. The relics were soon placed under the altar in a ceremony that inaugurated the current structure.

The south transept also features horseshoe arches atop slender columns, giving the transept the exotic flavor of a Muslim mosque. The door under the rose window leads directly from the Doge's Palace. On important occasions, the doge entered the church through here, ascended the steps of his pulpit, and addressed the people.

St. Mark's Three Museums

Inside the church are three sights, each requiring a separate admission. None is a must-see, but they provide the easiest way (outside of Istanbul or Ravenna) to soak up Byzantine ambience—and admission to the San Marco Museum (the best of the bunch) gives you access to great views over the inside of the church, as well as to the square outside.

⓮ Treasury (Tesoro)

• *The tiny Treasury is in the south transept. The admission fee includes an audioguide (when available)—ask for it. The collection is crammed into two small rooms.*

You'll see Byzantine chalices, silver reliquaries, monstrous monstrances (for displaying the Communion wafer), and icons done in gold, silver, enamels, gems, and semiprecious stones. Some pieces represent the fruit of labor by different civilizations over a thousand-year period. For example, an ancient rock-crystal chalice made by the Romans might be decorated centuries later with Byzantine enamels, and then finished still later with gold filigree by Venetian goldsmiths. This is marvelous handiwork, but all the

The Legend (Mixed with a Little Truth) of Mark and Venice

Mark (died c. A.D. 68) was a Jewish-born Christian, and he might have actually met Jesus. (The Bible mentions a "Mark"

and a "John Mark" who may have been him.) He traveled with fellow convert Paul, eventually settling in Alexandria as the city's first Christian bishop. On a trip to Rome, Peter—Jesus' right-hand man—asked him to write down the events of Jesus' life. This became the Gospel of Mark.

During his travels, Mark stopped in the lagoon (in Aquileia on the north coast of the Adriatic), where he dreamed of a Latin-speaking angel who said, *"Pax tibi Marce, evangelista meus"* ("Peace to you, Mark, my evangelist"), promising him rest after death. Back in Alexandria, Mark was attacked by an anti-Christian mob. They tied him with ropes and dragged his body through the streets until he died.

Eight centuries later, his body lay in an Alexandrian church that was about to be vandalized by Muslim fanatics. Two Venetian traders on a business trip saved the relics from desecration by hiding them in a basket of pork—a meat considered unclean by Muslims—and quickly setting sail. The perilous voyage home was only completed after many more miracles. The doge received the body, and in 828 they built the first church of St. Mark's to house it. During construction of the current church (1094), Mark's relics were temporarily lost, and it took another miracle to find them, hidden inside a column. Today, Venetians celebrate Mark on the traditional date of his martyrdom, April 25.

The events of Mark's life are portrayed vividly in many mosaics throughout the basilica. Unfortunately, most of them are either off-limits to tourists or in the dim reaches of the church. Enjoy them by buying a St. Mark's guidebook with photos.

ST. MARK'S BASILICA

more marvelous for having been done when Western Europe was still mired in mud. Here are some highlights.

• *Enter the main room, to the right. Start with the large glass case in the center of the room.*

Main Room: This display case holds the most precious Byzantine objects (mostly war booty brought here during the Fourth Crusade). The hanging lamp with the protruding fish features fourth-century Roman rock crystal framed in 11th-century

Byzantine metalwork. Just behind it, a black bucket, carved with scenes of satyrs chasing nymphs, epitomizes the pagan world that was fading as Christianity triumphed. Also in the case are blue-and-gold lapis lazuli icons of the Crucifixion and of the Archangel Michael, featuring a Byzantine specialty—enamel work (more on that craft at the Golden Altarpiece). See various chalices (cups used for the bread and wine during Mass) made of onyx, agate, and rock crystal, and an incense burner shaped like a domed church.

• *Along the walls, find the following displays (working counterclockwise around the room).*

The first three glass cases have bowls and urns made of glass or rock crystal, gold and silver, and precious stones, and laced with elaborate filigree (twisted wires). The styles blend elements from the three medieval cultures that cross-pollinated in the Eastern Mediterranean: Venetian, Byzantine, and Islamic. Next comes the Urn of Artaxerxes I (middle of the right wall), an Egyptian-made object that once held the ashes of the great Persian king who ruled 2,500 years ago (r. 465–425 B.C.). The next cases hold religious paraphernalia used for High Mass—chalices, reliquaries, candlesticks, bishops' robes, and a 600-year-old crosier (ceremonial shepherd staff) still used today by the chief priest on holy days.

Next is the Ciborio di Anastasia (far left corner), a small marble canopy that once arched over the blessed communion wafer during Mass. The object may be a gift from "Anastasia," the name carved on it in Greek. She was a lady-in-waiting in the court of the emperor Justinian (483–565). Christian legend has it that she was so beautiful that Justinian (a married man) pursued her amorously, so she had to dress like a monk and flee to a desert monastery.

Moving to the next wall, you'll see two large golden panels that once fronted an altar; flanking the panels are two golden candlesticks. What detail! The smiling angels at the top, the literary lion, the man with the weight on his shoulders, the row of queens... all the way down to the roots. Continuing counterclockwise, see a photo of a Madonna adorned with jewels, gold, and enamel. If you like this, it's just a taste of what the Pala d'Oro offers.

Next to the Madonna, notice the granite column that extends below current floor level—you can see how the floor has risen as things have settled in the last 1,000 years.

Relics/Sanctuary Room: Straight ahead, the glass case over the glowing alabaster altar contains elaborate gold-and-glass reliquaries holding relics of Jesus' Passion—his torture and execution. The reliquary showing Christ being whipped (from 1125) holds a stone from the column he was tied to. You may scoff, but of Europe's many "Pieces of the True Cross" and "Crown of Thorns" relics, these have at least some claim of authenticity. Legend has it that Christ's possessions were gathered up in the fourth century by Constantine's mother and taken to Constantinople. During the Crusade heist of 1204, Venetians brought them here. They've been paraded through the city every Good Friday for 800 years.

Back by the room's entrance is a glass reliquary with the bones of Doge Orseolo (r. 976–978), who built the church that preceded the current structure. Another contains the bones of St. George, legendary dragon slayer.

⓯ Golden Altarpiece (Pala d'Oro)

• *The Golden Altarpiece is located behind the main altar.*

Under the stone canopy sits the high altar. Inside the altar is an urn (not visible) with the mortal remains of Mark, the Gospel writer. (Look through the grate of the altar to read *Corpus Divi Marci Evangelistae,* or "Body of the Evangelist Mark.") He rests in peace, as an angel had promised him. Shh.

As you shuffle along, notice the marble canopy's support columns carved with New Testament scenes in the 13th century. (On the right-hand pillar closest to the altarpiece, fourth row from the bottom: Is that a genie escaping from a bottle while someone tries to stuff him back in?)

The Golden Altarpiece is a stunning golden wall made of 250 blue-backed enamels with religious scenes, all set in a gold frame

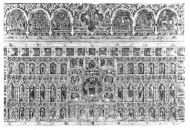
and studded with 15 hefty rubies, 300 emeralds, 1,500 pearls, and assorted sapphires, amethysts, and topaz. The Byzantine-made enamels (c. 1100) were part of the Venetians' plunder of 1204, subsequently pieced together by Byzantine craftsmen specifically for St. Mark's high altar. It's a bit much to take in all at once, but get up close and find several details you might recognize:

In the center, Jesus as Ruler of the Cosmos sits on a golden throne, with a halo of pearls and jewels. Like a good Byzantine Pantocrator, he dutifully faces forward and gives his blessing while stealing a glance offstage at Mark ("Marcus") and the other saints.

Along the bottom row, Old Testament prophets show off the books of the Bible they've written. With halos, solemn faces, and elaborately creased robes, they epitomize the Byzantine icon style.

Follow Mark's story in the panels along the sides. In the bottom left panel, Mark meets Peter (seated) at the gates of Rome. It was Peter (legend has it) who gave Mark the eyewitness account of Jesus' life that Mark wrote down in his Gospel. Mark's story ends in the bottom right panel with the two Venetian merchants returning by ship, carrying his coffin here to be laid to rest.

Byzantium excelled in the art of *cloisonné* enameling. A piece of gold leaf is stamped with a design, then filled in with pools of enamel paint, which are baked on. Look at a single saint to see the detail work: The gold background around the saint is the gold-leaf medallion that gets stamped. The golden folds in the robe are the raised edges of the impression. The different colors of the robe are different-colored paints in the recessed areas, each color baked on in a separate firing. Some saints even have pearl crowns or jewel collars pinned on. This kind of craftsmanship—and the social infrastructure that could afford it—made Byzantium seem like an enchanted world during Europe's dim Middle Ages.

After you've looked at some individual scenes, back up as far as this small room will let you and just let yourself be dazzled by the whole picture—this "mosaic" of Byzantine greatness. This magnificent altarpiece sits on a swivel (notice the mechanism at its base) and is swung around on festival Sundays so the entire congregation can enjoy it.

⑯ San Marco Museum (Museo di San Marco)— Mosaics, Bronze Horses, View of the Piazza, and More

• *The staircase up to the museum is in the atrium near the main entrance. The sign says* Loggia dei Cavalli, Museo. *Ascend the steps, buy your ticket, and enter. You'll see several models of the church at various stages of its history. From there, you'll spill out by the museum's three highlights: view of the interior (right), view of the square (out the door to the left), and bronze horses (directly ahead). Belly up to the stone balustrade to survey the interior.*

View of Church Interior

Scan the church, with its 8,000 square meters of mosaics, then take a closer look at the Pentecost Mosaic (first dome above you, described earlier). The unique design at the very top signifies the Trinity: throne (God), Gospels (Christ), and dove (Holy Spirit). The couples below the ring of apostles are the people of the world (I can find Asia, Judaea, and Cappadocia), who, despite their different languages, still understood the Spirit's message.

If you were a woman in medieval Venice, you'd enjoy this same close-up view, because in the Middle Ages, women climbed the same stairs you just did and found a spot along the balconies at your feet. The balcony was for women, the nave for men, and the altar for the priests. Back then the rood screen (the fence with the 15 figures on it) separated the priest from the public, and he officiated with his back to the people.

Appreciate the patterns of the mosaic floor—one of the finest in Italy—that covers the floor like a Persian carpet.

ST. MARK'S BASILICA

• *From here, the museum loops you to the far (altar) end of the church, then back to the bronze horses. Along the way, you'll see...*

Mosaic Fragments

These mosaics once hung in the church, but when they became damaged or aesthetically old-fashioned, they were replaced by new and more fashionable mosaics. These few fragments avoided the garbage can. You'll see mosaics from the church's earliest days (and most "Byzantine" style, c. 1070) to more recent times (1700s, realistic Renaissance detail). Many are accompanied by small photos that show where the fragment used to fit into a larger scene.

The mosaics—made from small cubes of stone or colored glass pressed into wet clay—were assembled on the ground, then cemented onto the walls. Artists draw the pattern on paper, lay it on the wet clay, and slowly cut the paper away as they replace it with cubes. The first mosaic on your left as you enter shows a reproduction of a paper "cast" of a mosaic.

• *Continuing on, you'll see other artwork and catch glimpses of the interior of the church from the north transept. Here you get a close-up view of the Tree of Jesse mosaic, showing Jesus' distant ancestor at the root and his mom at the top. Continue on to the Sala dei Banchetti (WCs near the room's entrance).*

Sala dei Banchetti

This large, ornate room—once the doge's banquet hall—is filled with religious objects, tapestries and carpets that once adorned the church, Burano lace vestments, illuminated music manuscripts, a doge's throne, and much more.

Try reading some music. The manuscripts date from the 16th century—before the age of treble and bass clefs. You'll see a C clef along the left margin of each staff (which could slide along the staff to locate middle C). From this, you could chant notes in proper relationship to each other, following the rhythm indicated.

In the center of the hall stands the most prestigious artwork here, the Pala Feriale, by Paolo Veneziano (1345). On ordinary workdays, these 14 scenes painted on wood covered the basilica's golden Pala d'Oro. The top row is seven saints (including crucified Christ). Below are seven episodes in Mark's life. In the first panel, Mark kneels before a red-robed Saint Peter and receives his calling. Next, he arrives in Alexandria and makes his first convert. Then Jesus appears to Mark. Mark is beaten to death and dragged through the streets. The panel of the sailboat tells the story of the Venetian merchants' trip home with Mark's relics. A storm at sea billows their sails, ripples the flag, churns the waves, and scares the crew as the ship heads toward the rocks. But then Mark himself appears miraculously at the stern and calms the storm, bringing the ship (and his own body) safely to Venice. Paolo proudly signed his name (along the bottom) and the names of his two assistants, his sons Luca and Giovanni. In the next panel, Mark's long-lost body is rediscovered hidden in a column. Finally, worshippers gather at Mark's tomb by the altar of the basilica.

• *Now double back toward the museum entrance, through displays of stone fragments from the church, finally arriving at...*

The Bronze Horses (La Quadriga)

Stepping lively in pairs and with smiles on their faces, they exude energy and exuberance. Art historians don't know how old they

are—they could be from ancient Greece (fourth century B.C.) or ancient Rome during its Fall (fourth century A.D.). Professor Carbon Fourteen says they're from around 175 B.C. Originally, the horses pulled a chariot *Ben-Hur* style. These bronze statues were not hammered and bent into shape by metalsmiths, but were cast from clay molds by using the lost-wax technique. The bronze is high quality, with 97 percent copper. Originally gilded, they still have some streaks of gold. Long gone are the ruby pupils that gave the horses the original case of "red eye."

Megalomaniacs through the ages have coveted these horses not only for their artistic value, but because they symbolize Apollo, the Greco-Roman god of the sun...and of secular power. The doge spoke to his people standing between the horses when they graced the balcony atop the church's facade (where the copies—which you'll see next—stand today).

Their expressive faces seem to say, "Oh boy, Wilbur, have we done some travelin'." Legend says they were made in the time of Alexander the Great, then taken by Nero to Rome. Constantine took them to his new capital in Constantinople to adorn the chariot racecourse. The Venetians then stole them from their fellow Christians during the looting of noble Constantinople (in 1204) and brought them to St. Mark's.

What goes around comes around, and Napoleon came around and took the horses when he conquered Venice in 1797. They stood atop a triumphal arch in Paris until Napoleon's empire was "blown-aparte" and they were returned to their "rightful" home.

The horses were again removed from their spot when they were attacked by their most dangerous enemy yet—modern man. The threat of oxidation from pollution sent them galloping for cover inside the church.

• *The visit ends outside on the balcony overlooking St. Mark's Square.*

The Loggia and View of St. Mark's Square

You'll be drawn repeatedly to the viewpoint of the square, but remember to look at the facade to see how cleverly all the looted

architectural elements blend together. Ramble among the statues of water-bearing slaves that serve as drain spouts. The horses are modern copies (note the 1978 date on the hoof of the horse to the right).

Be a doge, and stand between the bronze horses overlooking St. Mark's Square. Under the gilded lion of St. Mark, in front of the four great Evangelists (who once stood atop the columns), and flanked—like Apollo—by the four glorious horses, he inspired the Venetians in the square below to great things.

Admire the mesmerizing, commanding view of the center of this city, which so long ago was Europe's only superpower, and today is just a small town with a big history—one that's filled with tourists.

DOGE'S PALACE TOUR

Palazzo Ducale

Venice is a city of beautiful facades—palaces, churches, carnival masks—that can cover darker interiors of intrigue and decay. The Doge's Palace, with its frilly pink exterior, hides the fact that the "Most Serene Republic" (as Venice called itself—"serene" meaning stable) was far from serene in its heyday.

The Doge's Palace housed the fascinating government of this rich and powerful empire. It also served as the home for the Venetian ruler known as the doge (pronounced "dohzh"), or duke. For four centuries (about 1150–1550), this was the most powerful half-acre in Europe. The rest of Europe marveled at the way Venice could govern itself without a dominant king, bishop, or tyrant. The doges wanted their palace to reflect the wealth and secular values of the Republic, impressing visitors and serving as a reminder that the Venetians were Number One in Europe.

Orientation

Cost: Covered by the San Marco Museum Plus Pass (€13) or the Museum Pass (€18). You can't buy a ticket just for the Doge's Palace. For specifics, see "Passes for Venice" on page 24.

Hours: Daily April–Oct 8:30–18:30, Nov–March 9:00–18:00, last entry one hour before closing.

Getting There: The palace is next to St. Mark's Basilica, on the lagoon waterfront, and just off St. Mark's Square. Vaporetto stops: San Marco or San Zaccaria.

Crowd Control: To avoid the long peak-season line at the Doge's Palace, you have several options (the first is best).

    • Buy your pass at any of the less-crowded, included sights, such as the Correr Museum. Then go straight to the Doge's Palace turnstile, skirting along to the right of the

Doge's Palace

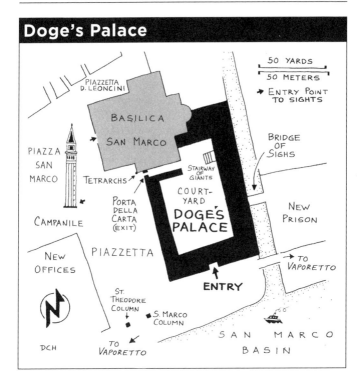

long ticket-buying line and entering at the "prepaid tickets" entrance.

• Buy your ticket online—at least 48 hours in advance—on the museum website (www.museicivicaveneziani.it).

• In peak season, visit the palace at about 17:00, when the line diminishes (but note that off-season, the museum closes at 18:00 rather than 18:30).

• Book a guided Secret Itineraries Tour (see "Tours," later).

Information: There are some English descriptions, and guidebooks are on sale in the bookshop. Tel. 041-271-5911, www.museicivicaveneziani.it.

Services: Some WCs are in the courtyard; more are halfway up the stairs to the balcony level. An elevator (off the courtyard) is available for those who have difficulty climbing stairs. Any bag bigger than a large purse must be checked (free) in the courtyard.

Tours: The **audioguide tour** is dry but informative (€5, €8/2 people, 1.5 hours, need ID or credit card for deposit). Pick it up after you pass through the turnstile after the ticket counter.

The fine **Secret Itineraries Tour** follows the doge's footsteps through rooms not included in the general admission price. Two or three English-language tours run each morning. Reserve ahead, as tours fill up as much as a month in advance in peak season—although you can try just showing up at the information desk (€18, includes Doge's Palace admission but not Correr Museum; discounted to €12 with San Marco Museum Plus Pass, which does cover Correr Museum; to reserve from the US dial 011-39-041-4273-0892, within Italy call 848-082-000, or reserve online at www.museicivici veneziani.it). Though the tour skips the main halls inside, you're welcome to visit the halls on your own afterward.

Length of This Tour: Allow 1.5 hours.

Cuisine Art: There's a sandwich-and-salad café in the palace courtyard (€4 *panini*, €9 salads, €2.50 cappuccino). Nearby are expensive cafés on St. Mark's Square, and good sandwich bars on Calle delle Rasse (two blocks behind the palace—see page 279).

Photography: Not allowed.

Starring: Big rooms bare of furnishings but crammed with history, Tintoretto masterpieces, and the doges.

The Tour Begins

Exterior

"The Wedding Cake," "The Tablecloth," or "The Pink House" is also sometimes known as the Doge's Palace. The style is called

Venetian Gothic—a fusion of Italian Gothic with a delicate Islamic flair. The columns originally had bases on the bottoms, but these were covered over as the columns sank, and the square was built up over the centuries. If you compare this lacy, top-heavy structure with

the massive fortress palaces of Florence, you realize the wisdom of building a city in the middle of the sea—you have no natural enemies except gravity. This unfortified palace in a city with no city wall was the doge's way of saying, "I am an elected and loved ruler. I do not fear my own people."

The palace was originally built in the 800s, but most of what we see came after 1300, as it was expanded to meet the needs of the empire. Each doge wanted to leave his mark on history with a new wing, but so much of the city's money was spent on the palace that finally a law was passed levying an enormous fine on anyone who even mentioned any new building. That worked for a while, until one brave and wealthy doge proposed a new wing, paid his fine...and started building again.

• *Enter the Doge's Palace from along the waterfront. After you pass through the turnstile, ignore the signs and cross the square to stand at the foot of the grand staircase topped by two statues.*

The Courtyard and the Stairway of Giants (Scala dei Giganti)

Imagine yourself as a foreign dignitary on business to meet the doge. In the courtyard, you look up a grand staircase topped

with two nearly nude statues of, I think, Moses and Paul Newman (more likely, Neptune and Mars, representing Venice's prowess at sea and at war). The doge and his aides would be waiting for you at the top, between the two statues and beneath the winged lion. No matter who you were—king, pope, or emperor—you'd have to hoof it up. The powerful doge would descend the stairs for no one.

Many doges were crowned here, between the two statues. The doge was something like an elected king—which makes sense only in the dictatorial republic that was Venice. Technically, he was just a noble selected by other nobles to carry out their laws and decisions. Many doges tried to extend their powers and rule more as divine-right kings. Many others just put on their funny hats and accepted their role as figurehead and ceremonial ribbon-cutter. Most were geezers, elected in their 70s and committed to preserving Venetian traditions.

The palace is attached to the church, symbolically welding church and state. Both buildings have ugly brick behind a painted-lady veneer of marble. In this tour, we'll see the similarly harsh inner workings of an outwardly serene, polished republic.

The courtyard is a hodgepodge of architectural styles, as the palace was refurbished over the centuries. There are classical statues in Renaissance niches, shaded by Baroque awnings, topped by Flamboyant Gothic spires, and crusted with the Byzantine onion domes of St. Mark's Basilica.

• *Cross back to near the entrance and follow the signs up the tourists' staircase to the first-floor balcony (loggia), where you can look back down on the courtyard (but not the backside of Paul Newman). From this point on, it's hard to get lost (though I've managed). It's a one-way system, so just follow the arrows.*

Midway along the balcony, you'll find a face in the wall, the...

Mouth of Truth

This fierce-looking androgyne opens his/her mouth, ready to swallow a piece of paper, hungry for gossip. Letterboxes like this (some

with lions' heads) were scattered throughout the palace. Originally, anyone who had a complaint or suspicion about anyone else could accuse him anonymously *(denontie secrete)* by simply dropping a slip of paper in the mouth. This set the blades of justice turning inside the palace.

• *Toward Paul Newman is the entrance to the...*

Golden Staircase (Scala d'Oro)

The palace was architectural propaganda, designed to impress visitors. This 24-karat gilded-ceiling staircase was something for them to write home about. As you ascend the stairs, look back at the floor below and marvel at its 3-D pattern.

• *Start up the first few steps of the Golden Staircase. Midway up, at the first landing, turn right, which takes you up into the...*

Doge's Apartments (Appartamento del Doge)

The dozen or so rooms on the first floor are where the doge actually lived. The blue-and-gold-hued Sala dei Scarlatti (Room 5) is typical of the palace's interior decoration: gold-coffered ceiling, big stone fireplace, velvety walls with paintings, and a spackled floor. There's very little original furniture, as doges were expected to bring their own. Despite his high office, the doge had to obey several rules that bound him to the city. He couldn't leave the palace unescorted, he couldn't open official mail in private, and he and his family had to leave their own home and live in the Doge's Palace.

The large Room 6, the Sala dello Scudo (Shield Hall), is full of maps and globes. The maps trace the eye-opening trip across Asia—from Italy to Greece to Palestine, Arabia, and "Irac"—of local boy Marco Polo (c. 1254–1325). Finally, he arrived at the other side of the world. This last map (at the far end of the room) is shown "upside-down," with south on top, giving a glimpse of the Venetian worldview circa 1550. It depicts China, Taiwan (Formosa), and Japan (Giapan), while America is a nearby island with California and lots of Terre Incognite.

In Room 7, the Sala Grimani, are several paintings of the lion

Paintings by Titian, Veronese, and Tintoretto

The doge had only the top Venetian painters decorate his palace. While the palace was once rich in Titians, fires in the late 1500s destroyed nearly all the work by the greatest Venetian master. As the palace was hastily reconstructed, the Titians were replaced with works by Veronese and Tintoretto. (Most of these canvases were painted in workshops, and quickly patched in to fill empty spaces.)

Veronese used the best pigments available—from precious stones, sapphires, and emeralds—and his colors have survived vividly. These Veronese paintings are by his hand and are fine examples of his genius. Tintoretto, on the other hand, didn't really have his heart in these commissions, and the pieces here were done by his workshop.

The paintings of the Doge's Palace are a study of old Venice, with fine views of the old city and its inhabitants. The extravagant women's gowns in the paintings by Veronese show off a major local industry—textiles. While the paintings are not generally of masterpiece quality, they're historically interesting. They prove that in the old days, Venice had no pigeons.

of St. Mark, including the famous one by Vittore Carpaccio of a smiling lion (on the long wall). The lion holds open a book with these words— *"Pax Tibi Marce..."* ("Peace to you, Mark")—which according to legend, were spoken by an angel welcoming St. Mark to Venice. In the background is the Doge's Palace and the Campanile.

DOGE'S PALACE

When you reach Room 10, the Sala dei Filosofi (Philosophers' Hall), pop up the humble stairway and look back at a Titian quickie, painted in just three days. This fresco of St. Christopher carrying the Christ child across the lagoon was made for a doge who believed that if you looked at St. Christopher, you wouldn't die that day.

• *After browsing the dozen or so private rooms of the Doge's Apartments, continue up the Golden Staircase to the third floor, which was the "public" part of the palace. The first room at the top of the stairs is the...*

Square Room (Atrio Quadrato)

The ceiling painting, ***Justice Presenting the Sword and Scales to Doge Girolamo Priuli,*** is by Tintoretto. (Stand at the top of the

painting for the full 3-D effect.) It's a late-Renaissance masterpiece. So what? As you'll soon see, this palace is wallpapered with Titians, Tintorettos, and Veroneses. Many have the same theme you see here: a doge, in his ermine cape, gold-brocaded robe, and funny one-horned hat with earflaps, kneeling in the presence of saints, gods, or mythological figures.

• *Enter the next room.*

Room of the Four Doors (Sala delle Quattro Porte)

This was the central clearinghouse for all the goings-on in the palace. Visitors presented themselves here and were directed to their destination—the courts, councils, or the doge himself.

The room was designed by Andrea Palladio, the architect who did the impressive Church of San Giorgio Maggiore, across the Grand Canal from St. Mark's Square. On the intricate stucco ceiling, notice the feet of the women dangling down below the edge (above the windows), extending the illusion.

On the wall next to the door you entered is a painting by (ho-hum) Titian, showing a **doge kneeling** with great piety before a woman embodying Faith holding the Cross of Jesus. Notice old Venice in the misty distance under the cross. This is one of many paintings you'll see of doges in uncharacteristically humble poses—paid for, of course, by the doges themselves.

G. B. Tiepolo's well-known ***Venice Receiving Neptune*** is now displayed on an easel, but it was originally hung on the wall above the windows where they've put a copy (you'll get closer to the painting as you progress through the museum). The painting shows Venice

as a woman—Venice is always a woman to artists—reclining in luxury, dressed in the ermine cape and pearl necklace of a doge's wife (dogaressa). Crude Neptune, enthralled by the

Executive & Legislative Rooms

```
ROOM II     ROOM 12
COLLEGIO    SENATE
  HALL       HALL

     ❻        ❾
                    ❽
  ❼
  ❺  ❹

ROOM OF THE 4 DOORS  ❸
        ❷
  ❶
   SQUARE
    ROOM         ROOM
                  15
   GOLDEN
  STAIRCASE
```

COURTYARD

DCH

❶ TINTORETTO – Justice
   Presenting the Sword and Scales

❷ TITIAN – Doge Kneeling

❸ TIEPOLO – Venice Receiving Neptune

❹ VERONESE – The Rape of Europa

❺ TINTORETTO – Bacchus and Ariadne

❻ VERONESE – Discussion

❼ VERONESE – Mars and Neptune
   with Campanile and Lion

❽ TINTORETTO – Triumph of Venice

❾ Clocks

First Lady's beauty, arrives bearing a seashell bulging with gold ducats. A bored Venice points and says, "Put it over there with the other stuff."

• *Enter the small room with the big fireplace and several paintings.*

Ante-Collegio Hall (Sala dell'Anticollegio)

It took a big title or bribe to get in to see the doge. Once accepted for a visit, you would wait here before you entered, combing your hair, adjusting your robe, popping a breath mint, and preparing the gifts you'd brought. While you cooled your heels and warmed your hands at the elaborate fireplace, you might look at some of the paintings—among the finest in the palace, worthy of any museum in the world.

The Rape of Europa (on the wall opposite the fireplace), by Paolo Veronese, most likely shocked many small-town visitors with its risqué subject matter. Here Zeus, the king of the Greek gods, appears in the form of a bull with a foot fetish, seducing a beautiful earthling, while cupids spin playfully overhead. The Venetian Renaissance looked back to pagan Greek and Roman art, a big change from the saints and crucifixions of the Middle Ages. This painting doesn't portray the abduction in a medieval condemnation of sex and violence, but rather as a celebration in cheery pastel colors of the earthy, optimistic spirit of the Renaissance.

Tintoretto's **Bacchus and Ariadne** (to the right of the fireplace) is another colorful display of Venice's sensual tastes. The God of Wine seeks a threesome, offering a ring to the mortal Ariadne, who's being crowned with stars by Venus, who turns slowly in zero gravity. The ring is the center of a spinning wheel of flesh, with the three arms like spokes.

But wait, the doge is ready for us. Let's go in.

• *Enter the next room and approach your imaginary doge.*

Collegio Hall (Sala del Collegio)

Flanked by his cabinet of six advisers—one for each Venetian neighborhood—the doge would sit on the wood-paneled platform at the far end to receive ambassadors, who laid their gifts at his feet and pleaded their countries' cases. All official ceremonies, such as the ratification of treaties, were held here.

At other times, it was the "Oval Office" where the doge and his cabinet (the executive branch) met privately to discuss proposals to give the legislature, pull files from the cabinets (along the right wall) regarding business with Byzantium, or rehearse a meeting with the pope. The wooden benches around the sides (where they sat) are original. The clock on the wall is a backward-running 24-hour clock with Roman numerals and a sword for hands.

The ceiling is 24-karat gold, with paintings by Veronese. These are not frescoes (painting on wet plaster), like those in the Sistine Chapel, but actual canvases painted in Veronese's studio and then placed on the ceiling. Within years, Venice's humidity would have melted frescoes like mascara.

The T-shaped painting of the woman with the spider web (on the ceiling, opposite the big window) represents the Venetian symbol of **Discussion.** You can imagine the webs of truth and lies woven in this room by the doge's scheming advisers.

In **Mars and Neptune with Campanile and Lion** (the ceiling painting near the entrance), Veronese presents four symbols of the Republic's strength—military, sea trade, city, and government (plus a cherub about to be circumcised by the Campanile).

• *Enter the large Senate Hall.*

Senate Hall (Sala del Senato)

While the doge presided from the stage, senators mounted the podium (middle of the wall with windows) to address their 120 colleagues. The legislators, chaired by the doge, debated and passed laws in this room.

Venice prided itself on its self-rule (independent of popes, kings, and tyrants), with most power placed in the hands of these annually elected men. Which branch of government really ruled? All of them. It was an elaborate system of checks and balances to make sure no one rocked the boat, no one got too powerful, and the ship of state sailed smoothly ahead.

Tintoretto's large *Triumph of Venice* on the ceiling (central painting, best viewed from the top) shows the city in all its glory. Lady Venice is up in heaven with the Greek gods, while barbaric lesser nations swirl up to give her gifts and tribute. Do you get the

feeling the Venetian aristocracy was proud of its city?

On the wall are two large clocks, one of which has the signs of the zodiac and phases of the moon. And there's one final oddity in this room, in case you hadn't noticed it yet. In one of the wall paintings (above the entry door), there's actually a doge... not kneeling.

• *Exiting the Senate Hall, you pass again through the Room of the Four Doors, then around the corner into a hall with a semicircular platform at the far end.*

Hall of the Council of Ten (Sala del Consiglio dei Dieci)

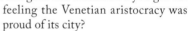

By the 1400s, Venice had a worldwide reputation for swift, harsh, and secret justice. The dreaded Council of Ten—10 judges, plus the doge and his six advisers—met here to dole out punishment to traitors, murderers, and "morals" violators. (Note the 17 wood panels where they presided.)

Slowly, they developed into a CIA-type unit with their own force of police officers, guards, spies, informers, and even assassins. They had their own budget and were accountable to no one, soon making them the de facto ruling body of the "Republic." It seemed no one was safe from the spying eye of the "Terrible Ten." You could be accused anonymously (by a letter dropped into a Mouth

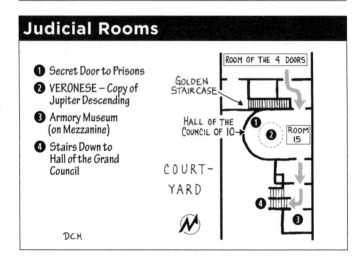

Judicial Rooms

1. Secret Door to Prisons
2. VERONESE – Copy of Jupiter Descending
3. Armory Museum (on Mezzanine)
4. Stairs Down to Hall of the Grand Council

ROOM OF THE 4 DOORS

GOLDEN STAIRCASE

HALL OF THE COUNCIL OF 10→

ROOM 15

COURT-YARD

DCH

of Truth), swept off the streets, tried, judged, and thrown into the dark dungeons in the palace for the rest of your life without so much as a Miranda warning.

It was in this room that the Council decided who lived or died, and who was decapitated, tortured, or merely thrown in jail. The small, hard-to-find **door** leading off the platform (the fifth panel to the right of center) leads through secret passages to the prisons and torture chambers.

The large, central, oval ceiling painting by Veronese (a copy of the original stolen by Napoleon and still in the Louvre) shows *Jupiter Descending from Heaven to Strike Down the Vices,* redundantly informing the accused that justice in Venice was swift and harsh. To the left of that, Juno showers Lady Venice with coins, crowns, and peace.

Though the dreaded Council of Ten was eventually disbanded, today their descendants enforce the dress code at St. Mark's Basilica.

• *Pass through the next room, turn right and head up the stairs to the Armory Museum.*

Armory Museum (L'Armeria)

The aesthetic of killing is beyond me, but I must admit I've never seen a better collection of halberds, falchions, ranseurs, targes, morions, and brigandines in my life. The weapons in these three rooms make you realize the important role the military played in keeping the East–West trade lines open.

Room 1: In the glass case on the right, you'll see the suit of armor worn by the great

DOGE'S PALACE

Venetian mercenary general, Gattamelata (far right, on horseback), as well as "baby's first armor" (how soon they grow up!). A full suit of armor could weigh 66 pounds. Before gunpowder, crossbows (look up) were made still more lethal by turning a crank on the end to draw the bow with extra force.

Room 2: In the thick of battle, even horses needed helmets. The hefty broadswords were brandished two-handed by the strongest and bravest soldiers who waded into enemy lines. Suspended from the ceiling is a large triangular banner captured from the Ottoman Turks at the Battle of Lepanto (1571).

Room 3: At the far (left) end of the room is a very, very early (17th-century) attempt at a 20-barrel machine gun. On the walls and weapons, the "C-X" insignia means that this was the private stash of the "Council of Ten."

Room 4: In this room, rifles and pistols enter the picture. Don't miss the glass case in the corner, with a tiny crossbow, some torture devices (including an effective-looking thumbscrew), the wooden "devil's box" (a clever item that could fire in four directions at once), and a nasty, two-holed chastity belt. These "iron breeches" were worn by the devoted wife of the Lord of Padua.

• *Exit the Armory Museum (enjoy a closer look at that early machine gun). Go downstairs, turn left, and pass through the long hall with a wood-beam ceiling. Now turn right and open your eyes as wide as you can to see the...*

Hall of the Grand Council (Sala del Maggiore Consiglio)

It took a room this size to contain the grandeur of the Most Serene Republic. This huge room (175 by 80 feet) could accommodate up to 2,600 people at one time. The engineering is remarkable. The ceiling is like the deck of a ship—its hull is the rooftop, creating a huge attic above that.

The doge presided from the raised dais, while the nobles—the backbone of the empire—filled the center and lined the long walls. Nobles were generally wealthy men over 25, but the title had less

DOGE'S PALACE

to do with money than with long bloodlines. In theory, the doge, the Senate, and the Council of Ten were all subordinate to the Grand Council of nobles who elected them.

On the wall over the doge's throne is Tintoretto's monsterpiece, *Paradise,* the largest oil painting in the world. At 570 square feet, it could be sliced up to wallpaper an apartment with

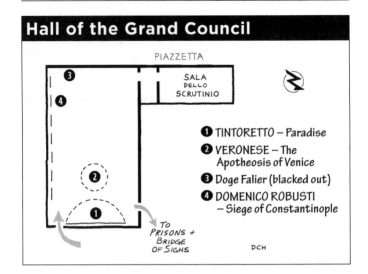

Hall of the Grand Council

PIAZZETTA

SALA DELLO SCRUTINIO

❶ TINTORETTO – Paradise
❷ VERONESE – The Apotheosis of Venice
❸ Doge Falier (blacked out)
❹ DOMENICO ROBUSTI – Siege of Constantinople

TO PRISONS & BRIDGE OF SIGHS

DCH

enough left over for placemats.

Christ and Mary are at the top of heaven, surrounded by 500 people. It's rush hour in heaven, and all the good Venetians made it. The painting leaves you feeling that you get to heaven not by being a good Christian, but by being a good Venetian. Tintoretto worked on this in the last years of his long life. On the day it was finished, his daughter died. He got his brush out again and painted her as saint number 501. She's dead center with the blue skirt, hands clasped, getting sucked up to heaven. (At least that's what an Italian tour guide told me.)

Veronese's *The Apotheosis of Venice* (on the ceiling at the Tintoretto end—view it from the top) is a typically unsubtle work showing Lady Venice being crowned a goddess by an angel.

Ringing the hall are portraits, in chronological order, of the first 76 doges. The one at the far end that's blacked out is the notorious **Doge Marin Falier,** who opposed the will of the Grand Council in 1355. He was tried for treason, beheaded, and airbrushed from history.

Along the entire wall to the right of Paradise, the *Siege of Constantinople* (by Tintoretto's son, Domenico Robusti) shows Venice's greatest military (if not moral) victory, the conquest of the fellow-Christian city of Constantinople during the Fourth Crusade (1204). The mighty walls of Constantinople repelled every attack for nearly a thousand years. But the sneaky Venetians (in the fifth painting) circled around back and attacked where the walls rose straight up from the water's edge. Skillful Venetian oarsmen cozied their galleys right up to the dock, allowing soldiers to scoot along crossbeams attached to the masts and on to the top of the city walls. In the foreground, an archer cranks up his crossbow. The gates are opened, the Byzantine emperor parades out to surrender, and tiny Doge Dandolo says, "Let's go in and steal some bronze horses."

But soon Venice would begin its long slide into historical oblivion. One by one, the Ottomans gobbled up Venice's trading outposts. In the West, the rest of Europe ganged up on Venice to reduce her power. By 1500, Portugal had broken Venice's East–West trade monopoly by finding a sea route to the East around the southern tip of Africa. To top it off, despite winning a famous victory in the bloody Battle of Lepanto in 1571 (depicted in paintings in the adjoining Sala dello Scrutinio), Venice's reputation as a naval power began to suffer; their ships could not compete with Spain's more modern, more effective armada. Over the centuries, Venice remained a glorious city, but not the world power she once was. Finally, in 1797, the French general Napoleon marched into town shouting *"Liberté, Egalité, Fraternité."* The Most Serene Republic was finally conquered, and the last doge was deposed in the name of modern democracy.

Out the windows (if they're open) is a fine view of the domes of the basilica, the palace courtyard below, and Paul Newman.

The adjoining **Sala dello Scrutinio** room overlooks the Piazzetta. From its balcony, a newly elected doge was presented to the people of Venice. A noble would announce, "Here is your doge, if it pleases you." That was fine, until one time when the people weren't pleased. From then on they just said, "Here is your doge."

• *Consider reading about the prisons here in the Grand Council Hall, where there are more benches and fewer rats.*

To reach the prisons, exit the Grand Hall by squeezing through the door to the left of Tintoretto's monsterpiece. Follow signs for Prigioni/ Ponte dei Sospiri, *passing through several rooms. In Room 31, pause at four fascinating paintings by Hieronymus Bosch (once hung in the Hall of the Council of Ten), showing sinners tortured in hell by genetic mutants and* Wizard of Oz *monkeys. In a room adjoining Room 31, you'll find a narrow staircase down, following signs to the prisons. (Don't miss it, or you'll miss the prisons altogether and end up at the bookshop near the exit.) Then cross the covered Bridge of Sighs over the canal to the prisons. Start your visit in the cells to your left.*

Prisons

The palace had its own dungeons. In the privacy of his own home, a doge could oversee the sentencing, torturing, and jailing of polit-

ical opponents. The most notorious cells were "the wells" in the basement, so-called because they were deep, wet, and cramped.

By the 1500s, the wells were full of political prisoners. New prisons were built across the canal (to the east of the palace) and connected with a covered bridge.

Medieval justice was harsh. The cells consisted of cold stone with heavily barred windows, a wooden plank for a bed, a shelf, and a bucket. (My question: What did they put on the shelf?) You can feel the cold and damp.

Circle the cells. Notice the carvings made by prisoners—from olden days up until 1930—on some of the stone windowsills of the cells, especially in the far corner of the building.

Explore the rest of the prisons. You can descend lower to the cells known as "the wells." Or stay on this floor, where there's a room displaying ceramic shards found in archaeological digs. Adjoining that are more cells, including the farthest cell, where you can see the bored prisoners' compelling and sometimes artistic graffiti.

• *Wherever you roam, you'll end up where you entered. Now re-cross...*

The Bridge of Sighs

According to romantic legend, criminals were tried and sentenced in the palace, then marched across the canal here to the dark prisons. On this bridge, they got one last look at Venice. They gazed out at the sky, the water, and the beautiful buildings.

• *Cross back over the Bridge of Sighs, pausing (if scaffolding allows) to look through the marble-trellised windows at all of the tourists and the heavenly Church of San Giorgio Maggiore. Heave one last sigh and leave the palace.*

DOGE'S PALACE

CORRER MUSEUM TOUR

Museo Civico Correr

A doge's hat, gleaming statues by Canova, and paintings by the illustrious Bellini family—for some people, that's a major museum; for others, it's a historical bore. But the Correr Museum has one more thing to offer, and that's a quiet refuge—a place to rise above St. Mark's Square when the piazza is too hot, too rainy, or too overrun with tourists. Besides, the museum is included if you've bought a ticket to the Doge's Palace. Those who enter are rewarded with an easy-to-manage overview of Venice's art and history.

Orientation

Cost: You can't buy an individual ticket just for the Correr. It's included in the San Marco Museum Plus Pass (€13) or the Museum Pass (€18), both of which also include the Doge's Palace, as well as the two lesser museums inside the Correr (National Archaeological Museum and the Monumental Rooms of the Marciana National Library—described briefly in this chapter). For specifics, see "Passes for Venice" on page 24.

If you visit the Clock Tower (€12, requires reservation, see page 40), that ticket also includes admission to the Correr Museum.

Hours: Daily April–Oct 9:00–19:00, Nov–March 9:00–17:00, last entry one hour before closing.

Getting There: The entrance is on St. Mark's Square in Napoleon's wing—the building at the far end of the square, opposite the basilica. Climb the staircase to the first-floor ticket office and bookstore.

Information: English descriptions are provided throughout. Tel. 041-240-5211, www.museiciviciveneziani.it.

Bag Check: Free and mandatory for bags bigger than a large purse.

Length of This Tour: Allow one hour.

Cuisine Art: The museum café has tables with a view of St. Mark's Square (€2.50 cappuccino, €4 *panini*, €1.50 pastries).

Photography: Not allowed.

Starring: Canova statues, Venetian historical artifacts, three Bellinis, and a Carpaccio.

The Tour Begins

The Correr Museum gives you admission and access to three connected museums—the Correr proper (which we'll see), the National Archaeological Museum, and the Marciana National Library.

The Correr itself is on three long, skinny floors that parallel St. Mark's Square. This tour covers the first two floors: The first floor contains Canova statues and Venetian history; the second floor displays a chronological overview of Venetian paintings.

First Floor

• *Buy your ticket. After entering, you'll likely find yourself in the long, skinny Room 3, the Loggia Napoleonica. From there, turn right into the large Ballroom (Room 2). Note that, because of temporary exhibits, you sometimes enter Room 2 directly from the bookshop, sometimes through Room 3, and sometimes Room 2 is closed altogether.*

Room 2 (Ballroom)
Canova—*Orpheus and Eurydice*
(*Orfeo,* 1775–1776; *Euridice,* 1775)

Orpheus is leading his beloved back from hell when she is tugged from behind by the cloudy darkness. She calls for help. Orpheus looks back and smacks his forehead in horror...but he can do nothing to help, and he has to hurry on.

In this youthful work, Venice's greatest sculptor, Antonio Canova, already shows elements of his later style: high-polished, slender, beautiful figures; an ensemble arrangement, with more than one figure; open space between the figures that's almost as compelling as the figures themselves; and a statue group that's interesting from many angles.

CORRER MUSEUM

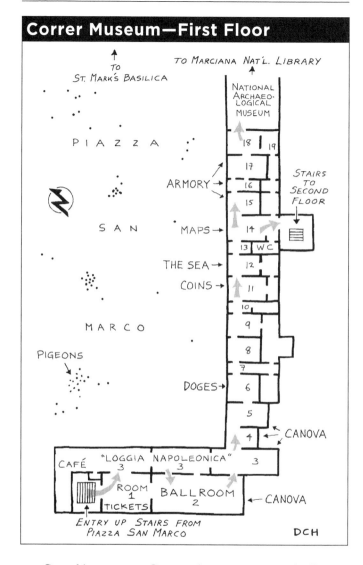

Carved by a teenage Canova, this piece captures the Rococo spirit of Venice in the late 1700s—elegant and beautiful, but tinged with bittersweet loss. Even Canova's later works—which were more sober, minimalist, and emotionally restrained—always retained the elegance and romantic sentiment of the last days of the Venetian Republic.

• *Enter the long hallway known as the Loggia Napoleonica, and admire its views over St. Mark's Square.*

Antonio Canova
(1757–1822)

Son of a Venetian stonemason, Canova grew up with a chisel in his hand in a studio along the Grand Canal, precociously mastering the sentimental, elegant Rococo style of the late 1700s. At 23, he went to Rome and beyond, studying ancient statues at then-recently discovered Pompeii. These archaeological finds inspired a new Renaissance-style revival of the classical style. Canova's pure, understated elegance and "neo"-classical style soon became the rage all over Europe.

Called to Paris, Canova became Napoleon's court sculptor and carved perhaps his best-known work: Napoleon's sister as Venus, reclining on a couch (now in the Borghese Gallery, Rome). Canova combined Rococo sentiment and elegance with the cool, minimal lines of classicism.

Room 3 (Loggia Napoleonica)

Find Canova's pyramid-shaped model of the *Monument to Titian (Monumento a Tiziano)*. This was Canova's design (based on the pyramid of Gaius Cestius in Rome) for a tomb he intended for the painter Titian. The design was not used for Titian, but instead for the tomb of an Austrian princess in Vienna, as well as for Canova's own memorial in the Frari Church (for more on Titian's and Canova's monuments, see page 148).

• *Continue on into Room 4.*

Room 4

Canova—*Daedalus and Icarus* (*Dedalo e Icaro*, 1778–1779)

Serious Daedalus straps wings, which he's just invented, onto his son's shoulders. The boy is thrilled with the new toy, not knowing what we know—that they will soon melt in the sun and plunge him to his death. Daedalus' middle-aged, sagging skin contrasts with Icarus' supple form. Canova, a stonemason's son, displays the tools of the family trade on the base.

Antonio Canova was only 20 when Venice's Procurator commissioned this work from the hometown prodigy. It was so realistic that it caused a stir—skeptics accused Canova of not really sculpting it, but making it from plaster casts of live humans.

Room 5
Canova—*Amor and Psyche*

Though not a great painting, this is Canova's 2-D version of a famous scene he set in stone (now in the Louvre). The two lovers spiral around each other in the never-ending circle of desire. The two bodies and Cupid's two wings form an X. But the center of the composition is the empty space that separates their hungry lips.

Canova—*Paris*
The guy with black measles is not a marble statue of Paris; it's a plaster of Paris, a life-size model that Canova used in carving the real one in stone. The dots are sculptor's "points," which tell the sculptor how far into the block he should chisel to establish the figure's rough outline.

Other Canovas
The other large statues in the Canova rooms are either lesser works or more plaster *(gesso)* studies for works later executed in marble. You'll also see small clay models, where Canova worked out ideas before chiseling into an expensive block of marble.

• *Enter the world of Venice's doges. On an easel in Room 6, find a doge portrait.*

Room 6: The Doge
Lazzaro Bastiani—*Portrait of Doge Francesco Foscari*
Doge Foscari, dressed in the traditional brocaded robe and cap with cloth earflaps, introduces us to the powerful, regal world of these "elected princes," who served as ceremonial symbols of the glorious Republic.

The Doge's World

While some doges were powerful dictators, and others merely doddering figureheads, all of Venice's rulers were expected to put on a good show at official events. St. Mark's Square was the site of many ceremonial parades. At the head came flag bearers and trumpet players sounding a fanfare. Next came the bigwigs, the archbishop, the bearer of the doge cap, the doge's chair, and finally Il Serenissimo himself, under an umbrella. Noble  ladies looked on from the windows above—the very windows of today's Correr Museum.

The process of electing a new doge was as baffling as the American Electoral College: Thirty nobles were chosen by casting lots, then 21 of them were eliminated by lots. The remaining nine elected 40 nobles, whose number was whittled down to 25 by lots...and so on through several more steps, until, finally, 41 electors—chosen by their peers and by chance—selected the next doge.

Foscari (1373–1457, buried in the Frari Church) inherited Venice at its historical peak as a prosperous sea-trading empire with

peaceful ties to eastern Ottomans and mainland Europeans. He has a serene look of total confidence...a look that would slowly melt as he led Venice on a 31-year war of expansion that devastated northern Italy, embroiled Venice in messy European politics, and eventually drained the city's coffers. Meanwhile, the Ottomans captured Constantinople. By the time the Venetian Senate "impeached" Foscari, forcing his resignation, Venice was sapped, soon to be surpassed by the new sea-trading powers of Spain and Portugal.

In the glass case, find doge memorabilia, including the funny **doge cap** with a single horn at the back, often worn over a cloth cap with earflaps.

• *High on the wall opposite the room's entrance, find the large painting by...*

CORRER MUSEUM

Andrea Michieli—*Arrival of Dogaressa Grimani (Lo Sbarco della Dogaressa Morosina Grimani)*

Although doges were men, several wives were crowned with ceremonial titles. This painting shows coronation ceremonies (1597) along the water by the Piazzetta. The lagoon is jammed with boats. Notice the Doge's Palace on the right, the Marciana National Library on the left (designed by Jacopo Sansovino), and the Campanile and Clock Tower in the distance. The dogaressa (left of center, in yellow, wearing her doge cap tilted back) arrives to receive the front-door key to the Doge's Palace.

The doge's private boat, the *Bucintoro* (docked at lower left, with red roof), has brought the First Lady and her entourage of red-robed officials, court dwarves, musicians, dancers, and ladies in formal wear. She walks toward the World Theater (on the right, in the water), a floating pavilion used for public ceremonies.

• *The displays in Rooms 7–10 change often. Browse the exhibits, but also appreciate the fact that these rooms were once government offices.*

Rooms 7–10: Government Offices

Some of the rich furnishings in these rooms—pictures of Doge processions (often in Room 7), rare books in walnut bookcases (Room 8), a Murano chandelier, wood-beamed ceiling, and portraits of political bigwigs—are reminders that this wing once housed the administrative offices of a wealthy, sophisticated, trade-oriented republic.

• *Move to Room 11 to view Venetian coins. The collection runs chronologically clockwise around the room.*

Room 11: Coins and the Treasury

The Venetian ducat weighed only a bit more than a US penny, but was mostly gold. (By decree, 99 percent pure gold, weighing 3.5

grams.) First minted around 1280 (find Giovanni Dandolo's *zecchino,* or "sequin," in the first glass case to the right of the door that leads into the next room), it became the strongest currency in all Europe for nearly 700 years, eventually replacing the Florentine florin. In Renaissance times, 100 ducats would be an excellent salary for a year, with a single ducat worth about $1,000. The most common design shows Christ on the "heads" side, standing in an oval of stars. "Tails" features the current doge kneeling before St. Mark, with the inscription "sacred money of Venice."

Also in Room 11, find **Tintoretto's painting** of three red-robed treasury officials, who handled ducats in these offices. The richness of their fur-lined robes suggests the almost religious devotion that officials were expected to have as caretakers of the "sacred money of Venice."

Room 12: Venice and the Sea

Venice's wealth came from its sea trade. Raw materials from Europe were exchanged for luxury goods from eastern lands controlled by Muslim Ottomans and Byzantine Christians.

Models of Galleys *(Modello di Galera)*

These fast oar- and wind-powered warships rode shotgun for Venice's commercial fleets plying the Mediterranean. With up to 150 men (four per oar, some prisoners, mostly proud professionals) and three horizontal sails, they could cruise from here to Constantinople in about a month. In battle, they specialized in turning on a dime to aim cannons, or in quickly building up speed to ram and board other ships with their formidable prows. Also displayed are large lanterns from a galley's stern.

• *Find two similar paintings depicting...*

The Battle of Lepanto *(Battaglia di Lepanto, 1571)*

The two paintings capture the confusion of a famous battle fought off the coast of Greece in 1571 between Muslim Ottomans and

a coalition of Christians. This battle ended Ottoman dominance at sea. Sort it out by their flags. The turbaned Ottomans fought under the crescent moon. On the Christian side, Venetians had the winged lion, the pope's troops flew the cross, and Spain was marked with the Habsburg eagle.

The fighting was fierce and hand-to-hand as they boarded each other's ships and cannons blasted away point-blank. Miguel de Cervantes fought in this battle; he lost his hand and had to pen *Don Quixote* one-handed.

The Christians won, sinking 113 enemy ships and killing up to 30,000. It was a major psychological victory, as it was a turning point in the Ottoman threat to Europe.

But for Venice, it marked the end of an era. The city lost 4,000 men and many ships, and never fully recovered its trading empire in Ottoman lands. Moreover, Spain's cannon-laden sailing ships proved to be masters of the waves, making Spain the next true naval power. Venice's shallow-hulled galleys, so swift in the placid Mediterranean, were no match on the high seas.

Room 13: The Arsenale

A pen-and-ink plan *(Pianta dell'Arsenale)* by Antonio di Natale shows a bird's-eye view of the shipbuilding factory located near the

tail of Venice. This rectangular, artificial harbor was surrounded by workshops where ships could be mass-produced as though on a modern assembly line (but it was the workers who moved). If needed, they could crank out a galley a day. The Arsenale's entrance (lower left of painting) is still guarded today by the two lions.

Room 14: The Map Room (Venezia Forma Urbis)

Old maps show a city relatively unchanged over the centuries, hemmed in by water. Find your hotel on Jacopo de' Barbari's big

black-and-white map from 1500. There's the Arsenale in the fish's tail. There's Piazza San Marco with a church standing where the Correr Museum entrance is today. The Accademia Bridge hadn't been built yet (nor had the modern train station). We'll see more about Barbari's impressive map upstairs.

Rooms 15–18: Armory

You'll find weapons from medieval times to the advent of gunpowder—maces, armor, swords, Ottoman pikes, rifles, cannons, shields, and a teeny-tiny pistol hidden in a book (in a glass case in Room 17).

• *Those interested in visiting the National Archaeological Museum (Greek and Roman statues) and the impressive Marciana National Library can reach them from Rooms 18 and 19 (included with Correr Museum admission). It's a bit of a detour to the library, and some may wish to skip ahead to "Venetian Painting."*

National Archaeological Museum and Marciana National Library

In the archaeological museum, you pass through room after room of ancient statues (mostly copies that aren't that ancient). You eventually reach the library, famous in Renaissance times because Venice was a major center of printing and secular knowledge. The library displays antique globes and manuscripts. On the ceiling are *tondi* (round) paintings of virtues and allegories of the liberal arts, such as mathematics, geometry, and music. The three *tondi* immediately above where you enter are by Paolo Veronese. The walls are richly decorated with portraits of renowned scholars and ancient philosophers who twist and turn in their niches in classical Baroque style. The smaller room at the end of the hall features Roman copies of Greek statuary and a trompe l'oeil ceiling that makes the wood-beam ceiling appear even higher. The painting in the center of the ceiling by Titian shows Lady Wisdom seated in the clouds reading a book and a scroll.

• *Backtrack to Room 14 (WCs nearby), then head upstairs to the second floor, following signs to* La Quadreria—Picture Gallery. *Enter Room 25.*

Second Floor

Venetian Painting

The painting highlights (the Bellinis) are located at the far end of this wing, and you have permission to hurry there. But along the way, trace the development of Venetian painting from golden Byzantine icons to Florentine-inspired 3-D to the natural beauty of Bellini and Carpaccio.

Room 25

Paolo Veneziano—*Six Saints* (c. 1310-1358)

Gold-backed saints combine traits from Venice's two cultural sources: Byzantine (serene, elongated, somber, and iconic, with gold background, like the mosaics in St. Mark's) and the Gothic of mainland Europe (curvy, expressive bodies posed at a three-quarters angle, colorful robes, and individualized faces).

Room 26

Lorenzo Veneziano—*Figures and Episodes of Saints* (*Figure e Storie di Santi,* c. 1356-1370)

Influence from the mainland puts icons in motion, adding drama

Correr Museum—Second Floor

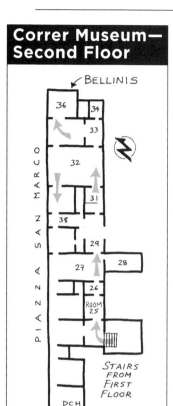

BELLINIS

36
34
33
32
31
38
29
28
27
26
ROOM 25

SAN MARCO
PIAZZA

STAIRS
FROM
FIRST
FLOOR

DCH

to the telling of saints' lives (in the small scenes above the three saints). St. Nicholas grabs the executioner's sword and lifts him right off the ground before he even knows what's happening.

Room 27: Ornate (Flamboyant) Gothic

Architectural fragments of Gothic buildings remind us that Venice's distinctive architecture is Italian Gothic, filtered through Eastern exoticism. You'll see examples, in paint as well as in stone, of pointed arches decorated with the "flame-like" curlicues that gave the Flamboyant Gothic style its name.

Room 29.II: International Gothic

Maestro dei Cassone Jarves—Two Painted Lids of a Hope Chest (c. 1425)

As humanism spread, so did art that was not exclusively religious. These scenes depict a story from Boccaccio's bawdy *Decameron*.

Done in the so-called International Gothic style, the painted lids emphasize decorative curves—curvy filigree patterns in clothes, curvy boats, curvy sails, curvy waves, curvy horses' rumps—all enjoyed as a decorative pattern.

CORRER MUSEUM

Room 31.I: Ferrarese Painters

Baldassare Estense—*Portrait of a Young Man (Ritratto di Gentiluomo, c. 1442–1564)*

The young man in red is not a saint, king, or pope, but an ordinary citizen painted, literally, wart and all. On the window ledge is a strongly foreshortened book. And behind the young man, the curtain opens to reveal a new world—a spacious 3-D vista courtesy of the Tuscan Renaissance.

Room 32

Jacopo de' Barbari—*Venetie MD* (1500)

How little Venice has changed in 500 years! Barbari's large, intricately detailed woodcut of the city put his contemporaries in a unique position—a mile up in the air, looking down on the rooftops. He chronicles nearly every church, alleyway, and gondola. Both the final product and the reverse-image woodcut are on display, a tribute to all of Barbari's painstaking labor.

Room 33: 15th-Century Flemish Artists

Pieter Brueghel the Younger—*Adoration (Adorazione dei Magi)*

Venetian artists were strongly influenced by the detailed, everyday landscapes of Northern masters. Lost in this snowy scene of the secular working world is baby Jesus in a stable (lower left), worshipped by the Magi. Venetians learned that landscape creates its own mood, and that humans don't have to be the center of every painting.

Room 34

Antonello da Messina—*Christ with Three Angels (Pietà con Tre Angeli, c. 1475)*

The Sicilian painter wowed Venice with this work when he visited in 1475, bringing a Renaissance style and new painting techniques. After a thousand years of standing rigidly on medieval crucifixes, Christ could finally let his body relax in a natural human

posture. The scene is set in a realistic, distant landscape.
Remember this work, as I'll refer to it later.

Room 36: The Bellini Family (I Bellini)

One family single-handedly brought Venetian painting into the
Renaissance—the Bellinis.

Jacopo Bellini—*Crucifixion (La Crocifissione)*

Father Jacopo (c. 1400–1470) had studied in Florence when
Donatello and Brunelleschi were
pioneering 3-D naturalism.

Daughter Cecilia (not a
painter) married the painter
Mantegna, whose precise lines and
statuesque figures influenced his
brothers-in-law.

Gentile Bellini—*Portrait of Doge Mocenigo*

Elder son Gentile (c. 1429–1507) took over
the family business and established a reputation for documenting Venice's rulers and
official ceremonies. His straightforward
style and attention to detail capture the
ordinary essence of this doge.

Giovanni Bellini—*Crucifixion (La Crocifissione)*

Younger son Giovanni (c. 1430–1516) became the most famous
Bellini, the man who pioneered new techniques
and subject matter, trained Titian and Giorgione,
and almost single-handedly invented the Venetian
High Renaissance.

Compare this early Crucifixion (young
Giovanni's earliest documented work) with his
father's version. Young Giovanni weeds out all
the crowded, medieval mourners, leaving only
Mary and John. Behind, he paints a spacious
(Mantegnesque) landscape, with a lake and mountains in the distance. Our eyes follow the winding
road from Christ to the airy horizon, ascending
like a soul to heaven.

Giovanni Bellini—*Christ Supported by Two Angels (Cristo Morto Sorreto da Due Angeli,* 1453–1455)

In another early work, Giovanni explores human anatomy, with

CORRER MUSEUM

exaggerated veins, a heaving diaphragm, and even a hint of pubic hair. Mentally compare this stiff, static work with Antonello da Messina's far more natural *Christ with Three Angels*, done 20 years later, to see how far Giovanni still had to go. In fact, Giovanni was greatly influenced by Antonello, appreciating the full potential of the new invention of oil-based paint. Armed with this more transparent paint, he could add subtler shades of color and rely less on the sharply outlined forms we see here.

Giovanni Bellini— *Madonna and Child (Madonna Frizzoni)*

Though the canvas is a bit wrinkled, it's a subject Giovanni would paint again and again—lovely, forever-young Mary (often shown from the waist up) holding rosy-cheeked baby Jesus. He portrayed the holiness of mother and child with a natural-looking, pastel-colored, soft-focus beauty.

Room 38

Vittore Carpaccio—*Two Venetian Ladies (a.k.a. The Courtesans, c. 1500–1510)*

Two well-dressed Venetians look totally bored, despite being surrounded by a wealth of exotic pets and amusements. One lady absentmindedly plays with a dog, while the other stares into space. Romantics imagined them to be kept ladies awaiting lovers, but the recent discovery of the once-missing companion painting tells us they're waiting for their menfolk to return from hunting. If you like Carpaccio, the Scuola Dalmata di San Giorgio (between St. Mark's Square and Arsenale) has the world's best collection; see page 55.

The colorful details and love of luxury are elements that would dominate the Venetian High Renaissance. Fascinating stuff, but my eyes—like theirs—are starting to glaze...

ACCADEMIA TOUR

Galleria dell'Accademia

The Accademia (ack-ah-DAY-mee-ah) is the greatest museum any-where for Venetian Renaissance art and a good overview of painters whose works you'll see all over town. Venetian art is underrated and, I think, misunderstood. It's nowhere near as famous today as the work of the florescent Florentines, but—with historical slices of Venice, ravishing nudes, and very human Madonnas—it's livelier, more colorful, and simply more fun.

Orientation

Cost: €6.50.

Hours: Mon 8:15–14:00, Tue–Sun 8:15–19:15, last entry 45 minutes before closing.

Crowd Control: Visit early or late to miss the crowds (300 people are allowed in at any one time), or reserve an entry time (€1) at least a day in advance. It's better to do this by phone (tel. 041-520-0345) than online (www.gallerieaccademia.org), since you can't cancel or change Internet reservations.

Getting There: The museum faces the Grand Canal, just over the Accademia Bridge (15-minute walk from St. Mark's Square—follow signs to *Accademia*). Vaporetto stop: Accademia.

Nearby: While you're in the Accademia neighborhood, consider visiting the ✪ Ca' Rezzonico, ✪ Peggy Guggenheim Collection, and historic ✪ La Salute Church.

Information: Some of the Accademia's rooms have information in English. The bookshop sells guidebooks for €8.20. Info tel. 041-520-0345 or 041-522-2247, www.gallerieaccademia.org.

Renovation: The museum is nearing the end of a years-long expansion. In 2011, some rooms may still be closed for construction, traffic may be rerouted, and some paintings may reside temporarily in other rooms. A few key works may not be on view at all. Expect changes, and be flexible.

Tours: The **audioguide** costs €5 (€7/2 people).

Length of This Tour: Allow one hour.

Bag Check: Purses and handbags are allowed, but large bags must be checked and may be subject to a charge of €0.50.

Photography: Not allowed.

Cuisine Art: Ristorante/Pizzeria Accademia Foscarini is a simple pizza joint with a great Grand Canal setting at the base of the Accademia Bridge (closed Tue).

Starring: Titian, Veronese, Giorgione, Bellini, and Tintoretto.

The Tour Begins

Venice—Swimming in Luxury

The Venetian love of luxury shines through in Venetian painting. We'll see grand canvases of colorful, spacious settings peopled with happy locals in extravagant clothes having a great time. The museum proceeds chronologically from the Middle Ages to the 1700s. But before we start at the medieval beginning, let's sneak a peek at a work by the greatest Venetian Renaissance master, Titian.

• *Buy your ticket, check your bag, and head upstairs to a large hall filled with gold-leaf altarpieces. Immediately past the turnstile, turn left and enter the small Room 24.*

Titian (Tiziano Vecellio)—*Presentation of the Virgin*

A colorful crowd gathers at the foot of a stone staircase. A dog eats a bagel, a mother handles a squirming baby, an old lady sells eggs, and people lean out the windows. Suddenly the crowd turns and points at something. Your eye follows up the stairs to a larger-than-life high priest in a jeweled robe.

But wait! What's that along the way? In a pale blue dress that sets her apart from all the other colored robes, dwarfed by the enormous staircase and columns, the tiny, shiny figure of the child Mary almost floats up to the astonished priest. She's unnaturally small, easily overlooked at first glance. When we finally notice

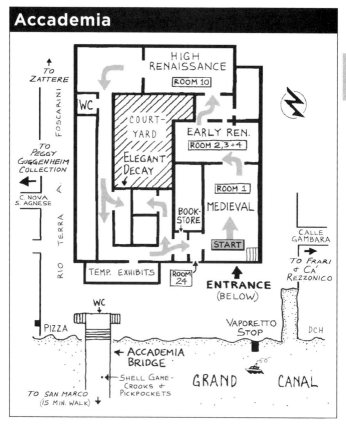

Accademia

HIGH RENAISSANCE
ROOM 10

TO ZATTERE

FOSCARINI

WC

COURT-YARD

ELEGANT DECAY

EARLY REN.
ROOM 2, 3+4

TO PEGGY GUGGENHEIM COLLECTION

C. NOVA S. AGNESE

ROOM 1

MEDIEVAL

TERRA

BOOK-STORE

RIO

TEMP. EXHIBITS

ROOM 24

START

CALLE GAMBARA

TO FRARI & CA' REZZONICO

ENTRANCE
(BELOW)

WC

PIZZA

VAPORETTO STOP

DCH

← ACCADEMIA BRIDGE

SHELL GAME- CROOKS & PICKPOCKETS

GRAND CANAL

TO SAN MARCO (15 MIN. WALK) ↓

ACCADEMIA

her, we realize all the more how delicate she is amid the bustling crowd, hard stone, and epic grandeur. Venetians love this painting and call it, appropriately enough, the "Little Mary."

The painting is a parade of colors. Titian (TEESH-un) leads your eyes from the massive buildings to the deep blue sky and mountains in the background to the bright red robe of the man in the crowd to glowing Little Mary. Titian painted the work especially for this room, fitting it neatly around the door on the right. The door on the left was added later, cutting into Titian's masterpiece.

This work is typical of Venetian Renaissance art. Here and throughout this museum, you will find: 1) bright, rich color; 2) big canvases; 3) Renaissance architectural backgrounds; 4) slice-of-life scenes of Venice; and 5) 3-D realism. It's a religious scene, yes, but it's really just an excuse to display secular splendor—Renaissance architecture, colorful robes, and human details.

Now that we've gotten a taste of Renaissance Venice at its

Accademia—Medieval Art

ACCADEMIA

ROOM 2
EARLY RENAISSANCE

COURT-
YARD

ROOM
1

③

BOOK-
STORE

ROOM
24

②

①

STAIRS FROM
GROUND FLOOR
(TICKETS & COATROOM)

DCH

① TITIAN – Presentation of the Virgin

② VENEZIANO – Madonna and Child with Two Donors

③ DEL FIORE – Coronation of the Virgin in Paradise

peak, let's backtrack and see some of Titian's predecessors.
• *Return to Room 1, stopping at a painting (near the turnstile) of Mary and baby Jesus.*

Medieval Art—Pre-3-D

Paolo Veneziano—*Madonna and Child with Two Donors (Madonna col Bambino e Due Committenti)*

Mary sits in heaven. The child Jesus is a baby in a bubble, a symbol of his "aura" of holiness.

Notice how two-dimensional and unrealistic this painting is. The sizes of the figures reflect their religious importance—Mary

is huge, being both the mother of Christ as well as "Holy Mother Church." Jesus is next, then the two angels who crown Mary. Finally, in the corner, are two mere mortals kneeling in devotion. The golden halos let us know who is holy. Medieval Venetians, with their close ties to the East, borrowed techniques such as

gold-leafing, frontal poses, and "iconic" faces from the religious icons of Byzantium (modern-day Istanbul).

Most of the paintings in Room 1 are altarpieces, intended to sit in the center of a church for the faithful to meditate on during services. Many feature the Virgin Mary being crowned in triumph. Very impressive. But it took Renaissance artists to remove Mary from her golden never-never land, clothe her in human flesh, and bring her down to the real world we inhabit.
• *In the far right corner of the room, you'll find...*

Ercole del Fiore—*Coronation of the Virgin in Paradise (Incoronazione della Vergine in Paradiso)*

This swarming beehive of saints and angels is an attempt to cram as much religious information as possible into one space. The architectural setting is a clumsy try at three-dimensionality (the railings of the wedding-cake structure are literally glued on). The color-coordinated saints are simply stacked one on top of the other, rather than receding into the distance as they would in real life.

ACCADEMIA

• *Enter Room 2 at the far end of this hall.*

Early Renaissance (1450–1500)

Only a few decades later, artists rediscovered the natural world and ways to capture it on canvas. With this Renaissance, or "rebirth," of the arts and attitudes of ancient Greece and Rome, painters took a giant leap forward. They weeded out the jumble of symbols, fleshed out cardboard characters into real people, and placed them in spacious 3-D settings.

Giovanni Bellini—*Madonna Enthroned with Child and Saints (Madonna in Trono col Bambino e Santi)*

Mary and the baby Jesus meet with saints beneath an arched half-dome, engaging in a sacred conversation *(sacra conversazione)*. A trio of musician angels jams at her feet. In its original church setting, the painting's pillars and arches matched the real ones in the church (there may be a photo reconstruction nearby), as though Bellini had blown a hole in the wall and built another chapel, allowing us mortals to mingle with holies.

Giovanni Bellini (bell-EE-nee) takes only a few figures, places them in this spacious architectural setting, and balances them, half on one side of Mary and half on the other. Left to right, you'll find St. Francis (medieval founder of an order of friars), John the Baptist, Job, St. Dominic (founder of another order of monks), St. Sebastian, and St. Louis.

The painting has a series of descending arches. At the top is a Roman arch. Hanging below that is a triangular canopy. Then comes a pyramid-shaped "arch" formed by the figures themselves, with Mary's head at the peak, echoed below by the pose of the three musicians. Subconsciously, this creates a mood of serenity, order, and balance, not the hubbub of the *Coronation*. Look at St. Sebastian—even arrows can't disturb his serenity.

Accademia—Early Renaissance

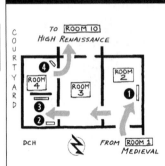

TO ROOM 10
HIGH RENAISSANCE

COURTYARD

ROOM 4

ROOM 3

ROOM 2

DCH

FROM ROOM 1
MEDIEVAL

❶ GIOVANNI BELLINI – Madonna Enthroned with Child and Saints

❷ MANTEGNA – St. George

❸ GIO. BELLINI – Madonna and Child between St. Catherine and Mary Magdalene

❹ GIORGIONE – The Tempest

In Bellini's long career, he painted many altarpieces in the *sacra conversazione* formula: Mary and Child surrounded by saints "conversing" informally about holy matters while listening to some tunes. The formula, developed largely by Fra Angelico (1400–1455), became a common Renaissance theme—compare this painting with other *sacras* by Bellini in the Frari Church (see page 146) and the Church of San Zaccaria (see page 229).

• *Climb the small staircase and pass through Room 3 into the small Room 4. (If Room 4 is closed for renovation, these paintings may be on display in Room 13.)*

Andrea Mantegna—*St. George (San Giorgio)*

This Christian dragon slayer is essentially a Greek nude sculpture with armor painted on. He rests his weight on one leg *(contrap-*

posto), the same as a classical sculpture, Michelangelo's *David,* or an Italian guy on the street corner. The doorway he stands in resembles a niche designed for a classical statue.

Mantegna (mahn-TAYN-yah) was trained in the Tuscan tradition, in which painters were like sculptors, "carving" out figures (like this) with sharp outlines, filling them in with color, and setting them in distant backdrops like the winding road behind George. When Mantegna married Giovanni Bellini's sister, he brought Florentine realism and draftsmanship to his in-laws.

St. George radiates Renaissance optimism—he's alert but relaxed, at rest but ready to spring into action, humble but confident. With the broken lance in his hand and the dragon at his feet, George is the strong Renaissance Man slaying the medieval dragon of superstition and oppression.

ACCADEMIA

• *Find three women and a baby on a black background.*

Giovanni Bellini—*Madonna and Child between St. Catherine and Mary Magdalene*

In contrast to Mantegna's sharp-focus 3-D, this painting features three female heads on a flat plane with a black velvet backdrop.

Their features are soft, hazy, and atmospheric, glowing out of the darkness as though lit by soft candlelight. It's not sculptural line that's important here, but color—warm, golden, glowing flesh tones. The faces emerge from the canvas like cameos.

Bellini painted dozens of Madonna and Childs in his day. (Others are nearby.) This Virgin Mary's pretty, but she's upstaged by the sheer idealized beauty of Mary Magdalene (on the right). Mary Magdalene's hair is down, like the prostitute that legend says she was, yet she has a childlike face, thoughtful and repentant. This is the perfect image of the innocent woman who sinned by loving too much.

Bellini was the teacher of two more Venetian greats, Titian and Giorgione, schooling them in the new medium of oil painting. Mantegna painted *St. George* using tempera paint (pigments dissolved in egg yolk), while Bellini pioneered oils (pigments in vegetable oil)—a more versatile medium. Applying layer upon transparent layer, Bellini painted creamy complexions with soft outlines, bathed in an even light. His gift to the Venetian Renaissance was the "haze" he put over his scenes, giving them an idealized, glowing, serene—and much copied—atmosphere. (You can see more of Bellini's work at the Correr Museum, Frari Church, and the Church of San Zaccaria.)

• *Around the partition, you'll find...*

Giorgione (Giorgio da Castelfranco)—*The Tempest*

It's the calm before the storm. The atmosphere is heavy—luminous but ominous. There's a sense of mystery. Why is the woman nursing her baby in the middle of the countryside? And the soldier—is he ogling her or protecting her? Will lightning strike? Do they know that the serenity of this beautiful landscape is about to be shattered by an approaching storm?

The mystery is heightened by contrasting elements. The armed soldier contrasts with the naked mother and her baby. The austere, ruined columns contrast with the lusciousness of Nature. And, most important, the stillness of the foreground scene is in direct opposition to the threatening storm in the background. The landscape itself is the main subject, creating a mood, regardless of what the painting is "about."

Giorgione (jor-JONE-ay) was as mysterious as his few paintings, yet he left a lasting impression. A student of Bellini, he learned to use haziness to create a melancholy mood of beauty. But nothing beautiful lasts. Flowers fade, Mary Magdalenes grow old, Giorgione died at 33, and, in *The Tempest,* the fleeting stillness is about to be shattered by the slash of lightning—the true center of the composition.

• *Exit and browse through several rooms. Check out the bookstore (there's another one later), then continue up the five steps to the large Room 10.*

Venetian High Renaissance (1500–1600)—Titian, Veronese, and Tintoretto

Paolo Veronese—*Feast of the House of Levi (Convito in Casa di Levi)*

Parrrrty!! Stand about 10 yards away from this enormous canvas, to where it just fills your field of vision...and hey, you're invited. Venice loves the good life, and the celebration is in full swing. You're in a huge room with a great view of Venice. Everyone's dressed to kill in colorful silk and velvet robes. Conversation roars and the servants bring on the food and drink.

This captures the Venetian attitude (more love, less attitude) as well as the style of Venetian Renaissance painting. Remember: 1) bright colors, 2) big canvases, 3) Renaissance architectural settings, 4) scenes of Venetian life, and 5) 3-D realism. Painters had

Accademia—High Renaissance

1 VERONESE – Feast of the House of Levi

2 TITIAN – Pietà

3 TINTORETTO – The Transporting of St. Mark's Body

DCH

mastered realism and now gloried in it.

The *Feast of the House of Levi* is, believe it or not, a religious work painted for a convent. The original title was *The Last Supper*. In the center of all the wild goings-on, there's Jesus, flanked by his disciples, sharing a final meal before his crucifixion.

This festive feast captures the optimistic spirit of Renaissance Venice. Life was a good thing and beauty was to be enjoyed. Renaissance men and women saw the divine in the beauties of Nature and glorified God by glorifying man.

Uh-uh, said the Church. In its eyes, the new humanism was the same as the old hedonism. The false spring of the Renaissance froze quickly after the Reformation, when half of Europe left the Catholic Church and became Protestant.

Veronese (vayr-oh-NAY-zay) was hauled before the Inquisition. What did he mean by painting such a bawdy Last Supper? With dwarf jesters? And apostles picking their teeth (between the columns, left of center)? And dogs and cats? And a black man, God forbid? And worst of all, some German soldiers—maybe even Protestants!—at the far right?

Veronese argued that it was just artistic license, so they asked to see his—it had expired. But the solution was simple. Rather than change the painting, just fine-tune the title. *Sì, no problema.* Veronese got out his brush, and *The Last Supper* became the *Feast of the House of Levi,* written in Latin on the railing to the left: "*FECIT D. COVI...*"

Titian—*Pietà*

Jesus has just been executed, and his followers grieve over his body before burying it. Titian painted this to hang over his own tomb.

Titian was the most famous painter of his day— perhaps even more famous

than Michelangelo. He excelled in every subject: portraits of dukes, kings, and popes; racy nudes for their bedrooms; solemn altarpieces for churches; and pagan scenes from Greek mythology. He was cultured and witty, a fine musician and businessman—an all-around Renaissance kind of guy.

Titian was old when he painted this. He had seen the rise and decline of the Renaissance and had experienced much sadness in his own life. Unlike Titian's colorful and exuberant "Little Mary," done at the height of the Renaissance, this canvas is dark, the mood more somber.

Jesus is framed by a Renaissance arch like the one in Bellini's *Sacred Conversation,* but here the massive stones overpower the figures, making them look puny and helpless. The lion statues are downright scary. Instead of the clear realism of Renaissance paintings, Titian uses rough, messy brushstrokes, a technique that would be picked up by the Impressionists three centuries later. Titian adds a dramatic compositional element—starting with the lion at lower right, a line of motion sweeps up diagonally along the figures, culminating in the grief-stricken Mary Magdalene, who turns away, flinging her arm and howling out loud.

Finally, the kneeling figure of old, bald Nicodemus is a self-portrait of the aging Titian, tending to the corpse of Jesus, who symbolizes the once powerful, now dead Renaissance Man. In the lower right, a painting-within-the-painting shows Titian and his son kneeling, asking the Virgin to spare them from the plague of 1576. Unfortunately, Titian's son died from it, and the heartbroken father passed away shortly after.

(For more Titians, visit the Frari Church, which houses the painter's tomb—❂ see the Frari Church Tour chapter; and the Doge's Palace—❂ see the Doge's Palace Tour chapter.)

• *On the opposite wall, find...*

Tintoretto (Jacopo Robusti)—*The Transporting of St. Mark's Body (Trafugamento del Corpo di San Marco)*

The event that put Venice on the map is frozen at its most dramatic moment. Muslim fundamentalists in Alexandria are about to burn Mark's body (there's the smoke from the fire in the center), when suddenly a hurricane appears miraculously, sending them running for cover. (See the wisps of baby-angel faces in the storm, blowing on the infidels? Look hard, on the left-hand side.) Meanwhile, the Venetian merchants whisk away the body.

Tintoretto makes us part of the

action. The square tiles in the courtyard run straight away from us, an extension of our reality, as though we could step right into the scene—or the merchants could carry Mark into ours.

Tintoretto would have made a great black-velvet painter. His colors burn with a metallic sheen, and he does everything possible to make his subject popular with common people.

In fact, Tintoretto was a common man himself, self-taught, who apprenticed only briefly with Titian before striking out on his own. He sold paintings in the marketplace in his youth and insisted on living in the poor part of town, even after he became famous.

Tintorettos abound here, in the next room and throughout Venice. Look for these characteristics, some of which became standard features of Mannerist and Baroque art that followed the Renaissance: 1) heightened drama, violent scenes, strong emotions; 2) elongated bodies in twisting poses; 3) strong contrasts between dark and light; 4) bright colors; and 5) diagonal compositions.

(Tintoretto fans will want to visit the Scuola San Rocco, Tintoretto's "Sistine Chapel"; ✪ see the Scuola San Rocco Tour chapter.)

• *Spend some time in this room, the peak of the Venetian Renaissance and the climax of the museum. After browsing, enter Room 11 and find a large, round painting. Stand underneath it for the full effect.*

Elegant Decay (1600–1800)

G. B. Tiepolo—*Discovery of the True Cross* (*La Scoperta della Vera Croce*)

Tiepolo blasts open a sunroof and we gaze up into heaven. We (the viewers) stand in the hole where they've just dug up Christ's cross,

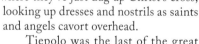

looking up dresses and nostrils as saints and angels cavort overhead.

Tiepolo was the last of the great colorful, theatrical Venetian painters. He took the colors, the grand settings, and the dramatic angles of previous Venetian masters and plastered them on the ceilings of Europe's Baroque palaces, such as the Royal Palace in Madrid, Spain; the Residenz in Würzburg, Germany; and the Ca' Rezzonico in Venice (✪ see the Ca' Rezzonico Tour chapter). This piece is from a church ceiling.

Tiepolo's strongly "foreshortened" figures are masterpieces of technical skill, making us feel as if the heavenly vision is taking place right overhead. Think back on those clumsy attempts at three-dimensionality we saw in the medieval room, and realize

Accademia—Elegant Decay

- **1** TIEPOLO – Discovery of the True Cross
- **2** CANALETTO – Perspective with Porch
- **3** GUARDI – San Giorgio Maggiore
- **4** GENTILE BELLINI – Procession in Piazza San Marco

how far painting has come. The fresco fragments hanging around the corners of this room were salvaged from a church bombed in World War I.

• *In the rooms branching off the long corridor to your left, you'll find works of the later Venetians. As you walk down the corridor, the first right leads to the WC. The first left is Room 17.*

Canaletto and Guardi: Views of Venice

By the 1700s, Venice had retired as a world power and become Europe's number-one tourist attraction. Wealthy offspring of the nobility traveled here to soak up its art and culture. They wanted souvenirs, and what better memento than a picture of the city itself?

Guardi and Canaletto painted "postcards" for visitors who lost their hearts to the romance of Venice. The city produced less art... as it became art itself. Here are some familiar views of a city that has aged gracefully.

Canaletto (Giovanni Antonio Canal)— *Perspective with Porch* *(Prospettiva con Portico)*

Canaletto gives us a sharp-focus, wide-lens, camera's-eye perspective on the city. Although this view of a porch looks totally realistic, Canaletto has compressed the whole scene to allow us to see more than the human eye could realistically take in. We see the porch as though we were standing underneath it, yet we also see the whole porch at one glance. The pavement blocks, the lines of columns, and the slanting roof direct our eye to the far end, which looks very far away indeed. Canaletto even paints a coat of arms (at right) at a very odd angle, showing off his mastery of 3-D perspective.

Francesco Guardi—*San Giorgio Maggiore (Il Bacino di San Marco con San Giorgio Maggiore e Giudecca)*

Unlike Canaletto, with his sharp-focus detail, Guardi sweetens Venice up with a haze of messy brushwork. In this familiar view  across the water from St. Mark's Square, he builds a boatman with a few sloppy smudges of paint. Guardi catches the play of light at twilight, the shadows on the buildings, the green of the water and sky, the pink light off the distant buildings, the Venice that exists in the hearts of lovers—an Impressionist work a century ahead of its time.

• *Return to the corridor, turn left at the end, then take another left, and then left again. Are you in Room 20? If so, find...*

Gentile Bellini—*Procession in Piazza San Marco (Processione in Piazza San Marco)*

A fitting end to our tour is a look back at Venice in its heyday. This wide-angle view by Giovanni's big brother—more than any human eye could take in at once—reminds us how little Venice  has changed over the centuries. There is St. Mark's gleaming gold with mosaics, the four bronze horses, the three flagpoles out front, the old Campanile on the right, and the Doge's Palace. There's the guy selling 10 postcards for a dollar. (But there's no Clock Tower with the two bronze Moors yet, the pavement's different, the church is covered with gold, and there are no café orchestras playing "New York, New York.") Every detail is in perfect focus, regardless of its distance from us, presented for our inspection. Take some time to linger over this and the other views of old Venice in this room. Then get outta here and enjoy the real thing.

• *To exit, backtrack to the main corridor and turn left past the bookstore. There are often temporary exhibits in Room 23, the large former chapel branching off the corridor. Say* ciao *to Titian's "Little Mary" on the way out.*

FRARI CHURCH TOUR

Chiesa dei Frari

For many travelers, this church offers the best art-appreciation experience in Venice, because so much of its great art is *in situ*—right where it was designed to be seen, rather than hanging in museums. And it's about the only Gothic church you'll tour here. Because Venice's spongy ground could never support a real stone Gothic church (like you'd find in France), the Frari Church is made of light and flexible brick. The white limestone foundation insulates the building from the wet soil.

The church was built by the Franciscan order, which arrived in Venice around 1230 (the present building was consecrated in 1492). Franciscan men and women were inspired by St. Francis of Assisi (c. 1182–1226), who dedicated himself to a nonmaterialist lifestyle—part of a reform movement that spread across Europe in the early 1200s. The Roman Church felt distant and corrupt, and there was a hunger for religious teaching that connected with everyday people. While some of these movements were dubbed heretical (like  the Cathars in southern France), the Franciscans (and Dominicans) eventually earned the Church's blessing.

The spirit of St. Francis of Assisi warms both the church of his "brothers" *(frari)* and the art that decorates it. The Franciscan love of all of creation—Nature and Man—later inspired Renaissance painters to capture the beauty of the physical world and human emotions, showing worshippers the glory of God in human terms.

Orientation

Cost: €3.

Hours: Mon–Sat 9:00–18:00, Sun 13:00–18:00, last entry 15 minutes before closing, no visits during services.

Dress Code: Modest dress is recommended.

Getting There: It's on the Campo dei Frari, near the San Tomà vaporetto and *traghetto* stops. From the dock, follow signs to *Scuola Grande di San Rocco*.

Nearby: For efficient sightseeing, combine your visit with the ✪ Scuola San Rocco, located behind the Frari Church. The ✪ Ca' Rezzonico is a seven-minute walk away: From the back end of the Frari Church, go through alleyway Sotoportego S. Rocco, turn left at the first T intersection, then right at the big white building. If you reach Campo San Barnaba, you've passed it—ask someone, *Dov'è Ca' Rezzonico?*" (doh-VEH kah ret-ZON-ee-koh).

Information: Tel. 041-272-8611, www.basilicadeifrari.it.

Tours: Audioguides are available (€2, €3/2 people). Those traveling with an iPod or other MP3 player can download a free **Rick Steves audio tour** of this chapter at www.ricksteves. com (or search for "Rick Steves Audio Tours" in iTunes).

Length of This Tour: Allow one hour.

Photography: Prohibited.

Cuisine Art: The church square is ringed with small, simple, reasonably priced cafés.

Concerts: The church occasionally hosts evening concerts (€15, buy ticket at church). For concert details, look for fliers, check the website, or call the church at 041-272-8618.

Starring: Titian, Giovanni Bellini, Paolo Veneziano, and Donatello.

The Tour Begins

• *Enter the church and turn right, finding a spot at the far end with a good view down the long nave toward the altar.*

❶ Church Interior and Choir (1250–1443)

The simple, spacious (110-yard-long), well-lit Gothic church—with rough wood crossbeams and a red-and-white color scheme—is truly a remarkable sight in a city otherwise crammed with exotic froufrou. Traditionally, churches in Venice were cross-shaped, but because the Franciscans were an international order, they weren't limited to Venetian tastes. This new T-shaped footprint featured a long, lofty nave—flooded with light and suited to large gatherings—where common people heard sermons.

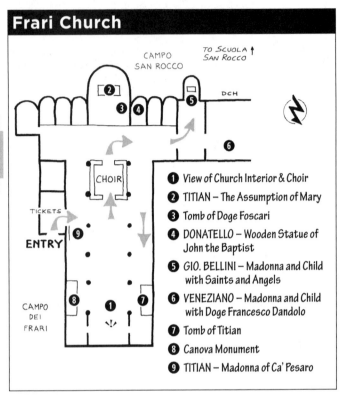

Frari Church

CAMPO
SAN ROCCO

TO SCUOLA
SAN ROCCO

DCH

❶ View of Church Interior & Choir

❷ TITIAN – The Assumption of Mary

❸ Tomb of Doge Foscari

❹ DONATELLO – Wooden Statue of
John the Baptist

❺ GIO. BELLINI – Madonna and Child
with Saints and Angels

❻ VENEZIANO – Madonna and Child
with Doge Francesco Dandolo

❼ Tomb of Titian

❽ Canova Monument

❾ TITIAN – Madonna of Ca' Pesaro

CHOIR

TICKETS

ENTRY

CAMPO
DEI
FRARI

The wooden choir area in the center of the nave allowed friars to hold smaller, more intimate services. As worshippers enter the church and look down the long nave to the altar, the sight that greets them—framed by the arch of the choir entrance—is Titian's altarpiece.

Walk prayerfully toward the Titian, stopping in the finely carved 1480s choir. Notice the fine inlay above the chairs, showing the Renaissance enthusiasm for Florentine-style 3-D. Surviving choirs such as this are rare. (In response to Luther's challenge, Counter-Reformation churches discarded the idea of the choirs and altar screens in order to get priests closer to their flocks.)

• *Approach Titian's heavenly vision.*

❷ Titian—*The Assumption of Mary* (1518)

Glowing red and gold like a stained-glass window, this altarpiece sets the tone of exuberant beauty found in this church. At the end of her life (though looking 17 here), Mary was miraculously "assumed" into heaven. As cherubs lift her up to meet a Jupiter-

like God, the stunned apostles on earth reach up to touch the floating bubble of light.

Look around. The church is littered with chapels and tombs "made possible by the generous financial support" of rich people who donated to the Franciscans for the good of their souls (and usually for tomb-topping statues of themselves, as well). But the Franciscans didn't sell their main altar; instead they hired the new whiz artist, Titian, to create a dramatic altar painting.

FRARI CHURCH

Unveiled in 1518, the work scandalized a Venice accustomed to simpler, more subdued church art. The rich colors, twisting poses, and mix of saccharine angels with blue-collar apostles were unheard of. Most striking, this Virgin is fully human, not a stiff icon on a throne. The Franciscans thought this Mary aroused excitement rather than spirituality. They agreed to pay Titian only after the Holy Roman Emperor offered to buy the altar if they refused.

In a burst of youthful innovation, Titian (1488–1576) had rewritten the formula for church art, hinting at changes to come with the Mannerist and Baroque styles. He energized the scene with a complex composition, overlapping a circle (Mary's bubble) and a triangle (draw a line from the apostle reaching up to Mary's face and down the other side) on three horizontal levels (God in heaven, Man on earth, Mary in between). Together, these elements draw our eyes from the swirl of arms and legs to the painting's focus—the radiant face of a triumphant Mary, "assumed body and soul into heaven."

• *Also in the apse (behind the main altar) are marble tombs lining the walls. On the wall to the right of the altar is the...*

❸ Tomb of Doge Foscari

In contrast to the poverty of the Franciscans, this heavy, ornate tomb marks the peak of Venice's worldly power. Doge Francesco Foscari (1373–1457) assumed control of Venice's powerful seafaring empire and then tried to expand it farther onto the mainland, battling Milan in a 31-year war of attrition that swept through northern Italy. Meanwhile, on the unprotected eastern front, the Ottomans took Constantinople (1453) and scuttled Venice's trade. Venice's long slide into historical oblivion had begun.

Financially drained city fathers forced Foscari to resign, turn in his funny hat, and hand over the keys to the Doge's Palace.

• *In the first chapel to the right of the altar, you'll find...*

❹ Donatello—Wooden Statue of John the Baptist

Emaciated from his breakfast of bugs 'n' honey and dressed in animal skins, the cockeyed prophet of the desert freezes mid-rant when he spies something in the distance. His jaw goes slack, he twists his face and raises his hand to announce the coming of...the Renaissance.

The Renaissance began in the Florence of the 1400s, where Donatello (1386–1466) created realistic statues with a full range of human emotions. This warts-and-all John the Baptist contrasts greatly with, say, Titian's sweet Mary. Florentine art (including painting) was sculptural, strongly outlined, and harshly realistic, with muted colors. Venetian art was painterly, soft-focus, and beautiful, with bright colors.

Florentine expatriates living in Venice commissioned Donatello to make this statue for their local chapel.

• *Enter the sacristy through the door at the far end of the right transept. You'll bump into an elaborate altar crammed with reliquaries. Opposite that (near the entrance door) is a clock, intricately carved from a single piece of wood. At the far end of the room, you'll find...*

❺ Giovanni Bellini—*Madonna and Child with Saints and Angels* (1488)

The Pesaro family, who negotiated an acceptable price and place for their family tomb, funded this delightful chapel dominated by a Bellini master-piece.

Mary sits on a throne under a half-dome, propping up baby Jesus (who's just learning to stand), flanked by saints and serenaded by musician angels. Giovanni Bellini (c. 1430–1516), the father of the Venetian Renaissance, painted fake columns and a dome to match the real ones in the gold frame, making the painting seem to be an extension of the room. He completes the illusion with glimpses of open sky in the background. Next, he fills the artificial niches with symmetrically posed, thoughtful saints—left to right, find Saints Nicholas, Peter, Mark, and Sean Connery (Benedict).

Bellini combined the meditative poses of the Venetian Byzantine tradition with Renaissance improvements in modern art. He pioneered painting in oil (pigments dissolved in vegetable oil) rather than medieval tempera (egg yolk–based). It allowed subtler treatment of colors, made with successive layers of paint. And because darker colors aren't so muddy when painted in oil, they "pop," effectively giving the artist a broader palette.

Bellini virtually invented the formula (later to be broken by his precocious pupil, Titian) for Venetian altarpieces. This type of "holy conversation" *(sacra conversazione)* between saints and Mary can also be seen in Venice's Accademia and Church of San Zaccaria.

Renaissance humanism demanded Madonnas and saints that were accessible and human. Bellini delivers, but places them in a physical setting so beautiful that it creates its own mood of serene holiness. The scene is lit from the left, but no one casts a harsh shadow—Mary and the babe are enveloped in a glowing aura of reflected light from the golden dome. The beauty is in the details, from the writing in the dome, to the red brocade backdrop, to the swirls in the marble steps, to the angels' dimpled legs.

• *In the adjoining room, find a Gothic-arch-shaped painting.*

❻ Paolo Veneziano—*Madonna and Child with Doge Francesco Dandolo* (c. 1339)

Bellini's Byzantine roots can be traced to Paolo Veneziano (literally, "the Venetian"), the first "name" artist in Venice, who helped

shape the distinct Venetian style. In turn, Veneziano was inspired by Byzantine artists who came to Venice in search of more freedom of expression. They had chafed under strict societies (both Byzantine and, in some locales, Islamic) that frowned on painting figurative images. In Venice, these expats found an eager community of rich patrons who indulged their love of deeper color, sentiment, movement, and decoration. (Venice clung to this style to the point that it eventually lagged behind Western Europe.)

In this altarpiece, Veneziano paints Byzantine icons, then sets them in motion. Baby Jesus turns to greet a kneeling Doge Dandolo, while Mary turns to acknowledge the doge's wife. None other than St. Francis presents "Francis" (Francesco) Dandolo to

FRARI CHURCH

the Madonna. Both he and St. Elizabeth (on the right) bend at the waist and gesture as naturally as 14th-century icons can.

• *Return to the nave and head toward the far end. Turn around and face the altar. The Tomb of Titian is in the second bay on your right.*

❼ Tomb of Titian (Titiano Ferdinandus MDCCCLII)

The tomb celebrates both the man (see a carved statue of Titian in the center with beard and crown of laurels) and his famous paintings (depicted in relief).

Titian was the greatest Venetian painter, excelling equally in inspirational altarpieces, realistic portraits, joyous mythological scenes, and erotic female nudes.

He moved to Venice as a child, studied first as a mosaic-maker and then under Giovanni Bellini, before establishing his own bold style, which featured teenage Madonnas (see a relief of *The Assumption of the Virgin* behind Titian). He became wealthy and famous, traveling Europe to paint stately portraits of kings and nobles, and colorful, sexy works for their bedrooms. Titian resisted the temptation of big money that drew so many of his contemporary Venetian artists to Rome. Instead he always returned to his beloved Venice (see winged lion on top)...and favorite Frari Church.

In his old age, Titian painted dark, tragic masterpieces, including the *Pietà* (see relief in upper left) that was intended for his tomb but ended up in the Accademia (see page 137). Nearing 90, he labored to finish the *Pietà* as the plague enveloped Venice. One in four people died, including Titian's son and assistant, Orazio. Heartbroken, Titian died soon afterward, probably of the plague, although his death was officially chalked up to influenza (to keep his body from being burned—a requirement for plague victims). His tomb was built three centuries later to remember and honor this great Venetian.

• *On the opposite side of the nave is the pyramid-shaped...*

❽ Canova Monument

Antonio Canova (1757–1822, see his portrait above the door) was Venice's greatest sculptor. He created gleaming, white, highly polished statues of beautiful Greek gods and goddesses in the Neoclassical style. (See several of his works at the Correr Museum.)

The pyramid shape is timeless, suggesting pharaohs' tombs

and the Christian Trinity. Mourners, bent over with grief, shuffle up to pay homage to the master artist. Even the winged lion is choked up.

Follow me here. Canova himself designed this pyramid-shaped tomb, not for his own use, but as the tomb of an artist he greatly admired: Titian. But the Frari Church used another design for Titian's tomb, so Canova used the pyramid for an Austrian princess...in Vienna. After his death, Canova's pupils reused the design here to honor their master. In fact, Canova isn't buried here—instead, he lies in southern Italy. But inside the tomb's open door, you can (barely) see an urn, which contains his heart.

• *Head back toward the altar. Halfway up the left wall is...*

❾ Titian—*Madonna of Ca' Pesaro* (1526)

Titian's second altarpiece for the Frari Church displays all of his many skills. Following his teacher, Bellini, he puts Mary (seated) and baby (standing) on a throne, sur-rounded by saints having a holy conver-sation. And, like Bellini, he paints fake columns that echo the church's real ones.

But wait. Mary is off-center, Titian's idealized saints mingle with Venetians sporting five o'clock shadows, and the stairs run diagonally away from us. Mary sits not on a throne, but on a pedestal. Baby Jesus is restless. The precious keys of St. Peter seem to dangle unnoticed. These things upset traditional Renaissance symmetry, but they turn a group of figures into a true scene. St. Peter (center, in blue and gold, with book) looks down at Jacopo Pesaro, who kneels to thank the Virgin for his recent naval victory over the Ottomans (1502). A flag-carrying lieutenant drags in a turbaned captive. Meanwhile, St. Francis talks to baby Jesus while gesturing down to more members of the Pesaro family. The little guy looking out at us (lower right) is the Pesaro descendant who administered the trust fund to keep prayers coming for his dead uncle.

Titian combines opposites: a soft-focus Madonna with photo-realist portraits, chubby winged angels with a Muslim prisoner, and a Christian cross with a battle flag. In keeping with the spirit of St. Francis' humanism, Titian lets mere mortals mingle with saints. And we're right there with them.

SCUOLA SAN ROCCO TOUR

Scuola Grande di San Rocco

The 50-plus paintings in the Scuola Grande di San Rocco—often called "Tintoretto's Sistine Chapel"—present one man's very personal vision of Christian history. Tintoretto spent the last 20 years of his life working practically for free, driven by the spirit of charity that the Scuola, a Christian organization, promoted. For Tintoretto fans, this is the ultimate. Even for the art-weary, his large, colorful canvases, framed in gold on the walls and ceilings of a grand upper hall, are an impressive sight.

Orientation

Cost: €7. (If you see an evening concert here, you can enjoy the art as a bonus; see page 296.)

Hours: Daily 9:30–17:30, last entry 30 minutes before closing.

Getting There: It's next to the Frari Church (see "Getting There" in previous chapter). Vaporetto: San Tomà. For an easy route on foot from the Rialto Bridge, ✪ take the Rialto to Frari Church Walk, following signs to *Scuola Grande di San Rocco.*

Nearby: Right next door is the Church of San Rocco, featuring still more Tintorettos (free, same hours as the Scuola).

Information: Tel. 041-523-4864, www.scuolagrandesanrocco .it. WCs are on the ground floor; get the key from the ticket clerk.

Audioguide Tours: €1 for the chapel's fine audioguide.

Mirrors: Use the mirrors scattered about the museum's Grand Hall, because much of this art is on the ceiling and a pain in the neck.

Length of This Tour: Allow one hour.

Starring: Tintoretto, Tintoretto, and Tintoretto.

The Tour Begins

The art of the Scuola is contained in three rooms—the Ground Floor Hall (where you enter) and two rooms upstairs, including the Great Upper Floor Hall, with the biggest canvases.

• *Enter on the ground floor, which is lined with big, colorful Tintoretto canvases. Begin with the first canvas on the left.*

❶ *The Annunciation*

An angel swoops through the doorway, dragging a trail of naked baby angels with him, to tell a startled Mary she'll give birth to Jesus. This canvas has many of Tintoretto's typical characteristics:

- **The miraculous and the everyday mingle side-by-side.** Glorious angels are in a broken-down house with stacks of lumber and a frayed chair.

- **Bright light and dark shadows.** A bright light strikes the brick column, highlighting Mary's face and the angel's shoulder, but casting dark shadows across the room.
- **Strong 3-D sucks you into the scene.** Tintoretto literally tears down Mary's wall to let us in. The floor tiles recede sharply into the distance, making Mary's room an extension of our real space.
- **Colors that are bright, almost harsh,** with a metallic "black-velvet" sheen, especially when contrasted with the soft-focus haze of Bellini, Giorgione, Veronese, and (sometimes) Titian.
- **Twisting, muscular poses.** The angel turns one way, Mary turns the other, and the baby angels turn every which way.
- **Diagonal composition.** Shadows run diagonally on the floor as Mary leans back diagonally.
- **Rough brushwork.** The sketchy pattern on Mary's ceiling contrasts with the precise photo-realism of the brick column.

And finally, *The Annunciation* exemplifies the general theme of the San Rocco paintings—God intervenes miraculously into our everyday lives in order to save us.

• *We'll return to the ground floor later, but let's get right to the highlights. Climb the staircase (taking time to admire the plague scenes that are not by Tintoretto) and enter the impressive Great Hall.*

Wow! Before we tackle the big canvases in this huge room, let's start where Tintoretto did, in the Albergo Hall—the small room in the left

Scuola San Rocco

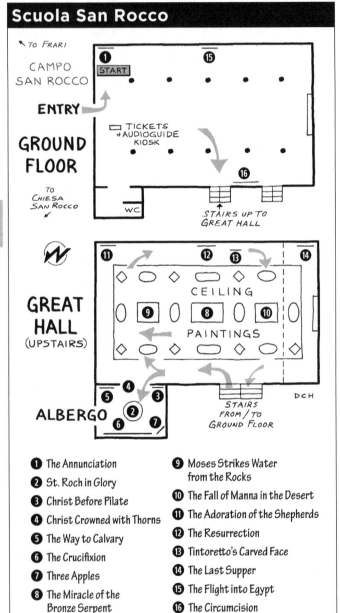

SCUOLA SAN ROCCO

❶ The Annunciation

❷ St. Roch in Glory

❸ Christ Before Pilate

❹ Christ Crowned with Thorns

❺ The Way to Calvary

❻ The Crucifixion

❼ Three Apples

❽ The Miracle of the Bronze Serpent

❾ Moses Strikes Water from the Rocks

❿ The Fall of Manna in the Desert

⓫ The Adoration of the Shepherds

⓬ The Resurrection

⓭ Tintoretto's Carved Face

⓮ The Last Supper

⓯ The Flight into Egypt

⓰ The Circumcision

Jacopo Tintoretto
(1518–1594)

The son of a silk dyer ("Tintoretto" is a nickname meaning "little dyer"), Tintoretto applied a blue-collar work ethic to painting, becoming one of the most prolific artists ever. He trained briefly under Titian, but their egos clashed. He was influenced more by Michelangelo's recently completed *Last Judgment,* with its muscular, twisting, hovering nudes and epic scale.

By age 30, Tintoretto was famous, astounding Venice with the innovative *St. Mark Freeing the Slave* (now in the Accademia). He married, had eight children (three of whom became his assistants), and dedicated himself to work and family, shunning publicity and living his whole life in his old Venice neighborhood.

Twenty years of his life were spent decorating the Scuola di San Rocco. It was a labor of love, showing his religious faith, his compassion for the poor, and his artistic passion.

corner of the Great Hall. On the ceiling of the Albergo Hall is an oval painting of St. Roch, best viewed from the doorway.

Albergo Hall (Sala d'Albergo)— Christ's Passion

❷ *St. Roch in Glory* (1564)

Start at the feet of St. Roch (San Rocco), a French medical student in the 1300s who dedicated his short life to treating plague victims. The Scuola di San Rocco was a kind of Venetian "Elks Club" whose favorite charity was poor plague victims.

This is the first of Tintoretto's 50-plus paintings in the Scuola. It's also the one that got him the job, beating entries by Veronese and others.

Tintoretto amazed the judges by showing the saint from beneath, as though he hovered above in a circle of glory. This Venetian taste for dramatic angles and illusion would later become standard in

Baroque ceilings. Tintoretto trained by dangling wax models from the ceiling and lighting them from odd angles.

• *On the walls are scenes of Christ's trial, torture, and execution. Work counterclockwise around the room, starting by the door with...*

❸ Christ Before Pilate (Ecce Homo)

Jesus has been arrested and brought before the Roman authorities in a cavernous hall. Although he says nothing in his own defense, he stands head and shoulders above the crowd, literally "rising above" the slanders. Tintoretto shines a bright light on his white robe, making Christ radiate innocence.

At Christ's feet, an old, bearded man in white stoops over to record the events on paper—it's Tintoretto himself.

❹ Christ Crowned with Thorns

Jesus was beaten, whipped, then mocked by the soldiers, who dressed him as a king "crowned" with thorns. Seeing the bloodstains on the cloth must have touched the hearts of Scuola members, generating compassion for those who suffer.

❺ The Way to Calvary

Silhouetted against a stormy sky, Jesus and two other prisoners trudge up a steep hill, carrying their own crosses to the execution site. The cycle culminates with...

❻ The Crucifixion

The crucified Christ is the calm center of this huge and chaotic scene that fills the wall.

Workers struggle to hoist crosses, mourners swoon, riffraff gamble for Christ's clothes, and soldiers mill about aimlessly. Scarcely anyone pays any attention to the Son of God...except us, because Tintoretto directs our eye there.

All the lines of sight point to Christ at the center: the ladder on the ground, the cross being raised, the cross still on the ground, the horses on the right, and the hillsides that slope in. In a trick of multiple perspectives, the cross being raised seems to suck us in toward the center, while the cross still on the ground seems to cause the figures to be sucked toward us.

Above the chaos stands Christ, high above the horizon, higher than everyone, glowing against the dark sky. Tintoretto lets us appreciate the quiet irony lost on the frenetic participants—that this minor criminal suffering such apparent degradation is, in fact, triumphant.

• *Displayed on an easel to the left of and beneath* The Crucifixion *is a small fragment of...*

❶ *Three Apples*

This fragment, from the frieze around the upper reaches of the Albergo Hall, was discovered folded under the frieze in 1905. Because it was never exposed to light, it still retains Tintoretto's original bright colors. All of his paintings are darker today, despite cleaning, due to the irreversible chemical alteration of the pigments.

• *Now step back out into the Great Upper Hall.*

Great Upper Hall—Understanding What You're Standing Under

Thirty-four enormous oil canvases, set into gold frames on the ceiling and along the walls of this impressive room, tell biblical history from Adam and Eve to the Ascension of Christ. Tintoretto's storytelling style is straightforward, and anyone with knowledge of the Bible can quickly get the gist. Tintoretto's success in the Albergo Hall won him the job of the enormous Great Upper Hall.

The ceiling displays Old Testament scenes; the walls show events from the New Testament. Beyond that, the layout is not chronological but symbolic, linked by common themes. Tintoretto shows how God leads mankind to salvation. Evil enters the world with the Original Sin of *Adam and Eve* (at the Albergo end of room, on the ceiling). From there, man must go through many trials, as the ceiling shows—the struggles of Moses and the Israelites, Jonah, and Abraham. But God is always there to help. In the three largest paintings on the ceiling, God saves man from thirst *(Moses Strikes Water from the Rocks)*, illness *(The Miracle of the Bronze Serpent)*, and hunger *(The Fall of Manna in the Desert)*. Christ's story (along the walls) parallels the struggles of men (on the ceiling). But while the first humans *(Adam and Eve)* succumb to Satan's temptation, Christ does not (see *Christ Tempted by Satan*, on the wall nearby). And ultimately—at the altar—mankind is saved by Christ's sacrifice (*The Passover* overhead on the ceiling, and *The Last Supper* on the wall to the left). The art captures the charitable spirit of the school—just as God has helped those who suffer, so should we.

• *Let's look at a few pieces in depth. Start with the largest painting, in the center of the ceiling. View it from the top (the Albergo end), not directly underneath.*

❽ The Miracle of the Bronze Serpent

The tangle of half-naked bodies (at the bottom of the painting) represents the children of Israel, wrestling with poisonous snakes

and writhing in pain. At the top of the pile, a young woman gestures toward Moses (in pink), who points to a pole carrying a bronze serpent sent by God. Those who looked at the statue were miraculously healed. His work all done, God (above in the clouds) high-fives an angel.

This was the first of the Great Hall panels Tintoretto painted in response to a terrible plague that hit Venice in 1576. One in four died. Four hundred a day were buried. (They say that Titian, Tintoretto's colleague, died of heartbreak soon after his son died of the plague.) Like today's Red Cross, the Scuola sprang into action, raising funds, sending doctors, and giving beds to the sick—and aid to their families. Tintoretto saw the dead and dying firsthand. While capturing their suffering, he gave a ray of hope that help is on the way: Turn to the cross, and be saved by your faith.

There are dozens of figures in the painting, shown from every conceivable angle. Tintoretto was well aware of where it would hang and how it would be viewed. Walk around beneath it and see the different angles come alive. The painting becomes a movie, and the children of Israel writhe like snakes.

• *The rectangular panel at the Albergo end of the hall is...*

❾ Moses Strikes Water from the Rocks

Moses (in pink, in the center) hits a rock in the desert with his staff, and it miraculously spouts water, which the thirsty Israelites catch in jars. The water spurts like a ray of light. Moses is a strong, calm center to a spinning wheel of activity.

SCUOLA SAN ROCCO

Tintoretto worked fast, and, if nothing else, his art is exuberant. He trained in fresco painting, which must be finished before the plaster dries. With these paintings, he sketched an outline right onto the canvas, then improvised details as he went.

The sheer magnitude of the San Rocco project is staggering. This canvas alone is 300 square feet—like painting a bathroom with an artist's tiny brush. The whole project, counting the Albergo Hall, Great Upper Hall, and the Ground Floor Hall together, totals some 8,500 square feet—more than enough to cover a typical house, inside and out. (The Sistine Chapel ceiling, by comparison, is 5,700 square feet.)

• *The rectangular panel at the altar end of the hall is...*

❿ *The Fall of Manna in the Desert*

It's snowing bread, as God feeds the hungry Israelites with a miraculous storm. They stretch a blanket to catch it and gather it

up in baskets. Up in the center of the dark cloud is a radiant, almost transparent God, painted with sketchy brushstrokes to suggest he's an unseen presence.

Tintoretto tells these Bible stories with a literalness that was very popular with the poor, uneducated sick who sought help from the Scuola. He was the Spielberg of his day, with the technical know-how to bring imagination to life, to make the miraculous tangible.

• *You could grow old studying all the art here, so we'll select just a couple of the New Testament paintings on the walls. Start at the Albergo end with...*

⓫ *The Adoration of the Shepherds*

Christ's glorious life begins in a straw-filled stable with cows, chickens, and peasants who pass plates of food up to the new parents. It's night, with just a few details lit by phosphorescent

moonlight: the kneeling shepherd's forehead and leggings, the serving girl's shoulders, the faces of Mary and Joseph...and little baby Jesus, a smudge of light.

Notice the different points of view. Tintoretto clearly has placed us on the lower floor, about eye level with the cow, looking up through the roof beams at the night sky. But we also see Mary and Joseph in the loft above as though they were at eye level. By using multiple perspectives (and ignoring the laws of physics), Tintoretto could portray every detail at its perfect angle.

• *In the middle of the long wall, find...*

⑫ The Resurrection

Angels lift the sepulchre lid, and Jesus springs forth in a blaze of light. The contrast between dark and light is extreme, with great dramatic effect.

• *Head for* The Last Supper, *in the corner to the left of the altar. On the way there, look on the wall for a wood carving of Tintoretto (⑬, third statue from altar, directly opposite entry staircase). The artist holds the tools of his trade. His craggy, wrinkled face peers out from under a black cap and behind a scraggly beard.*

⑭ The Last Supper

A dog, a beggar, and a serving girl dominate the foreground of Christ's final Passover meal with his followers. More servants work

in the background. The disciples themselves are dining in the dark, some with their backs to us, with only a few stray highlights to show us what's going on. Tintoretto emphasizes the human, everyday element of that gathering, in contrast to, say, Leonardo da Vinci's more stately version. And he sets the scene at a diagonal for dramatic effect.

The table stretches across a tiled floor, a commonly used device to create 3-D space. But Tintoretto makes the more distant tiles unnaturally small to exaggerate the distance. Similarly, the table and the people get proportionally smaller and lower until, at the far end of the table, tiny Jesus (with glowing head) is only half the size of the disciple at the near end.

Theatrically, Tintoretto leaves it to us to piece together the familiar narrative. The disciples are asking each other, "Is it I who will betray the Lord?" Jesus, meanwhile, unconcerned, hands out Communion bread.

• *Browse the Great Upper Hall and notice the various easel paintings by other artists. Contrast Titian's placid, evenly lit, aristocratic*

Annunciation *(displayed on an easel by the altar) with the blue-collar Tintoretto version downstairs. After you've gotten your fill of the Great Upper Hall, head back downstairs for Tintoretto's last works.*

Ground Floor Hall—The Life of Mary

⓯ *The Flight into Egypt*

There's Mary, Joseph, and the baby, but they're dwarfed by palm trees. Tintoretto, in his old age, returned to composing a

Venetian specialty—landscapes—after years as champion of the Michelangelesque style of painting beefy, twisting nudes. The leafy greenery, the still water, the super-natural sunset, and the hut whose inhabitants go about their work tell us better than any human action that the holy family has found a safe haven.

⓰ *The Circumcision*

This painting, bringing the circumcision of the baby Jesus into sharp focus, is the final canvas that Tintoretto did for the Scuola. He collaborated on this work with his son Domenico, who carried on the family business.

In his long and prolific career, Tintoretto saw fame and many high-paying jobs. But at the Scuola, the commission became an obsession. It stands as one man's very personal contribution to the poor, to the Christian faith, and to art.

CA' REZZONICO TOUR

*Museum of 18th-Century Venice
(Museo del Settecento Veneziano)*

> *Endowed by nature with a pleasing physical appearance, a confirmed gambler, a great talker, far from modest, always running after pretty women...I was certain to be disliked. But, as I was always willing to take responsibility for my actions, I decided I had a right to do anything I pleased.*
> —from *The Memoirs of Giacomo Casanova* (1725–1798)

Venice in the 1700s was the playground for Europe's aristocrats, including the wealthy Rezzonico family, who owned this palace. Today, the Ca' Rezzonico (ret-ZON-ee-koh) contains furniture, decoration, and artwork from the period. This grand home on the Grand Canal is the best place in town to experience the luxurious, decadent spirit of Venice in the Settecento (the 1700s).

Orientation

Cost: €7, can be covered by San Marco Museum Plus Pass if you choose, or free with Museum Pass (see page 24).

Hours: April–Oct Wed–Mon 10:00–18:00, Nov–March Wed–Mon 10:00–17:00, closed Tue, last entry one hour before closing.

Getting There: The museum is located on the west bank of the Grand Canal, right where the canal makes its hairpin turn. There are a number of ways to reach the museum: Vaporetto #1 has a Ca' Rezzonico stop (between Rialto and Accademia). From the east side of the Grand Canal (near the Palazzo Grassi), take the quick Sana Samuele *traghetto* ride across the canal (daily 8:30–13:30). From the Accademia, it's a 10-minute walk heading northwest: When you reach Campo San Barnaba, cross the bridge in the far right corner and turn right immediately on Fondamenta Rezzonico. From the Rialto Bridge, it's a 20-minute walk heading southwest. It's seven minutes from the Frari Church (directions on page 143).

Information: The Ca' Rezzonico is also known as the Museo del Settecento Veneziano. On the ground floor, you'll find a bookstore and WCs. Tel. 041-241-0100, www.museicivici veneziani.it.

Bag Check: Required and free for bags larger than a purse.

Audioguide Tours: They cost €4 (€6/2 people) and last 1.5 hours.

Length of This Tour: Allow 1.5 hours.

Cuisine Art: The museum's café has simple fare (€4 *panini*). For restaurants near Campo San Barnaba, see page 280.

Photography: Prohibited.

Starring: A beautiful palace with 18th-century furnishings and paintings by G. B. Tiepolo, Canaletto, and Guardi.

The Tour Begins

Our Ca' Rezzonico tour covers two floors. The first floor has rooms decorated with period furniture and ceiling frescoes by

G. B. Tiepolo. The second floor displays paintings by Canaletto, Guardi, G. D. Tiepolo, Longhi, and others. (The third floor painting gallery—which we won't visit—shows lots of flesh in lots of rooms.)

First, step onto the dock on the Grand Canal and admire Ca' Rezzonico's heavy stone facade. This dock was, of course, the main entrance back in the 1700s. Next, admire the 1700s-era covered gondola in the courtyard. Picture this arriving at the Ca's dock for a party during Carnevale. A charcoal heater inside kept the masked and caped passengers warm, as they sipped Prosecco and chatted in French, enjoying their winter holiday away from home....

First Floor

• *Buy tickets on the ground floor, then ascend the grand staircase to the first floor (where you show your ticket), entering the ballroom.*

Room 1: Ballroom

A great place for a wedding reception. At 5,600 square feet, it's the biggest private venue in the city. Stand in the center, and the room gets even bigger, with a ceiling painting that opens up to

Ca' Rezzonico—First Floor

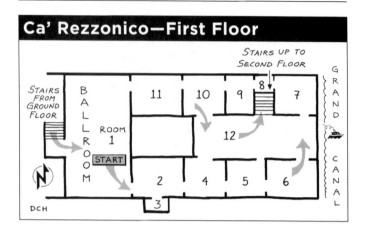

the heavens and painted, trompe l'oeil (optical illusion) columns and arches that open onto fake alcoves.

Imagine dancing under candlelit chandeliers to Vivaldi's *Four Seasons*. Servants glide by with drinks and finger foods. The gentlemen wear powdered wigs, silk shirts with lacy sleeves, tight velvet coats and breeches, striped stockings, and shoes with big buckles. They carry snuff-boxes with dirty pictures inside the lids. The ladies powder their hair, pile it high, and weave in stuff—pictures of their children or locks of a lover's hair. And everyone carries a mask on a stick to change identity in a second.

The chandeliers of gold-covered wood are original. But while most of the furniture we'll see is from the 1700s, it's not from the Rezzonico family collection.

• *Promenade across the floor into the next room.*

Room 2: Nuptial Allegory Room

In fact, there *was* a wedding here—see the happy couple on the ceiling, arriving in a chariot pulled by four white horses and ser-enaded by angels, cupids, and Virtues. In 1757, Ludovico Rezzonico exchanged vows with Faustina Savorgnan in this room, under the bellies of the horses painted for the occa-sion by Giovanni Battista ("John the Baptist") Tiepolo. G. B. Tiepolo (1696–1770), the best-known decorator of Europe's palaces, was at the height of his fame and technique. He knocked this off in 12 days. His bright colors, mastery of painting figures from every possible angle, wide knowledge of classical literary subjects, and sheer, unbridled imagination made his frescoes blend seamlessly with ornate Baroque and Rococo furniture.

The Rezzonicos were a family of *nouveaux riches* who bought their way into the exclusive club of Venetian patrician families. The ***Portrait of Clement XIII*** (on easel), pink-cheeked and well-fed, shows the most famous Rezzonico. As pope (elected 1758), Clement spent his reign defending the Jesuit society from anti-Catholic European nobles. A prayer kneeler (in the tiny adjoining chapel, Room 3) looks heavily used, dating from the sin-and-repent era of Settecento Venice.

Room 4: Pastel Room

Europe's most celebrated painter of portraits in pastels was a Venetian, Rosalba Carriera (1675–1757). Wealthy French and English tourists on holiday wanted a souvenir of Venice, and Carriera obliged, with miniature portraits on ivory rather than the traditional vellum (soft animal skin). She progressed to portraits in pastel, a medium that caught the luminous, pale-skin, white-haired, heavy-makeup look that was considered so desirable. Still, her ***Portrait (Ritratto) of Sister Maria Caterina*** has a warts-and-all realism that doesn't hide the nun's heavy eyebrows, long nose, and forehead vein, which only intensifies the spirituality she radiates.

At age 45, Carriera was invited by tourists whom she'd befriended to visit them in Paris. There she became the toast of the town. Returning triumphantly to Venice, she settled into her home on the Grand Canal and painted until her eyesight failed.

Also in the room is the portrait of Cecilia Guardi Tiepolo: wife of famous painter Giovanni Battista Tiepolo, sister of famous painter Francesco Guardi, and mother of not-very-famous painter Lorenzo Tiepolo, who painted this when he was 21.

Room 5: Tapestry Room

Tapestries, furniture, a mirror, and a door with Asian themes that shows an opium smoker on his own little island paradise (lower panel) give a sense of the Rococo luxury of the wealthy. In a century dominated by the French court at Versailles, Venice was one of the few cities that could hold its own. The furniture ensemble of gilded wood chairs, tables, and chests hints at the Louis XIV (claw-foot) style, but the pieces were made in a Venetian workshop.

Despite Venice's mask of gaiety, in the 1700s it was a poor, politically bankrupt, dirty city. Garbage floated in the canals, the streets were either unpaved or slippery with slime, and tourists could hardly stand visiting St. Mark's Basilica or the Doge's Palace because of the stench of mildew. But its reputation for decay and sleaze was actually romanticized into a metaphor for adventures into shady morality. With licensed casinos and a reputed "20,000 courtesans" (prostitutes), it was a fun city for foreigners freed from hometown blinders.

Room 6: Throne Room

"Nowhere in Europe are there so many and such splendid fêtes, ceremonies, and public entertainments of all kinds as there are in Venice," wrote a visitor from France. As you check out the view of the Grand Canal, imagine once again that you're attending a party here. You could watch the *Forze d'Ercole* (Force of Hercules) acrobats, who stood in boats and kept building a human pyramid—of up to 50 bodies—until they tumbled laughing into the Grand Canal. At midnight the hosts would dim the mirrored candleholders on the walls, so you could look out on a fireworks display over the water.

Carnevale, Venice's prime party time, stretched from the day after Christmas to Lent. Everyone wore masks. Frenchmen, dressed as turbaned Ottoman Turks, mingled with Turkish traders dressed as harlequins. Fake Barbary pirates fought playfully with skin-blackened "Moors." And long-nosed Pulcinella clowns were everywhere, reveling in the time when all social classes partied as one because "the mask levels all distinctions."

The **ceiling fresco**, again by Giovanni Battista Tiepolo, certainly trompes my oeil. (It's best viewed from the center.) Tiepolo opens the room's sunroof, allowing angels to descend to earth to pick up the Rezzonico clan's patriarch. The old, bald, bearded fellow is crowned with laurels and begins to rise on a cloud up to the

Famous 18th-Century Venetians

Canaletto (Giovanni Antonio Canal): Painter of Venice views

Antonio Canova: Neoclassical sculptor

Giacomo Casanova: Gambler, womanizer, revolutionary

Carlo Goldoni: Playwright of realistic comedies

Francesco Guardi: Painter of romantic Enlightened ideas

Giovanni Battista (G. B.) Tiepolo: Painter of Rococo ceilings

Giovanni Domenico (G. D.) Tiepolo: Painter son of famous Tiepolo

translucent temple of glory. The angels hold Venice's Golden Book, where the names of the city's nobles were listed. In 1687, the Rezzonico family bought their way into the exclusive club. Tiepolo captures the moment just as the gang is exiting out the "hole" in the ceiling. The leg of the lady in blue hangs over the "edge" of the fake oval. Tiepolo creates a zero-gravity universe that must have astounded visitors. Walk in circles under the fresco, and watch the bugling angel spin.

• *Pass through the large next room and into...*

Room 7: Tiepolo Room

The ceiling painting by G. B. Tiepolo depicts Nobility and Virtue as a kind of bare-breasted, Thelma-and-Louise duo defeating Treachery, who tumbles down. The painting—which is on canvas, not a fresco like the others—was moved here from another palazzo.

Portraits around the room are by Tiepolo and his sons, Lorenzo and Giovanni Domenico. The paintings are sober and down-to-earth, demonstrating the artistic range of this exceptional family. Giovanni Battista ("G. B.") was known for his flamboyance, but he passed to his sons his penchant for painting wrinkled, wizened old men in the Rembrandt style. In later years, G. B. had the pleasure

of traveling with his sons to distant capitals, meeting royalty, and working on palace ceilings. Giovanni Domenico ("G. D.") contributed some of the minor figures in the Ca' Rezzonico ceilings and went on to a successful artistic career of his own. (We'll see his work upstairs.)

This room was the Rezzonicos' game room, and you can see a card table in the center. The big walnut cabinet along the wall is one of the few original pieces of furniture from the Rezzonicos' collection.

Room 8: Passage

This narrow corridor displays vessels for serving three foreign stimulants that became popular beverages in 1700s Venice—coffee, tea, and hot chocolate.

Room 9: Library

Ca' Rezzonico was the home of the English poet Robert Browning (1812–1889) in his later years. Imagine him here in this study, in a melancholy mood after a long winter, reading a book and thinking of words from a poem of his: "Oh to be in England, now that April's there...." Antonio Corradini's marvelous bust of the **Veiled Woman (Dama Velata/Puritas)** adds to the somber mood.

Room 10: Lazzarini Room

The big, colorful paintings are by Gregorio Lazzarini (1655–1730), Tiepolo's teacher. Tiepolo took Lazzarini's color, motion, and twisted poses and suspended them overhead.

Room 11: Brustolon Room

Andrea Brustolon (1662–1732) carved Baroque fantasies into the custom-made tables, chairs, and vase stand that he crafted in his Venice workshop. In black ebony, reddish boxwood, and brown walnut, they overwhelm with the sheer number of figures, yet each carving is a gem worth admiring. The big vase stand is a harmony of different colors: a white vase supported by ebony slaves in chains and a brown boxwood Hercules. The slaves' chains are carved from a single piece of wood—a racist motif, but an impressive artistic feat.

The room's flowery Murano glass chandelier—of pastel pinks,

Giacomo Casanova
(1725–1798)

I began to lead a life of complete freedom, caring for nothing except what pleased me.
—from *The Memoirs of Giacomo Casanova*

Casanova, a real person who wrote an exaggerated autobiography, typifies the Venice that so entranced the rest of Europe.

In his life, he adopted many personae, worked in a number of professions, and always took the adventurous path.

Casanova was born just across the Grand Canal from the Ca' Rezzonico. The son of an actor, Casanova trained to be a priest, but was expelled for seducing nuns. To Venetians he was first known as a fiery violinist at fancy parties in palaces such as the Ca' Rezzonico. He would later serve time in the Doge's Palace prison, accused of being a magician.

As a professional gambler and charmer, he roamed Europe's capitals seducing noblewomen, dueling with fellow men of honor, and impressing nobles with his knowledge of Greek literature, religion, politics, and the female sex. His memoirs, published after his death, cemented his reputation as a genial but cunning rake, rogue, and rapscallion.

blues, and turquoise—is original.

• *Backtrack to Room 10, then turn right into the large, sparsely decorated room called the...*

Room 12: Portego

That funny little cabin in the room is a sedan chair, a servant-powered taxi for Venice's nobles. Four strong-shouldered men ran poles through the iron brackets on either side, then carried it on their shoulders, while the rich rode in red-velvet luxury above the slimy streets.

• *The staircase to the second floor is here in Room 12, in the middle of the long wall. On the second floor, you emerge into Room 13 and find the two Canaletto paintings on the opposite wall.*

Second Floor

The first floor showed the rooms and furniture of the 1700s. The second-floor paintings depict the people who sat in those chairs.

Ca' Rezzonico—Second Floor

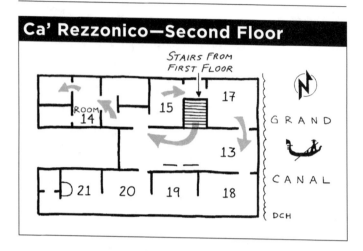

Room 13: Painting Portego—Canaletto

Rich tourists wanting to remember their stay in Venice sought out Canaletto (1697–1768) for a "postcard" view. The ***Grand Canal from***

Palazzo Balbi to Rialto (by Giovanni Antonio Canal, called Il Canaletto) captures the view you'd see from the palazzo two doors down. With photographic clarity, Canaletto depicts buildings, boats, and shadows on the water, leading the eye to the tiny, half-hidden Rialto Bridge on the distant horizon.

The ***View of Rio dei Mendicante*** chronicles every chimney, every open shutter, every pair of underwear hanging out to dry.

Canaletto was a young theater-set painter working on Scarlatti operas in Rome when he decided his true calling was painting reality, not Baroque fantasy. He moved home to Venice, set up his easel outside, and painted scenes like these two, directly from nature. It was considered a very odd thing to do in his day.

Despite the seeming photo-realism and crystal clarity, these wide-angle views are more than any human eye could take in without turning side to side. Canaletto, who meticulously studied the mathematics of perspective, was not above tweak-

ing those rules to compress more of Venice into the frame. In the *Grand Canal from Palazzo Balbi to Rialto,* notice there are shadows along both sides of the canal—physically impossible, but more picturesque. His paintings still have a theater-set look to them, but here, the Venice backdrop is the star.

To meet the demand for postcard scenes of Venice, Canaletto resorted in later years to painting from engravings or following formulas. But these two early works reflect his pure vision to accurately paint the city he loved.

• *From here, we'll move roughly clockwise around the second floor. Head for the door behind your right shoulder. Room 14 is actually a maze of several rooms.*

Room 14: G. D. Tiepolo's Frescoes from the Villa in Zianigo

The son of G. B. Tiepolo decorated the family villa with frescoes for his own enjoyment. They're far more down-to-earth than G.

B.'s high-flying fantasies. *New World* features butts, as ordinary folk crowd around a building with a peep-show window. The only faces we see are the two men in profile—Giovanni Domenico Tiepolo (far right, with eyeglass) and his father, G. B. Tiepolo (arms folded)—and baby brother Lorenzo (center). The **Pulcinella Room** (far right corner) has several scenes (including one overhead) of the hook-

nosed, white-clothed, hunchbacked clown who, at Carnevale time, represented the lovable country bumpkin. But here, he and his similarly dressed companions seem tired, lecherous, and stupid. The decadent gaiety of Settecento Venice was at odds with the *Liberté, Egalité,* and *Fraternité* erupting in France.

• *Backtrack through the maze of Room 14, winding your way into a room with a harpsichord, or spinet, cleverly named the...*

Room 15: Spinet Room

The 1700s saw the development of new keyboard instruments that would culminate by century's end in the modern piano. This particular specimen has strings that are not hammered (like a piano) but plucked (like a mechanical guitar). The spacing of "white" keys and "black" keys is chromatic like a modern piano. This newly invented "tempered" scale of evenly spaced notes let you play in all keys without retuning.

Room 17: Parlor Room

Francesco Guardi (1712–1793), like Canaletto, supplied foreigners with scenes of Venice. But Guardi uses rougher brushwork that casts a romantic haze over the decaying city.

The Parlor (Il Parlatorio delle Monache di S. Zaccaria) is an interior landscape featuring visiting day at a convent school. The girls, secluded behind grills, chat and have tea with family members, friends, ladies with their pets, and potential suitors. Convents were like finishing schools for aristocratic girls, where they got an education and learned manners before re-entering the world. Note the puppet show (starring spouse-abusing Pulcinella).

Guardi's *Il Ridotto di Palazzo Dandolo* shows partygoers in masks at a Venetian palace licensed for gambling. Casanova and others claimed that these casino houses had back rooms for the private use of patrons and courtesans. The men wear the traditional *bautta*—a three-piece outfit consisting of a face mask, three-cornered hat, and cowl. This getup was actually required by law in certain seedy establishments to ensure that every sinner was equally anonymous. The women wear Lone Ranger masks, and parade a hint of cleavage to potential customers.

• *Continuing along, you'll pass back through the Painting Portego and into...*

Room 18: Longhi Room

There is no better look at 1700s Venice than these genre scenes by Pietro Longhi (1702–1785), depicting everyday life among the upper classes. See ladies and gentlemen going to the hairdresser or to the dentist, dressed in the finery that was standard in every public situation.

Contrast these straightforward

scenes with G. B. Tiepolo's sumptuous ceiling painting of nude gods and goddesses. The Rococo fantasy world of aristocrats was slipping increasingly into the more prosaic era of the bourgeoisie.

• *Pass through several rooms to the far corner.*

Room 21: The Alcove

Casanova daydreamed of fancy boudoirs like this one, complete with a large bed (topped with a Madonna by Rosalba Carriera), a walnut dresser, Neoclassical wallpaper, and silver toiletries. Even the presence of the baby cradle would not have dimmed his ardor.

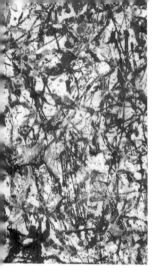

PEGGY GUGGENHEIM COLLECTION TOUR

Peggy Guggenheim (1898–1979)—an American-born heiress to the Guggenheim fortune and niece of Solomon Guggenheim (who built New York's modern-art museum of the same name)—made her mark as a friend, lover, and patron of modern artists.

As a gallery owner, she introduced Europe's avant-garde to a skeptical America. As a collector, she gave instant status to modern art that was too radical for serious museums. As a patron, she fed starving artists such as Jackson Pollock. And as a person, she lived larger than life, unconventional and original, with a succession of lovers that enhanced her reputation as a female Casanova.

In 1948, Peggy "retired" to Venice, moving into a small, unfinished palazzo on the Grand Canal. Today it's a museum, decorated much as it was during her lifetime, with one of the best collections anywhere of 20th-century art. It's the only museum I can think of where the owner is buried in the garden.

Orientation

Cost: €12, generally includes temporary exhibits (displayed near the café and museum shop).

Hours: Wed–Mon 10:00–18:00, closed Tue, last entry 15 minutes before closing.

Getting There: The museum, overlooking the Grand Canal, is at Dorsoduro 704, a five-minute walk from the Accademia Bridge (vaporetto: Accademia) or from La Salute Church (vaporetto: Salute). A cool way to cross the Grand Canal is via the S.M. del Giglio *traghetto* (runs 9:00–18:00, see map on page 60) or the Dogana *traghetto* from St. Mark's Square (9:00–14:00, see map on page 72; both *traghetti* €0.50).

Nearby: If you like contemporary art, this is your neighborhood.

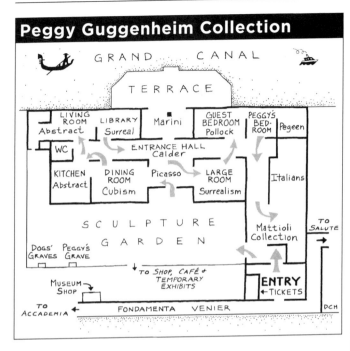

Browse the art galleries, and visit the Punta della Dogana museum (next to La Salute, see page 48).

Information: The museum shop sells an excellent €6 mini-guidebook. Tel. 041-240-5411, www.guggenheim-venice.it.

Tours: Audioguides cost €7. You can book a 1- to 1.5-hour **guided tour** (€60) by calling the museum. Art interns guarding the works are happy to tell you about particular pieces if you ask.

Length of This Tour: Allow one hour.

Baggage Check: Free and required for anything bigger than a small purse.

Photography: Permitted only in garden and terrace.

Cuisine Art: Pricey café on site (€10–20 dishes). See page 280 in the Eating in Venice chapter for recommendations in the Dorsoduro neighborhood.

Starring: Picasso, Kandinsky, Mondrian, Dalí, Pollock...and Peggy herself.

The Tour Begins

After passing through a garden courtyard sprinkled with statues, you enter the palazzo. There's a wing to the left and a wing to the right, plus a modern annex. The collection is (very) roughly chronological, starting to the left with Cubism and ending to the right with young, post-World War II artists.

The collection's strength is its Abstract, Surrealist, and Abstract-Surrealist art. The placement of the paintings may change, so use this chapter as an overview, not a painting-by-painting tour. What makes this collection unique is that it hangs here in Peggy's home, much as it did in her lifetime. As you tour, keep an eye out for black-and-white photos of Peggy standing alongside her art, now hanging in the very same rooms in which they were taken.

• *Walk through Peggy's collection and her life. From the sculpture garden, head into the...*

Entrance Hall: Meet Peggy Guggenheim

Picture Peggy Guggenheim greeting guests here—standing under the **trembling-leaf mobile by Alexander Calder,** flanked by two Picasso paintings, surrounded by her yapping dogs and meowing cats, and wearing her Calder-designed earrings, Mondrian-print dress, and "Catwoman" sunglasses.

During the 1950s and 1960s, this old palazzo on the Grand Canal was a mecca for "Moderns," from composer Igor Stravinsky to actor Marlon Brando, from painter Mark Rothko to writer Truman Capote, from choreographer George Balanchine to Beatle John Lennon and performance artist Yoko Ono. They came to sip cocktails, tour the great art, talk about ideas, and meet the woman who had become a living legend.

Pablo Picasso—*On the Beach* (1937)

Curious, balloon-animal women play with a sailboat while their friend across the water looks on. Of all Peggy's many paintings, this was her favorite.

By the time Peggy Guggenheim first became serious about modern art (about the time this was painted), Pablo Picasso—the most famous and versatile modern artist—had already been through his Blue, Rose, Fauve, Cubist, Synthetic Cubist, Classical, Abstract, and Surrealist phases, finally arriving at a synthesis of these styles. Peggy had some catching up to do.

• *Enter the first room to the left, and you'll see a dining-room table in the center.*

1900–1920: Cubists in the Dining Room

Peggy's dining-room table reminds us that this museum was, indeed, her home for the last 30 years of her life. Most of the furniture is now gone, but the walls are decorated much as they were when she lived here, with paintings and statues by her friends, colleagues, and mentors. Here, she entertained countless artists and celebrities (more name-dropping), from actor Paul Newman to poet Allen Ginsberg, from sculptor Henry Moore to playwright Tennessee Williams, from James Bond creator Ian Fleming to glass sculptor Dale Chihuly.

Most of the art in the dining room dates from Peggy's childhood, when she was raised in the lap of luxury in New York, oblivious to the artistic upheavals going on in Europe.

In 1912, the *Titanic* went down, taking Peggy's playboy tycoon father with it...and leaving his 14-year-old daughter with a small but comfortable trust fund and a man-sized hole in her life.

Approaching adulthood, Peggy rejected her traditional American upbringing, hanging out at a radical bookstore, getting a nose job (a botched operation, leaving her with a rather bulbous schnozz)...and planning a trip to Europe.

In 1920, 21-year-old Peggy arrived in Paris, where a revolution in art was taking place.

• *Find the following early 20th-century art (or similar pieces) in the Dining Room and surrounding rooms—the Kitchen, the Living Room, the Entrance Hall, and the Library.*

Pablo Picasso—*The Poet* (1911)

Picasso, a Spaniard living in Paris, shattered the Old World into brown shards ("cubes") and reassembled it in Cubist style. It's a vaguely recognizable portrait of a man from the waist up—tapering to a head at the top, smoking a pipe (?), and cradling the traditional lyre of a poet. While the newfangled motion-picture camera could capture a moving image, Picasso suggests motion with a collage of stills.

Marcel Duchamp—*Nude (Study), Sad Young Man on a Train* (1911–1912)

In a self-portrait, Duchamp poses gracefully with a cane, but the moving train jiggles the image into a blur of brown. Duchamp is best known, not for paintings like this, but for his outrageous conceptual pieces: his urinal-as-statue *(Fountain)* and his moustache on the *Mona Lisa* (titled *L.H.O.O.Q.*, which—when spoken aloud in French—is a pun that translates loosely as "she has a hot ass"). In a 2004 poll of

British artists, Duchamp's urinal was named the most influential modern artwork of all time.

Umberto Boccioni—*Dynamism of a Speeding Horse + Houses* (assemblage, 1915)

This statue captures the blurred motion of the modern world—accelerated by technology, then shattered by World War I, which left nine million Europeans dead and everyone's moral compass spinning. (In fact, this statue was shattered by the destructive force of Boccioni's own kids, who scattered the cardboard "houses" while using it as a rocking horse.)

Constantin Brancusi—*Maiastra* (bronze statue, c. 1912)

For the generation born before air travel, flying was magical. This high-polished bird is the first of many by Brancusi, who dreamed of flight. But this bird just sits there. For centuries, a good sculptor was one who could capture movement in stone. Brancusi reverts to the style of "primitive" African art, in which even the simplest statues radiate mojo.

Marc Chagall—*Rain* (1911)

The rain clouds gather over a farmhouse, the wind blows the trees

and people, and everyone prepares for the storm. Quick, put the horse in the barn, grab an umbrella, take a leak, and round up the goats in the clouds.

Marc Chagall, a Russian living in France, found the romantic, weightless, childlike joy of topsy-turvy Paris.

1920s: Abstraction and Various "-Isms"

In the Roaring Twenties, Peggy spent *her* twenties right in the center of avant-garde craziness: Paris. For the rest of her life, Europe—not America—would be her permanent address.

In Paris, trust-funded Peggy lived the bohemian life. Post–WWI Paris was cheap and, after the bitter war years, ready to party. Days were spent drinking coffee in cafés, talking ideas with the likes of activist Emma Goldman, writer Djuna *(Nightwood)* Barnes, and photographer Man Ray. Nights were spent abusing the drug forbidden in America (alcohol), dancing to jazz music into the wee hours, and talking about Freud and s-e-x.

One night, at the top of the Eiffel Tower, a dashing artist and intellectual nicknamed "The King of Bohemia" popped the question. Peggy and Laurence Vail soon married and had two children, but the partying only slowed somewhat. This thoroughly modern couple dug the wild life and the wild art it produced.

Wassily Kandinsky—*White Cross* (1922)

I see white, I see crosses, but where's the white cross? Oh, there it is on the right, camouflaged among black squares.

Like a jazz musician improvising from a set scale, Kandinsky plays with new patterns of related colors and lines, creating something that's simply beautiful, even if it doesn't "mean" anything. As Kandinsky himself would say, his art was like "visual music—just open your eyes and look."

Piet Mondrian—*Composition with Red* (1938–1939)

Like a blueprint for Modernism, Mondrian's T-square style boils painting down to its basic building blocks—black lines, white canvas, and the three primary colors (red, yellow, and blue) arranged in orderly patterns. This stripped-down canvas even omits yellow and blue.

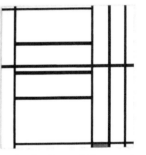

Mondrian started out painting realistic landscapes of the orderly fields in his native Holland. Increasingly, he simplified things into horizontal and vertical patterns, creating rectangles of different proportions. This one has horizontal lines to the left, vertical ones to the right. The horizontals appear to dominate, until we see that they're balanced by the tiny patch of red.

For Mondrian, who was heavily into Eastern mysticism, up vs. down and left vs. right were metaphors for life's ever-shifting dualities: good vs. evil, man vs. woman, fascism vs. communism. The canvas is a bird's-eye view of Mondrian's personal landscape.

1930s: Abstract Surrealists

In 1928, Peggy's marriage to Laurence Vail ended, and she entered into a series of romantic attachments—some loving and stable, others sexual and impersonal. Though not stunningly attractive,

Abstract Art

Abstract art simplifies. A man becomes a stick figure. A squiggle is a wave. A streak of red expresses anger. Arches

make you want a cheeseburger. These are universal symbols that everyone from a caveman to a banker understands. Abstract artists capture the essence of reality in a few lines and colors, even things a camera can't—emotions, abstract concepts, musical rhythms, and spiritual states of mind.

Most 20th- and 21st-century paintings are a mix of the real world ("representation") and the colorful patterns of "abstract" art. Artists purposely distort camera-eye reality to make the resulting canvas more decorative.

she was easy to be with, and she truly admired artistic men.

In 1937, she began an on-again, off-again (so to speak) sexual relationship with playwright Samuel *(Waiting for Godot)* Beckett. Beckett steered her toward Modern painting and sculpture—things she'd never paid much attention to.

She started hanging out with the French Surrealists, from artist Marcel Duchamp to writer André Breton to filmmaker/artist Jean *(Beauty and the Beast)* Cocteau. Duchamp, in particular, mentored her in modern art, encouraging her to use her money to collect and promote it. Nearing 40, she moved to London and launched a new career.

Yves Tanguy—*The Sun in Its Jewel Case* (1937)

In May 1938, this painting was featured at Guggenheim Jeune, the art gallery Peggy opened in London. Tanguy's painting sums up the turbulent art that shocked a sleepy London during that first season.

Weird, phallic, tissue-and-bone protuberances cast long shadows across a moody, dreamlike landscape—the landscape of the mind. (Peggy said the picture "frightened" her, but added, "I got over my fear...and now I own it.")

The figures are Abstract (unrecognizable), and the mood is Surreal, producing the style cleverly dubbed Abstract Surrealism.

Peggy was drawn to Yves Tanguy and had a short but intense affair with the married man. Tanguy, like his art, was wacky and spontaneous, occasionally shocking friends by suddenly catching and gobbling up a spider and washing it down with white wine. The Surrealists saw themselves as spokesmen for Freud's "id," the untamed part of the personality that thinks dirty thoughts when the "ego" goes to sleep.

The Guggenheim Jeune gallery exhibited many of the artists we see in this museum, including Kandinsky, Mondrian, and Calder. Guggenheim Jeune closed as a financial flop after just two years, but its shocking paintings certainly created a buzz in the art world, and as the years passed the gallery's failure gained a rosy glow of success.

1939–1940: Peggy's Shopping Spree in Paris

Peggy moved back to Paris and rented an apartment on the Ile St. Louis. In September, Nazi Germany invaded Poland, sparking World War II. All of France waited...and waited...and waited for the inevitable Nazi attack on Paris.

Meanwhile, Peggy spent her days shopping for masterpieces. Using a list compiled by Duchamp and others, she personally visited artists in their studios—from Brancusi to Dalí to Giacometti—often negotiating directly with them. (Picasso initially turned Peggy down, thinking of her as a gauche, bargain-hunting housewife. When she entered his studio he said, "Madame, you'll find the lingerie department on the second floor.") In a few short months, she bought 37 of the paintings now in the collection, perhaps saving them from a Nazi regime that labeled such art "decadent."

In 1941, with the Nazis occupying Paris and most of Europe, Peggy fled her adopted homeland. With her stash of paintings and a new companion—painter Max Ernst—she sailed from Lisbon to safety in New York.

• *Pass back through the Entrance Hall—where Peggy welcomed celebrity guests, from writer Somerset Maugham to actor Rex Harrison to painter Marc Chagall—and into the east wing. The right entryway leads to a room filled with Surrealist canvases.*

1941–1945: Surrealists Invade New York

Trees become women, women become horses, and day becomes night. Balls dangle, caves melt, and things cast long shadows across film-noir landscapes—Surrealism. The world was moving fast, and Surrealists caught the jumble of images. They scattered seemingly unrelated things on the canvas, leaving us to trace the connections in a kind of connect-the-dots game without numbers.

Peggy spent the war years in America. She married Max Ernst, and their house in New York City became a gathering place for exiled French Surrealists and young American artists.

In 1942, she opened a gallery/museum in New York called Art of This Century that featured, well, essentially the collection we see here in Venice. But patriotic, gung-ho America was not quite ready for the nonconformist, intellectual art of Europe.

Max Ernst—*The Antipope* (c. 1942)

The horse-headed nude in red is a portrait of Peggy—at least, that's what she thought when she saw it. She loved the painting and insisted that Max give it to her as a wedding present, renamed *The Mystic Marriage*.

Others read more into it. Is the horse-headed warrior (at right) Ernst himself? Is he being wooed by one of his art students? Is that Peggy's daughter, Pegeen (center), watching the scene, sadly, from a distance? And is Peggy turning toward her beloved Max, subconsciously suspicious of the young student...

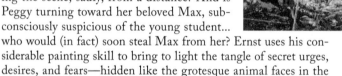

who would (in fact) soon steal Max from her? Ernst uses his considerable painting skill to bring to light the tangle of secret urges, desires, and fears—hidden like the grotesque animal faces in the reef they stand on.

Paul Delvaux— *The Break of Day* (1937)

Full-breasted ladies with roots cast long shadows and awaken to a mysterious dawn. If you're counting boobs, don't forget the one reflected in the nightstand mirror.

René Magritte— *Empire of Light* (1953–1954)

Magritte found that, even under a sunny blue sky, suburbia has its dark side.

Salvador Dalí— *The Birth of Liquid Desires* (1931–1932)

Salvador Dalí could draw exceptionally well. He painted "unreal" scenes with photographic realism, making us believe they could truly happen. This creates an air of mystery—

the feeling that anything is possible—that's both exciting and unsettling. His men explore the caves of the dream world and morph into something else before our eyes.

Personally, Peggy didn't like Dalí or his work, but she dutifully bought this canvas (through his wife, Gala) to complete her collection.

• *Across the hall is the Guest Bedroom, with a fireplace and works by Pollock.*

1945–1948, The Postwar Years: Pollock in the Guest Bedroom

Certain young American painters—from Mark Rothko to Robert Motherwell to Robert De Niro, Sr. (the actor's father)—were strongly influenced by Peggy's collection. Adopting the Abstract style of Kandinsky and Mondrian, they practiced Surrealist spontaneity to "express" their personal insights. The resulting style (duh): Abstract Expressionism.

Jackson Pollock—*Enchanted Forest* (1947)

"Jack the Dripper" attacked America's postwar conformity with a can of paint, dripping and splashing a dense web onto the canvas. Picture Pollock in his studio, jiving to the hi-fi, bouncing off the walls, throwing paint in a moment of alcohol-fueled enlightenment.

Peggy helped make Pollock a celebrity. She bought his earliest works (which show Abstract-Surrealist roots), exhibited his work at her gallery, and even paid him a monthly stipend to keep experimenting.

By the way, if you haven't yet tried the Venetian specialty *spaghetti al nero di seppia* (spaghetti with squid in its own ink), it looks something like this.

In 1946, Peggy published her memoirs, titled *Out of This Century: The Informal Memoirs of Peggy Guggenheim.* The front cover was designed by Max Ernst, the back by Pollock. Peggy herself was now a celebrity.

• *The room on the other side of the fireplace was Peggy's Room.*

1950s: Peggy in the Bedroom

As America's postwar factories turned swords into kitchen appliances, Peggy longed to return "home" to Europe. The one place that kept calling to her was Venice, ever since she visited here with Laurence Vail in the 1920s. "I decided Venice would be my future home," she wrote. "I felt I would be happy alone there."

In 1947, after a grand finale exhibition by Pollock, she closed the Art of This Century gallery, crated up her collection, and moved to Venice. In 1948, she bought this palazzo and moved in.

This was Peggy's bedroom. She painted it turquoise. She commissioned the **silver headboard by Alexander Calder** for her canopy bed, using its silver frame to hang her collection of earrings, handmade by the likes of Calder and Tanguy. Venetian mirrors hung on the walls, along with a sentimental portrait of herself and her sister as children. Ex-husband Laurence Vail's collage-decorated bottles sat on the nightstand.

In 1951, Peggy met the last great love of her life, an easygoing, blue-collar Italian with absolutely no interest in art. She was 53, Raoul was 30, and their relationship, though rather odd, was tender and mutually satisfying. When Raoul died in 1954 in a car accident, Peggy comforted herself with her pets.

• *The tiny corner room adjoining the bedroom displays paintings by Pegeen.*

Pegeen

Peggy's daughter, Pegeen, inherited some of Laurence Vail's artistic talent, painting childlike scenes of Venice, populated by skinny Barbie dolls with antennae.

The guest bedroom (where the Pollocks are) was a busy place. Pegeen and her brother, Sinbad, visited their mother, as did Peggy's ex-husbands and their new loves. Other overnight guests ranged from sculptor Alberto Giacometti (who honeymooned here), to author and cultural explorer Paul Bowles, to artist Jean Arp.

• *Cross the hall and go down a few steps into the wing perpendicular to the palazzo, the Mattioli Annex.*

Italians in the Annex

You'll find paintings by well-known Italians **(Modigliani, Boccioni),** as well as the less-famous postwar generation of young Italians who were strongly influenced by Peggy's collection. In 1948, Peggy showed her collection in its own pavilion at the Biennale, Venice's "world's fair of art," and it was the hit of the show. Europeans were astounded and a bit dumbfounded, finally seeing the kind of "degenerate" art forbidden during the fascist years, plus the radical new stuff coming out of New York City.

Peggy sponsored young artists, including **Tancredi**—just one name, back when that was odd—who was given a studio in the palazzo's basement. Tancredi had a relationship with daughter

Pegeen, with her mother's blessing. (Pegeen died in 1967 of a bar-biturates overdose.)

• *Return to the Entrance Hall, then go out onto the Terrace, overlooking the Grand Canal.*

Exhibitionists on the Terrace

> *You fall in love with the city itself. There is nothing left over in your heart for anyone else.*
>
> —Peggy Guggenheim

Marino Marini's equestrian statue, *The Angel of the City* **(1948),** faces the Grand Canal, spreads his arms wide, and tosses his head back in sheer joy, with an eternal hard-on for the city of Venice. Every morning, Peggy must have felt a similar exhilaration as she sipped coffee with this unbelievable view.

Marini originally designed his bronze rider with a screw-off penis (which sounds dirtier than it is) that could be removed for prudish guests or by curious ones. Someone stole it for some unknown purpose, so the current organ is permanently welded on.

The palazzo—called Palazzo Venier dei Leoni—looks modern but is old. Begun in 1748, construction was halted after only the ground floor was built. Legend has it that members of the rival family across the canal in Palazzo Corner squelched the plans for the upper stories to prevent their home from being upstaged. The palazzo remained unfinished until Peggy bought it in 1948 and spruced it up. She added the annex in 1958. The **lions** *(leoni)* of the original palace still guard the waterfront entrance.

Peggy's outlandish and rather foreign presence in Venice—drinking, dressing up outrageously, and sunbathing on her rooftop for all to see—was not immediately embraced by the Venetians. But for artists in the 1950s and 1960s, Peggy's palazzo was *the* place to be, especially when the Biennale brought the jet set. Everyone from actor Alec Guinness, to political satirist Art Buchwald, to gossip columnist Hedda Hopper signed her guest book. Picture Peggy and guests, decked out in evening clothes, hopping into her custom-built gondola (nicknamed *La Barchessa,* after the doge's private boat) to ride slowly down the canal for a martini and a Bellini at Harry's Bar.

• *Pass back through the Entrance Hall, then outside to the...*

GUGGENHEIM COLLECTION

Sculpture Garden

Peggy opened her impressive collection of sculpture to the Venetian public for free. It features first-rate works by all the greats, from Brancusi to Giacometti. After so much art already, you might find the trees—so rare in urban Venice—more interesting.

If, after your visit here, you still don't like modern art, think of what Peggy used to tell puzzled visitors: "Come back again in 50 years."

• *In the southwest corner of the garden (along the brick wall), find...*

Peggy's Grave and Her Dogs' Graves

"Here Lie My Beloved Babies," marks the grave of her many dogs that were her steady companions as she grew old. Note the names of some of these small, long-haired Lhasa Apsos. Along with  "Cappuccino" and "Baby," you'll see "Pegeen," after her daughter, and "Sir Herbert," for Herbert Read, the art critic who helped Peggy select her collection.

Peggy's ashes are buried alongside, marked with a simple plaque: "Here Rests Peggy Guggenheim 1898–1979."

Over your right shoulder, the flourishing olive tree is a gift from one of Peggy's old traveling buddies—Yoko Ono.

In the nonconformist 1960s, Peggy's once shocking art and unconventional lifestyle became more acceptable, even commonplace. By the 1970s, she was universally recognized as a major force in early modern art and was finally even honored by the Venetians with a nickname—"The Last Dogaressa" *(L'Ultima Dogaressa)*. When she died in a Padua hospital in 1979, she was mourned by the art world, from composer Virgil Thomson, to choreographer Jerome Robbins, to writer George Plimpton, to composer John Cage, to...

LA SALUTE CHURCH TOUR

Santa Maria della Salute

Where the Grand Canal opens up into the lagoon stands one of Venice's most distinctive landmarks, the church dedicated to Santa Maria della Salute (Our Lady of Health). The architect, Baldassare Longhena—who also did St. Mark's Square's "New" wing and the Ca' Rezzonico—remade Venice in the Baroque style. Crown-shaped La Salute was his crowning achievement, and the last grand Venetian structure built before Venice's decline began.

Orientation

Cost and Hours: Free entry to church, daily 9:00–12:00 & 15:00–17:30. Sacristy (€2) may have shorter hours than the church. Vespers service with organ music Mon–Fri at 15:30.

Getting There: The church is on the Grand Canal, near the point where the canal spills into the lagoon. It's a 10-minute walk from the Accademia Bridge (past the Peggy Guggenheim Collection). By boat, vaporetto #1 delivers you to its doorstep (€2 from San Marco, 5 minutes). The Dogana *traghetto* (runs 9:00–14:00) and S.M. del Giglio *traghetto* (9:00–18:00) both stop nearby (each cost €0.50). If it's November 21, you can walk directly to the church across the Grand Canal on a floating, pontoon-like bridge.

Information: Tel. 041-274-3928.

Length of This Tour: Allow 30 minutes.

Photography: Allowed, but no flash in the church, and no photos at all in the Sacristy.

Starring: Baldassare Longhena's church, minor works by Titian and Giordano, and Sacristy with major works by Tintoretto and Titian.

The Tour Begins

Exterior

The white stone church has a steep dome that rises above a circular structure. It's encrusted with Baroque scrolls, leafy Corinthian columns, and 125 statues, including the lovely ladies lounging over the central doorway. The architect conceived of the church "in the shape of a crown."

During the bitter plague of 1630, the Virgin Mary took pity on the city of Venice, miraculously allowing only one in three Venetians (46,000 souls) to die. During this terrible time, Venetians built this church in honor of Our Lady of Health. Her statue tops the lantern, and she's dressed as an admiral, hand on a rudder, welcoming ships to the Grand Canal.

Even today, Mary's intercession is celebrated every November 21, when a floating bridge is erected across the Grand Canal and Venetians can walk from San Marco across the water and right up the seaweed-covered steps to the front door.

At age 32, architect Baldassare Longhena (1598–1682) supported the city's heaviest dome by sinking countless pilings (locals claim over a million) into the sandy soil to provide an adequate foundation. The 12 Baroque scrolls at the base function as buttresses to help support the mammoth dome.

Interior

❶ View from the Entrance

The church has a bright, healthy glow, with white stone (turned gray because of a fungus) illuminated by light filtering through the dome's windows. The church is circular, surrounded by chapels. In contrast to the ornate Baroque exterior, the inside is simple, with only some Corinthian columns and two useless balcony railings up in the dome. The red, white, and yellow marble of the floor adds a cheerful note.

Longhena focuses our immediate attention on the main altar. Every other view is blocked by heavy pillars. Longhena, a master of "theatrical architecture," only reveals the side chapels one by one as we walk around and explore.

The church is an octagon surrounding a circular nave that's topped by the dome. Viewed from the center of the church, the altar and side chapels are framed by arches.

Some of the "marble" is actually brick covered with marble

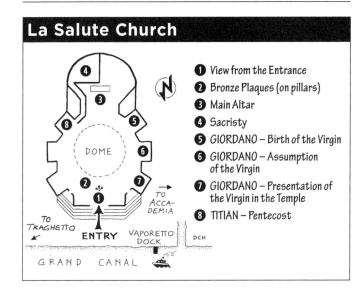

La Salute Church

- ❶ View from the Entrance
- ❷ Bronze Plaques (on pillars)
- ❸ Main Altar
- ❹ Sacristy
- ❺ GIORDANO – Birth of the Virgin
- ❻ GIORDANO – Assumption of the Virgin
- ❼ GIORDANO – Presentation of the Virgin in the Temple
- ❽ TITIAN – Pentecost

dust. The windows are the simple shape that a drop of molten glass makes, to bring in maximum light.

• *Look at the pillars near the entrance, opposite the altar, to find the...*

❷ Bronze Plaques

The church is dedicated not just to physical health but to spiritual health as well. The plaques tell us that on September 16, 1972, the future Pope John Paul I—the predecessor of John Paul II—visited here and paid homage to the Virgin of Health (six years later, he fell sick and died after only 30 days in office).

❸ Main Altar

The marble statues on the top tell the church's story: Mary and Child (center) are approached for help by a kneeling, humble Lady Venice (left). Mary shows compassion and sends an angel baby (right) to drive away Old Lady Plague.

The icon of a black, sad-eyed Madonna with a black baby (12th-century Byzantine) is not meant to be ethnically accurate. Here, a "black" Madonna means an otherworldly one.

• *Find the entrance to the Sacristy, if it's open (entry location varies). It costs €2 to get in, but cheapskates can get a glimpse of the paintings for free by standing outside the entry.*

❹ Sacristy

Along the wall is Tintoretto's big and colorful *Marriage at Cana*. The dinner table leads the eye to Jesus, who is surrounded by the bustle of a wedding. On the right, the host (in gray) orders the servant to bring more wine. The apostles at the table portray leading Venetian artists of the day.

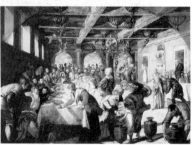

On the ceiling are three ultra-dramatic paintings by Titian, with gruesome subjects: *Cain Clubbing Abel, Abraham Sacrificing His Son,* and *David Slaying Goliath.* The panels—featuring stormy clouds, windblown hair, colorless tones, and overwrought poses—date from Titian's "Mannerist crisis." After visiting Rome and seeing the work of Michelangelo in the Sistine Chapel, Titian left his standard, sweet, and tested style (such as the small painting over the Sacristy altar) and painted big, statuesque, and dramatic works in the Mannerist style. Contrast these with Titian's stately *St. Mark Enthroned with Saints* to appreciate his range of styles.

• *Back in the circular nave, there are six side chapels—three to the left, three to the right. Start near the altar, on the right side (to your right as you face the altar).*

Side Chapel Paintings

Luca Giordano (1632–1705) celebrates the Virgin in three paintings with a similar composition—heaven and angels above, dark earth below.

Giordano, a prolific artist from Naples, was known as "Luca fa presto" (Fast Luke) for his ambidextrous painting abilities.

• *In the chapel to the right of the altar is...*

❺ Giordano—*Birth of the Virgin* (1674)

Little baby Mary in her mom's arms seems like nothing special. But God the Father looks down from above and sends the dove of the Spirit.

• *In the middle chapel, look for...*

❻ Giordano—*Assumption of the Virgin*

Mary, at the end of her life, is being taken gloriously by winged babies, up from the dark earth to the golden light of heaven. The apostles cringe in amazement. A later artist thought his statue was better and planted it right in our way.

• *In the chapel closest to the entrance, see...*

❼ Giordano—*Presentation of the Virgin in the Temple*

Notice how the painting fits the surrounding architecture. It's great to enjoy art *in situ*. The child Mary (in blue, with wispy halo) ascends a staircase that goes diagonally "into" the canvas. Giordano places us viewers at the foot of the stairs. The lady in the lower left asks her kids, "Why can't you be more like her?!"

• *From here, look directly across to the other side of the nave at Titian's* Pentecost, *in the chapel closest to the main altar. The painting looks its best from this distance and angle.*

❽ Titian (Tiziano Vecellio)—*Pentecost* (1546)

The dove of the Holy Spirit sends spiritual rays that fan out to the apostles below, giving them tongues of fire above their heads. They

gyrate in amazement, each one in a different direction. Using floor tiles and ceiling panels, Titian has created the 3-D illusion of a barrel-arched chapel, with the dove coming right into the church through a fake window. But the painting was not designed for this location and, up close, the whole fake niche looks...fake.

SAN GIORGIO MAGGIORE TOUR

San Giorgio in Isola

This dreamy church-topped island is a five-minute vaporetto ride away from St. Mark's Square. Even if you're not interested in Palladio's influential architecture, Tintoretto's famous *Last Supper*, or the stunning bell-tower views of Venice and the lagoon, it's worth a trip just to escape from tourist-mobbed St. Mark's Square.

Orientation

Cost: Admission to the church is free. It costs €3 to go up the bell tower. Bring €0.50 coins to light the artwork.

Hours: Church open May–Sept Mon–Sat 9:30–12:30 & 14:30–18:00, Sun 8:30–11:00 & 14:30–18:00; Oct–April until 16:30. The elevator up the bell tower runs from 30 minutes after the church opens to 30 minutes before it closes.

Avoiding Crowds: The church is never crowded, but the bell tower and elevator can be. Come early or late to have it to yourself.

Getting There: San Giorgio Maggiore is the impressive church you see across the lagoon from St. Mark's Square. The only way to reach it is by the five-minute ride on vaporetto #2. It leaves from the San Zaccaria-M.V.E. stop, located east of the Bridge of Sighs by the equestrian statue (€2, 6/hour, ticket valid for 1 hour, direction: Tronchetto, stop: San Giorgio). To get back to St. Mark's Square, take the #2 headed the opposite way (direction: San Marco).

Gregorian Mass: A Gregorian Mass is sung Mon–Sat at 8:00 and Sun at 11:00. The church is closed to sightseers during Sunday Mass. To attend Mass, held in the Conclave, ring the bell at the door to the right of the main entrance.

Length of This Tour: Allow one hour, more with a trip to the café.

Cuisine Art: A fine little harborside café, rarely used by tourists, is about 150 yards around the left of the church. Its terrace is peaceful—except at lunchtime, when it's mobbed by librarians (€7 pastas, salads, daily 10:00–20:00, off-season 11:00–15:00).

Services: A WC is at the base of the elevator, inside the church.

The Rest of the Island: There's no access to the rest of the monastery complex. You can walk along the left side of the church to the café, and see pleasure boats in the marina, but that's it. If you want to see inside the monastery complex, inquire about weekend tours at tel. 041-524-0119 or www.cini.it.

Starring: Palladio, Tintoretto, and views of Venice.

The Tour Begins

Exterior

The facade looks like a Greek temple, a style well-known today because of its architect, Andrea Palladio (1508–1580). Palladio's hugely influential treatise on architecture inspired centuries of architects in England and America with its expert application of Greco-Roman styles. Countless villas, palaces, and churches look like this. They are "Palladian."

Palladio's facade is similar to two temple fronts overlapping. The four tall columns topped by a triangular pediment resemble a Greek porch, marking the entryway to the tall, central nave. This is superimposed over the facade of the lower side aisles. Behind the facade rises a dome topped with a statue of St. George (the Christian slayer of medieval dragons) holding a flag. The whole complex is completed by the bell tower, which echoes the Campanile in St. Mark's Square across the water.

This church feels so striking because it just doesn't fit with old-school Venice. Palladio makes no concession to the Byzantine legacy of Venice that you see across the water at the Doge's Palace.
• *Walk into the interior of the church.*

❶ View down the Nave, then up the Nave

The interior matches the outer facade, with a high nave flanked by lower side aisles. The walls are white (Palladio's favorite color); the

San Giorgio Maggiore

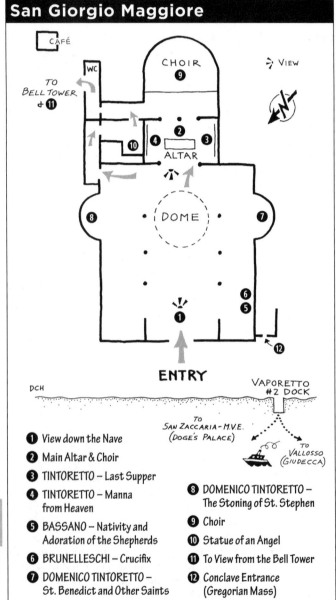

1 View down the Nave

2 Main Altar & Choir

3 TINTORETTO – Last Supper

4 TINTORETTO – Manna from Heaven

5 BASSANO – Nativity and Adoration of the Shepherds

6 BRUNELLESCHI – Crucifix

7 DOMENICO TINTORETTO – St. Benedict and Other Saints

8 DOMENICO TINTORETTO – The Stoning of St. Stephen

9 Choir

10 Statue of an Angel

11 To View from the Bell Tower

12 Conclave Entrance (Gregorian Mass)

windows have clear, rather than stained, glass; and the well-lit church has a clarity, orderliness, and mathematical perfection that exudes the classical world. In keeping with Palladio's classical sensitivity, all decor is in order (compared to the relative chaos of, say, the Frari Church). Oh, the stout, stony symmetry and mathematical purity—with light spilling in from the canal—it's enough to give a Renaissance architect a...never mind.

❷ Main Altar and Choir

The altar is topped with a bronze globe of the world. The monks who once lived on this island congregated in the choir area behind

the main altar. The choir is designed with acoustics in mind, and the barrel-vault ceiling is backed up with a woofer-shaped apse—all to amplify the Gregorian chants that still fill this church daily. (Suddenly I feel a cough coming on... my, the echoes.)

• On the wall to the right of the altar is...

❸ Tintoretto—*Last Supper*

This is the last of several versions of the Last Supper by Tintoretto (1518–1594) that decorate Venice, each one different and inventive

(compare it with the Scuola San Rocco version, pictured on page 158). Here, the table stretches diagonally away from us on a tiled floor. The convincing 3-D effect is theatrical, engaging the viewer. The scene is crowded— servants and cats mingle with wispy, unseen angels. A blazing lamp, radiating supernatural light, illuminates the otherwise dark interior. At the far left, a beggar is fed, illustrating Christ's concern for the poor. The devilish guy on the right turns away from a simple meal (basket of communion wafers) toward a hedonistic banquet. Your eyes go straight to a well-lit Christ, serving his faithful with both hands—wholeheartedly.

San Giorgio was the church for a Benedictine monastery, an order that stressed a simple lifestyle and concern for the poor. They hired Tintoretto (a common-man's painter) and worked closely with him to hone the message that all are welcome—saints, servants, beggars, sinners—into the Christian faith. The monks appreciated Tintoretto's jumble of the spiritual with the mundane, proclaiming that God works miraculously with us on an everyday level.

This canvas works together theologically with the other canvas flanking the altar.

• On the wall to the left of the altar is...

❹ Tintoretto—*Manna from Heaven*

This painting illustrates the Benedictine motto: Work and pray. Here we see the sunny morning after the storm, when God rained bread down on the hungry Israelites. Some work, others relax prayerfully, and others gather the heavenly meal in baskets, basking in the glow of the miracle. The message: Work and pray, and God will take care of you.

❺-❿ More Art Inside the Church

As long as you're here, check out a few more works. They're minor pieces in art-drenched Venice, but they'd be stars in any American museum.

Back near the entrance, in the first chapel on the right, is ❺ **Jacopo Bassano's** *Nativity and Adoration of the Shepherds,* where a radiant baby Jesus lights the dim canvas. In the next chapel is a carved ❻ *Crucifix* by Florentine dome-builder Filippo Brunelleschi.

In the transepts are two works by Jacopo Tintoretto's son, Domenico. In the right transept, the static ❼ *St. Benedict and Other Saints* shows the early monk (to left, in black, bald and bearded) along with Pope Gregory (who wrote about him) having a heavenly vision. ❽ *The Stoning of St. Stephen* (left transept) shows that Domenico had his father's raw talent, but not his flair for dramatic compositions that recede into the distance.

Behind the altar, the ❾ **choir** features 82

View from San Giorgio Maggiore

AIRPORT

LAGOON

TORCELLO

BURANO

MESTRE

CAUSEWAY

SAN MICHELE (CEMETERY)

MURANO

TRONCHETTO

RIALTO

SAN GIOVANNI

GRAND CANAL

SAN MARCO

ARSENALE

SALUTE

G I U D E C C A

REDENTORE

SAN GIORGIO

BIENNALE PARK

DCH

SAN SERVOLO

LIDO

ADRIATIC SEA

NOT TO SCALE— SAN GIORGIO TO:
TORCELLO = 6 MILES
MESTRE = .5 MILES
LIDO   = 2 MILES

N

stalls elaborately carved in walnut. Here, the monks stand and sing, carrying on the prayers, chants, and traditions of the Benedictine order, as they've done since this church was founded in A.D. 982. ⓾

On your way to the bell tower, you'll pass the original ⓾ **statue of an angel** that once stood atop the tower (a copy stands there today). Made in the 18th century of laminated wood covered in lead, it was destroyed by lightning in 1993. Restorers have done their best to piece it back together.

• *You'll find the lift to the top of the bell tower in the far left corner of the church.*

⓫ View from the Bell Tower

The bell tower has no grill (unlike the Campanile at St. Mark's, which has one to keep suicidal people from jumping) and gives a grand view in all directions. Start by looking at the city (to the north), and go clockwise:

Facing North (toward the city): This is the famous view

of Venice's skyline, with St. Mark's Campanile dominating. The big, long, brick church farther inland is Santi Giovanni e Paolo. Farther to the right (east) is the barely visible basin of the Arsenale, the former ship factory, which in its medieval heyday bragged that it was capable of producing a ship a day. Farther still is the green parkland where the Biennale International Art Exhibition is held every odd-numbered year (including 2011). North of Venice, in the hazy distance, you can glimpse several islands. Tiny San Michele (with cypress trees) is the city's cemetery—from here, the island looks connected to Venice. Murano is the next-closest, appearing to be connected to the forested cemetery. Burano is to the distant right, with its leaning bell tower. And Torcello (trust me) is just beyond Burano.

Facing East and South: Look out at the lagoon, which leads to the open Adriatic. This tower was once used to spot approaching enemy boats. The lagoon is too shallow for serious shipping; posts mark the channels dredged to let boats pass through. There's a strict speed limit: 5 kph on the small canals, 7 kph on the Grand Canal, and 11 kph around the perimeter of the island city.

The long, narrow island of Lido in the distance is six miles long and only a half-mile wide (with cars and ferry service to the mainland). The green dome on the island marks the Lido's town center, home to modern hotels and beaches. The Lido serves as a natural breakwater against the wind and waves of the Adriatic Sea, helping create the placid waters of the Venetian lagoon. At the right end of the Lido (visible from here,  but not obvious) is the narrow opening to the Adriatic, where the proposed, long-delayed, underwater flood barriers are to be built. Designed to block the *acqua alta* flooding, the multibillion-dollar Moses Project involves the construction of a series of hinged barriers that will rise up to block high tides threatening the lagoon.

Once a year, the mayor of Venice sails to the opening of the Adriatic to celebrate the ritual marriage of Venice and the sea—the same ritual performed centuries ago by the doges in their gold-leaf boat.

Between the Lido and San Giorgio are several smaller islands, which have been home over the centuries to monasteries and hospitals. The plain, rectangular white building on San Servolo, the little island just before the Lido, was an 18th-century hospital for the insane that now houses a university.

At your feet are the green gardens and the cloisters of the Abbey of San Giorgio.

Facing West: Below is the church, with its dome topped by a green St. George carrying a flag (or is his arm still missing?). You  can see the back sides of the white statues atop Palladio's facade. Stretching to the left is the island of Giudecca, which is oh-so-close to the island you're on, but must be reached by a short swim or vaporetto #2. The Giudecca, which has always been isolated from the rest of the city, was a popular place to build villas in Venice's heyday. The island's separation also made it a perfect place for exiles such as Michelangelo, who found refuge and peace here between commissions. Today, except for a few churches, a youth hostel, and a couple of luxury hotels, the Giudecca is home to locals going about their quiet lives, oblivious to the tourism that dominates the rest of Venice. You can see the swimming pool of the jet-setty Ciprani Hotel, the domes of other Palladian churches (the only sights on this otherwise residential island), and, at the far end, the Molino Stucky, an old, industrial flour mill that reopened in 2007 as the Hilton Hotel.

Directly across from you is the grand dome of La Salute Church. At the head of the Grand Canal stands the golden globe of the old Customs House, now the Punta della Dogana contemporary art museum. And in the far distance, through the smog, are the burning smokestacks and cranes of lovely Mestre, on the mainland.

Looking Up: The bells chime the hours, and ring especially loudly at noon. You're warned.

VENICE'S LAGOON TOUR

San Michele, Murano, Burano, and Torcello

Interesting islands hide out in Venice's lagoon, a calm section of the Adriatic protected from wind and waves by the natural breakwater of the Lido. The brackish marsh—a mix of fresh water and silt from the mainland's rivers, plus the tide-driven saltwater of the Adriatic—is set among a maze of sandbars. The lagoon is big (212 square miles) and so shallow that you could walk across most of it without getting your hair wet. Centuries ago, the shallow water and treacherous sandbars made the Isle of Venice safe from attack by land or sea. Venice is the only great medieval city that never needed a wall.

Cradled by the lagoon north of the city are four islands easily laced together in a half-day trip, a nice escape from the hubbub of Venice. Murano is known for glass, Burano for lace and photogenic pastel houses, and tranquil Torcello for its church. San Michele (a.k.a. Cimitero) is the cemetery island, the last stop for its residents but the first stop for the vaporetto from Venice.

Orientation

Transportation: We'll travel by vaporetto, but there are other options (see "More Transportation Options" sidebar on page 210). Since single vaporetto tickets (€6.50) expire after one hour, using a vaporetto pass for this lagoon excursion makes more sense (e.g., a €16, 12-hour pass; see page 31 for more on vaporetto tickets).

Sightseeing Costs: Murano's Glass Museum costs €5.50, and all of Torcello's sights together cost €10, including the audioguide (€3 for individual sights). The Museum Pass covers the Glass Museum; you can also choose to use the San Marco Museum Plus Pass here (see page 24).

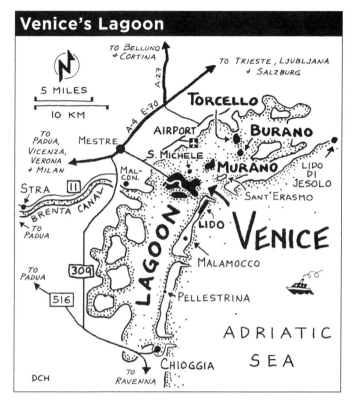

Venice's Lagoon

When to Go: If you want to visit all the lagoon sights, keep in mind that Torcello's church museum is closed Monday.

Information: Pick up a free map of the lagoon and its islands from any TI.

Length of This Tour: Since it takes a minimum of three hours round-trip from St. Mark's to Torcello, allow at least five hours to see all four islands. For an hour-by-hour itinerary, see page 22.

Starring: World-famous Venetian glass and lace, the mosaics of the oldest Venetian church, and the quieter side of Venice.

The Route

We'll sail from Venice to Murano (stopping at San Michele on the way) to Burano (lace and ambience) to Torcello (rural ruins). Here's our plan:

Venice to Murano (via San Michele, takes 40 minutes): From St. Mark's Square, catch vaporetto #41 to Murano. Boats leave every 10 minutes from the San Zaccaria-Jolanda dock, located just past the Bridge of Sighs along the Riva. They travel around the

Lagoon Tour

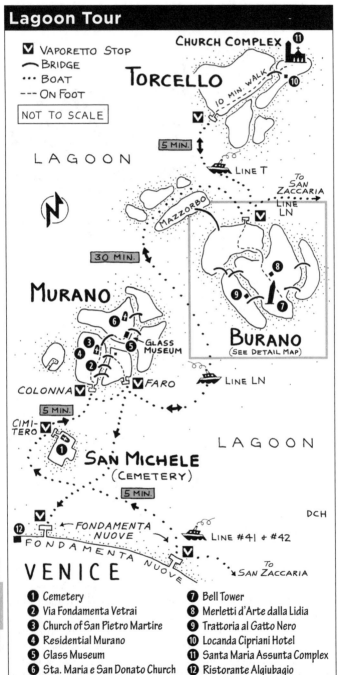

Legend:
- ☑ Vaporetto Stop
- ⌒ Bridge
- ••• Boat
- --- On Foot

NOT TO SCALE

CHURCH COMPLEX

TORCELLO

10 MIN. WALK

5 MIN. Line T

To San Zaccaria

LAGOON

N

MAZZORBO

Line LN

30 MIN.

MURANO

BURANO
(See Detail Map)

Glass Museum

COLONNA

FARO

Line LN

5 MIN.

CIMI-TERO

SAN MICHELE
(Cemetery)

LAGOON

5 MIN.

DCH

FONDAMENTA NUOVE

Line #41 & #42

FONDAMENTA NUOVE

To San Zaccaria

VENICE

1. Cemetery
2. Via Fondamenta Vetrai
3. Church of San Pietro Martire
4. Residential Murano
5. Glass Museum
6. Sta. Maria e San Donato Church
7. Bell Tower
8. Merletti d'Arte dalla Lidia
9. Trattoria al Gatto Nero
10. Locanda Cipriani Hotel
11. Santa Maria Assunta Complex
12. Ristorante Algiubagio

"tail" of fish-shaped Venice, making several stops (including the Cimitero stop on San Michele) before reaching Murano-Colonna.

If you're already on the north shore of Venice (the "back" of the fish), you could catch the #41 or #42 from the Fondamenta Nuove vaporetto stop. Five minutes later, it stops at San Michele (Cimitero stop), then continues on to Murano-Colonna. (Fondamenta Nuove is a 15-minute walk from Rialto and 25 minutes from St. Mark's Square.)

From Murano to Burano (30 minutes): To continue on to Burano, catch the LN vaporetto, which leaves from the Murano-Faro stop twice hourly. Our tour takes us from the Murano-Colonna stop on foot to the Murano-Faro stop (the #41 and #42 *vaporetti* stop at both Murano stops).

From Burano to Torcello (5 minutes): Line T shuttles between Burano and Torcello, on the hour and half-hour.

From Torcello to Venice (75 minutes): Return to Burano (5 minutes) and catch the LN back to Venice, either on a 70-minute trip through the lagoon to San Zaccaria near St. Mark's Square (hourly), or on a 45-minute trip to Fondamenta Nuove (leaves twice an hour; from there you can catch the #42 back to San Zaccaria—leaves every 10 minutes, takes 30 minutes).

Got all that? If not, you can just catch your first boat and follow the tour I've laid out here. Ahoy, matey, we're off!

The Tour Begins

• *From St. Mark's Square (San Zaccaria-Jolanda stop), catch the #41 vaporetto to Murano-Colonna. (Or, from Fondamenta Nuove, you could take the #41 or #42.) On the way, you can hop off for a short visit at the stop called Cimitero, on the island of...*

San Michele

Boats connecting Venice and Murano stop at San Michele, the

cemetery island (its location—directly across the water from the emergency room of Venice's San Giovanni e Paolo hospital—is just a coincidence). Consider a quick stopover, since boats come every 10 minutes. If you enjoy wandering through old cemeteries, you'll dig this one (daily April–Sept 7:30–18:00, Oct–March 7:30–16:30; reception is to the left as you enter, WC to the right).

The island, which is dedicated to St. Michael and holds a Renaissance church, became Venice's cemetery in 1806 when

Pound in Italy

How did an Idaho boy end up in a Venetian cemetery? Poet Ezra Pound (1885-1972), who spent much of his life in Europe, settled in Italy in the 1920s, becoming infatuated with Mussolini's Modernist outlook...and his politics. By the early 1940s, Pound was a leading pro-Fascist propagandist, for which he was indicted for treason by the US once the war was over. He was spared execution by successfully (though controversially) pleading insanity, and eventually returned to Italy.

Nevertheless, Pound's most lasting legacy is his poetry. Scholars consider him one of the form's most influential Modernist voices. While Pound's own masterwork was the series of poems called *The Cantos*, his greatest literary contribution was arguably his heavy-handed editing of his friend T. S. Eliot's *The Waste Land*.

This excerpt of one of Pound's *Cantos* was inspired by Venice—a city of stone reflected in the water during a boat ride at night.

From **Canto XVII**

A boat came,
One man holding her sail,
Guiding her with oar caught over gunwale, saying:
"There, in the forest of marble,
The stone trees—out of water—
the arbours of stone...
the gilt beams flare of an evening..."

And the waters richer than glass...
Dye-pots in the torch-light...
The flash of wave under prows...
Stone trees, white and rose-white in the darkness...
Drift under hulls in the night.
"In the gloom the gold
Gathers the light about it."

Napoleon decreed that it was unhygienic to bury bodies within a city. As a result, Venice's coffins were shipped out to San Michele, and since then, Venetians have been buried here. You'll find the dearly departed (often with their photos) sorted into sections of priests *(preti)*, nuns *(suore)*, monks *(frati)*, children *(bambini)*, civilian victims of war, soldiers, military sailors *(marinai)*, and so on.

Foreign Romantics and artists who made Venice their adopted hometown have also chosen this spot as their final resting place. To find the graves of the most famous foreigners, go straight

VENICE'S LAGOON

ahead from the entrance to the far end and follow the signs. In the Evangelico (Protestant) section lies Idaho-born poet Ezra Pound (to the left; using an imaginary clock as a compass, he's at about 10 o'clock from the Evangelico gate). His large plot is overgrown with shrubs that obscure the gravestone (for more on Pound, see the sidebar).

Ten yards from Pound's grave, find Nobel Laureate and onetime US Poet Laureate Joseph Brodsky (1940–1996), who was expected from Soviet Russia, lived the rest of his life in America, and asked to be buried here in Venice.

In the Greco (Orthodox) section, find Russian-born Modernist composer Igor Stravinsky (far right corner, alongside his wife) and the Russian dancer/choreographer Diaghalev (the canopied tomb along the far wall).

• *Catch the vaporetto (#41 or #42, both leave every 10 minutes) to the Murano-Colonna stop (5 minutes). While you're waiting, look for the blue funeral boat with a rack on wheels for the coffin. It's usually moored next to the vaporetto.*

As you approach the island of Murano, you'll see its ghostly lighthouse (faro). *In centuries past, the* faro *guided boats from the open sea into town.*

Murano

Murano is famous for its glass factories. A 1292 law restricted glass production (and its dangerous furnaces) to the isle of Murano to

prevent fires on the main island... and to protect the secrets of Venetian glassmaking. Originally, glassmakers made mosaic tiles, later branching out to produce the ornate vases, beaded necklaces, glass sculptures, and wine decanters you'll see here today.

While Murano seems dominated by the glassworks that line its main canal (and their respective showrooms), there's more to the island than glass. If you take time to wander, you'll find impressive churches, restaurants, and untouristed residential areas.

From the Colonna vaporetto stop, wander up "main street"— **Via Fondamenta Vetrai**—along the canal of the glassmakers. The canal/street is lined with factories *(fabriche)* and their furnaces *(fornaci)*. The brick buildings give the city a 19th-century, Industrial

Age look and feel.

Each **factory** offers a similar, usually free, 20-minute glassblowing demonstration of an artisan in action. He sticks a rod with raw glass on the end into a furnace, melts the glass, and expands it by blowing through the hollow rod. Then he shapes it with tongs into a vase, a glass, or a piece of art. This is followed by an almost comically high-pressure sales pitch in the showroom. (The spiel is brief, and there's absolutely no obligation to buy anything.) If you do buy something, see page 291 for tips on having a purchase shipped home.

The glassworks at #7—the first on the canal—is welcoming, and does a good glassblowing demonstration. Be sure to check out the venerable Venini shop, at #47, which shows off the ultimate in modern Venetian glass design.

Continue up Via Fondamenta Vetrai to the far (north) end of the canal, to the **Church of San Pietro Martire** (Mon–Sat 9:00–18:00, Sun 12:00–17:00). The

church features Giovanni Bellini's solid-color *Virgin Enthroned with Mark and a Kneeling Doge* (right wall of the nave in the center, see photo at top of next page). This votive painting—showing a doge being introduced to the Virgin Mary by St. Mark—was the doge's way of thanking Mary for

his position of power. The doge wears a luxurious ermine cloak (a symbol of royalty) and a ducal crown hat. The sacristy/museum (€1.50) has ornately carved caryatids (human pillars, c. 1660) with expressive faces and arms posed every which way. The carved panels between the caryatids depict scenes from the life of John the Baptist, culminating in his beheading in the far corner. In the next rooms, see ceremonial religious objects and statues, then check out the photos (midway up the steps) of these objects being used in modern-day Venetian parades. Upstairs are piles of relics in glass cases.

Exiting the church, look across the canal at the cute little **tower,** built as a fire lookout in this city of furnaces.

For a slice of **residential Murano,** circle counterclockwise around the back of the church and down Ramo da Mula street. In this old shell, there's a new vibrancy, as tourist-swamped Venice's high rents and real-estate prices drive locals to the outlying islands. Murano is a workaday community of 6,000 residents. It has real neighborhoods, with moms shopping at markets, schools filled with noisy children, bikes in the front yards, and benches warmed by Venetian old-timers. All of this gives Murano a "Venice without the tourism" charm.

At the Grand Canal of Murano, cross the big, green metal bridge and head right 150 yards for the **Glass Museum** (following signs for *Museo Vetrario*). While the display is musty and antiquated, it's well-described in English. The first room, on the lower level, shows ancient glass and glassmaking techniques in order to illustrate how Venice has carried on making the same colors and using the same techniques from its earlier days. Upstairs, on one floor, the museum displays the very best of 500 years of Venetian glassmaking (€6.50, covered by passes—see page 24, April–Oct Thu–Tue 10:00–18:00, Nov–March Thu–Tue 10:00–17:00, last entry 30 minutes before closing, tel. 041-739-586, www.museicivicivenezia.it).

One hundred yards farther along the canal is **Santa Maria e San Donato Church,** the architectural highlight of Murano (erratic opening hours). Before entering, note the fine Byzantine Romanesque exterior—especially the stonework of its apse, facing the canal. The interior takes you back to the 12th century. Built when St. Mark's Basilica was under construction, the highlights are its inlaid stone floor and the gorgeous mosaic above the altar. It features Mary as God's mother, gliding in from heaven on her carpet, blessing the faithful with two open hands. Her three stars symbolize her virginity: before, during, and after giving birth to Jesus.

A WWI monument lies at the base of the church's bell tower, and next to that, the Snack Bar Da Ice serves good salads and sandwiches.

When you're ready to leave Murano, return to the main street, and walk south along the other side. Turn left on Bressagio street, which takes you to the white-stone lighthouse *(faro)* and its Murano-Faro vaporetto dock.

• *To continue our tour, from Murano-Faro, catch the LN vaporetto to* **Burano** *(2/hour, 30 minutes).*

Or, if you want to head back to **Venice,** several *vaporetti* can take you there. The #42 returns to Fondamenta Nuove (by way of Murano-Colonna and San Michele) and continues on to San

Boating in Venice

Italian law stipulates that a luxury tax is levied on all boats—except in Venice, where they're considered a necessity.

Venetians go everywhere by boat. Calling a taxi? A boat comes. Going to the hospital to have a baby? Just hop on the vaporetto. Garbage day? You put your bag on the canal edge, and a garbage boat mashes it and takes it away.

Many residents own a boat, though it's not always practical for everyday activities. If you want to cruise to the grocery store, you first have to check the tide table to make sure your boat can fit beneath certain bridges. And parking is always a huge problem everywhere—either you know a friend nearby with a grandfathered parking space, or your partner has to "circle the block" while you shop.

Locals rely more on the public *vaporetti* and *traghetti*. While tourists pay plenty for these boats, Venetians ride cheap and easy. An all-year pass costs less than €1 a day.

Gondolas are strictly for tourists these days, but in earlier times, these flat-bottomed boats were the only way to negotiate the tricky, shallow lagoon. The oarsman had to stand up in the back of the boat to see oncoming sandbars. Today, boats ply confidently between the shifting sandbanks of the lagoon, thanks to thoroughfares defined by modern pilings.

While many Venetians own a car for driving on the isle of Lido or the mainland, they admit, "We're not very much beloved on the road."

Zaccaria, near St. Mark's Square. The #41 also goes to Fondamenta Nuove, but continues on around the other side of Venice, via the Ferrovia (train station) stop, before returning to San Zaccaria. The DM (Diretto Murano) vaporetto heads directly to the train station (after a quick loop around the island).

Burano

Burano has three vaporetto docks side-by-side (*vaporetti* in and out, and the shuttle to Torcello). Upon arrival, note departure times—most boats leave twice an hour.

Famous for its lace and picturesque pastel houses, Burano is a sleepy island with a sleepy community (pop. 2,700)—village Venice without the glitz. Its colorfully painted homes look like Venice before the plaster peeled off. Each adjoining townhouse is painted its own color. While Venice is a showy city of merchants,

Burano

TO TORCELLO
LINE T

To
SAN MARCO
VIA LIDO

Line LN

MAZZORBO

✓ VAPORETTO STOP

100 YARDS
100 METERS

SAN MAURO

LINE LN

TO
MURANO

TERRANOVA

F.S. MAURO

VIA B. GALUPPI

PITONA

POST

VIGNA

❶

F. TERRA

❷

FISH
MKT

WC

PIZZO

LAGOON

F. PIZZO

PARK

PIAZZA
GALUPPI

❶ Merletti d'Arte dalla Lidia
   Lace Shop & Museum

❷ Trattoria al Gatto Nero

DCH

SAN MARTINO CHURCH &
LEANING BELL TOWER

Burano is a humble town of fishermen. While Burano's main drag is mobbed with tourists by day, at night the island is quiet. Laundry

hangs over alleyways, and sunshades (typical of the area) cover the doors of residents' homes. The church's bell tower leans at a five-degree angle...the same as Pisa's.

This town's history is ancient, explained in part by its name. "Burano" comes from the Venetian word for "breeze"—and a breeze meant survival on the lagoon. It kept away the malaria-carrying mosquitoes that made other places (like Torcello) less habitable.

The island can be covered in a five-minute stroll. From the vaporetto dock, follow the crowds into the center. Turn left at the canal. A bridge leads to Piazza Galuppi, and beyond that—on the far side of the little island—is Burano's famous leaning church **bell tower.** The church has a fine, restored Tiepolo painting of the Crucifixion.

The main drag from the vaporetto stop into town is packed

with tourists and lined with shops, some of which sell Burano's locally produced white wine. Wander to the far side of the island, and the mood shifts. Explore to the right of the leaning tower for a peaceful yet intensely pastel, small-town lagoon world. Benches lining a little promenade at the water's edge make another pretty picnic spot.

Most tourists visit Burano for its lace, and they're not disappointed. Lace is cheaper in Burano than in Venice, and serious

shoppers should comparison-shop in Venice before visiting Burano. Of the many lace shops, I like **Merletti d'Arte dalla Lidia** for its fine private museum (in the rear of the shop and upstairs). Paola, who speaks English, gives visitors a warm welcome as she shows off the masterpieces of lace from all over Europe. Ask her for

a magnifying glass to marvel at the intricate knots, and be sure to go upstairs (daily 9:30–18:00, just off the big square opposite the leaning tower at Via Galuppi 215, tel. 041-730-052).

For a picnic, the park next to Burano's only vaporetto dock is hard to beat. And you'll find plenty of touristy eateries on Burano, all enthusiastic about their fish. While you have plenty of options for a quick bite, if you want to dine, consider **Trattoria al Gatto Nero.** They serve good traditional dishes outside overlooking the peaceful canal, or in the dressy interior (€15 pastas, €20 *secondi*, closed Mon, crisp service, 3-minute walk from the ferry dock and from the thriving main tourist drag at Via Giudecca 88, tel. 041-730-120).

• *To reach our tour's next stop,* **Torcello,** *take the shuttle boat (Line T) that runs on the hour and the half-hour back and forth (five-minute trip). (If you want to skip Torcello and head right back to* **Venice,** *see the very end of this chapter.)*

Torcello

This is the birthplace of Venice, where the first mainland refugees settled, escaping the barbarian hordes. Yet today, it's the least-developed island (pop. 20) in its most natural state, marshy and shrub-covered. There's little for tourists to see except the church (a 10-minute walk from the dock), which claims to be the oldest in Venice and has impressive mosaics.

From the vaporetto dock, walk through a salty landscape and think of the original inhabitants. Romanized farmers came here, escaping the Germanic barbarians who started streaming through the mainland in the fifth century. By the 11th century, the teeny island had 11 churches. But one look around tells you that this place was inhospitable—the farming was poor, there was no fresh water, and mosquitoes and malaria were big problems. Even though residents diverted the flow of mainland rivers, the lagoon silted up around them anyway, and the island was slowly abandoned.

Approaching the church, you'll pass by the remote yet fancy **Locanda Cipriani Hotel** next door. With just five rooms, it's hosted Thomas Mann, Queen Elizabeth II, and Princess Diana. The hotel has a delightful garden that's (kind of) open to the public.

The **Santa Maria Assunta Church** complex consists of four sights: the church itself, the bell tower (behind the church, climb a  ramped stairway for great lagoon views), a sacristy, and a small museum (facing the church, in two separate buildings) that displays Roman sculpture and medieval sculpture and manuscripts. Tickets cost €3 for any one sight, or €10 for all sights, including an audioguide (most open daily March–Oct 10:30–17:30, Nov–Feb 10:00–17:00, museum closed Mon, last entry 30–60 minutes before closing, museum tel. 041-730-761, church/bell tower tel. 041-730-119). There's a pay WC between the museum's two buildings.

The ruins in front of the church used to be a baptistery from the ninth century; in those days when you couldn't enter a church until you were baptized.

Inside the church, the brick walls and wood-beam ceiling are classic Venetian building materials—that is, flexible—to accommodate the ever-shifting sands underneath. The altar has the relics of St. Heliodorus (d. 390), a local-born bishop who was the travel partner of the famed St. Jerome on a trip to the Holy Land. The columns of the rood screen (separating the altar area from the congregation) were obviously scavenged from elsewhere—note the variety of capitals. You can see a bit of the church's original black-and-white mosaic floor (ninth century) under a small glassed-over section on the right side of the nave. In the 12th century, flooding forced them to rebuild 12 inches higher. The apse mosaic (over the altar) shows Mary and baby Jesus above and the 12 apostles below. In the right apse, with its sumptuous vault, find Christ Pantocrator,

More Transportation Options

If you'd like to tailor your trip, you have a number of ways to get around the lagoon: cheap public *vaporetti*, private paid speedboat tours, or free boats that come with a sales pitch. All of these boats travel at roughly the same pace, since even speedboats must obey strict speed limits designed to reduce boat wakes.

By Speedboat Tour: The easiest—and priciest—way to see Murano, Burano, and Torcello is to pay €20 for a rushed and touristy 3- to 5-hour speedboat tour. They leave twice a day in summer from the San Marco-Giardinetti dock; look and listen for guides calling out for potential passengers (€20, April–Oct usually at 9:30 and 14:30, Nov–March at 14:00 only, tel. 041-240-1711). The tours are speedy indeed—live guides race through the commentary in up to five languages—and boats stop for roughly 40 minutes at each island. The stops are for glassblowing and lacemaking demonstrations followed by sales spiels, leaving no time left to explore on your own.

A Free Ride with a Sales Pitch: You can get to Murano for free on a speedboat shuttle (a 35-minute trip from St. Mark's). Tourists are practically kidnapped from St. Mark's Square by the aggressive sales reps who approach them. Your only obligation is to sit through a fairly interesting 20-minute glassmaking demonstration and sales pitch. After that, there's no obligation to actually buy, and then you're on your own. (In fact, they don't promise you a trip back to Venice.)

Other Vaporetto Options: A handful of different *vaporetti* ply the four islands. Lines #41 and #42 go between Venice (Fondamenta Nuove or San Zaccaria-Jolanda, near St. Mark's Square) and Murano, with a stop at San Michele (Cimitero stop). Which boat is best depends on your exact itinerary: Ask at the dock you're leaving from. If Burano is your chief destination, take the LN, which travels between Burano and the San  Zaccaria-Pietà dock near St. Mark's Square (70 minutes). It also connects Burano and Fondamenta Nuove (via Murano, 45 minutes). The DM (Diretto Murano) vaporetto connects Murano directly with the train station and Piazzale Roma, but doesn't stop at the cemetery. Finally, the tiny T connects Burano with Torcello.

Take your choice of boats, or just follow along the tour I've laid out in this chapter.

ruler of all, flanked by archangels Michael and Gabriel. On the ceiling, Christ is represented by the sacrificial lamb.

The mosaic on the back wall is famous. Six horizontal bands depict the Last Judgment (and other scenes). From top to bottom, see:

1. The Crucifixion.

2. A striding Christ pulling a soul out from Limbo while stepping on a devil.

3. Christ, in an almond-shaped bubble, as the Creator, flanked by souls in Paradise. From the bottom of the bubble pours a river of fire, which runs down the wall to hell.

4. Angels preparing the Throne of Judgment—empty except for a book. Note Adam and Eve kneeling below.

5 and 6. Archangel Michael (over the door) weighing souls on a scale, while mischievous devils try to tip the scales in their favor.

On the right are the fires of hell, where sinners—many of them turbaned Muslims—are tormented by black-skinned demons. A crude display of the seven deadly sins appears at the lower right: pride (crowned heads in flames), lust (bodies in flames), gluttony (guys eating even their fingers), envy (skulls with worms eating out their coveting eyes), greed (fancy earrings), laziness (useless hands and cut-off feet), and anger (a man waist-deep in cold water to cool down).

• *Avoid the eighth deadly sin—missing your vaporetto—by allowing at least 10 minutes to get from the church back to the boat dock. Boats generally depart at :15 and :45 past the hour. Your quickest way back to Venice is to return to Burano (5 minutes), and from there, catch one of two LN vaporetti back to Venice. One LN line sails from Burano to Lido (via Punta Sabbioni on the island of Sant'Erasmo) and then St. Mark's Square (at the San Zaccaria-Pietà dock). It's slow (70 minutes to St. Mark's) and leaves only once an hour, but is often a big double-decker boat, and by taking it you get a fine lagoon cruise experience. The other LN line leaves twice an hour (at :26 and :56) and gets you back to Venice faster (45 minutes from Burano to Fondamenta Nuove via Murano-Faro), but ultimately takes just as long to get you back to St. Mark's Square (change at Fondamenta Nuove for #42 vaporetto to San Zaccaria).*

ST. MARK'S TO RIALTO WALK

Two rights and a left (simple!) can get you from St. Mark's Square to the Rialto Bridge via a completely different route from the one most tourists take. Along the way, take in some lesser sights in the area west of St. Mark's Square. You finish where many fish do—at the market.

Orientation

Length of This Walk: Allow one hour for a leisurely walk (30 minutes with no stops).

San Moisè Church: Free, Mon–Sat 9:30–12:30, Sun Mass only at 11:00, tel. 041-296-0630.

La Fenice Opera House: €7, includes 45-minute audioguide, generally open daily 10:00–19:30, but the schedule varies greatly depending on rehearsal and performance schedules (concert box office open daily 9:30–18:30, call center open daily 7:30–20:00, tel. 041-2424, www.teatrolafenice.it).

Scala Contarini del Bovolo: It's viewable for free any time from the outside. However, it can't currently be climbed, as the tower is closed for renovation. It's scheduled to reopen in 2012.

Rialto Market: The souvenir stalls are open daily; the produce market is closed on Sunday and Monday; and the fish market is closed on Sunday. The market is lively only in the morning.

Overview

There are actually three easy routes from St. Mark's Square to Rialto:

1. Along the crowded Mercerie (follow the tourists underneath the Clock Tower).

2. A straight shot on Calle dei Fabbri (exit St. Mark's Square next to Gran Caffè Quadri).

3. The slightly longer but more interesting route described in this chapter.

The Walk Begins

Start at St. Mark's Square

• *From the square, walk to the waterfront and turn right. You're walking on recently raised Venice—in 2006, the stones were taken up and six inches of extra sand put down, to minimize flooding. Continue along the water toward the white TI pavilion.*

Along the waterfront, you'll see the various boats that ply Venice's waters. The gondolas here are often more expensive than

elsewhere. Water taxis, in classic wooden motorboats, are pricey (about €60 from here to the train station), but they are a classy splurge if you can split the fare with four others. Hotel shuttle boats bring guests from distant, $700-a-night hotels.

Run the gauntlet of souvenir stands to the entrance to the gardens. The Giardinetti Reali (Royal Gardens) offers some precious greenery in a city built of stone on mud. Nearby are €1.50 WCs, a TI in a cute 18th-century former coffeehouse pavilion, and public pay phones where you can call home just to tell everyone where you are right now. From atop the bridge by the TI, look across the mouth of the Grand Canal to view the big dome of La Salute Church, and the guy balancing a bronze ball on one foot—the old Customs House, which is now a contemporary art museum (the Punta della Dogana, described on page 48).

• *Twelve steps down and 20 yards ahead on the right is...*

❶ Harry's American Bar

Hemingway put this bar on the map by making it his hangout in the late 1940s. If Brad and Angelina are in town, this is where they'll be. If they're not, you'll see plenty of dressed-up Americans looking around for celebrities. The discreet (and overpriced) restaurant upstairs is where the glitterati hang out. The street-level bar is for gawkers. If you wear something a bit fancy (or artsy bohemian), you can pull up a stool at the tiny bar by the entrance and pay too much for a Bellini (Prosecco and peach juice), which was invented right here.

• *Head inland down Calle Vallaresso, one of Venice's most exclusive*

*streets, past fancy boutiques such as Pucci, Gucci, and Roberto Cavalli.
At the T intersection, turn left and head west on Salizada S. Moisè
(which becomes Calle Larga XXII Marzo). You'll pass the fine
Mondadori Bookstore, then continue to the first bridge and a square
dominated by the fancy facade of a church. Climb the bridge, and against
a soundtrack of tourists negotiating with hustling gondoliers, look back
at the ornate...*

❷ San Moisè Church

This is the parish church for St Mark's; because of tourist crowds at
the basilica, this is where the community actually worships. While
it's one of Venice's oldest churches, dat-
ing from the 10th century (note the old
tower on the right), its busy facade is
17th-century Baroque. This was an age
when big shots who funded such projects expected to see their faces featured
(see the bust of Mr. Fini in the center).
Moses *(Moisè)* caps the facade.

Inside, the altarpiece depicts
Mount Sinai, with Moses (kneeling)
receiving the two tablets with the Ten
Commandments. The alcove to the
left of the altar has Tintoretto's *Christ
Washing the Disciples' Feet.*

The ugly modern building on the right marks the former
Venice headquarters of the Nazis during World War II. Its fascist
facade still gives locals the Mussolini-creeps. Now a five-star hotel,
it's one of the few modern buildings in town.

• *Continue past the bridge, down Calle Larga XXII Marzo, a big
street that seems too wide and large for Venice. It was created during
the 19th century by filling in a canal. You can make out the outline of
the sidewalks that once flanked the now-gone canal. Pass by the Vivaldi
look-alikes selling concert tickets and immigrants selling knockoffs of
Prada bags.*

*Halfway down the street, turn right on tiny Calle del Sartor da
Veste. Go straight, crossing a bridge, and passing the* **Matteo lo Greco
Studio** *(❸ on map), with his plump people in bronze celebrating life
with a lighter-than-air joy. Then, at the next square, you'll find...*

❹ La Fenice Opera House
(Gran Teatro alla Fenice)

Venice's famed opera house, built in 1792 (read the MDCCXCII
on the facade), was reduced to a hollowed-out shell by a disastrous fire in 1996. After a vigorous restoration campaign, "The
Phoenix"—true to its name—has risen again from the ashes. La

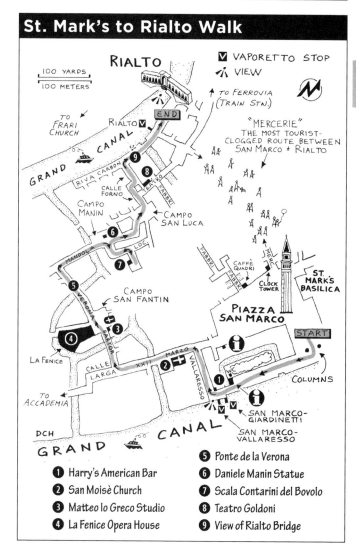

St. Mark's to Rialto Walk

☑ VAPORETTO STOP
⚲ VIEW

100 YARDS
100 METERS

RIALTO
↑ TO FERROVIA (TRAIN STN.)

"MERCERIE"
THE MOST TOURIST-CLOGGED ROUTE BETWEEN SAN MARCO & RIALTO

TO FRARI CHURCH

RIALTO ☑

GRAND CANAL

END

RIVA CARBON

CALLE FORNO

CAMPO MANIN

CAMPO SAN LUCA

CALLE FABBRI

❾

❽

❻

❼

LOC

MANDOLA

❺

VERONA

CAMPO SAN FANTIN

CAFFÈ QUADRI

FABBRI

MERC

CLOCK TOWER

ST. MARK'S BASILICA

PIAZZA SAN MARCO

❸

❹

LA FENICE

CALLE LARGA

XXII MARZO

VALLARESSO

❷

START

ℹ

WC

ℹ

COLUMNS

TO ACCADEMIA

DCH

GRAND CANAL

☑

SAN MARCO-GIARDINETTI

SAN MARCO-VALLARESSO

❶ Harry's American Bar
❷ San Moisè Church
❸ Matteo lo Greco Studio
❹ La Fenice Opera House
❺ Ponte de la Verona
❻ Daniele Manin Statue
❼ Scala Contarini del Bovolo
❽ Teatro Goldoni
❾ View of Rialto Bridge

Fenice resumed opera productions in 2004, opening with *La Traviata*. The theater is usually open daily to the public (for information, see beginning of this chapter).

Venice is one of the cradles of the art form known as opera. An opera is a sung play and a multimedia event, blending music, words, story, costume, and set design. Some of the great operas were first performed here in this luxurious setting. Verdi's *Rigoletto* (1851) and *La Traviata* (1853) were actually commissioned by La Fenice. The man who put words to Mozart's tunes was a Venetian who drew inspiration from the city's libertine ways and joie de vivre. In recent years, La Fenice's musical reputation was overshadowed by its reputation as a place for the wealthy to parade in furs and jewels.

• *Continue north along the same street (though its name is now Calle de La Verona), to a small bridge over a quiet canal.*

❺ Ponte de la Verona

Pause atop this bridge, with reflections that can make you wonder which end is up. Looking above you, see bridges of stone prop-

ping up leaning buildings, and there's a view of the "Leaning Tower" of Santo Stefano.

People actually live in Venice. See their rooftop gardens, their laundry, their plumbing, electricity lines snaking into their apartments, and the rusted iron bars and bolts that hold their crumbling homes together. On one building, find centuries-old relief carvings—a bearded face and a panel of an eagle with its prey.

While many Venetians own (and love) their own boat, parking a boat is a huge problem. Getting a spot is tough, and when you finally find one, it's very expensive and rarely near your apartment. (For more on boating in Venice, see page 206.) People once swam freely in the canals. Find the sign that reads *Divieto di Nuoto* ("swimming not allowed").

• *Continue north. At the T intersection, you reach a main thoroughfare connecting the Accademia (left) and St. Mark's Square (right). Turn right on Calle de la Mandola. You'll cross over a bridge into a spacious square dominated by a statue and an out-of-place modern building.*

❻ Campo Manin

The centerpiece of the square is **a statue of Daniele Manin** (1804–1857), Venice's fiery leader in the battle for freedom from Austria and eventually a united Italy (the Risorgimento). The statue faces the red house he lived in. Chafing under Austrian rule, the Venetians rose up. The Austrians laid siege to the city (1848–1849) and bombed it into surrender. Manin was banished and spent his final years in Paris, still proudly drumming up support for modern Italy. In a rare honor, he's buried in St. Mark's Basilica.

• *Scala Contarini del Bovolo is a block south of here, with yellow signs pointing the way. Facing the Manin statue, turn right and exit the square down an alley. Follow yellow signs to the left, then immediately to the right, into a courtyard with one of Venice's hidden treasures...*

❼ Scala Contarini del Bovolo

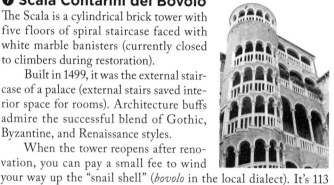

The Scala is a cylindrical brick tower with five floors of spiral staircase faced with white marble banisters (currently closed to climbers during restoration).

Built in 1499, it was the external staircase of a palace (external stairs saved interior space for rooms). Architecture buffs admire the successful blend of Gothic, Byzantine, and Renaissance styles.

When the tower reopens after renovation, you can pay a small fee to wind your way up the "snail shell" (*bovolo* in the local dialect). It's 113

steps to the top, where you're rewarded with views of the Venetian skyline.

• *Return to the Manin statue. Continue east, circling around the big Cassa di Risparmio bank, marveling at its Modernist ugliness. At Campo San Luca, turn left (north) on Calle del Forno. Note the* 24-hour pharmacy vending machine that dispenses shower gel, Band-Aids, bug repellant, toothbrushes, toothpaste, condoms, and other after-hours necessities. Heading north, glance 20 yards down the street to the right at the flag-bedecked...

❽ Teatro Goldoni

Though this theater looks modern, it dates from the 1500s, when Venice was at the forefront of secular entertainment. Many of Carlo Goldoni's (1707–1793) groundbreaking comedies got their first performance here, and the theater was renamed in his honor. It's still a working theater of mainly Italian productions.

• *Continue north on Calle del Forno. You're very close to the Grand Canal. Keep going north, jogging to the right at the small square, then left down a teeny-tiny alleyway. Pop! You emerge on the Grand Canal, about 150 yards downstream from the...*

❾ Rialto Bridge

Of Venice's more than 400 bridges, only five cross the Grand Canal. Rialto was the first among these five.

The original Rialto Bridge, dating from 1180, was a platform supported by boats tied together. It linked the political side (Palazzo Ducale) of Venice with the economic center (Rialto). Rialto, which takes its name from *riva alto* (high bank), was one of the earliest Venetian settlements. When Venice was Europe's economic superpower, this  was where bankers, brokers, and merchants conducted their daily business.

Rialto Bridge II was a 13th-century wooden drawbridge. It was replaced in 1588 by the current structure, with its bold single arch (spanning 160 feet) and arcades on top designed to strengthen the stone bridge. Its immense foundations stretch 650 feet on either side. Heavy buildings were then built atop the foundations to hold everything in place. The Rialto remained the only bridge crossing the Grand Canal until 1854.

Reliefs of the Venetian Republic's main mascots, St. Mark and St. Theodore, crown the arch. Barges and *vaporetti* run the busy waterways below, and merchants vie for tourists' attention on top.

The Rialto has long been a symbol of Venice. Aristocratic inhabitants built magnificent palaces just to be near it. The poetic Lord Byron swam to it all the way from Lido Island. And thousands of marriage proposals have been sealed right here, with a kiss, as the moon floated over *La Serenissima*.

• *From here, you can return to St. Mark's Square, or walk over the bridge into the fish market—following my Rialto to Frari Church Walk (next chapter).*

RIALTO TO FRARI CHURCH WALK

Cross the Rialto Bridge, and dive headlong into Venice's thriving market area. The area west of the Grand Canal is less touristy—the place where "real" Venetians live. This 20-minute walk is the most direct route from the Rialto Bridge to the Frari Church and Scuola San Rocco. This chapter is less a collection of sights than it is a tour of the Rialto market area, followed by a convenient, easy-to-follow route through the San Polo area. After exploring the lively produce and stinky fish markets, you'll see pubs and squares that are at least a bit off the tourist path.

Orientation

Length of This Walk: Allow about one hour.

When to Go: The markets are lively only in the morning. The produce market is closed on Monday, and both markets (produce and fish) are closed on Sunday.

Church of San Polo: €3, Mon–Sat 10:00–17:00, closed Sun, last entry 15 minutes before closing.

"Tragicomica" Mask Shop: Daily 10:00–19:00, tel. 041-721-102.

Eateries: Many pubs and restaurants in the Rialto area are recommended in the Eating in Venice chapter.

Overview

- Head west from the Rialto Bridge one long block, and explore the colorful Rialto produce market and nearby fish market.
- When you're ready to move on, head down Ruga Vecchia San Giovanni. Walk southwest along the Ruga (paralleling the Grand Canal) about a quarter-mile to spacious Campo San Polo.
- From Campo San Polo, continue southwest another 200

Rialto to Frari Church Walk

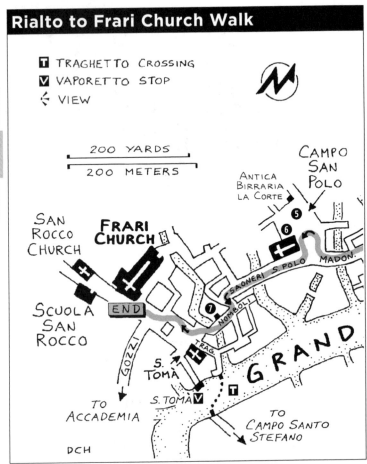

T TRAGHETTO CROSSING
V VAPORETTO STOP
↢ VIEW

200 YARDS
200 METERS

CAMPO SAN POLO

ANTICA BIRRARIA LA CORTE

SAN ROCCO CHURCH

FRARI CHURCH

SCUOLA SAN ROCCO

END

SAONERI S. POLO MADON

NOMBOLI

GOZZI

S. TOMA

TRAG.

S. TOMA V

T

G R A N D

TO ACCADEMIA

TO CAMPO SANTO STEFANO

DCH

yards, then jog left, then right, where you'll see *Scuola Grande di San Rocco* signs pointing you to the Scuola San Rocco and the Frari Church next door.

The Walk Begins

• *From the top of the Rialto Bridge, walk (away from the St. Mark's side) about fifty yards until you see an old square on your right. Go to its fountain.*

❶ Campo San Giacometto

This square, named for the church that faces it, looks today much like it did in the 16th century. The buildings lining the square are High Renaissance, mostly built after a 1514 fire devastated this

TO FERROVIA (TRAIN STN.)

TO FERROVIA (TRAIN STN.)

CAMPO BECC

CASARIA

SPEZIALI

RIALTO MERCATO

CICCHETI BAR AREA

S. APONAL

RUGA VECC.

START

POST

OLIO RAVANO S. GIOV

S. SILV.

FOND. DEL VIN

RIALTO

MEL.

S. SILV.

CANAL

RIALTO

↓ TO SAN MARCO

❶ Campo San Giacometto
❷ Produce Market
❸ Fish Market
❹ The Ruga
❺ Campo San Polo
❻ Church of San Polo
❼ "Tragicomica" Mask Shop

area. Find the MDXX date on the arcade: It was built in 1520. Only the church predates that fire. The square is designed to col-

lect rainwater and store it in a cistern that once fed this fountain (for more on this system, see page 48).

Back when the Rialto Bridge was a drawbridge (until the 1590s), big ships would dock alongside this historic market. Imagine the commotion as ships tied up to load and unload their spices, oil, wine, and jewels. The line of buildings between Campo San Giacometto and the canal was once a strip of banks. It's still called Bancogiro, which means the place where letters of credit were endorsed. Back when carrying cash meant carrying gold and silver—heavy and dangerous—letters of credit were a godsend. Behind today's trashy jewelry stands are real jewelry shops. In fact, the street across from the market has been called "Street of Jewelers" for over 500 years.

Opposite the church, a hunchback supports steps leading to a

column. Until the 1550s, when a financial crisis knocked it for an economic loop, Venice was Europe's trading capital. You could call this neighborhood the "Wall Street of medieval Europe." In those days, this column was the closest thing they had to a *Wall Street Journal.* This was where the daily news from the doge was read aloud each noon: which ships had docked, which foreign ambassadors were in town, the price of pepper, and so on. Behind the hunchback, the lane called Calle de la Sicurtà is named for the maritime insurance companies that once did business here.

The church facade is one of the oldest in town. Back before clocks had minute hands (like this church's), its porch was a shelter for the poor. St. James the Minor, for whom the church is named, looked out on the business community, encouraging honesty in a time when banking regulations were non-existent.

Walk along the canal side of the church. The huge building behind the church

was and still is the city's fiscal administration building. Notice how the building tilts out (probably because the bridge's huge foundation is compressing the mud beneath it).

Now walk along the canal to a little canalside dead-end that's as close as you can get to the Rialto Bridge. Take in the great view of the bridge. The former post office (directly across from you) was originally the German merchants' hall (see the seal). It's about to be reincarnated as a Benetton-owned shopping center.

You're standing under a former prison. Study the iron grills over the windows. Notice the interlocking pipes with alternating joints—you can't cut just one and escape.

• *From the prison, walk back along the canal. Ahead of you are today's central criminal courts. Your canalside path is blocked by modern black bars, which herd local criminals from police boats into the courts. Walk around the court building and into a square called Casaria (named for the historic cheese market). Today, this is Venice's...*

❷ Produce Market (Erberia)

Colorful stalls offer fresh fruit and vegetables, some quite exotic. Nothing is grown on the island of Venice, so everything is shipped

in daily from the mainland. The Mercato Rialto vaporetto stop is a convenient place for boats to unload their wares, here in the heart of fish-shaped Venice. At #205, the shop called Macelleria Equina sells horse and donkey *(asino)* meat. Continue along the canal, exploring all the produce stalls.

RIALTO TO FRARI CHURCH

• *Follow your nose to Campo de la Pescaria, the open-air arcade that houses the...*

❸ Fish Market (Pescheria)

This is especially vibrant and colorful in the morning. The open-air stalls have the catch of the day—Venice's culinary specialty. Find eels, scallops, crustaceans with five-inch antennae, and squid destined for tonight's risotto soaking in their own ink. This is the Venice that has existed for centuries: Workers toss boxes of fish from delivery boats while shoppers step from the *traghetto* (gon-

dola shuttle) into the action. It's a good peek at workaday Venice. Shoppers are exacting and expect to know if the fish is fresh or frozen, farmed or wild. Local fish are small and considered particularly tasty because of the high concentration of salt at this end of the Adriatic. It's not unusual to pay €30 per kilo (about 2.2 pounds) for the best fish.

Locate a white Istrian stone on a wall between the two arcades. It lists the minimum length permitted for a fish to be sold. Sardines must be seven centimeters; *peocio* (mussels) must be three centimeters. (Below that, someone has added a penis joke: *El Mio 3.7 cm*..."Mine's two inches").

Behind the fish market is Campo de la Beccarie (Butchers' Square). Within 40 yards of here (find Calle delle Do Spade) are several of my favorite local bars serving the Venetian version of tapas, *cicchetti*. If it's lunchtime, consider dropping by a few of these for a mobile feast: Cantina Do Mori, Bar all'Arco, Ostaria ai Storti, and Cantina Do Spade (for descriptions, see page 271).

And, if the market has you ready for a fishy nibble, drop by the hole-in-the-wall Pesce Pronto for tasty fish hors d'oeuvres (Calle de le Beccarie o Panataria 319; see listing on page 273).

From here, follow Ruga degli Speziali (Spice Road) back toward Rialto. Along the way, pop into Antica Drogheria Mascari, which hides a vast enoteca holding 600 different Italian wines arranged by region, plus spices and lots of gifty edibles.

• *Ruga degli Speziali eventually leads to Ruga Vecchia San Giovanni, which runs parallel to the canal. Turn right and follow the crowds.*

❹ The Ruga

This busy street is lined with shops that get progressively less touristy and more practical. As you walk, you'll see fewer trinkets and more clothes, bread, shoes, watches, shampoo, and underwear.

• *The Ruga changes names as you go—from Ruga to Calle, and so on. Just keep heading southwest. When in doubt, follow signs pointing to* Ferrovia *(train station).*

❺ Campo San Polo

One of the largest squares in Venice, Campo San Polo is shaped  like an amphitheater, with its church tucked away in the corner (just ahead of you). Antica Birraria la Corte, a fine and family-friendly pizzeria/ristorante, is located at the far side (see listing on page 274). The square's amphitheater shape was determined by a curved canal at the base of the buildings. Today, the former canal is now a *rio terra*—a street made of landfill. There are a few rare trees in the square, and rare benches occupied by grateful locals. In the summer, bleachers and a screen are erected for open-air movies, a true *Cinema Paradiso* experience.

• *On the square is the...*

❻ Church of San Polo (S. Polo Apostolo)

This church is one of the oldest in Venice, dating from the ninth century (€3, English description at ticket desk). The wooden boat-shaped ceiling recalls the earliest basilicas built after Rome's fall. While the church is skippable for many, art enthusiasts visit to see Tintoretto's *Last Supper*, G. B. Tiepolo's *Virgin Appearing to St. John of Nepomuk* and *Stations of the Cross*, and Veronese's *Betrothal of the Virgin with Angels.*

• *From the Church of San Polo, continue about 200 yards (following* Ferrovia *signs). Jog left when you have to, then right, onto Calle dei Nomboli. On the right, directly across the alley from the Casa Goldoni museum, you'll see the...*

❼ "Tragicomica" Mask Shop

One of Venice's best mask stores, this is also a workshop that offers a glimpse into the process of mask-making. Venice's masks

have always been a central feature of the celebration of Carnevale—the local pre-Lent, Mardi Gras–like blowout. (The translation of Carnevale is "goodbye to meat," referring to the lean days of Lent.) You'll see Walter and Alessandra hard at work.

Many masks are patterned after standard characters of the theater style known as commedia dell'arte: the famous trickster Harlequin, the beautiful and cunning Columbina, the country bumpkin Pulcinella (who later evolved into the wife-beating "Punch" of marionette shows), and the solemn, long-nosed Doctor *(dottore).*

• *Continuing along, cross the bridge and veer right. You'll soon see purple signs directing you to* Scuola Grande di San Rocco. *Follow these until you bump into the back end of the Frari Church, with Scuola San Rocco next door.*

❖ See the Frari Church Tour chapter; also see the Scuola San Rocco Tour chapter.

ST. MARK'S TO SAN ZACCARIA WALK

San Zaccaria, one of the oldest churches in Venice, is just a few minutes on foot from St. Mark's Square. The church features a Bellini altarpiece, and a submerged crypt that might be the oldest place in Venice. This short walk gets you away from (some of) the bustle of St. Mark's, includes a stroll along the waterfront, and brings you right back to where you started.

Orientation

Length of This Walk: Allow about an hour for a leisurely walk (though the actual distance is short).

Church of San Zaccaria: Free, Mon–Sat 10:00–12:00 & 16:00–18:00, Sun 16:00–18:00. Mass is held Mon–Sat at 18:30, and Sun at 10:00 and 12:00. Admission to the crypt costs €1. A €0.50 coin illuminates Bellini's altarpiece.

The Walk Begins

❶ Start at St. Mark's— Piazzetta dei Leoncini

Facing St. Mark's Basilica, start in the small square to the left of the church (Piazzetta dei Leoncini), with the 18th-century stone lions that kids love to sit on. The white building at the east end of the square houses the offices of Venice's "patriarch," the special title given to the local bishop (see the yellow-and-white Vatican flag). In the 1950s, this is where the future Pope John XXIII presided as Venice's patriarch and cardinal.

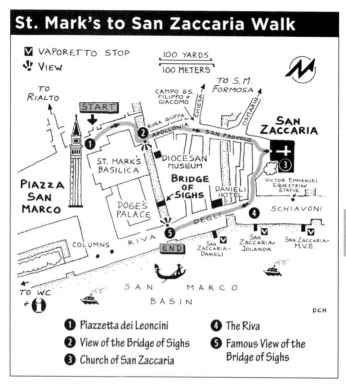

St. Mark's to San Zaccaria Walk

☑ VAPORETTO STOP
⚜ VIEW

100 YARDS
100 METERS

TO RIALTO

START

TO S.M. FORMOSA

CAMPO S.S. FILIPPO & GIACOMO

CHIESA

RUGA GIUFFA

APOLLONIA

OSMARIN

SAN PROVOLO

SAN ZACCARIA

ST. MARK'S BASILICA

DIOCESAN MUSEUM

PIAZZA SAN MARCO

BRIDGE OF SIGHS

DOGE'S PALACE

DANIELI HOTEL

VICTOR EMMANUEL EQUESTRIAN STATUE

SCHIAVONI

COLUMNS

RIVA

DEGLI

END

SAN ZACCARIA-DANIELI

SAN ZACCARIA-JOLANDA

SAN ZACCARIA-M.V.E.

TO WC

SAN MARCO BASIN

DCH

1 Piazzetta dei Leoncini
2 View of the Bridge of Sighs
3 Church of San Zaccaria
4 The Riva
5 Famous View of the Bridge of Sighs

ST. MARK'S TO SAN ZACCARIA

The popular, warm-hearted bishop went on to become the "Sixties Pope," who oversaw major reforms in the Catholic Church. You'll see a plaque dedicated to "Papa Giovanni XXIII" on the building to the left of the basilica.

• *Head east along Calle de la Canonica, circling behind the basilica. You'll reach a bridge with a...*

❷ View of the Bridge of Sighs

This lesser-known view of the Bridge of Sighs (probably behind scaffolding when you visit) also lets you see the tourists who are ogling it, with cameras cocked.

On the near side of the bridge is a common sight in neighborhood Venice: a street-side altarpiece and donation box. As the street signs tell you, the bridge you're on marks the boundary between two traditional neighborhoods, the *sestiere* (district) of San Marco and that of Castello. Throughout this walk, you'll pass relics of a fast-fading era: newspaper stands, public telephones, and a 24-hour cigarette vending machine.

• *Continue east. You'll cross another bridge with a view of a "Modern Bridge of Sighs," which connects two wings of the exclusive Danieli Hotel. Continue east another 50 yards, through the former gate of a cloistered Benedictine convent, until you run into the...*

❸ Church of San Zaccaria

Back in the ninth century, when Venice was just a collection of wooden houses and before there was a St. Mark's Basilica, a stone church and convent stood here. This is where the doges worshipped, public spectacles occurred, and sacred relics were kept. Today's structure dates mostly from the 15th century.

The tall facade by Mauro Codussi (who also did the Clock Tower in St. Mark's Square) is early Renaissance. The "vertical" effect produced by the four support pillars that rise up to an arched crown is tempered by the horizontal, many-layered stories and curved shoulders.

In the northwest corner of Campo San Zaccaria (near where you entered) is a plaque from 1620 listing all the things that were prohibited "in this square" *(in questo campo),* including games, obscenities, dishonesty, and robbery, all "under grave penalty" *(sotto gravis pene).*

• *Enter the church. The second chapel on the right holds the...*

Body of Zechariah (S. Zaccaria, Patris S. Jo: Baptista)

Of the two bodies in the chapel, the upper one in the glass case

(supported by stone angels) is the reputed body of Zechariah, the father of John the Baptist. Back when mortal remains were venerated and thought to bring miracles to the faithful, Venice was proud to own the bones of St. Zechariah ("San Zaccaria," also known as Zacharias).

• *The church is virtually wall-papered with art. On the opposite side of the nave (second chapel on the left), you'll find...*

Giovanni Bellini—*Madonna and Child with Saints* (*Sacra Conversazione,* 1505)

Mary and the baby, under a pavilion, are surrounded by various saints engaged in a so-called "holy conversation," which in this painting is more like a quiet meditation. The saints' mood is melancholy, with lidded eyes and downturned faces. A violinist angel plays a sad solo at Mary's feet.

This is one of the last of Bellini's paintings in the *sacra conversazione* formula. Compare this to his other variations on this theme in the Accademia (see page 133) and Frari Church (see page 146). The life-size saints stand in an imaginary extension of the church—the pavilion's columns match those of the real church. We see a glimpse of trees and a cloudy sky beyond. He establishes a 3-D effect using floor tiles. The four saints pose symmetrically, and there's a harmony in the big blocks of richly colored robes—blue, green, red, white, and yellow. A cool white light envelops the whole scene, casting no dark shadows.

The 75-year-old Bellini was innovative and productive until the end of his long life. The German artist Albrecht Dürer said of him: "He is very old, and still he is the best painter of them all."

• *On the right-hand side of the nave is the entrance (€1 entry fee) to...*

The Crypt

Before you descend into the crypt, the first room (Chapel of the Choir) contains **Tintoretto's *Birth of John the Baptist*** (on the altar), which tells the back-story of Zechariah. In the background, old Zechariah's wife Elizabeth props herself up in bed while nurses hold and coo over her newborn son, little John the Baptist. The birth was a miracle, as she was past childbearing age. On the far right, Zechariah—the star of this church—witnesses the heavens opening up, bringing this miracle to earth.

The five **gold thrones** (displayed in this room or one of the next rooms) were once seats for doges. Every Easter, the current doge would walk from St. Mark's Square to this religious center and thank the nuns of San Zaccaria for giving the land for the square.

The small next room contains religious objects, as well as an engraving of the doge parading into Campo San Zaccaria.

Next comes the Chapel of Gold, dominated by an impressive (but likely scaffolded) 15th-century prickly gold altarpiece by Vivarini. The predella (seven small scenes beneath the altarpiece) may be by Paolo Veneziano, the grandfather of Venetian painting. Look down through glass in the floor to see the 12th-century mosaic floor from the original church. In fact, these rooms were parts of the earlier churches.

Finally, go downstairs to the **crypt**—the foundation of a church built in the 10th century. The crypt is low and the water table high, so the room is often flooded, submerging the bases of the columns. It's a weird experience, calling up echoes of the Dark Ages.

• *Emerge from the Church of San Zaccaria into the small campo. Before leaving the campo, check out the small art gallery (free), the pink Carabinieri police station (a former convent), and the thirst-quenching water fountain. Now, turn left and head south—past that cigarette machine—until you pop out at the waterfront.*

❹ The Riva

The waterfront promenade known as the "Riva" provides a great view of the Church of San Giorgio Maggiore. To get there, catch vaporetto #2 from the San Zaccaria-M.V.E. stop nearby. (For more on the handy *vaporetti* departing from San Zaccaria, see page 30.)

The big equestrian monument depicts Victor Emmanuel II, who helped lead Italy to unification, becoming the country's first king in 1861. Beyond that (over the

bridge) is the four-columned La Pietà Church, where Antonio Vivaldi once directed the music. A bit beyond that (not visible from here) is the Arsenale.

The Riva is lined with many of Venice's most famous luxury hotels. For a peek at the *most* famous and luxurious, turn right, cross over one bridge, and nip into the **Danieli Hotel.** Tuck in your shirt, stand tall and aristocratic, and (with all the confidence of a guest) be swept by the revolving door into the sumptuous interior of what was once the Gothic Palazzo Dandolo. As you check out the Danieli's restaurant menu (that's why you're there, isn't it?), admire the lobby, the old-style chandeliers, water-taxi drive-up entrance, and the occasional celebrity. Since 1820, the Danieli has been Venice's most exclusive hotel. Exquisite as all this is, it still gets flooded routinely in the winter.

• *Facing the water, turn right and head west toward St. Mark's Square. The commotion atop a little bridge marks the...*

❺ Famous View of the Bridge of Sighs

The Bridge of Sighs will likely be covered by scaffolding for several years for renovation. From this historic bridge (according to romantic legend), prisoners took one last look at Venice before entering the dark and dank prisons. And sighed. Lord Byron picked up on the legend in the early 1800s and gave the bridge its famous nickname, making this sad little span a big stop on the Grand Tour. Look high up on your left—while that rogue Casanova wrote of the bridge in his memoirs, he was actually imprisoned here in the Doge's Palace. Nowadays the bridge is a human traffic jam of gawking tourists and clever pickpockets during the day, though it's breathtakingly romantic in the lonely late-night hours.

• *From here, you can take one last look at the lagoon, then ponder the billboards on the Bridge of Sighs and the sweaty crowds of St. Mark's Square...and sigh.*

ST. MARK'S TO SAN ZACCARIA

SLEEPING IN VENICE

For hassle-free efficiency and the sheer magic of being close to the action, I favor hotels that are handy to sightseeing activities. I've listed rooms in four neighborhoods: St. Mark's bustle, the Rialto action, the quiet Dorsoduro area behind the Accademia art museum, and near the train station (handy for train travelers, but far from the action). I also mention several apartment rentals, big fancy hotels, cheap dorms, and places on the mainland.

A major feature of this book is its extensive listing of good-value rooms. I like places that are clean, small enough to have a hands-on owner and stable staff, central yet not in the tourist flood zone, relatively quiet at night (except for the song of gondoliers), reasonably priced, friendly, and run with a respect for Venetian traditions.

Outside of holidays and weekends, it's possible to visit Venice without booking ahead, but it's smart, simple, and less stress-ful to have a reservation in place (see "Making Reservations," later). Book a room as soon as you know when you'll be in town. Contact the hotel directly, not through any tourist information room-finding service (they can't give opinions on quality). If everything's full, don't despair. Call a day or two in advance and fill in a cancellation.

If you arrive on an overnight train, your room probably won't be ready first thing in the morning. You should be able to drop your bag safely at the hotel and dive right into Venice.

Note that hotel websites are particularly valuable for Venice, because they often show the hotel's location on a map.

Types of Accommodations

Hotels

Double rooms listed in this book will range from about €90 (very simple, toilet and shower down the hall) to €450 (plush Grand Canal views and maximum plumbing), with most clustered around €130–170 (with private bathrooms).

Solo travelers find that the cost of a *camera singola* (single room) is often only 25 percent less than a *camera doppia* (double room). Three or four people can economize by requesting one big room. (If a Db is €110, a Qb would be about €150.) Most listed hotels have rooms for anywhere from one to five people. If there's room for an extra cot, they'll cram it in for you (charging you around €25). English works in all but the cheapest places.

Nearly all places offer private bathrooms. Generally rooms with a bath or shower also have a toilet and a bidet (which Italians use for quick sponge baths). The cord that dangles over the tub or shower is not a clothesline. You pull it when you've fallen and can't get up.

Double beds are called *matrimoniale,* even though hotels aren't interested in your marital status. Twins are *due letti singoli.* Even if a single or triple room isn't listed, ask—they can accommodate you.

When you check in, usually the receptionist will ask for your passport and keep it for a couple of hours. Italian hotels are legally required to register each guest with the local police. Relax. Americans are notorious for making this chore more difficult than it needs to be.

Assume that breakfast is included in the prices I've listed, unless otherwise noted. If breakfast is included but optional, you may want to skip it. While convenient, it's usually expensive—€5–8 for a simple continental buffet with ham, cheese, yogurt, and unlimited *caffè latte.* A picnic in your room followed by a coffee at the corner café can be lots cheaper.

More pillows and blankets are usually in the closet or available on request. In Italy, towels and linens aren't always replaced every day. Hang your towel up to dry. Budget hotels often use "waffle" or very thin, tablecloth-type towels that take less water and electricity to launder.

Most hotel rooms have a TV and phone, and Internet access (usually Wi-Fi) is increasingly common. Simpler places rarely have a phone. Pricier hotels usually come with a small stocked mini-fridge called a *frigo bar* (FREE-goh bar; pay for what you use).

Hoteliers can be a great help and source of advice. Most know Venice well, and can assist you with everything from public transit and airport connections to finding a good restaurant, the nearest

Chill Out

All but the cheapest hotels have air-conditioning. Because Europeans are generally careful with energy use, you'll find government-enforced limits on air-conditioning and heating. There's a one-month period each spring and fall when neither is allowed. Air-conditioning sometimes costs an extra per-day charge, is worth seeking out in summer (though it may be on only at certain times of the day), and is rarely available from fall through spring. Fancier hotel rooms usually include air-conditioning in the price.

Most hotel rooms with air conditioners come with a control stick (like a TV remote) that generally has the same symbols and features: fan icon (click to toggle through wind power, from light to gale); louver icon (choose steady airflow or waves); snowflake and sunshine icons (cold air or heat, depending on season); clock ("O" setting: run x hours before turning off; "I" setting: wait x hours to start); and the temperature control (20–21 degrees Celsius is comfortable).

launderette, or an Internet café.

Even at the best hotels, mechanical breakdowns occur: air-conditioning malfunctions, sinks leak, hot water turns cold, and toilets gurgle and smell. Report your concerns clearly and calmly at the front desk. For more complicated problems, don't expect instant results.

If you suspect night noise will be a problem, ask for a quiet room in the back or on an upper floor. To guard against theft in your room, keep valuables out of sight. Some rooms come with a safe, and other hotels have safes at the front desk. Use them if you're concerned.

Checkout can pose problems if surprise charges pop up on your bill. If you settle up your bill the night before you leave, you'll have time to discuss and address any points of contention.

Apartments

Many Venetians rent out their apartments, which can be a great value for families or multiple couples traveling together. Rentals are generally by the week, with prices starting around €100 per day. A bigger place for a family of four to five rents for around €200 per day. Apartments typically offer a couple of bedrooms, a sitting area, and a teensy *cucinetta* (kitchenette), usually stocked with dishes and flatware. After you check in, you're basically on your own. While you won't have a doorman to carry your bags or a maid to clean your room each day, you will get an inside peek at a

Venetian home, and you can save lots of money—especially if you take advantage of the cooking facilities—with no loss of comfort.

Several of these recommended hotels, all listed later in this chapter, rent apartments (with small kitchens) on the side. **$$$ Hotel Campiello,** east of St. Mark's Square, has three modern, upscale, and quiet family apartments for up to six people, just steps away from their hotel. **$$ Pensione Guerrato,** west of the Rialto Bridge, has apartments for four to eight people. **$$ Locanda la Corte,** east of the Rialto Bridge, has two quads for up to eight (in hotel, no kitchen). **$ Alloggi Henry,** located close to the train station, can accommodate up to nine in their apartment.

Practicalities

Pricing and Discounts

Over the past decade, Venice has seen the opening of several big new hotels, countless little boutique hotels, and the conversion of many private homes to short-term rental apartments. Capacity has jumped from 13,000 rooms in 2000 to 23,000 rooms in 2010. Now the city is overbuilt for hotels. Demand is soft and, therefore, so are prices.

These days, it seems no Venetian hotel expects to actually get its published "rack rate." While I wish I could promise a set price or a discount for readers of this book, it's a pricing free-for-all; hotels have tossed straight pricing out the window. Smart travelers will email several places and see who offers the best rates. It's important to email the hotel directly (rather than going through a booking service) and to say you are a Rick Steves reader and expect their best price. Then survey your results, and pick what you think is the best value for that day.

You may save more if you do any of the following: offer to pay cash, stay at least three nights, offer to skip breakfast, or ask if there are cheaper rooms. To save money during a relatively slow time, consider arriving without a reservation and dropping in at the last minute. Big, fancy hotels put empty rooms on an aggressive push list, offering great prices.

I've done my best to predict prices for peak season: April, May, June, September, and October. Prices will be higher during festivals, and almost all places drop prices from November through March (except during Carnevale and Christmas) and in July and August.

Many hotels in Venice list rooms on www.venere.com, especially for last-minute vacancies (two to three weeks before the date). Before you bite, check to see if rates are lower than the prices in this book.

Phoning

To call Italy from the US or Canada, dial 011-39, and then the local number. (The 011 is our international access code, and 39 is Italy's country code.) If calling Italy from another European country, dial 00-39-local number. (The 00 is Europe's international access code.) To call a Venice hotel from anywhere in Italy (including Venice), simply dial the 10-digit local number. Land lines start with 0, mobile lines start with 3. For more tips on calling, see page 370.

Making Reservations

Given the quality of the accommodations I've found for this book, I'd recommend that you reserve your rooms in advance, particularly if you'll be traveling during peak season. Book several weeks ahead, or as soon as you've pinned down your travel dates. Note that some national holidays jam things up and merit your making reservations far in advance (see "Major Holidays and Weekends" sidebar on page 4).

Requesting a Reservation: To reserve, contact hotels directly by email, phone, or fax. Email is the clearest and most economical way to make a reservation. Or you can go straight to the hotel website; many have secure online reservation forms and can instantly inform you of availability and any special deals. But be sure you use the hotel's official site and not a booking agency's site—otherwise you may pay higher rates than you should. If you're phoning from the US, be mindful of time zones. Most recommended hotels are accustomed to guests who speak only English.

Your hotelier wants to know these key pieces of information (also included in the sample request form in the appendix):

- number and type of rooms
- number of nights
- date of arrival
- date of departure
- any special needs (e.g., bathroom in the room or down the hall, twin beds vs. double bed, air-conditioning, quiet, view, ground floor, etc.)

When you request a room, use the European style for writing dates: day/month/year. Hoteliers need to know your arrival and departure dates. For example, for a two-night stay in July, I would request "1 double room for 2 nights, arrive 16/07/11, depart 18/07/11." (Consider carefully how long you'll stay; don't just assume you can tack on extra days after you arrive.)

Confirming a Reservation: If the hotel's response tells you its room availability and rates, it's not a confirmation. You must tell them that you want that room at the given rate. Many hoteliers will request your credit-card number to hold the room. While you can email your credit-card information (I do), it's safer to share

Sleep Code

(€1 = about $1.25, country code: 39)

Price Rankings

To help you easily sort through these listings, I've divided the rooms into three categories based on the price for a standard double room with bath during high season:

$$$ Higher Priced—Most rooms €180 or more.

$$ Moderately Priced—Most rooms between €130–180.

$ Lower Priced—Most rooms €130 or less.

I always rate hostels as $, whether or not they have double rooms, because they have the cheapest beds in town. Prices can change without notice; verify the hotel's current rates online or by email. For other updates, see www.ricksteves .com/update.

Abbreviations

To give you maximum information in a minimum of space, I use the following code to describe the accommodations. Prices listed are per room, not per person. When a price range is given for a type of room (such as double rooms listing for €100–150), it means the price fluctuates with the season, size of room, or length of stay.

S = Single room (or price for one person in a double).

D = Double or Twin room. "Double beds" are often two twins sheeted together, and are usually big enough for nonromantic couples.

T = Triple (generally a double bed with a single).

Q = Quad (usually a double bed and 2 small singles).

b = Private bathroom with toilet and shower or tub.

s = Private shower or tub only (the toilet is down the hall).

According to this code, a couple staying at a "Db-€140" hotel would pay a total of €140 (about $175) for a double room with a private bathroom. Unless otherwise noted, breakfast is included, hotel staff speak basic English, and credit cards are accepted.

If I mention "Internet access," there's a public terminal in the lobby for guests to use. If I specify "Wi-Fi" or "cable Internet," you can generally access it in your room, but only if you have your own laptop.

that personal info via phone call, fax, or secure online reservation form (if the hotel has one on its website).

Canceling a Reservation: If you must cancel your reservation, it's courteous to do so with as much advance notice as possible. Simply make a quick phone call or send an email. Hotels lose money if they turn away customers while holding a room for someone who doesn't show up. Understandably, many hoteliers bill no-shows for one night.

Cancellation policies can be strict: For example, you might lose a deposit if you cancel within two weeks of your reserved stay, or you might be billed for the entire visit if you leave early. Ask about cancellation policies before you book.

If canceling via email, request confirmation that your cancellation was received to avoid being accidentally billed.

Reconfirm Your Reservation: Always call to reconfirm your room reservation a few days in advance from the road. If you'll be arriving late (after 17:00), alert your hotelier. On the small chance that a hotel loses track of your reservation, bring along a hard copy of their confirmation.

Reserving Rooms as You Travel: If you enjoy having a flexible itinerary, you can make reservations as you travel, calling hotels a few days to a week before your visit. If you'd rather travel without any reservations at all, you'll have greater success snaring rooms if you arrive at your destination early in the day. When you anticipate crowds (weekends are worst), call hotels at about 9:00 on the day you plan to arrive, when the hotel clerk knows who'll be checking out and just which rooms will be available. If you encounter a language barrier, ask the fluent receptionist at your current hotel to call for you.

Accommodations

Hotels in Venice can be tricky to locate. While I've tried to give clear directions, you'll do best by following the arrival instructions provided on your hotel's website. Most sites have a good map. (If yours does, print it out.) Remember that Venice has six districts: San Marco, Castello, Cannaregio, San Polo, Santa Croce, and Dorsoduro. Each district has about 6,000 address numbers.

If you're on a tight budget, you could focus on these recommended budget hotels and B&Bs, which have clean, simple rooms and are a good value: $ Corte Campana B&B and $ Alloggi Barbaria.

Near St. Mark's Square

Located near the Bridge of Sighs, just off the Riva degli Schiavoni waterfront promenade, these places rub drainpipes with Venice's most palatial five-star hotels. To get here from the train station or Piazzale Roma bus stop, ride the vaporetto to San Zaccaria—either the slow #1 or the fast #2 (from the Tronchetto parking lot, it's #2 only). Consider using your ride to follow my tour of the Grand Canal (❷ see Grand Canal Cruise chapter); to make sure you arrive via the Grand Canal, confirm that your boat goes "*via Rialto*."

Nearby Laundry: Lavanderia Gabriella offers full service a few streets north of the square (€15/load wash and dry, Mon–Fri 8:00–12:30, closed Sat–Sun; with your back to the door of San Zulian Church, go over Ponte dei Ferali, take first right down Calle dei Armeni, then first left on Rio Terra de le Colonne to #985; tel. 041-522-1758, Elisabetta).

$$$ Hotel Campiello, lacy and bright, was once part of a 19th-century convent. Ideally located 50 yards off the waterfront, on a tiny square, its 16 rooms offer a tranquil, friendly refuge for travelers who appreciate comfort and professional service (Sb-€130, Db-€180, 10 percent discount with cash and this book, air-con, elevator, Wi-Fi; from the waterfront street—Riva degli Schiavoni—take Calle del Vin, between pink Hotel Danieli and Hotel Savoia e Jolanda, to #4647, Castello; tel. 041-520-5764, fax 041-520-5798, www.hcampiello.it, campiello@hcampiello.it; family-run for four generations, currently by Thomas, Monica, Nicoletta, and Marco). They also rent three modern family apartments, under rustic timbers just steps away (up to €380/night).

$$ Locanda al Leon is a basic place renting 14 decent rooms just off Campo S.S. Filippo e Giacomo (Db-€135–150, Tb-€170, Qb-€220, these prices with cash and this book, air-con, Internet access and Wi-Fi, Campo S.S. Filippo e Giacomo 4270, Castello, tel. 041-277-0393, fax 041-521-0348, www.hotelalleon.com, leon @hotelalleon.com, Giuliano and Marcella). From the San Zaccaria-Danieli vaporetto stop, take Calle dei Albanesi (two streets left of pink Hotel Danieli) to its far end.

$$ Hotel Fontana is a two-star, family-run place with 15 rooms near a school, two bridges behind St. Mark's Square. Their annex across the street has much lower ceilings and slightly lower prices (Sb-€110, Db-€140–170, family rooms, 10 percent cash discount, quieter rooms on garden side, 2 rooms have terraces for €10 extra, air-con, elevator, Internet access and Wi-Fi, Campo San Provolo 4701, Castello, tel. 041-522-0579, fax 041-523-1040, www .hotelfontana.it, info@hotelfontana.it, Diego and Gabriele). From the San Zaccaria vaporetto dock, take Calle delle Rasse—to the left of pink Danieli Hotel—then turn right at the end, and continue to the first square.

$$ Hotel la Residenza is a grand old palace facing a peaceful square. It has 15 great rooms on three levels and a huge, luxurious old lounge. This is a great value for romantics—you'll

Hotels near St. Mark's Square

N

TO RIALTO

TO RIALTO

10

R. COLONNE

C. FIUBERA

FABBRI

TRON

RAMO SELVA

FRENZARIA

POST
WC

SAL.

SAN MOISÈ

CALLE VALLARESSO

SAN
MOISÈ

TO
ACCADEMIA

MERCERIE

SPADARIA

SAN
ZULIAN

LARGA   S. MARCO

9

8

PIAZZETTA
D. LEONCINI

OLD OFFICES

CLOCK
TOWER

ST. MARK'S
BASILICA

CAMPA-
NILE

PIAZZA
SAN MARCO

CORRER
MUSEUM
+ Napoleon's
Wing

NEW OFFICES

DOGE'S
PALACE

PIAZZETTA

S. MARCO
COLUMN

GIARDINETTI
REALI

WC

G

S.
THEODORE
COLUMN

SAN MARCO –
GIARDINETTI

SAN MARCO –
VALLARESSO

S A N   M A R C O

T

TO
SALUTE

← ENTRANCES TO SIGHTS
V VAPORETTO STOP
T TRAGHETTO CROSSING
G GONDOLA STATION

100 YARDS
100 METERS

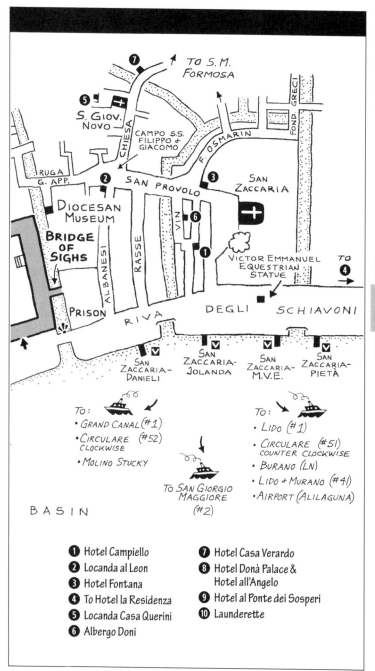

1 Hotel Campiello

2 Locanda al Leon

3 Hotel Fontana

4 To Hotel la Residenza

5 Locanda Casa Querini

6 Albergo Doni

7 Hotel Casa Verardo

8 Hotel Donà Palace & Hotel all'Angelo

9 Hotel al Ponte dei Sosperi

10 Launderette

feel like you're in the Doge's Palace after hours. Hang out in the living room and you become royalty (Sb-€100, Db-€130–165, air-con, Wi-Fi, Campo Bandiera e Moro 3608, Castello, tel. 041-528-5315, fax 041-523-8859, www.venicelaresidenza.com, info @venicelaresidenza.com, Giovanni). From the Bridge of Sighs, walk east along Riva degli Schiavoni, cross three bridges, and take the first left up Calle del Dose to Campo Bandiera e Moro.

$$ **Locanda Casa Querini** rents six bright, high-ceilinged rooms on a quiet square tucked away behind St. Mark's. You can enjoy your breakfast or a sunny picnic/happy hour sitting at their tables right on the sleepy little square (Db-€150, third person-€20–25, one cheaper small double, ask for cash discount, air-con, Wi-Fi, halfway between San Zaccaria vaporetto stop and Campo Santa Maria Formosa at Campo San Giovanni in Oleo 4388, Castello, tel. 041-241-1294, fax 041-523-6188, www.locandaquerini .com, casaquerini@hotmail.com, Patrizia and Silvia). From the San Zaccaria vaporetto stop, take the street to the right of the Bridge of Sighs to Campo S.S. Filippo e Giacomo, continue on Calle drio la Chiesa, take the second left, and curl around to the left into the little square, Campo San Giovanni Novo.

$ **Albergo Doni** is dark, clean, and quiet—a bit of a time-warp—with 13 dim but once-classy rooms run by a likable smart aleck named Gina, her niece Tessa, and her nephew, an Italian stallion named Nikos (D-€90, Db-€115, T-€120, Tb-€155, reserve with credit card but pay in cash, ceiling fans, three Db rooms have air-con, avoid their overflow apartment, Fondamenta del Vin 4656, Castello, tel. & fax 041-522-4267, www.albergodoni.it, albergodoni@hotmail.it). From the San Zaccaria vaporetto stop, cross one bridge to the right and take the first left (marked Calle del Vin), then turn left at the little square named Ramo del Vin, jog left, and find the hotel ahead on Fondamenta del Vin.

Near the Rialto Bridge
Vaporetto #2 quickly connects the Rialto with the train station, the Piazzale Roma bus stop, and the Tronchetto parking lot. The slower vaporetto #1 connects everything but Tronchetto.

Nearby Laundry: Effe Erre, a modern self-service *lavan-deria,* is near recommended Hotel al Piave at Ruga Giuffa 4826 (open daily, self-service 6:30–23:00, €11/small load wash and dry; full-service for just a couple euros more, 9:00–13:00, winter hours may be shorter, mobile 349-058-3881, Massimo).

West of the Rialto Bridge
$ **Pensione Guerrato,** above the colorful Rialto produce market and just two minutes from the Rialto Bridge, is run by friendly, creative, and hardworking Roberto and Piero. Their 800-year-

old building—with 24 spacious, air-conditioned, and charming rooms—is simple, airy, and wonderfully characteristic (D-€90, Db-€130, Tb-€150, Qb-€170, Quint/b-€185, these prices with this book and cash, check website for special discounts, Rick Steves readers can ask for €5/night discount below Web specials, Wi-Fi, Calle drio la Scimia 240a, San Polo, tel. & fax 041-528-5927, www .pensioneguerrato.it, hguerrat@tin.it, Monica and Rosanna). From the train station, take vaporetto #1 to the Mercato Rialto stop (comes before the "Rialto" stop), exit the boat to your right, and follow the waterfront. Calle drio la Scimia (not simply Scimia, the block before), is on the left—you'll see the hotel sign. My tour groups book this place for 50 nights each year. Sorry. The Guerrato also rents family apartments in the old center (great for groups of 4–8) for around €55 per person.

East of the Rialto Bridge

$$$ **Hotel al Ponte Antico** is exquisite, professional, and small. With nine plush rooms and a velvety royal living/breakfast room, it's perfect for a romantic anniversary. Because its wonderful terrace overlooks the Grand Canal, Rialto Bridge, and market action, its non-canal-view rooms may be a better value (Db-€290, superior Db-€380, deluxe canal-front Db-€450, air-con, Wi-Fi; 100 yards from Rialto Bridge, follow Salizzada S. Grisostomo behind post office and past Coin department store, turn left down the dark and empty Calle del Aseo to #5768, Cannaregio; tel. 041-241-1944, fax 041-241-1828, www.alponteantico.com, info @alponteantico.com).

$ **Locanda la Corte,** a three-star hotel, is perfumed with elegance. Its 19 attractive, high-ceilinged, wood-beamed rooms—done in earthy pastels—circle a small, quiet courtyard (Sb-€100, standard Db-€120, superior Db-€150, 10 percent discount with cash, ask for Rick Steves discount, suites and family rooms available, air-con, Wi-Fi, Castello 6317, tel. 041-241-1300, fax 041-241-5982, www.locandalacorte.it, info@locandalacorte.it, Marco, Raffaela, and Tommy the cat). Take vaporetto #52 from the train station to Fondamenta Nuove, exit the boat to your left, follow the waterfront, and turn right after the second bridge to reach S.S. Giovanni e Paolo. Facing the Rosa Salva bar, take the street to the left (Calle Bressana); the hotel is a short block away at #6317, before the bridge.

$ **Casa Pisani Canal Hotel** is a sweet little place renting five rooms (Db-€100–120, huge Db suite overlooking canal-€240, air-con, Wi-Fi, Calle de le Erbe 6105, Cannaregio, tel. 041-724-1030, www.casapisanicanal.it, info@casapisanicanal.it, Tortorelle family). It's just off Campo S.S. Giovanni e Paolo, on Calle de le Erbe.

Hotels near the Rialto Bridge

TO GHETTO
& TRAIN STN.

TO TRAIN STN.

TO TRAIN STN.

STRADA NOVA

CA' D'ORO

FISH MARKET BLDG.

VEG. MKT.

CANAL

CAMPO BECC.

PISTOR

SS. APOST.

CAMPO SS. APOST.

CAMPO CORN. S.

MERCATO RIALTO

ASEO

GRIST.

RIALTO BRIDGE

S. MATTIA

SPEZIALI

S. GIOV.

OREFICI

CAMPO S. GIAC.

POST

SAL.

STATUE

CAMPO S. BART.

BISSA

RUGA VECCHIA S. GIOV.

TO CAMPO SAN POLO & FRARI CHURCH

FONDAMENTA

VIN

FERRO

RIALTO

MAZZINI

2 APRILE

STAGNERI

SAN SILV.

GRAND

RIVA

CARBON

BEMBO

MERCERIE

MERC.

FABBRI

BALLOTTE

REGINA

CAMPO S. LUCA

TO ACCADEMIA

TO SAN MARCO

DCH

① Pensione Guerrato
② Hotel al Ponte Antico
③ Locanda la Corte
④ Casa Pisani Canal Hotel
⑤ Alloggi Barbaria
⑥ Hotel al Piave
⑦ Hotel Riva

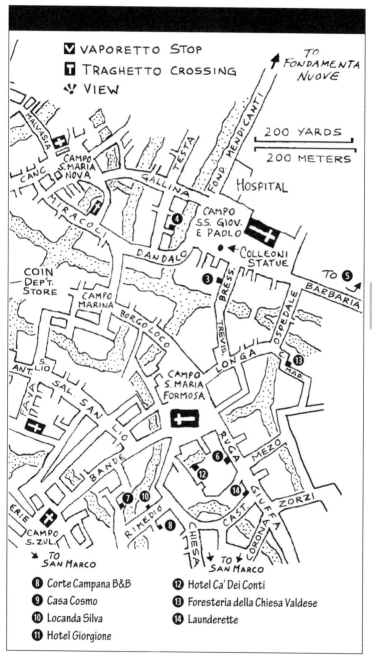

VAPORETTO STOP

TRAGHETTO CROSSING

VIEW

TO FONDAMENTA NUOVE

200 YARDS

200 METERS

HALVASIA

CAMPO S. MARIA NOVA

CANC.

MIRACOLI

TESTA

GALLINA

FOND. MENDICANTI

HOSPITAL

CAMPO S.S. GIOV. E PAOLO

COLLEONI STATUE

DANDALO

BRESS.

TO BARBARIA

COIN DEP'T. STORE

CAMPO MARINA

BORGOLOCO

TREVIS.

OSPEDALE

MAR.

ANT.

S. LIO

SAL. SAN

LONGA

CAMPO S. MARIA FORMOSA

FAVA

LIO

BANDE

RUGA

MEZO

CAMPO

CAST.

GIUFFA

ZORZI

ERIE

CAMPO S. ZUL.

RIMEDIO

CHIESA

CORONA

TO SAN MARCO

TO SAN MARCO

SLEEPING IN VENICE

8 Corte Campana B&B

9 Casa Cosmo

10 Locanda Silva

11 Hotel Giorgione

12 Hotel Ca' Dei Conti

13 Foresteria della Chiesa Valdese

14 Launderette

$ **Alloggi Barbaria** rents eight quiet, spacious, backpacker-type rooms on one floor around a bright and institutional-feeling common area. Beyond Campo S.S. Giovanni e Paolo, this Ikea-style place is a long walk from the action but a good value and a chance to see the real Venice (Db-€90–100, third or fourth person-€25 each, pay cash for best price, family deals, air-con, tel. 041-522-2750, fax 041-277-5540, www.alloggibarbaria.it, info @alloggibarbaria.it, Giorgio and Fausto). Take vaporetto #52 to Ospedale stop, turn left as you get off the boat, then right down Calle de le Capucine to #6573.

Southeast of the Rialto Bridge

$$ **Hotel al Piave,** with 27 fine air-conditioned rooms above a bright and classy lobby, is fresh, modern, and comfortable. You'll enjoy the neighborhood and always get a cheery welcome (Db-€150, Tb-€200; family suites-€280 for 4, €300 for 5, or €320 for 6; cash discount, Internet access and Wi-Fi, Ruga Giuffa 4838/40, Castello, tel. 041-528-5174, fax 041-523-8512, www.hotelalpiave .com, info@hotelalpiave.com, Mirella, Paolo, and Ilaria speak English). From the San Zaccaria vaporetto stop, take the street to the right of the Bridge of Sighs to Campo S.S. Filippo e Giacomo, and continue on Calle drio la Chiesa. Cross the bridge, continue straight, then turn left onto Ruga Giuffa until you find the hotel on your left at #4838.

$ **Hotel Riva,** with gleaming marble hallways, big exposed beams, fine antique furnishings, and bright rooms, is romantically situated on a canal along the gondola serenade route. You could actually dunk your breakfast rolls in the canal (but don't). Ten of the 30 rooms come with air-conditioning for the same price—request one when you reserve. Or, if you prefer lots of light but no air-conditioning, you can ask Sandro to hold a corner *(angolo)* room for you (Sb-€90, D-€100, Db-€120, Tb-€170, €20 extra for view, reserve with credit card but pay with cash only, Ponte dell'Angelo, tel. 041-522-7034, fax 041-528-5551, www.hotelriva .it, info@hotelriva.it, Daniella). Facing St. Mark's Basilica, walk behind it on the left along Calle de la Canonica, take the first left (at blue *Pauly & C* mosaic in street), continue straight, go over the bridge, and angle right to the hotel at Ponte dell'Anzolo.

$ **Corte Campana B&B,** run by enthusiastic and helpful Riccardo, rents three quiet and characteristic rooms just behind St. Mark's Square, plus two apartments (Db-€125, Tb or Tb apart-ment-€165, Qb-€190, prices are soft, cash only, 2-night minimum, €10/night less for stays of 4 nights, air-con, Internet access, Calle del Remedio 4410, Castello, tel. & fax 041-523-3603, mobile 389-272-6500, www.cortecampana.com, info@cortecampana.com). From nearby Locanda Silva—described below—go 30 yards down

Flexible Floors

All over town, from palaces to cheap, old hotels, you'll find speckled floors *(pavimento alla Veneziana)*. While they

might look like cheap linoleum, these are historic—protected by the government and a pain for Venetian landlords to maintain. As Venice was built, it needed flexible flooring to absorb the inevitable settling of the buildings. Through an expensive and laborious process, several layers of material were built up and finished with a broken marble top that was shaved and polished to what you see today. While patterns were sometimes designed into the flooring, it's often just a speckled hodgepodge. Keep an eye open for this. Once a year, the floor is rubbed with natural oil to maintain its flexibility, and craftspeople still give landlords fits when repairs are needed.

the canal, turn right onto Calle del Remedio, follow it to #4410, and ring the bell at the black gate.

$ Casa Cosmo is a humble little five-room place run by Davide and his parents. While it comes with minimal services and no public spaces, it's air-conditioned, very central, inexpensive, and quiet (Db-€110, cash discount, no breakfast, Calle di Mezo 4976, San Marco, tel. & fax 041-296-0710, www.casacosmo.com, info @casacosmo.com). From the Rialto vaporetto stop, head inland on Larga Mazzini (which becomes Merceria). Turn right onto San Salvador, then immediately left onto tiny Calle di Mezo to #4976 (it's just behind Foot Locker).

$ Locanda Silva is a big, basic, beautifully located, institutional-feeling place renting 23 decent old-school rooms (S-€65, Sb-€80, D-€85, weekday Db-€110, weekend Db-€130, substantially less during slow times, request 10 percent Rick Steves discount, closed Dec–Jan, Fondamenta del Remedio 4423, tel. 041-522-7643, fax 041-528-6817, www.locandasilva.it, info@locanda silva.it, Sandra and Massimo). From San Marco, head north toward Campo Santa Maria Formosa, go down Calle del Remedio, and turn left at the canal to Fondamenta del Remedio.

Near the Accademia Bridge

When you step over the Accademia Bridge, the commotion of touristy Venice is replaced by a sleepy village laced with canals. This quiet area, next to the best painting gallery in town, is a

15-minute walk from the Rialto or St. Mark's Square.

The fast vaporetto #2 connects the Accademia Bridge with the train station (15 minutes), Piazzale Roma bus stop (20 minutes), Tronchetto parking lot (25 minutes), and St. Mark's Square (5 minutes). For hotels south of the Accademia Bridge, vaporetto #51 to Zattere (or the Alilaguna speedboat from the airport to Zattere) are good options.

South of the Accademia Bridge

$$$ Hotel Belle Arti has a grand entry and a formal, stern staff. With the ambience of a modern American hotel, its 64 rooms feel out of place in musty Old World Venice (Sb-€130, Db-€240, Tb-€280, air-con, elevator; 100 yards behind Accademia art museum: facing museum, jog left, then right, down Via Dorsoduro to #912, Dorsoduro; tel. 041-522-6230, fax 041-528-0043, www .hotelbellearti.com, info@hotelbellearti.com).

$$$ Pensione Accademia fills the 17th-century Villa Maravege like a Bellini painting. Its 27 rooms are comfortable, elegant, and air-conditioned. You'll feel aristocratic gliding through its grand public spaces and lounging in its wistful, breezy gardens (Sb-€145, standard Db-€235, bigger "superior" Db-€280, Qb-€330, ask for discount when you book; facing Accademia art museum, go right, cross the bridge, go right to where the small canal hits the big one, Dorsoduro 1058; tel. 041-521-0188, fax 041-523-9152, www .pensioneaccademia.it, info@pensioneaccademia.it).

$$$ Hotel Agli Alboretti is a cozy, family-run, 23-room place in a quiet neighborhood a block behind the Accademia art museum. With red carpeting and wood-beamed ceilings, it feels classy (Sb-€115, Db-€200, Tb-€225, Qb-€250, air-con, elevator, 100 yards from the Accademia vaporetto stop on Rio Terra A. Foscarini at #884, Dorsoduro, tel. 041-523-0058, fax 041-521-0158, www.aglialboretti.com, info@aglialboretti.com, Anna).

$$ Pensione la Calcina, the home of English writer John Ruskin in 1876, maintains a 19th-century formality. It comes with all the three-star comforts in a professional yet intimate package. Its 32 rosy, perfumed rooms are squeaky clean, with nice wood furniture, hardwood floors, and a peaceful canalside setting facing Giudecca Island (Sb-€140, Sb with view-€150, Db-€150–310 depending on size and view, Qb-€280, air-con, Wi-Fi, rooftop terrace, floating buffet-breakfast terrace, near Zattere vaporetto stop at south end of Rio di San Vio at #780, Dorsoduro, tel. 041-520-6466, fax 041-522-7045, www.lacalcina.com, info@lacalcina .com). Guests get discounted meals at their La Piscina restaurant.

$$ Casa Rezzonico is a silent getaway far from the madding crowds. Its private garden terrace has perhaps the lushest grass in Italy, and its seven spacious, very Venetian rooms have garden/

canal views (Sb-€120, Db-€160, Tb-€190, Qb-€220, ask for discount when you book, air-con, Wi-Fi, Fondamenta Gherardini 2813, Dorsoduro, tel. 041-277-0653, fax 041-277-5435, www .casarezzonico.it, info@casarezzonico.it). Take vaporetto #1 to Ca' Rezzonico, head up Calle del Traghetto, cross Campo San Barnaba to the canal, and continue on Fondamenta Gherardini to #2813.

$$ Hotel Galleria has nine tight, velvety rooms, most with views of the Grand Canal. Some rooms are quite narrow. It's run with a family feel by Luciano and Stefano (S-€85, D-€120, skinny Grand Canal view Db-€150, palatial Grand Canal view Db-€180, includes breakfast in room, fans, 30 yards from Accademia art museum, next to recommended Foscarini pizzeria, Dorsoduro 878a, tel. 041-523-2489, fax 041-520-4172, www.hotelgalleria.it, galleria@tin.it).

$$ Don Orione Religious Guest House is a big cultural center dedicated to the work of a local man who became a saint in modern times. Filling an old monastery, it feels institutional, like a modern retreat center—clean, peaceful, and strictly run, with 74 rooms. It's beautifully located, comfortable, and a fine value (Sb-€84, Db-€140, Tb-€180, profits go to mission work in the developing world, groups welcome, air-con, Dorsoduro, tel. 041-522-4077, fax 041-528-6214, www.donorione-venezia.it, info @donorione-venezia.it). From the Zattere vaporetto stop, turn right, then turn left. It's just after the church at #909a.

$ Ca' San Trovaso rents seven simple, spacious rooms split between the main hotel and a nearby annex. The location is peaceful, on a small canal (Sb-€90, Db-€115, Db with bigger canal view and air-con-€130, Tb-€145, these prices with cash, includes breakfast in your room, air-con, small roof terrace, Dorsoduro 1350/51, tel. 041-277-1146, mobile 339-445-8821, fax 041-277-7190, www .casantrovaso.com, s.trovaso@tin.it, Mark and his son Alessandro). From the Zattere vaporetto stop, exit left, and cross a bridge. Turn right at tiny Calle Trevisan, cross another bridge, cross the adjacent bridge, take an immediate right, and then the first left. Nearby, Mama Cristina's **Casa di Sara** is a brightly colored B&B with quiet rooms, a tiny roof terrace, and the same prices (mobile 345-070-8547, www.casadisara.com, info@casadisara.com).

Between the Accademia Bridge and St. Mark's Square

$$$ Hotel Flora sits buried in a sea of fancy designer boutiques and elegant hotels almost on the Grand Canal. It's formal, with uniformed staff and grand public spaces, yet the 43 rooms have a homey warmth and the garden oasis is a sanctuary for foot-weary guests (generally Db-€260, check website for special discounts or email Sr. Romanelli for 10 percent Rick Steves discount off

SLEEPING IN VENICE

Hotels near the Accademia Bridge

TO FRARI
& RIALTO

CAMPO
S. MARG.

CA'
REZZONICO

SAN
SAM.

PALAZZO
GRASSI

16

BOTT.

CA'
REZZ.

CAMPO
SANTO
STEFANO

TO
5

CAMPO S.
BARNABA

TRAGHETTO

GRAND

FRUTT

15

CALLE

TOLETTA

2

CORFU GAMB

ACC

ACCADEMIA
BRIDGE

ROMITE

BORGO

ACCADEMIA
MUSEUM

PISTOR

CAMPO
S. VIO

6

CAMPO
SAN
TROVASO

NUOVA

8

BONILI

GONDOLA
WORKSHOP

NANI

POMP.

3

CHIESA

ZATTERE

S. MARIA
GESUATI

FOSCA

RINI

1

CAMPO S.
AGNESE

CARITA
VENIER

BRAGADIN

ALILAGUNA
DOCK

PONTE LONGO

7

ZATTERE

ZATTERE

4

DRIO INC.

200 YARDS

200 METERS

G I U D E C C A

① Hotel Belle Arti
② Pensione Accademia
③ Hotel Agli Alboretti
④ Pensione la Calcina
⑤ To Casa Rezzonico

⑥ Hotel Galleria
⑦ Don Orione Religious
   Guest House
⑧ Ca' San Trovaso &
   Casa di Sara

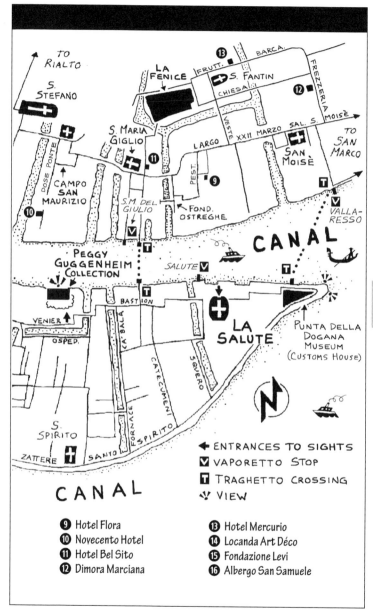

TO RIALTO

S. STEFANO

LA FENICE

S. MARIA GIGLIO

CAMPO SAN MAURIZIO

DOSE PONTE

S.M. DEL GIULIO

FOND. OSTREGHE

S. FANTIN

CHIESA

FRUTT.

BARCA.

VESTE

LARGO XXII MARZO

SAL. S. MOISÈ

FREZZERIA

TO SAN MARCO

SAN MOISÈ

PEST.

VALLA-RESSO

PEGGY GUGGENHEIM COLLECTION

SALUTE

CANAL

VENIER

OSPED.

BASTION

CA BALA

LA SALUTE

PUNTA DELLA DOGANA MUSEUM (CUSTOMS HOUSE)

CATECUMENI

SEVERO

S. SPIRITO

ZATTERE

SANTO

FORNACE

ESPIRITO

CANAL

SLEEPING IN VENICE

← ENTRANCES TO SIGHTS

Ⓥ VAPORETTO STOP

Ⓣ TRAGHETTO CROSSING

⚡ VIEW

⑨ Hotel Flora
⑩ Novecento Hotel
⑪ Hotel Bel Sito
⑫ Dimora Marciana

⑬ Hotel Mercurio
⑭ Locanda Art Déco
⑮ Fondazione Levi
⑯ Albergo San Samuele

standard prices, air-con, elevator, Calle dei Bergamaschi 2283a, San Marco, tel. 041-520-5844, fax 041-522-8217, www.hotelflora .it, info@hotelflora.it). It's at the end of Calle dei Bergamaschi, a long, skinny dead-end lane just off Calle Larga XXII Marzo.

$$$ Novecento Hotel rents nine plush rooms. Owned by Hotel Flora (described above), this boutique hotel is decorated circa-1900 throughout, with a big lounge and an elegant living room (Db-€240–260, air-con, Wi-Fi, Calle del Dose 2683, off Campo San Maurizio, San Marco, tel. 041-241-3765, fax 041-521-2145, www.novecento.biz, info@novecento.biz).

$$$ Hotel Bel Sito offers pleasing yet well-worn Old World character, 38 rooms, generous public spaces, a peaceful courtyard, and a picturesque location—facing a church on a small square between St. Mark's Square and the Accademia (Sb-€110, Db-€185, air-con, Wi-Fi, elevator; catch vaporetto #1 to Santa Maria del Giglio stop, take street inland to square, hotel is at far end to your right at Santa Maria del Giglio 2517, San Marco; tel. 041-522-3365, fax 041-520-4083, www.hotelbelsito.info, info@hotelbelsito.info, manager Rossella).

$$ Dimora Marciana, a mod place furnished in a traditional Venetian style, has seven rooms in a quiet alley just a two-minute walk from St. Mark's Square (Db-€165, Tb-€190, 2-room Qb-€230, mention Rick Steves when you book to get the best prices, cash discount, air-con, Wi-Fi, small bar, tel. 041-522-0755, www.dimoramarciana.com, info@dimoramarciana.com, Daniel). From behind the Correr Museum, turn right on Frezzeria, then take Calle Bognolo—the second street on the left—to #1604.

$$ Hotel Mercurio offers 19 peaceful, comfortable, and recently renovated rooms near La Fenice Opera House. Some rooms offer canal views (Sb-€130, Db-€170, Tb-€200, €10 less with cash, less mid-June–Aug and Nov–Feb except Christmas week, air-con, Wi-Fi, Calle del Fruttariol 1848, San Marco, tel. 041-522-0947, fax 041-582-5270, www.hotelmercurio.com, info @hotelmercurio.com, Monica, Vittorio, and Natale). From the San Marco-Vallaresso vaporetto stop, follow Calle Vallaresso to Calle Frezzaria, turn right, and follow it over a bridge as it becomes Calle del Frutariol. The hotel is on the left just before La Fenice Opera House.

$$ Locanda Art Déco is a charming little place. While the Art Deco theme is scant, a wrought-iron staircase leads from the inviting lobby to six thoughtfully decorated rooms (Db-€150–170, Tb-€200, 3-night minimum on weekends, 5 percent cash discount, air-con, free Wi-Fi, just north of the Accademia Bridge off Campo Santo Stefano at Calle delle Botteghe 2966, San Marco, tel. 041-277-0558, fax 041-270-2891, www.locandaartdeco.com, info @locandaartdeco.com). They also rent loft apartments.

$ **Fondazione Levi,** run by a foundation that promotes research on Venetian music, offers 35 quiet, institutional yet comfortable and spacious rooms (Sb-€70, Db-€110 or less, Tb-€120, Qb-€140, twin beds only, elevator, San Vidal 2893, San Marco, tel. 041-786-711, fax 041-786-766, www.fondazionelevi.it, foresteria levi@libero.it). It's 80 yards from the Accademia Bridge on the St. Mark's side. Leaving the bridge (opposite the Accademia vaporetto stop), take an immediate left, cross the bridge, and go down Calle Giustinian straight to the Fondazione. Buzz the *Foresteria* door to the right.

$ **Albergo San Samuele's** is a backpacker place: dumpy but in a great locale. It rents 12 basic rooms in a crumbling old palace near Campo Santo Stefano. Sleep here only if their price is far less than other listings (S-€60, D-€80, Db-€100, extra bed-€30, no breakfast, Salizada San Samuele 3358, San Marco, tel. 041-520-5165, fax 041-522-8045, www.albergosansamuele.it, info @albergosansamuele.it).

Near the Train Station

I don't recommend the train station area. It's crawling with noisy, disoriented tourists with too much baggage and people whose life's calling is to scam visitors out of their money. It's so easy just to hop a vaporetto upon arrival and sleep in the Venice of your dreams. Still, some like to park their bags near the station, and if so, these places work well.

Nearby Laundry: Orange, the nearest self-service laundry, is across the Grand Canal from the station (daily 7:30–22:30, €5/small load, follow directions to recommended Albergo Marin, on the right at Ramo delle Chioverete 665a/b).

$$$ **Hotel Abbazia,** in the dreary hotel zone near the train station, fills a former abbey with both history and class. The refectory makes a grand living room for guests, a garden fills the old courtyard, and the halls leading to 50 rooms are monkishly wide (Db-€180–200, larger superior rooms-€25 extra—choose Venetian or modern style, ask for Rick Steves discount when you book direct, air-con, Wi-Fi, no elevator but plenty of stairs, fun-loving staff, 2 blocks from the station on the very quiet Calle Priuli dei Cavaletti 68, tel. 041-717-333, fax 041-717-949, www.abbaziahotel .com, info@abbaziahotel.com).

$ **Locanda Herion** rents 17 basic rooms for a decent price (Db-€100–120, 10 percent discount with cash, air-con, tel. 041-275-9426, fax 041-275-6647, www.locandaherion.com, info @locandaherion.com). Exiting the train station, turn left to follow Rio Terra Lista de Spagna. Cross the Ponte di Guglie bridge and turn right at the yellow *San Marcuola traghetto* sign to find Campiello Picutti o del Magazen 1697a.

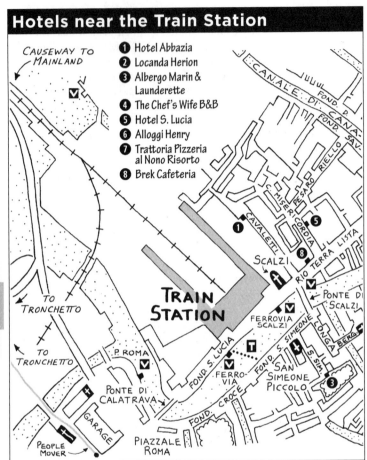

Hotels near the Train Station

1. Hotel Abbazia
2. Locanda Herion
3. Albergo Marin & Launderette
4. The Chef's Wife B&B
5. Hotel S. Lucia
6. Alloggi Henry
7. Trattoria Pizzeria al Nono Risorto
8. Brek Cafeteria

$ Albergo Marin and its staff offer 17 good-value, quiet rooms handy to the train station (Sb-€110, D-€90, Db-€120, Tb-€150, 5 percent cash discount, fans on request, Ramo delle Chioverete #670b, Santa Croce, tel. 041-718-022, fax 041-721-485, www.albergomarin.it, info@albergomarin.it). From the station, cross the Grand Canal and turn immediately right. Take the first left, then the first right, then right again to Ramo delle Chioverete.

$ The Chef's Wife B&B is run by American Stacy Gibboni. The "chef" is her Venetian husband, who runs a restaurant next door. Together they rent one sprawling and very cozy apartment for two to four people (Db-€100, Qb-€150, ask for Rick Steves rate, 2-night minimum, huge living room, no air-con, Wi-Fi, adjacent to Stacy's art studio, Corte del Pegoloto 1801, Cannaregio,

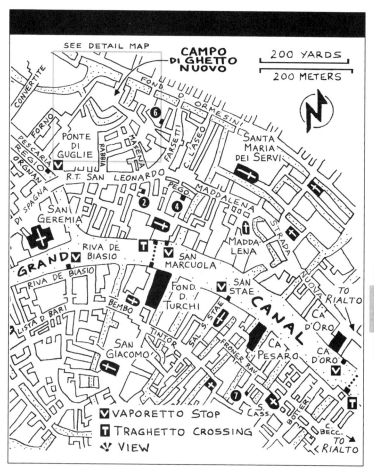

SEE DETAIL MAP

CAMPO DI GHETTO NUOVO

200 YARDS
200 METERS

N

mobile 328-365-8753, www.thechefswife.eu, stacysguesthouse
@hotmail.it). It's near the San Marcuola vaporetto stop—see
Stacy's website for directions.

$ Hotel S. Lucia, 150 yards from the train station, is oddly
modern and sterile, with bright and spacious rooms and tight
showers. Its 15 rooms are simple and clean. Guests enjoy their
sunny garden area out front (S-€60, Db-€105, Tb-€145, discounts
for three or more nights, 5 percent cash discount, breakfast-€5,
air-con, Calle della Misericordia 358, Cannaregio, tel. 041-715-
180, fax 041-710-610, www.hotelslucia.com, info@hotelslucia.com,
Gianni and Alessandra). Exit the station, head left, then take the
second left onto Calle della Misericordia. The hotel is 100 yards
ahead on the right.

$ Alloggi Henry, a homey little family-owned hotel, rents 15 simple and flowery rooms in a quiet residential neighborhood. It's a 10-minute walk from the train station (D-€80, Db-€100, Tb-€130, prices good with cash and this book through 2011, no breakfast, air-con, Calle Ormesini 1506e, Cannaregio, tel. 041-523-6675, fax 041-715-680, www.alloggihenry.com, info@alloggi henry.com, Manola and Henry). From the station, follow Lista de Spagna, San Leonardo, and Farsetti. Turn left on Calle Ormesini, then turn right into tiny Campiello Briani. They also rent a three-room apartment that sleeps up to nine.

Big, Fancy Hotels that Discount Shamelessly

Here are several big, plush, four-star places with greedy, sky-high rack rates (around Db-€300) that often have great discounts (as low as Db-€120) for drop-ins, off-season travelers, or online booking through their websites. If you want sliding-glass-door, uniformed-receptionist kind of comfort and formality in the old center, these are worth considering: **$$$ Hotel Giorgione** (big, garish, shiny, near Rialto Bridge, www.hotelgiorgione.com, see map on page 244); **$$$ Hotel Casa Verardo** (elegant and quietly parked on a canal behind St. Mark's, more stately, www.casaverardo.it, see map on page 240); **$$$ Hotel Donà Palace** (sitting like Las Vegas in the touristy zone a few blocks behind St. Mark's Basilica, works with neighbors **$$$ Hotel all'Angelo** and **$$$ Hotel al Ponte dei Sosperi** to rent 100 overpriced but often discounted rooms, all on Calle Larga San Marco, www.donapalace.it, see map on page 240); and **$$$ Hotel Ca' Dei Conti** (five minutes northeast of St. Mark's Square, palatial and perfectly located but €500 rooms worth it only when deeply discounted, www.cadeiconti.com, see map on page 244).

Cheap Dormitory Accommodations

$ Foresteria della Chiesa Valdese, run by the Methodist Church, offers 60 beds in doubles and 6- to 8-bed dorms, halfway between St. Mark's Square and the Rialto Bridge. This chilly, run-down yet charming old place has elegant ceiling paintings (dorm bed-€28, Db-€92, Tb-€111, Qb-€136, discount for stays of 2 nights or more; includes breakfast, sheets, towels, and lockers; room lock-out 10:00–13:30, must check in and out when office is open—8:30–20:00, reservations by phone only—no email, Fondamenta Cavagnis 5170, Castello, tel. 041-528-6797, fax 041-241-6238, www .foresteriavenezia.it, info@foresteriavenezia.it). From Campo Santa Maria Formosa, walk past Bar all'Orologio to the end of Calle Longa and cross the bridge onto Fondamenta Cavagnis.

$ Venice's youth hostel, on Giudecca Island with 260 beds and grand views across the Bay of San Marco, is a godsend for backpackers shell-shocked by Venetian prices (€25 beds with sheets and breakfast in 8- to 20-bed dorms, cheaper for hostel members, lockers, room lock-out 10:30–13:30, office open daily 7:00–24:30, catch vaporetto #2 from station to Zittele, tel. 041-523-8211, can reserve online at www.ostellovenezia.it).

On the Mainland

$ Villa Dolcetti, about 12 miles from Marco Polo Airport, is a 1635 building with nine comfortable rooms. Art lovers Diego and Tatiana provide a buffet breakfast, free parking, and lots of sight-seeing advice (Db-€70, superior Db-€80, Tb-€90–110, request discount, Internet access and Wi-Fi, tel. 041-563-1077, fax 041-563-1139, www.villadolcetti.com, info@villadolcetti.com). It's on the Venice–Padua road in the Venetian suburb of Oriago di Mira, at Via Venezia 85. Email them for driving and bus directions (buses run to/from Piazzale Roma, 2/hour, 25 minutes).

   $ Villa Mocenigo Agriturismo, about 10 miles from Marco Polo Airport, is a working, family-run farm in a peaceful rural location between Venice and Padua. Its 10 rooms are furnished with antiques, and regional specialties are served for dinner (Sb-€40–60, Db-€60–80, extra bed-€15–25, dinner and wine-€15–25 per person, air-con, Via Viasana 59 in Mirano-Venezia, tel. & fax 041-433-246, mobile 335-547-4728, www.villamocenigo.com, info@villamocenigo.com). Email them for directions by car or bus. Buses to Venice leave directly from the villa (3/hour, 45 minutes).

EATING IN VENICE

The Italians are masters at the art of fine living. That means eating...long and well. Lengthy, multicourse lunches and dinners and endless hours sitting in outdoor cafés are the norm. Americans eat on their way to an evening event and complain if the check is slow in coming. For Italians, dining is an end in itself, and only rude waiters rush you. When you want the bill, mime-scribble on your raised palm or ask for it: *"Il conto?"* You may have to ask for it more than once. To save time, you could ask for the check when you receive the last item you order.

Even those of us who liked dorm food will find that the cafés, cuisine, and wines become a highlight of our Italian adventure. Trust me: This is sightseeing for your palate, and even if the rest of you is sleeping in cheap hotels, your taste buds will relish an occasional first-class splurge. You can eat well without going broke. But be careful: You're just as likely to blow a small fortune on a disappointing meal as you are to dine wonderfully for €25.

Restaurants

Looking for an "untouristy restaurant" in Venice is like looking for the same thing at Disneyland. Venice restaurants exist to feed tourists. Still, some cater to groups and sloppy big spenders, while others respect their clientele—both locals and travelers. Avoid the places with big signs boasting, "We speak English and accept credit cards." High-rent restaurants parked on famous squares or canals must pass on their costs, and they generally serve tourists bad food at high prices. The natives eat better at low-rent holes-in-the-wall, which need to be good to be known. While Venetians still eat out and have their favorites, a restaurateur once confided in me that no restaurant in Venice can be truly untouristy: They all want and need the tourist euro.

Eating with the Seasons

Italian cooks love to serve you fresh produce and seafood at its tastiest. If you must have porcini mushrooms outside of

October and November, they'll be frozen. Each region in Italy has its own specialties, which you'll see displayed in open-air markets. To get the freshest veggies at a fine restaurant, request *"Un piatto di verdure della stagione, per favore"* (A plate of seasonal vegetables, please).

Here are a few examples of what's fresh when:

April–May:	Squid, green beans, asparagus, artichokes, and zucchini flowers
April–May, Sept–Oct:	Black truffles
May–June:	Asparagus, zucchini, cantaloupe, and strawberries
May–Aug:	Eggplant
Oct–Nov:	Mushrooms, white truffles, and chestnuts
Nov–Feb:	Radicchio
Fresh year-round:	Clams, meats

EATING IN VENICE

A trattoria or *osteria* (which historically meant a simple restaurant) can now be just as elegant and pricey as a *ristorante*.

For unexciting but basic values, look for a *menù turistico*, a three- or four-course set-price meal (also called *menù del giorno*—menu of the day); the price includes a service charge, and there's no need to tip. While set-price meals can be cheap and easy, galloping gourmets order à la carte with the help of a menu translator. (The *Rick Steves' Italian Phrase Book & Dictionary* has a menu decoder with enough phrases for intermediate eaters.)

A full meal consists of an appetizer (antipasto, €4–6), a first course (*primo piatto*, pasta, rice, or soup, €5–12), and a second course (*secondo piatto*, expensive meat and fish dishes, €10–20). Vegetables *(contorni, verdure)* may come with the *secondo* or cost extra (€4–6) as a side dish. The euros can add up in a hurry. Light and budget eaters get a

Tipping

In Italy, the "service" charge (*servizio*) is usually built into your bill's grand total in one of two ways: If the menu says *servizio incluso*, the listed prices already include this fee; if it says *servizio non incluso*, a fixed percentage (usually 10–15 percent of the total) will be added as a line item to the bottom of the bill. In either case, the total you pay already includes a basic tip. If you're pleased with the service, you can round up the bill by a euro or two (though most Italians rarely add this additional tip). Even if you pay your bill with a credit card, it's best to tip in cash—leave it on the table or hand it directly to your server.

Tipping is an issue only at restaurants that have waiters and waitresses. If you order your food at a counter, don't tip.

primo piatto each and share an antipasto.

Note that seafood and steak may be sold by weight (priced by the kilo—1,000 grams, or just over two pounds; or by the *etto*—100 grams). The letters "s.q." means according to quantity. Fish is usually served whole with the head and tail; you can't just get half a fish or a filet unless it already comes prepared as just a filet (*filetto*, sometimes *trancio*—slice, as in tuna or swordfish). However, you can ask your waiter to select a smaller fish for you. Sometimes, especially for steak, restaurants require a minimum order of four or five *etti*. Beware, or be shell-shocked by €50 entrées. Make sure you're really clear on the price before ordering.

Some special dishes come in large quantities meant for two people; the shorthand way of showing this on a menu is "x2" (meaning "times two"), and the price listed generally indicates the cost per person.

Restaurants normally pad the bill with a cover charge (*pane e coperto*—"bread and cover charge") of around €2, which is not negotiable, even if you don't eat the bread.

Cheap Meals

The keys to eating affordably in Venice are pizza, bars/cafés, and picnics. *Panini* and *tramezzini* (sandwiches, described on page 264) are sold fast and cheap at bars everywhere and can stave off midmorning hunger. There's a great "sandwich row" of cheap cafés near St. Mark's Square (see page 279). For speed, value, and ambience, you can get a filling plate of typically Venetian appetizers at nearly any bar. For budget eating, I like small, stand-up mini-meals at **cicchetti bars** best (many are recommended in this chapter).

EATING IN VENICE

Pizzerias

Pizza is cheap and readily available. Key pizza vocabulary: *capricciosa* (generally ham, mushrooms, olives, and artichokes), *funghi* (mushrooms), *marinara* (tomato sauce, oregano, garlic, no cheese), *quattro formaggi* (four different cheeses), and *quattro stagioni* (different toppings on each of the pizza's four quarters, for those who can't choose just one menu item). If you ask for pepperoni on your pizza, you'll get *peperoni* (green or red peppers, not sausage); request *diavola* instead (the closest thing in Italy to American pepperoni). Kids like the simple *margherita* (cheese with tomato sauce).

Bars/Cafés

Italian "bars" are not taverns, but cafés. These neighborhood hang-outs serve coffee, mini-pizzas, sandwiches, and drinks from the cooler. Many dish up plates of fried cheese and vegetables from under the glass counter, ready to reheat. This budget choice is the Italian equivalent of English pub grub. Unique to Venice, *cicchetti* bars specialize in finger foods and appetizers that can combine to make a quick and tasty meal. See "The Stand-Up Progressive Venetian Pub-Crawl Dinner" on page 272.

For quick meals, bars usually have trays of cheap, ready-made sandwiches (*panini* or *tramezzini*)—some are delightful grilled. (Others are lots of mayo between crustless slices of Wonder Bread.) To save time for sightseeing and room for dinner, consider a ham-and-cheese *panino* at a bar (called *toast*, have it grilled twice if you want it really hot) for lunch.

To get food "for the road," say, *"Da portar via"* (or *"da portar canale"*...for the canal). Many bars are small—if you can't find a table, you'll need to stand up. Most charge extra for table service. All bars have a WC *(toilette, bagno)* in the back, and customers (and the discreet public) may use it.

Bars serve great drinks—hot, cold, sweet, caffeinated, or alcoholic. Chilled bottled water, still *(naturale)* or carbonated *(frizzante),* is sold cheap to go.

Coffee: Take some time to learn Italian coffee lingo—the names and the rituals are a little different from those at your hometown java joint. If you ask for *"un caffè,"* you'll get espresso. If you ask for a latte, you'll get just that—a glass of hot milk. Starbucks-style mochas aren't on the menu at all.

Cappuccino is served to locals before noon and to tourists at any time of day. (To an Italian, cappuccino is a breakfast drink and a travesty after anything with tomatoes.) Italians like their coffee only warm—to get it hot, request *"Molto caldo"* (MOHL-toh KAHL-doh; very hot) or *"Più caldo, per favore"* (pew KAHL-doh, pehr fah-VOH-ray; hotter, please).

Experiment with a few of the options:

- *Cappuccino:* Espresso with foamed milk on top
- *Caffè latte:* Tall glass with espresso and hot milk mixed, no foam
- *Caffè hag:* Instant decaf (you can order decaffeinated versions of any coffee drink—ask for it *decaffeinato;* day-kah-fay-ee-NAH-toh)
- *Macchiato* (mah-kee-AH-toh): Espresso with only a little milk (*macchiato* means "marked" or "stained")
- *Latte macchiato:* Hot milk with a shot of espresso
- *Caffè americano:* Espresso diluted with water
- *Caffè freddo:* Sweet and iced espresso
- *Cappuccino freddo:* Iced cappuccino
- *Caffè corretto:* Espresso with a shot of liqueur, usually grappa or Sambuca, but amaretto is also good

Other Hot Drinks: *Cioccolato* is hot chocolate. *Tè* is hot tea. *Tè freddo* (iced tea) is usually from a can—sweetened and flavored with lemon or peach.

Juice: *Spremuta* means freshly squeezed as far as *succo* (fruit juice) is concerned (order *una spremuta*); it's usually orange juice, and February through April it's almost always made from blood oranges. (Note: *Spumante* means champagne.)

Beer: Beer on tap is *alla spina*. Get it *piccola* (33 cl, 11 oz), *media* (50 cl, about a pint), or *grande* (a liter, about 2 pints). Italians drink mainly lager beers. You'll find local brews (Peroni or Moretti) and imports such as Heineken as well. A *lattina* is a can and a *bottiglia* (boh-TEEL-yah) is a bottle.

Wine: To order a glass (*bicchiere;* bee-kee-AY-ree) of red *(rosso)* or white *(bianco)* wine, say, *"Un bicchiere di vino rosso/bianco."* *Secco* is dry, *corposo* means full-bodied, and *frizzante* is fizzy. House wine *(vino della casa)* comes in a carafe: quarter-liter (8.5 oz, *un quarto*), half-liter pitcher (17 oz, *un mezzo*), or one-liter pitcher (34 oz, *un litro*). An *ombra* is the smallest glass.

Prices: You'll notice a two-tiered pricing system. It's cheapest to drink a cup of coffee while standing at the bar; you'll pay more for that same cup to sit at an indoor table, and often still more at an outdoor table. Many places have a *listino prezzi* (price list) with two columns—*al bar* and *al tavolo*—posted somewhere by the bar or cash register. If you're on a budget, don't sit without first checking out the financial consequences. Ask, "Same price if I sit or stand?" by saying, *"Costa uguale al tavolo o al banco?"* (KOH-stah oo-GWAH-lay ahl TAH-voh-loh oh ahl BAHN-koh?). A cup of coffee at any bar generally costs only a euro if you stand.

If the bar isn't busy, you can probably just order and pay when you leave. Otherwise: 1) decide what you want; 2) find out the price by checking the price list on the wall, the prices posted near the food, or by asking the barista; 3) pay the cashier; and 4) give the receipt to the barista (whose clean fingers handle no dirty euros) and tell him what you want.

Picnics

Picnicking saves lots of euros and is a great way to sample regional specialties. Unfortunately, the only legal place to picnic in public in Venice is Giardinetti Reali, the waterfront park near St. Mark's Square.

An *alimentari* is your one-stop corner grocery store (most will slice and stuff your sandwich for you if you buy the ingredients there).

Juice-lovers can get a liter of O.J. for the price of a Coke or coffee. Look for "100% *succo*" (juice) on the label or be surprised by something diluted and sugary sweet. Hang onto the half-liter plastic mineral-water bottles (sold everywhere for about €1). Buy juice in cheap liter boxes, drink some, and store the extra in your water bottle. You'll also save money by buying water in big bottles (a third the price of small bottles—even cheaper in supermarkets) to keep in your hotel room and use to refill your smaller, more portable bottle. (I drink the tap water—*acqua del rubinetto*.)

Picnics can be adventures in high cuisine. Be daring. Try the

fresh mozzarella, presto pesto, shriveled olives, marinated eggplant or artichokes, sun-dried tomatoes, and any UFOs the locals are excited about. Shopkeepers are happy to sell small quantities of produce. Rather than pick your own produce, it is customary to let the merchant choose the produce for you. Say, *"Per oggi"* (pehr OH-jee, "for today"), and he or she will grab you something ready to eat, weigh it, and make the sale. If you suspect you're being overcharged, know the cost per kilo and study the weighing procedure as if you're doing the arithmetic.

A typical picnic for two might be fresh rolls, 100 grams of meat (about a quarter pound, called *un etto* in Italy), 100 grams of cheese, two tomatoes, three carrots, two apples, yogurt, and a liter box of juice. Total cost—about €10.

Near the Rialto: The **produce market** that sprawls for a few blocks just past the Rialto Bridge is a fun place to assemble a picnic (best Mon–Sat 8:00–13:00, closed Sun). The adjacent **fish market** is wonderfully slimy (closed Sun–Mon). Side lanes in this area are speckled with fine little hole-in-the-wall munchie bars, bakeries, and cheese shops.

A tiny *alimentari* just around the corner from the Rialto market has *salumi*, cheese, bread, and an intriguing (and spicy!)

concoction of cheese, kalamata olives, sun-dried tomatoes, olive oil, and hot peppers. It goes great with a fresh roll. To get there from the market, walk to the end of Ruga degli Orefici, turn left onto Ruga Vecchia S. Giovanni, and then right under Sotoportego dei Do' Mori—it's just on your left (open daily).

Near the Accademia Bridge: A small deli hides along the main route between the Accademia and St. Mark's Square (on the zig-zag bridge near the Church of Santa Maria del Giglio).

Near St. Mark's Square: To find the produce stand near the square, face St. Mark's Basilica, then walk along its left side, heading east down Calle de la Canonica. Cross the bridge and turn left at Campo S.S. Filippo e Giacomo.

Supermarkets: The handy **SuVe** supermarket is between St. Mark's and Campo Santa Maria Formosa, on the corner of Salizada San Lio and Calle del Mondo Novo. It has a great selection of picnic supplies, including prepackaged salads for less than €2 (Mon–Sat 9:00–19:30, closed Sun). **Billa** supermarket is at the far west end of Dorsoduro, on the corner of Zattere al Ponte Longo and Calle della Massena (Mon–Sat 8:00–20:00, Sun 9:00–19:00, tel. 041-522-6187). Assemble your picnic, and then dine in style overlooking Giudecca Canal.

Venetian Cuisine

Even more so than the rest of Italy, Venetian cuisine relies heavily on fish, shellfish, risotto, and polenta. Along with the usual pizza and pasta fare, here are some typical foods you'll encounter.

Bar Snacks

Venetians often eat a snack—*cicchetti* or *panini*—while standing at a bar. (Remember, you'll usually pay more if you sit, rather than stand.)

Cicchetti: Generic name for various small finger foods served in some pubs—like appetizers or tapas, Venetian-style. Designed as a quick meal for working people, the selection and ambience are best on workdays (Mon–Sat lunch and early dinner). See "The Stand-Up Progressive Venetian Pub-Crawl Dinner," page 272.

Panini: Sandwiches made with rustic bread, filled with meat, vegetables, and cheese, served cold or toasted—*riscaldato* (ree-skahl-DAH-toh). You can eat your sandwich at the bar or take it with you.

Tramezzini: Crustless, white bread sandwiches served cold and stuffed with a variety of fillings (e.g., egg, tuna, or shrimp), mixed with a mayonnaise dressing. The selection is best in the morning and skimpy by afternoon.

Appetizers *(Antipasti)*

Antipasto di mare: A marinated mix of fish and shellfish served chilled.

Asiago cheese: The Veneto region's specialty, a cow's-milk cheese that's either *mezzano*—young, firm, and creamy; or *stravecchio*—aged, pungent, and granular.

Sarde in saor: Sardines marinated with onions.

Rice *(Riso)*, Pasta, and Polenta

Risotto: Short-grain rice, simmered in broth and often flavored with fish and seafood. For example, *risotto nero* is risotto made with squid and its ink, and *risotto ai porcini* contains porcini mushrooms.

Risi e bisi: Rice and peas.

Pasta e fagioli: Bean and pasta soup.

Bigoli in salsa: A long, fat, whole-wheat noodle (one of the few traditional pastas) with anchovy sauce.

Polenta: Cornmeal boiled into a mush and served soft or cut into firm slabs and grilled. Polenta is a standard accompaniment with cod *(baccalà)*, or calf liver and onions *(fegato alla veneziana)*.

Seafood *(Frutti di Mare)*

Some sea creatures found in the Adriatic are slightly different from their American cousins. Generally, Venetian fish are smaller than American salmon and trout (think sardines and anchovies). The shellfish are more exotic. The weirder the animal (eel, octopus, frogfish), the more local it is. Remember that seafood can be sold by weight rather than a set price (if you see "100 g" or *"l'etto"* by a too-good-to-be-true price on the menu, that's the cost per 100 grams—about a quarter pound). As noted earlier, the abbreviation "s.q." means according to quantity (you pay for the weight of the particular piece).

Baccalà: Reconstituted dried salt cod served with polenta, or chopped up and mixed with mayonnaise as a topping for *cicchetti* (appetizers).

Branzino: Sea bass, grilled and served whole (with head and tail).

Calamari: Squid, usually cut into rings and either deep-fried or marinated.

Cozze: Mussels, often steamed in an herb broth with tomato.

Gamberi: The generic name for shrimp. *Gamberetti* are small shrimp, and *gamberoni* are large shrimp. (Language tip: *-etti* signifies little, and *-oni* indicates big.)

Moleche col pien: Fried soft-shell crabs.

Orata: Sea bream, a common European game fish.

Pesce fritto misto: Assorted deep-fried seafood (often calamari and prawns).

Pesce spada: Swordfish.

Rombo: Delicately flavored flat fish.

Rospo: Frogfish, a small marine fish.

Seppia: Cuttlefish, a squid-like creature that sprays black ink when threatened. *Seppia al nero* is the squid in its own ink, often served over spaghetti. It's sweet and tender when grilled—either *grigliata* or *alla griglia* (without its ink).

Sogliola: Sole, served poached or oven-roasted.

Vitello di mare: "Sea veal," like swordfish—firm, pink, mild, and grilled.

Vongole: Small clams steamed with fresh herbs and wine, or served as a first course, such as *spaghetti alle vongole*.

Zuppa di pesce: Seafood stew.

Dessert *(Dolci)*

Tiramisù: Spongy ladyfingers soaked in coffee and marsala, layered with mascarpone cheese and bitter chocolate. Arguably Venetian in origin, the literal meaning of the word is "pick-me-up."

Venetian cookies: There are numerous varieties, due perhaps to Venice's position in trade (spices) and the Venetians' love of celebrations. Many treats were created for certain feast days and religious holidays. *Pinza*, a sweet made with corn, wheat flour, and raisins (and sometimes figs, almonds, and lemon), is made for Epiphany, January 6. *Fritole* are tiny doughnuts associated with Carnevale (Mardi Gras). *Bussola* rings are made for Easter. Other popular treats are *bisse* (seahorse-shaped cookies) and *croccante* (made with toasted corn and almonds, similar in texture to peanut brittle).

Cocktails

Spritz: The dominant predinner drink *(aperitivo)* among Venetians is the *spritz*. This refreshing *aperitivo* mixes white wine, soda, and ice with a liquor of your choice and is garnished with an olive or skewer of fruit. Most popular with Venetians are *uno spritz con Campari* (bitter—traditionally the man's choice) or *con Aperol* (sweeter, a supposedly feminine choice). Between

18:00 and 20:00, this happy pink drink seems to dominate Venice's watering holes.

Bellini: A cocktail of Prosecco and white-peach puree; invented (and drunk by Hemingway) at the pricey Harry's American Bar (near San Marco-Vallaresso vaporetto stop).

Tiziano: Grape juice and Prosecco.

Sgroppino: A traditional drink of squeezed lemon juice, lemon gelato, and vodka, designed to finish off a meal.

Top Local Wines

Prosecco: Sparkling wine, usually a predinner drink, but can be ordered any time. It's neutral-tasting, making it easy to drink too much.

Soave: Crisp white (great with seafood) from near Verona. *Soave Classico* designates a higher quality.

Valpolicella: Light, dry, fruity red from the hills north of Verona. It's likely what you're drinking if you ordered the house wine *(vino della casa).*

Bardolino: Also made from Valpolicella grapes, it's a similar wine but grown near Lake Garda.

Amarone: Rich, intense red, with alcohol content at about 16 percent, made from Valpolicella grapes.

Fragolino: A sweet, slightly fizzy dessert wine made from a strawberry-flavored grape.

Grappa: Distilled *vinacce* (grape skins and stems left over from winemaking) make this powerful firewater. A *stravecchio* is an aged grappa, making it somewhat mellower.

Restaurants

While touristy restaurants are the scourge of Venice, these places are still popular with actual Venetians and respect the tourists who happen in. First trick: Walk away from triple-language menus. Second trick: Order the daily special. Third trick: For freshness, eat fish. Most seafood dishes are the catch-of-the-day. Remember that a place may feel really touristy at 19:00, but if you come back at 21:00 it could be filled with locals. Tourists eat barbarically early, which is fine with the restaurants because they fill tables that would otherwise be used only once in an evening.

Near the Rialto Bridge

North of the Bridge

These restaurants are located between Campo S.S. Apostoli and Campo Santa Maria Nova.

Trattoria da Bepi, bright and alpine-paneled, feels like a classic. Owner Loris scours the market for only the best

EATING IN VENICE

Restaurants near the Rialto Bridge

TO GHETTO & TRAIN STN.

TO TRAIN STN.

TO TRAIN STN.

TO CAMPO SAN POLO & FRARI CHURCH

STRADA NOVA

CA' D'ORO

FISH MARKET BLDG.

Veg. MKT.

CANAL

CAMPO BECC.

SPEZIALI

C. DO SPADE

S. MATTIA

ARCO

S. GIOVANNI

RUGA VECC.

FONDAMENTA

SANSONI

BOTERI

CAMPO S.S. APOST.

PISTOR

S.S. APOST.

CAMPO CORN. S.

MERCATO RIALTO

GRISTO

RIALTO BRIDGE

CAMPO S. GIAC.

OREFICI

POST

SAL

STATUE

FERRO

VIN

MAZZINI

RIALTO

CAMPO S. BART.

BISSA

2 APRILE

STAGNERI

MERCERIE

MERC.

REGINA

BALLOTTE

DCH

SAN SILV.

GRAND

RIVA

CARBON

BEMBO

FABBRI

CAMPO S LUCA

TO ACCADEMIA

TO SAN MARCO

- ❶ Trattoria da Bepi
- ❷ Vini da Gigio
- ❸ Trattoria Ca' d'Oro
- ❹ Osteria al Bomba
- ❺ Osteria "Alla Botte"
- ❻ Osteria di Sta. Marina
- ❼ Rost. S. Bartolomeo
- ❽ Osteria al Portego
- ❾ Cantina Do Mori, Bar all'Arco & Ostaria ai Storti
- ❿ Cantina Do Spade
- ⓫ Pesce Pronto
- ⓬ Bancogiro Bar
- ⓭ Al Marcà
- ⓮ Antica Ostaria Ruga Rialto

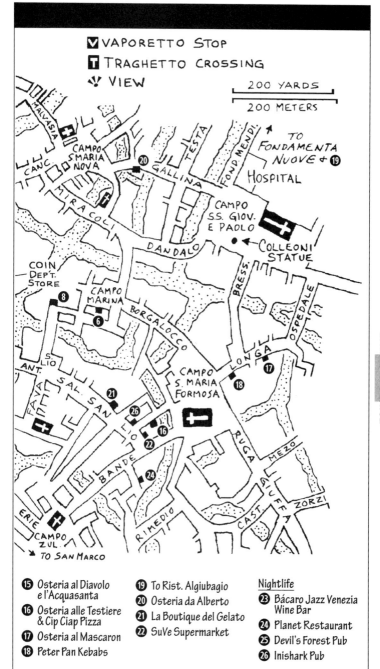

EATING IN VENICE

15 Osteria al Diavolo e l'Acquasanta

16 Osteria alle Testiere & Cip Ciap Pizza

17 Osteria al Mascaron

18 Peter Pan Kebabs

19 To Rist. Algiubagio

20 Osteria da Alberto

21 La Boutique del Gelato

22 SuVe Supermarket

Nightlife

23 Bácaro Jazz Venezia Wine Bar

24 Planet Restaurant

25 Devil's Forest Pub

26 Inishark Pub

ingredients—especially seafood—and takes good care of the hungry clientele. Ask for his seasonal specialties—the crab dishes are excellent. There's good seating inside and out (€10 pastas, €15 *secondi*, Fri–Wed 12:00–14:30 & 19:00–22:00, closed Thu, near Rialto Bridge, half a block north of Campo Santi Apostoli on Salizada Pistor, tel. 041-528-5031).

Little **Vini da Gigio** has a passion for good food, serving traditional Venetian dishes (€13 pastas, €20 *secondi*, no cover, Wed–Sun 19:00–late, last order at 22:30, closed Mon–Tue, 4 blocks from Ca' d'Oro vaporetto stop, behind the church on Campo San Felice, tel. 041-528-5140).

Trattoria Ca' d'Oro, while a little less accessible and inviting to the tourist, is a venerable favorite with a small, appealing menu and an enthusiastic following. Just to sip wine and enjoy *cicchetti* at the bar is a treat—their *polpette* (tuna and potato meatballs) are famous, and the house wine will set you back just €0.50. It's also fine for a meal (€9 pastas, €10 *secondi*, closed Thu, reservations recommended; from the Ca' d'Oro vaporetto dock, walk 100 yards directly away from the canal, cross Strada Nuova, and you'll hit it; tel. 041-528-5324).

Osteria al Bomba is a *cicchetti* bar with a female touch, thanks to Giovanna. It's unusual (clean, no toothpicks, no cursing) and quite good, with lots of veggies. You can stand and eat at the bar—try a little €3 *crostino* with polenta and cod—or oversee the construction of the house *"antipasto misto di cicchetti"* plate (€15, enough fish and vegetables for two) and choose your wine by the glass from the posted list. A seat at the long table comes with a €2 *coperto* (daily 12:00–15:00 & 18:00–23:00, near Campo S.S. Apostoli, go a block off Strada Nuova down a small alley, then take the first right on Calle dell'Oca, tel. 041-520-5175).

East of the Rialto Bridge, near Campo San Bartolomeo

Osteria "Alla Botte," despite being located a minute from the Rialto Bridge, is packed with a casual neighborhood clientele in two simple, woody rooms. For a classic Venetian taste, try the €18 all-seafood *antipasto misto* (daily 12:00–15:00 & 19:00–23:00, two short blocks off Campo San Bartolomeo in the corner behind the statue—down Calle de la Bissa, notice the "day after" photo showing a debris-covered Venice after the notorious 1989 Pink Floyd open-air concert, tel. 041-520-9775, Cristiano).

Osteria di Santa Marina, on the wonderful Campo Marina, serves pricey, near-gourmet cuisine in a dressy dining room. The presentation is impressive, but you feel there's more pretense than love of food. Cheap-eating tricks are frowned on in this elegant, borderline stuffy restaurant (enticing menu with €15 pastas and

€25 *secondi,* Tue–Sat 12:30–14:30 & 19:30–22:00, closed Sun, reserve for dinner, eat indoors or outdoors on pleasant little square, between Rialto Bridge and Campo Santa Maria Formosa on Campo Marina, tel. 041-528-5239).

Rosticceria San Bartolomeo is a cheap—if confusing—self-service diner, a throwback budget eatery with a likeably surly staff. Take out, grab a table, munch at the bar, or pay a bit more to eat at the restaurant upstairs (good €6–7 pasta, great fried *mozzarella al prosciutto* for €1.50, delightful fruit salad, €1 glasses of wine, prices listed on wall behind counter, no cover or service charge, daily 9:00–21:30, tel. 041-522-3569). To find it, imagine the statue on Campo San Bartolomeo walking backward 20 yards, turning left, and going under a passageway—now, follow him.

If you're pub crawling from Rosticceria San Bartolomeo, continue over a bridge to Campo San Lio. Here, turn left, passing Hotel Canada on your right, and follow Calle Carminati straight about 50 yards over another bridge. On the left is the pastry shop *(pasticceria),* and straight ahead is Osteria al Portego (at #6015).

Osteria al Portego is a friendly neighborhood bar—one of the best in town. Carlo serves good meals and excellent *cicchetti*—best enjoyed early, around 18:00 (from 19:00 to 21:00, tables are reserved for those ordering from the menu; the *cicchetti* are picked over by 21:00). Prices for food and wine are posted clearly on the wall. The *cicchetti* here can make a great meal, but you should also consider sitting down for a dinner from their fine menu. This place can get very busy, so reserve ahead if you want a table (€13 pastas, €2 glasses of wine, Mon–Sat 10:30–15:00 & 18:00–21:30, Sun 18:00–21:30, near Campo Marina at Calle Malvasia 6015, tel. 041-522-9038).

West of the Rialto Bridge

All of these places are informal, serving *cicchetti* and/or light meals. The first bars listed are within 200 yards of each other, a few steps behind the Rialto fish market; the rest are a short walk from this hive of eateries (see map on page 268). This area is very crowded by day, nearly empty early in the evening, and crowded with young Venetians later.

Cicchetti and Light Meals West of the Rialto

Most bars are closed 15:00–18:00 (though Cantina Do Mori and Ostaria ai Storti stay open all day), and offer glasses of house wine for under €1, better wine for around €2, and *cicchetti* for €1–2. At each place, look for the list of snacks and wine by the glass at the bar or on the wall. If you're ready for desert, try dipping a Burano biscuit in a glass of strawberry-flavored *fragolino* or another sweet dessert wine.

The Stand-Up Progressive Venetian Pub-Crawl Dinner

My favorite Venetian dinner is a pub crawl *(giro d'ombra)*—a tradition unique to Venice, where no cars means easy crawling. (*Giro* means stroll, and *ombra*—slang for a glass of wine—means shade, from the old days when a portable wine bar scooted with the shadow of the Campanile bell tower across St. Mark's Square.)

Venice's residential back streets hide plenty of character-istic bars *(bacari)* with countless trays of interesting toothpick munchies *(cicchetti)* and blackboards listing the wines that are uncorked and served by the glass. This is a great way to mingle and have fun with the Venetians. Bars don't stay open very late, and the *cicchetti* selection is best early, so start your evening by 18:00. Most bars are closed on Sunday. For a stress-free pub crawl, consider taking a tour with the charming Alessandro Schezzini (see page 33).

Cicchetti **bars** have a social stand-up zone and a cozy gaggle of tables where you can generally sit down with your *cicchetti* or order from a simple menu. In some of the more popular places, the crowds happily spill out into the street. Food generally costs the same price whether you stand or sit.

I've listed plenty of pubs in walking order for a quick or extended crawl. If you've crawled enough, most of these bars make a fine one-stop, sit-down dinner.

While you can order a plate, Venetians prefer going one-by-one...sipping their wine and trying this...then give me one of those...and so on. Try deep-fried mozzarella cheese, gorgonzola, calamari, artichoke hearts, and anything ugly on a toothpick.

EATING IN VENICE

Cantina Do Mori has been famous with locals (since 1462) and savvy travelers (since 1982) as a convivial place for fine wine. You'll choose from a forest of little edibles on toothpicks and *francobolli* (a spicy selection of 20 tiny, mayo-soaked sandwiches nicknamed "stamps"). Go here to be abused in a fine atmosphere—the frowns are part of the shtick (Mon–Sat 8:00–20:00, closed Sun, stand-up only, arrive early before the *cicchetti* are gone, San Polo 429, tel. 041-522-5401). From the Rialto Bridge, walk 200 yards down Ruga degli Orefici, away from St. Mark's Square—then turn left on Ruga Vecchia S. Giovanni, then right at Sotoportego Do Mori.

Bar all'Arco, a bustling one-room joint across from Cantina Do Mori, is particularly enjoyable for its tiny open-face sandwiches (closed Sun, tel. 041-520-5666).

Ostaria ai Storti serves lots of veggies and a few homemade pastas (check the daily specials) at great prices. With a homey feel, it's a fun place to congregate. Check out the photo of the market in

Crostini (small toasted bread with something on it) are popular, as are marinated seafood, olives, and prosciutto with melon. Meat and fish (*pesce;* PESH-ay) munchies can be expensive; veggies *(verdure)* are cheap, at about €3 for a meal-sized plate. In many places, there's a set price per food item (e.g., €1.50). To get a plate of assorted appetizers for €8 (or more, depending on how hungry you are), ask for *"Un piatto classico di cicchetti misti da €8"* (oon pee-AH-toh KLAH-see-koh dee cheh-KET-tee MEE-stee dah OH-toh ay-OO-roh). Bread sticks *(grissini)* are free for the asking.

Bar-hopping Venetians enjoy an *aperitivo,* a before-dinner drink. Boldly order a Bellini, a *spritz con Aperol,* or a Prosecco, and draw approving looks from the natives.

Drink the house wines. A small glass of house red or white wine *(ombra rosso* or *ombra bianco)* or a small beer *(birrino)* costs about €1. The house keg wine is cheap—€1 per glass, about €4 per liter. *Vin bon,* Venetian for fine wine, may run you from €1.50 to €6 per little glass. There are usually several fine wines uncorked and available by the glass. A good last drink is *fragolino,* the local sweet wine—*bianco* or *rosso.* It often comes with a little cookie *(biscotti)* for dipping.

1909, below the bar. Alessandro speaks English and enjoys helping educate travelers while serving *fragolino* (daily 9:00–22:30, 20 yards from Cantina Do Mori on Calle delle Do Spade 819, tel. 041-523-6861).

Cantina Do Spade is run by Sebastiano, who clearly lists the *cicchetti* and wines of the day (daily 11:00–15:00 & 18:00–21:00, 30 yards down Calle delle Do Spade from Ostaria ai Storti at Calle delle Do Spade 19, tel. 041-521-0583).

At **Pesce Pronto,** you can actually sample fish while watching the market action. Bruno and Umberto serve artful fish hors d'oeuvres, *sfornato con pesce* (a savory baked pastry), and many other fresh fish tidbits—all at a fair price. This fancy hole-in-the-wall is fun for a quick bite—eat standing up or take it to go. At 12:30, they serve €10–12 "express plates" of pasta and other choices (Tue–Sat 9:00–14:30 & 17:00–19:30, closed Sun-Mon, facing the fish market at Calle de le Beccarie o Panataria 319, tel. 041-822-0298).

Youthful *Cicchetti* Bars near Campo San Giacometto

A strip of five places between Campo San Giacometto and the Grand Canal, several with canal-front tables, together make a thriving youth *spritz* scene that's worth a look even if you don't eat or drink there.

The **Bancogiro Bar** is good for strong cheese and its canalside tables (€3.50/person cover, €15 cheese plate, wine by glass is listed on board, Tue–Sun 12:00–23:00, closed Mon, tel. 041-523-2061).

Al Marcà, a few steps away and off the canal, is an even livelier little nook with a happy crowd, where young locals gather to grab drinks and little snacks. The price list is clear, and I've found the crowd to be welcoming to tourists interested in connecting (Mon–Sat 9:00–15:00 & 18:00–21:00, closed Sun, on Campo Cesare Battisti).

More *Cicchetti* Bars West of the Rialto Bridge

Antica Ostaria Ruga Rialto, a.k.a. "the Ruga," is a neighborhood fixture where Giorgio and Marco serve great bar snacks and wine to a devoted clientele. Treats here are their polenta, sardine with onions, and veggies. Bar or table, no problem—they're happy to make you a €3, €6, or €10 mixed plate (daily 11:00–14:30 & 19:00–24:00, easy to find—just past the Chinese restaurant at Ruga Vecchia San Giovanni 692, tel. 041-521-1243).

Osteria al Diavolo e l'Acquasanta, three blocks west of the Rialto Bridge, serves good—if pricey—Venetian-style pasta, and makes a handy lunch stop for sightseers and gondola riders. Though they list *cicchetti* and wine by the glass on the wall, I'd come here for a light meal rather than for appetizers (Mon 12:00–14:30, Wed–Sun 12:00–21:30, closed Tue, hiding on Calle della Madonna—a quiet street just off Ruga Vecchia San Giovanni, tel. 041-277-0307).

Pizza and Pasta Farther West of the Rialto Bridge

Antica Birraria la Corte is an everyday eatery on the delightful Campo San Polo, between the Rialto Bridge and the Frari Church. Popular with locals for its pizza, calzones, and salads, it fills the far side of this cozy, family-filled square. While the interior is a sprawling beer hall, it's a joy to eat on the square, where metal tables teeter on the cobbles, the wind plays with the paper mats, and children run free (daily 12:00–14:30 & 19:00–22:30, Campo San Polo 2168, see map on page 220, tel. 041-275-0570).

Trattoria Pizzeria al Nono Risorto is unpretentious, inexpensive, youthful, and famous for serving some of the best pizza in town. You'll sit in a gravelly garden under a leafy canopy, surrounded by an enthusiastic waitstaff and Italians enjoying huge €8 salads, pastas, and pizzas, and €12 grilled meat or fish dishes

(Thu–Tue 12:00–14:30 & 19:00–22:30, closed Wed, reservations smart on weekends; from Rialto fish market, walk 3 minutes to Campo San Cassiano—it's just over the bridge on Sotoportego de Siora Bettina; see map on page 254; tel. 041-524-1169).

Near Campo Santa Maria Formosa

Campo Santa Maria Formosa is one of my favorite community scenes. While the restaurants fronting the square aren't much, several good options for dining lie a short walk away. For locations, see the map on page 268.

Osteria alle Testiere is my top dining recommendation in Venice. Hugely respected, they are dedicated to quality, serving up creative, artfully presented market-fresh seafood (there's no meat on the menu), homemade pastas, and fine wine in what the chef calls a "Venetian Nouvelle" style. With only 22 seats, it's tight and homey, yet elegant. They have daily specials, 10 wines by the glass, and one agenda: a great dining experience. Luca, the owner/host, is gracious and passionate about his food. This is one place to let loose and trust your host. Reservations are required for their three seatings: 12:30, 19:00, and 21:30 (€19 pastas, €25 *secondi,* plan on spending €50 for dinner, closed Sun–Mon, just off Campo Santa Maria Formosa at Calle del Mondo Novo 5801, tel. 041-522-7220).

Osteria al Mascaron is where I've gone for years to watch Gigi, Momi, and their food-loving band of ruffians dish up rustic-yet-sumptuous pastas with steamy seafood to salivating foodies. The pastas, while pricey, are for two (it's OK to ask for single portions). The €16 *antipasto misto* plate—have fun pointing—and two glasses of wine make a terrific light meal, and their seafood pastas make beautiful memories (Mon–Sat 12:00–15:00 & 19:00–23:00, closed Sun, reservations smart Fri–Sat, a block past Campo Santa Maria Formosa at Calle Longa Santa Maria Formosa 5225, tel. 041-522-5995).

Fast and Cheap Eats: The Campo Santa Maria Formosa area has plenty of ways to sit and munch cheap. The veggie stand on the square is a fixture. For *döner kebabs* to go, head down Calle Longa to **Peter Pan** (€3.50). For pizza to go, it's **Cip Ciap** (next to Osteria alle Testiere at the bridge).

Near St. Mark's Square

For locations, see the map on page 276.

Dining near St. Mark's Square

The following three places are a few blocks east of St. Mark's Square and offer classy dining experiences. The first two listings are the best canalside dining values I've found in Venice. Both specialize in fish, and have a reasonable-for-the-romantic-setting

EATING IN VENICE

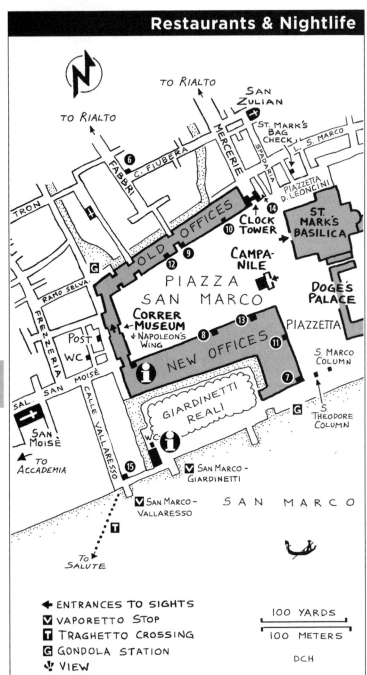

Restaurants & Nightlife

TO RIALTO

TO RIALTO

SAN ZULIAN

ST. MARK'S BAG CHECK

S. MARCO

MERCERIE

SPADARIA

PIAZZETTA D. LEONCINI

C. FIUBERA

FABBRI

6

TRON

OLD OFFICES

14

10 CLOCK TOWER

ST. MARK'S BASILICA

9

12

CAMPA-NILE

PIAZZA SAN MARCO

DOGE'S PALACE

RAMO SELVA

FRENZERIA

CORRER MUSEUM + Napoleon's Wing

13

8

NEW OFFICES

11

PIAZZETTA

POST WC

7

S. MARCO COLUMN

i

SAN MOISÈ

MOISÈ

CALLE VALLARESSO

SAL. SAN

GIARDINETTI REALI

WC

i

G

S. THEODORE COLUMN

SAN MOISÈ

TO ACCADEMIA

15

V San Marco - Giardinetti

V San Marco - Vallaresso

SAN MARCO

T

TO SALUTE

← ENTRANCES TO SIGHTS
V VAPORETTO STOP
T TRAGHETTO CROSSING
G GONDOLA STATION
⚘ VIEW

100 YARDS

100 METERS

DCH

near St. Mark's Square

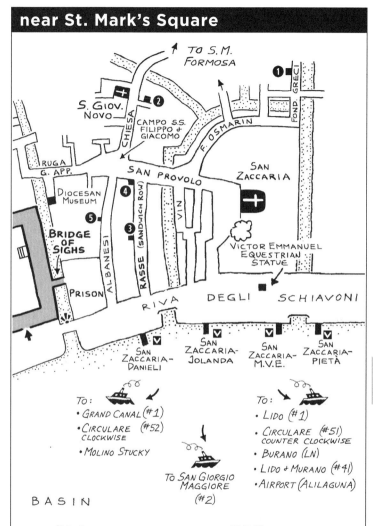

Eateries

❶ Ristorante alla Conchiglia
   & Trattoria da Giorgio ai Greci
❷ Ristorante Antica Sacrestia
❸ "Sandwich Row": Birreria Forst
❹ Bar Verde
❺ Ristorante alla Basilica
❻ Rizzo
❼ Todaro Gelateria

Nightlife

❽ Caffè Florian
❾ Gran Caffè Quadri
❿ Gran Caffè Lavena
⓫ Gran Caffè Chioggia
⓬ Eden Bar
⓭ Caffè Aurora
⓮ American Bar
⓯ Harry's American Bar

Romantic Canalside Settings

Of course, if you want a meal with a canal view, it generally comes with lower quality or a higher price. But if you're aiming for a canalside memory, these places can be great. I've listed the better-value places below, along with advice for coping with the tourist traps.

Near the Rialto Bridge: Several *cicchetti* bars line the Grand Canal, with front tables just off **Campo San Giacometto,** between the market and the Rialto Bridge (described on page 274). You can get good light meals in this area, but these bars don't offer romantic dining per se.

Rialto Bridge Tourist Traps: Venetians are embarrassed by the lousy food and aggressive "service" at the string of joints dominating the best romantic, Grand Canal–fringing real estate in town. Still, if you want to linger over dinner with a view of the most famous bridge and the songs of gondoliers oaring by (and don't mind eating with other tourists), this can be enjoyable. Don't trust the waiter's recommendations for special meals. The budget ideal would be to get a simple pizza or pasta and a drink for €15, and savor the ambience without getting ripped off. But few restaurants will allow you to get off that easy. To avoid a dispute over the bill, ask if there's a minimum charge—before you sit down (most places have one).

East of St. Mark's Square: Ristorante alla **Conchiglia** and **Trattoria da Giorgio ai Greci,** a few blocks behind St. Mark's, have the best canalside dining I've found anywhere in town (see page 279).

Overlooking the Giudecca Canal: **Terrazza del Casin dei Nobili,** located in Zattere—on the Venice side of the wide Giudecca Canal—gets the warm, romantic evening sun (page 280).

On Fondamenta Nuove with a View of the Open Lagoon: Ristorante Algiubagio is a good opportunity to eat well while overlooking the lagoon (page 281).

On Burano: Trattoria al **Gatto Nero** sits on a tranquil canal under a tilting bell tower in the pastel townscape of Burano. If you're touring the lagoon and want to enjoy Burano without the crowds, go late and consider a dinner here (see page 208).

menu; if you want a canalside seat for dinner, call to reserve it. To reach these from St. Mark's Square, head behind the basilica to Campo San Provolo, then follow Calle Osmarin to Fondamenta dei Greci. To get to the third, head up Chiesa from Campo San Provolo.

Ristorante alla Conchiglia seats its guests at lovely tables that line the sleepy canal (€10 pizzas, big €14 salads, €15 fixed-price meals, daily specials, daily, closed Dec and Jan, Fondamenta dei Greci, tel. 041-528-9095).

Trattoria da Giorgio ai Greci, right next door, is enthusiastically run by Giorgio and sons Davide and chatty Roberto (€17–21 fixed-price meals, daily 12:00–22:30, Ponte dei Greci 4988, tel. 041-528-9780).

Ristorante Antica Sacrestia is a classic restaurant where the owner, Pino, takes a hands-on approach to greeting guests. His staff serve a delightful antipasto spread (€18), are proud of their fish, and offer €20–45 fixed-price meals of fish, meat, or vegetarian dishes. It's also a local favorite for pizza. This is the kind of place where you are best off going with the waiters' suggestions. My readers are welcome to a free *sgroppino* (lemon vodka after-dinner drink) upon request (immediately behind San Giovanni Novo Church at Calle della Sacrestia 4442, Castello, tel. 041-523-0749).

Budget Eateries near St. Mark's Square

Picnicking isn't allowed on St. Mark's Square, but you can legally take your snacks to the nearby Giardinetti Reali, the small park along the waterfront west of the Piazzetta.

"Sandwich Row": On Calle delle Rasse, just steps away from the tourist intensity at St. Mark's Square, is a strip I call "Sandwich Row." Lined with sandwich bars, it's the closest place to St. Mark's to get a decent sandwich at an affordable price with a place to sit down (most places open daily 7:00–24:00, €1 extra to sit; from the Bridge of Sighs, head down the Riva and take the second lane on the left). I particularly like **Birreria Forst,** which serves a selection of meaty €2.70 sandwiches with tasty sauce on wheat bread, or made-to-order sandwiches for around €3.50 (daily 10:00–20:30, air-con, rustic wood tables, Calle delle Rasse 4540, tel. 041-523-0557) and **Bar Verde,** a more modern sandwich bar with fun people-watching views from its corner tables (big €4 sandwiches, splittable €8 salads, fresh pastries including Sicilian cannoli, at the end of Calle delle Rasse, facing Campo S.S. Filippo e Giacomo).

Ristorante alla Basilica, just one street behind St. Mark's Basilica, is a church-run, institutional-feeling place serving a solid €13 three-course lunch daily from 11:45 to 15:00 (modern, air-con, Calle degli Albanesi 4255, tel. 041-522-0524).

Rizzo is a convenient bar/*alimentari* market located north of St. Mark's Square on the main drag of Calle dei Fabbri. Grab €4.50 homemade lasagna and other reasonably priced snacks, such as yogurt, sautéed spinach, or fried sandwiches. It's stand-and-eat only—there's no seating (Mon–Sat 8:00–20:00, closed Sun, Calle dei Fabbri 933A, tel. 041-522-3388).

In Dorsoduro

Near the Accademia Bridge

Ristorante/Pizzeria Accademia Foscarini, next to the Accademia Bridge and Galleria, offers decent €8–11 pizzas in a great canalside setting. Their toasted *fareiti* sandwich is a local favorite (€6.50 at the table). Though the pizzas may be forgettable, this place is both scenic and practical—on each visit to Venice, I grab a pizza lunch here while I ponder the Grand Canal bustle (May–Oct Wed–Mon 7:00–21:30, Nov–April until 20:00, closed Tue, Dorsoduro 878C, tel. 041-522-7281).

Enoteca Cantine del Vino Già Schiavi is much-loved for its €1 *cicchetti* and €3.50 sandwiches (order from list on board). It's also a good place for a €2 glass of wine and appetizers (Mon–Sat 8:00–20:30, closed Sun, 100 yards from Accademia art museum on San Trovaso canal; facing Accademia, take a right and then a forced left at the canal to the second bridge—S. Trovaso 992, tel. 041-523-0034). You're welcome to enjoy your wine and finger food hanging out at the bar, sitting on the bridge out front, or in the nearby square—which actually has grass. This is primarily a wine shop with great prices for bottles to go—and plastic glasses for picnickers.

Terrazza del Casin dei Nobili, located in Zattere (on the Venice side of the Giudecca Canal), takes full advantage of the warm, romantic evening sun. They serve finely crafted, regional specialties with creativity at reasonable prices. The canalside seating is breezy and beautiful, but comes with the rumble of *vaporetti* from the nearby stop. The interior is bright and hip (good €10 pizzas, €10 pastas, €15 *secondi*, €2 cover, Fri–Wed 12:00–23:00, closed Thu, exit vaporetto at Zattere stop and turn left to Zattere 924/5, tel. 041-520-6895). For more on Zattere (including the free live music on Wed and Sun evenings), see page 298.

Near Campo San Barnaba

A number of restaurants are near this small square, a short walk from the Accademia. As these are each within a few steps of each other and the energy and atmosphere can vary, I like to survey the options before choosing (although reservations may be necessary later in the evening).

Casin dei Nobili ("Pleasure Palace of Nobles")—related to the Terrazza del Casin dei Nobili, listed above—has a high-energy, informal, modern setting. The patio is filled with simple tables, happy tourists, and inviting €11 daily lunch specials (€12 pastas, €20 *secondi*, good pizzas, and "fantasy salads," Tue–Sun 12:00–15:00 & 19:00–23:00, closed Mon, cash only, a half-block south of Campo San Barnaba at Calle delle Casin 2765, tel. 041-241-1841, Damiano).

Pane Vino e San Daniele is a busy little place that feels real, with the TV on, an enticing blackboard listing the day's specials, and the kitchen action filling its dining room (€7 pastas, €10 salads and *secondi*, Calle Longa San Barnaba 2861, tel. 041-243-9865).

Enoteca e Trattoria la Bitta is dark and woody, with a soft-jazz bistro feel and a small, forgettable back patio. They serve beautifully presented, traditional Venetian food with—proudly—no fish. Their helpful waitstaff and small menu are clearly focused on quality. Reservations are required (€10 pastas, €15 *secondi*, dinner only, Mon–Sat 18:30–23:00, closed Sun, cash only, between previous two listings at Calle Longa San Barnaba 2753, tel. 041-523-0531).

Elsewhere in Venice

On Fondamente Nuove: **Ristorante Algiubagio** is a good place to eat well overlooking the lagoon. The name is a combination of the owners' four names—Alberto, Giulio, Barbara, and Giovanna—who strive to impress visitors with quality, creative Venetian cuisine made using the best ingredients. Reserve a table on the lagoon facing the island of San Michele or in their classy cantina dining room (€16 pastas, €25 *secondi*, €3 cover, Wed–Mon 12:00–15:00 & 19:00–22:30, closed Tue, to the left of the vaporetto dock as you face the water at Fondamenta Nuove 5039, Cannaregio, tel. 041-523-6084). This is a convenient place to eat if you're taking the vaporetto out to the islands in the lagoon (described in Venice's Lagoon Tour chapter; see map on page 200).

Near Campo Santa Maria Nova: **Osteria da Alberto,** with excellent daily specials, €13 seafood plates, €10 pastas, a good house wine, and a woody and characteristic interior, is one of my standbys. It's smart to reserve at night—I'd request a table in the front (Mon–Sat 12:00–15:00 & 18:00–23:00, closed Sun, midway between Campo S.S. Apostoli and Campo S.S. Giovanni e Paolo, next to Ponte de la Panada on Calle Larga Giacinto Gallina, tel. 041-523-8153, run by Graziano and Giovanni).

Near the Train Station: There are piles of eateries near the

Restaurants near the

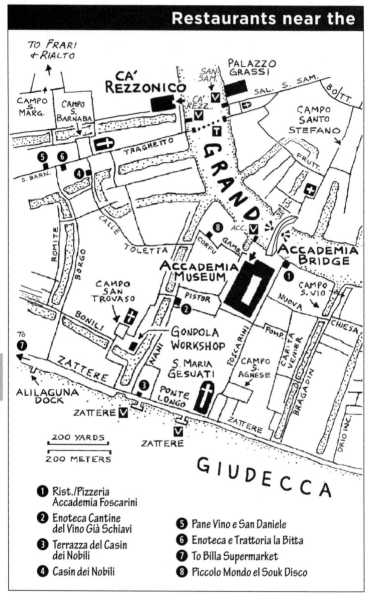

1 Rist./Pizzeria Accademia Foscarini

2 Enoteca Cantine del Vino Già Schiavi

3 Terrazza del Casin dei Nobili

4 Casin dei Nobili

5 Pane Vino e San Daniele

6 Enoteca e Trattoria la Bitta

7 To Billa Supermarket

8 Piccolo Mondo el Souk Disco

Accademia Bridge

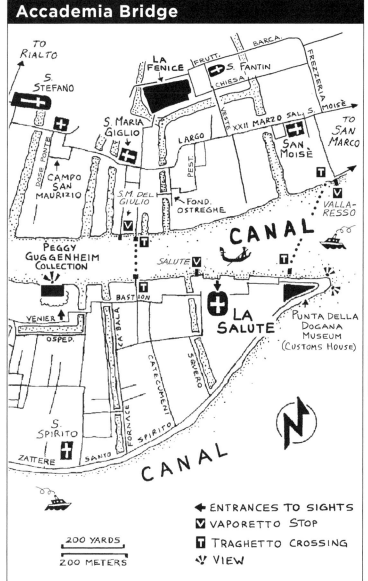

TO RIALTO

S. STEFANO

LA FENICE

FRUTT.

BARCA

S. FANTIN

CHIESA

FREZZERIA

S. MARIA GIGLIO

VESTE

XXII MARZO

SAL. S. MOISÈ

TO SAN MARCO

LARGO

PEST.

SAN MOISÈ

DOSE PONTE

CAMPO SAN MAURIZIO

S.M. DEL GIULIO

FOND. OSTREGHE

T

VALLA-RESSO

PEGGY GUGGENHEIM COLLECTION

CANAL

SALUTE

T

VENIER

OSPED.

BASTION

CA BALA

LA SALUTE

PUNTA DELLA DOGANA MUSEUM (CUSTOMS HOUSE)

CATECUMENI

S. GREGORIO

S. SPIRITO

FORNACE

SPIRITO

ZATTERE

SANTO

CANAL

200 YARDS

200 METERS

➤ ENTRANCES TO SIGHTS

V VAPORETTO STOP

T TRAGHETTO CROSSING

VIEW

EATING IN VENICE

station. The **food circus** in the station is quite good, with peaceful garden seating out back. A block away is the efficient and economic **Brek,** a popular self-service cafeteria chain (daily 11:30–22:00, head left as you leave the station and walk about 50 yards past the bridge to Rio Terra Lista di Spagna 124).

Gelato

La Boutique del Gelato, as lines attest, is considered the best *gelateria* in Venice. They dish up generous €1.20 scoops (daily 10:00–22:00, closed Dec–Jan, located on map on page 268, leave Campo Santa Maria Formosa from the corner with the bell tower, cross the bridge, turn right on Salizada San Lio, and find it next to Hotel Bruno at #5727).

On St. Mark's Square, there are two venerable *gelaterie:* **Gran Caffè Lavena** (daily until 24:00, first café to left of the Clock Tower, behind the first orchestra) and **Todaro Gelateria** (on the corner of the Piazzetta, near the Grand Canal and just under St. Theodore slaying the dragon, tel. 041-528-5165).

VENICE WITH CHILDREN

Some of the best fun I've had with my kids has been in Venice. The city doesn't need an amusement park...it is one big fantasy world. It's safe and like nothing else your kids have ever seen. Though there's lots of pavement and few parks or playgrounds, just being there—and free to wander—can be delightful.

If you're bringing the family, consider these tips:

• Don't overdo it. Tackle just one or two key sights each day and mix in a healthy dose of enjoyable activities. A vaporetto ride is a great way to start your visit.

• Follow this book's crowd-beating tips. Kids dislike long lines even more than you do.

• Eat dinner early (19:00 at restaurants), and skip the romantic places. Try self-service cafeterias, out-of-the-way bars (children are welcome), or fast-food restaurants, where kids can move around without bothering others. For pizza, favorite choices for kids include *margherita* (tomato and cheese) and spicy *diavola*, which is the closest thing on the menu to sliced pepperoni sausage (if you ask for *peperoni*, you'll get bell peppers). Picnic lunches and dinners work well. For ready-made picnics, drop by the *rosticcerie* (delis). For fast and kid-friendly meals in the center, you'll find a couple of American hamburger joints between the Rialto Bridge and St. Mark's Square, great pizzerias on squares everywhere, and plenty of gelato.

• Give your kid a cheap camera. Venice turns anyone into a photographer.

• Look for family and child discounts. If buying the San

Marco Museum Plus Pass (or its off-season version, the Museum Card of the Museums of St. Mark's Square), which includes the Doge's Palace, ask for the family discount (available to two adults with at least two children up to age 18). A family ticket is also available for the Chorus Pass. The "Rolling Venice" Youth Discount Pass gives discounts on many sights and transportation for travelers under 30. See "Passes for Venice," on page 24, for details.

• Venice is great for older children and teens, but presents challenges if traveling with infants or toddlers. Keep in mind that there are rarely any fences or walls between the sidewalk and the water, so keep toddlers safely in hand. You won't have much use for strollers—with hundreds of stepped bridges, Venice is a frustrating obstacle course. Try toting your baby in a carrier instead. The Campo Santa Maria Formosa is a rare place in Venice where you'll find railings.

• While Venice is short on parks, its many small squares have served as playgrounds for local children for centuries. Let your kids run around while you take a seat at a café or bench.

• Turn the city into a scavenger hunt. Look on buildings for a winged lion, search the shop windows for a mask with a long nose, scour the canal for a fire boat—and extra points for a (yuck) dead pigeon! Wait for the world's first digital clock (on the Clock Tower in St. Mark's Square) to flip over. Find pickpockets in action at the viewing point for the Bridge of Sighs. Wave at romantics in gondolas from bridges over popular gondola routes.

• In Venice, pick up a copy of *VivaVenice: A Guide to Exploring, Learning, and Having Fun* by Paola Zoffoli. It's full of interesting facts, and it's sold at many bookstores in the city. *Venice for Kids*, by Elisabetta Pasqualin, is a great guidebook for tweens and up, available at many museum bookshops. *A Walk Thru Venice* (purchase locally) is a fun history book for older kids.

• Involve your children in the trip. Let them lead you through the maze of Venice's back streets. Get lost together. If your children are old enough, they can be the tour guides and read this book's self-guided tours. (Standard tip for good guides: a two-scoop gelato.)

• If you're taking the train to another city, ask for the family discount *("Offerta Familia")* when buying tickets at a counter; or, at a ticket machine, click "Yes" to the "Do you want ticket issue?" cue, then click "Familia." With the discount, families of three to five people with at least one kid under age 12 get 50 percent off for the kids under 12, and 20 percent off for adults. The deal doesn't apply to all trains at all times, but it's certainly worth checking out.

Sights and Activities

Watch the pigeons on St. Mark's Square. (Though feeding them is now against the law, they're still around.) If you yell, the birds will just ignore you, but tossing a sweater into the air kicks off a pigeon evacuation. And anyone of any age enjoys the magic of **St. Mark's Square at night.**

Ride the elevator to the top of the **Campanile** bell tower to enjoy the grand view, and be there as the huge bells whip into ear-shattering action at the top of each hour (see St. Mark's Square Tour chapter).

Take in a **glassblowing demonstration** at Galleria San Marco (just off St. Mark's Square, see page 291). Part of the **Doge's Palace** tour includes the dark, dank prison and a creative armory.

Ride lots of **boats** (vaporetto, gondola, *traghetto,* or speedboat tours of the lagoon). Sit in the front seat of a vaporetto for my Grand Canal Cruise. See how many kinds of service boats you can spot while on the canal (UPS, police, fire, and so on).

The Rialto **fish market** is as fishy as they get (closed Sun, on the canal two blocks west of Rialto Bridge). Watch the people unload the boats at the market. You can leave by *traghetto* and cross the Grand Canal (*traghetto* dock at market).

Be choosy when taking kids to museums. The venerable and fascinating (to adults) Accademia will probably bore children. But don't skip art entirely. Kids like holding mirrors to see the ceiling paintings at the **Scuola San Rocco.** The **Peggy Guggenheim Collection** has colorful modern art, by Picasso and others, that interests kids.

A **children's park** is near the train station (facing the canal with your back to station, walk down the stairs and a block left past the shops to a small opening in wall on left—you'll see the playground inside). The bigger **Giardini park** has swings and playground equipment (on the far end of town—in Venice's "fish tail," near Giardini vaporetto stop). The **Lido** (beach) island sounds more intriguing than it is, though it can be a kid-friendly place to visit or stay, given the beaches and bike-riding possibilities.

If your kids are likely to enjoy a **soccer game,** consider a trip to the stadium located in the Santa Elena district. Venice's team is currently in the fifth-ranked Italian Serie D league (not so good), so the crowds aren't as enthusiastic as usual, but games are fun nonetheless. Matches take place on Sundays from September to June (ask at the TI). Buy a scarf with the team colors—black, orange, and green—and join the fun. Goal!

Make a point to include some **Venetian history.** Taking advantage of the information in this book, explain St. Mark (look for winged lions, page 74), the birth of the city (page 358), how and why the city floods (page 34), and the story of the gondolas (page 294).

SHOPPING IN VENICE

Long a city of aristocrats, luxury goods, and merchants, Venice was built to entice. While no one claims it's great for bargains, it has a shopping charm that makes paying too much strangely enjoyable. Carnevale masks, lace, glass, antique paper products, designer clothing, fancy accessories, and paintings are all popular with tourists visiting Venice.

Shops are generally open from 9:00 to 13:00 and from 15:00 to 19:30. In touristy Venice, more shops are open on Sunday than in the rest of the country. If you're buying a substantial amount from nearly any shop, bargain—it's accepted and almost expected. Offer less and offer to pay cash; merchants are very conscious of the bite taken by credit-card companies. Anything not made locally is pricey to bring in and therefore generally more expensive than elsewhere in Italy. The shops near St. Mark's Square charge the most.

For ordinary items (not high-priced tourist baubles), the best all-purpose department store is the Coin store on the St. Mark's Square side of the Rialto Bridge. (From the bridge, head north toward Ferrovia, the train station.)

For information on VAT refunds and customs regulations, see page 12.

Shopping Streets

Here's the best route to kick off your Venetian shopping spree:

St. Mark's Square: Walk the entire colonnaded square past pricey jewelry, glass, lace, and clothing stores. A half-block detour out the far end leads to several high-fashion shops along Calle de Vallaresso.

Mercerie: This is the main street between St. Mark's Square (leave the square under the Clock Tower) and the Rialto, noted

Mask Making

In the 1700s, when Venice was Europe's party town, masks were popular—sometimes even mandatory— to preserve the anonymity of visiting nobles doing things forbidden back home. At Carnevale (the weeks-long Mardi Gras leading up to Lent), everyone wore masks. The most popular were based on characters from the lowbrow comedic theater called commedia dell'arte. We all know Harlequin (simple, Lone Ranger-type masks), but there were also long-nosed masks for the hypo- critical plague doctor, pretty Columbina masks, and so on.

Masks are made with the simple technique of papier- mâché. You make a mold of clay, smear it with Vaseline (to make it easy to remove the finished mask), then create the mask by draping layers of paper and glue atop the clay mold.

You'll see mask shops all over town. Just behind St. Mark's Square, on a quiet canal just inland from the Church of San Zaccaria (on Fondamenta dell'Osmarin), is a corner with two fascinating mask and costume shops. The **Ca' del Sol** mask and costume shop (two showrooms connected by a little bridge) and **Atelier Marega** are both worth a look. After you cross the bridge to the second Ca' del Sol shop, head to the next door farther on, the wood-carving shop of **Paolo Brandolisio** (Mon–Fri 9:30–13:00 & 15:30–19:00, tel. 041-522-4155, http://paolobrandolisio.altervista.org). You can pop in to watch Paolo carving traditional oars and *forcola* (the oar- lock of the gondola, a symbol of Venetian life and a popular art piece). To check out Paolo virtually, search for "forcole e remi" on YouTube to watch videos of him working.

Out near the Frari Church, the **"Tragicomica" Mask Shop** is highly respected and likely to have artisans at work (daily 10:00–19:00, 200 yards past Church of San Polo on Calle dei Nomboli, tel. 041-721-102).

for its high rent, high prices, fancy windows, and designer labels. Then, go over the...

Rialto Bridge: The streets at either side are a cancan of shop- ping temptations. Continue down the street to...

Ruga Vecchia San Giovanni (a.k.a. Ruga): Away from the intensity of the tourist center, you'll enter the San Polo neighbor- hood (west side of Rialto Bridge) with plenty of inviting shops, but fewer crowds and better prices.

Elsewhere in Venice: Art-lovers browse the **art galleries** between the Accademia and the Peggy Guggenheim Collection.

Venetian Glass

Popular Venetian glass is available in many forms: vases, tea sets, decanters, glasses, jewelry, lamps, mod sculptures (such as solid-glass aquariums), and on and on. Shops will ship it home for you, but you're likely to pay as much or more for the shipping as you are for the item(s). Make sure the shop insures their merchandise *(assicurazione)*, or you're out of luck if it breaks. If your item arrives broken and it has been insured, take a photo of the pieces, send it to the shop, and they'll replace it for free. For a cheap, packable souvenir, consider the glass-bead necklaces sold at vendors' stalls throughout Venice.

If you're serious about glass, visit the small shops on **Murano Island.** Their glassblowing demonstrations are fun; you'll usually see a vase and a "leetle 'orse" made from molten glass. You'll find greater variety on Murano, but prices are usually the same as in Venice.

Around St. Mark's Square, various companies offer glass-blowing demos for tour groups. **Galleria San Marco,** a tour-group staple just off St. Mark's Square, offers great demos every few minutes. They have agreed to let individual travelers flashing this book sneak in with tour groups to see the show (and sales pitch). And, if you buy anything, show this book and they'll take 20 percent off the listed price. The gallery faces the square behind the orchestra nearest the church; at #139, go through the shop and climb the stairs (daily 9:00–18:00, tel. 041-271-8650, manager Ferdinando).

Souvenir Ideas

The most popular souvenirs and gifts are Murano glass (described above), Burano lace (fun lace umbrellas for little girls), Carnevale masks (fine shops and artisans all over town), art reproductions (posters, postcards, and books), prints of Venetian scenes, traditional stationery (pens and marbled paper products of all kinds), calendars with Venetian scenes, silk ties, scarves, and plenty of goofy knickknacks (Titian mousepads, gondolier T-shirts, and little plastic gondola condom holders).

Along Venice's many shopping streets, you'll notice fly-by-night street vendors selling knockoffs of famous-maker handbags (Louis Vuitton, Gucci, etc.). These vendors are willing to bargain. But buyer beware: If you're caught purchasing fakes, you could get hit with a fine. Legitimate manufacturers are raising a stink about these street merchants, and the government  is trying to rid the city of them. Authorities frustrated in their attempts to actually arrest the merchants have made it illegal to buy counterfeit items. Their hope: The threat of a huge fine will scare potential customers away—so unlicensed merchants will be driven out of business and off the streets.

NIGHTLIFE IN VENICE

You must experience Venice after dark. The city is quiet at night, as tour groups stay in the cheaper hotels of Mestre on the mainland, and the masses of day-trippers return to their beach resorts and cruise ships.

Do what you must to reserve energy for evening: Take a nap, or skip a few sights during the day. When the sun goes down, a cool breeze blows in from the lagoon, the lanterns come on, the peeling plaster glows in the moonlight, and Venice resumes its position as Europe's most romantic city.

Though Venice comes alive after dark, it does not party into the wee hours. By 22:00, restaurants are winding down; by 23:00, many bars are closing; and by midnight, the city is shut tight. Evenings are made for wandering—even Venice's dark and distant back lanes are considered very safe after nightfall. Enjoy the orchestras on St. Mark's Square. Experience Vivaldi's *Four Seasons* in a candlelit 17th-century church. Pop into small bars for an appetizer and a drink. Lick gelato. As during the day, it's the city itself that is the star. But Venice under a cloak of darkness has an extra dose of magic and mystery—the ambience that has attracted visitors since the days of Casanova.

Sightseeing

You can stretch your sightseeing day at the Doge's Palace and Correr Museum (daily until 19:00 April–Oct), Accademia (Tue–Sun until 19:15), Punta della Dogana (Wed–Mon until 19:00), and the Campanile (the bell tower on St. Mark's Square, daily until 21:00 July–Sept). The self-guided walks in this book are most enjoyable in the evening.

Gondolas

Two hundred years ago, there were 10,000 gondolas in Venice. Although the aristocracy preferred horses to boats through the early Middle Ages, begin-ning in the 14th century, when horses were outlawed from the streets of Venice, the noble class embraced gondolas as a respectable form of transpor-tation.

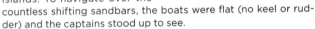

The boats became *the* way to get around the lagoon's islands. To navigate over the countless shifting sandbars, the boats were flat (no keel or rud-der) and the captains stood up to see.

Today, there are only 500 gondolas, used only by tourists. The boats are prettier now, but they work the same way they always have. Single oars are used both to propel and to steer the boats, which are built curved a bit on one side so that an oar thrusting from that side sends the gondola in a straight line.

These sleek yet ornate boats typically are about 35 feet long and 5 feet wide, and weigh about 1,100 pounds. They travel about three miles an hour (same as walking) and take the same energy to row as it does to walk. They're always painted black (six coats)—the result of a 17th-century law a doge enacted to elimi-nate competition between nobles for the fanciest rig. But each has unique upholstery, trim, and detailing, such as the squiggly shaped, carved-wood oarlock *(forcula)* and metal "hood orna-

Gondola Rides

Gondolas cost lots more after 19:00 but are also more romantic and relaxing under the moon. A rip-off for some, this is a tra-ditional must for romantics. Gondoliers charge about €80 for a 40-minute ride during the day; from 19:00 on, figure on €100. To add *musica* (a singer and an accordionist), it'll cost an addi-tional €110 before 19:00, or €130 after 19:00. You can divide the cost—and the romance—among up to six people per boat, but you'll need to save two seats for the musicians if you choose to be serenaded. Only two seats (the ones in back) are next to each other. If you want to haggle, you'll find softer prices during the day. (Note that gondoliers have a trick where one guy says "No," and another, acting secretive, comes to you a bit later and says, "OK, but don't let my friend know I'm offering you this incredible price.") Establish the price and duration before boarding, enjoy your ride, and pay only when you're finished.

If you've hired musicians and want to hear a Venetian song

ment" *(ferro)*. The six horizontal lines and curved top of the *ferro* represent Venice's six *sestieri* (districts) and the doge's funny cap. All in all, it takes about two months to build a gondola.

The boats run about €35,000–50,000, depending on your options (air-con, cup holders, etc.). Every 40 years, the boat's hull must be treated with a new coat of varnish to protect against a lagoon-dwelling creature that eats into wood. A gondola lasts about 15 years, after which it can be refinished (once) to last another 10 years.

You can see Venice's most picturesque gondola workshop (from the outside; it's not open to the public) in the Accademia

neighborhood. (Walk down the Accademia side of the canal called Rio San Trovaso; as you approach Giudecca Canal, you'll glimpse the beached gondolas on your right across the canal.) The workmen, traditionally from Italy's mountainous Dolomite region (because they need to be good with wood), maintain this refreshingly alpine-feeling little corner of Venice.

There are about 400 licensed gondoliers. When one dies, the license passes to his widow. And do the gondoliers sing, as the popular image has it? My mom asked our gondolier that very question, and he replied, "Madame, there are the lovers and there are the singers. I do not sing."

(un canto Veneziano), try requesting *"Venezia La Luna e Tu."* Asking to hear *"O Sole Mio"* (which comes from Naples) is like asking a bartender in Cleveland to sing "The Eyes of Texas."

Glide through nighttime Venice with your head on someone's shoulder. Follow the moon as it sails past otherwise unseen buildings. Silhouettes gaze down from bridges while window glitter spills onto the black water. You're anonymous in the city of masks, as the rhythmic thrust of your striped-shirted gondolier turns old crows into songbirds. This is extremely relaxing (and, I think, worth the extra cost to experience at night). Because you might get a narration plus conversation with your gondolier, talk with several and choose one you like who speaks English well.

Women, beware...while gondoliers can be extremely charming, local women say that anyone who falls for one of these Romeos "has slices of ham over her eyes."

For cheap gondola thrills during the day, stick to the €0.50 one-minute ferry ride on a Grand Canal *traghetto*. At night, *vaporetti* are nearly empty, and it's a great time to cruise the Grand Canal on the slow boat #1. Or hang out on a bridge along the gondola route and wave at romantics.

St. Mark's Square

For tourists, St. Mark's Square is the highlight, with lantern light and live music echoing from the cafés. Just being here after dark is a thrill, as **dueling café orchestras** entertain (see sidebar on page 75).

Every night, enthusiastic musicians play the same songs, creating the same irresistible magic. Hang out for free behind the tables (allowing you to move easily on to the next orchestra when the musicians take a break), or spring for a seat and enjoy a fun and gorgeously set concert. If you sit a while, it can be €12–20 well spent (for a drink and the cover charge for music). Dancing on the square is free (and encouraged).

Streetlamp halos, live music, floodlit history, and a ceiling of stars make St. Mark's magic at midnight. You're not a tourist, you're a living part of a soft Venetian night...an alley cat with money. In the misty light, the moon has a golden hue. Shine with the old lanterns on the gondola piers, where the sloppy lagoon splashes at the Doge's Palace...reminiscing.

Entertainment

Venice has a busy schedule of events, festivals, and entertainment. Check at the TI for listings, and keep an eye out for publications such as the free *Un Ospite di Venezia* magazine (monthly, bilingual, available at top-end hotels and the TI, www.aguestinvenice.com).

Baroque Concerts

Venice is a city of the powdered-wig Baroque era. For about €25 (prices vary), you can take your pick of traditional Vivaldi concerts in churches throughout town. Homegrown Vivaldi is as ubiquitous here as Strauss is in Vienna and Mozart is in Salzburg. In fact, you'll find frilly young Vivaldis hawking concert tickets on many

corners. The TI has a list of this week's Baroque concerts. Shows start at 21:00 and generally last 1.5 hours. You'll see posters in hotels all over town (hotels sell tickets at face-value). A one-stop shop for concerts is the Vivaldi Store, at the east end of Rialto Bridge (5537 Salizada del Fontego dei Tedeschi). Tickets for Baroque concerts in Venice can usually be bought the same day as the concert, so don't bother with websites that sell tickets with a surcharge.

Consider the venue carefully. The general rule of thumb: Musicians in wigs and tights offer better spectacle; musicians in black-and-white suits are better performers. **San Vitale Church** (at the north end of Accademia Bridge) and the **Interpreti Veneziani orchestra** (which often plays there) are reliably top-notch (tel. 041-277-0561, www.interpretiveneziani.com). For the latest on church concerts, check any TI or visit www.turismovenezia.it.

If you're attending a concert at **Scuola San Rocco** (tickets €15–30), arrive 30 minutes early to enjoy the art (which you'd have to pay €7 to see during the day).

Other Performances

Venice's most famous theaters are **La Fenice** (grand old opera house, box office tel. 041-786-5111, see page 45), **Teatro Goldoni** (mostly Italian live theater), and **Teatro della Fondamenta Nuove** (theater, music, and dance).

Musica a Palazzo is a unique evening of opera at the Doge's Palace. You'll spend about 45 minutes in three sumptuous rooms as eight musicians (generally four instruments and four singers) perform. With these kinds of surroundings, under Tiepolo frescoes, you'll be glad you dressed up. As there are only 70 seats, you must book by phone or online in advance. Opera-lovers find this to be a wonderful evening (€50, nightly shows at 20:30, Palazzo Barbarigo-Minotto, Fondamenta Duodo o Barbarigo—on the Grand Canal next to the Santa Maria del Giglio vaporetto stop, mobile 340-971-7272, www.musicapalazzo.com).

Venezia is advertised as "the show that tells the great story of Venice" and "simply the best show in town." I found the performance to be slow-moving and a bit cheesy, and the venue to be disappointing (€40, nightly at 19:00, 80 minutes, ticket includes a 30-minute video on Venice at 18:00, Teatro San Gallo, just off St. Mark's Square on Campo San Gallo, tel. 041-241-2002, www.teatrosangallo.net).

Movies

Venetian cinema is rarely in the original language; expect to hear it in Italian. Every September, Venice's **film festival** (with some English-language films) doubles the viewing choices and brings the stars out to Venice's Lido, a 10-minute vaporetto ride from St. Mark's Square.

Eating and Drinking

In the evening, locals and those spending the night in Venice fill the piazzas, restaurants, and bars.

Dining

The local way to spend an evening is to enjoy a slow and late dinner in a romantic canalside or piazza setting (see the Eating in Venice chapter). Another option is a fast-paced, stand-up dinner of *cicchetti* in a pub (or in several—see pub-crawl sidebar, page 272).

Zattere Neighborhood

At the south end of Dorsoduro is a canalfront strip called Zattere (near the Zattere vaporetto stop). With a fun youthful vibe, the pizzerias, gelaterias, and bars do a good job of entertaining. **El Chioschetto alle Zattere,** a simple bar, offers a free live music program right on the promenade—especially enjoyable as the sun sets over the cruise ships and sinks behind the industrial zone on the mainland in the distance (cocktails, sandwiches, and drinks; April–Sept Wed and Sun 18:00–21:00; just west of Zattere vaporetto dock at 1406 Zattere—see map on page 282, mobile 348-396-8466).

Pubs, Clubs, and Late-Night Spots

While a pub-crawl dinner is fun and colorful, most serious eating is finished early to make way for drinking.

Near the Rialto Bridge

Located near each other in the center, these bars and jazz clubs are good spots for night owls (see map on page 268).

Bácaro Jazz Venezia wine bar, with bras upholstering its ceiling, offers food until 1:30 in the morning (on St. Mark's side of Rialto Bridge, just north of Campo San Bartolomeo).

Planet Restaurant shows sports coverage on TV while serving up pizzas and pastas until 1:00 in the morning and drinks until 2:00 (3 blocks north of St. Mark's Square at Calle Casselleria 5281).

Also open late are several Irish pubs, including the **Devil's Forest Pub** (fine prices, daily 11:00–24:00, pasta served 12:00–

14:30, sandwiches available all the time, no cover or service charge at night, a block off Campo San Bartolomeo on Calle dei Stagneri, tel. 041-520-0623) and **Inishark Pub** (until 1:30 in the morning, closed Mon, just west of Campo Santa Maria Formosa off Salizada San Lio at Calle del Mondo Nuovo 5787).

Other Late-Night Haunts

The university student zone of **Campo Santa Margherita** is likely to be lively late. This popular-with-Venetians square has a good restaurant, café, and bar scene—especially May through September (Bar Rosso is particularly popular).

Paradiso Perduto, on Fondamenta della Sensa (on Rio della Sensa) in Cannaregio, is notorious for being noisy late at night. When locals complain, night owls say there's got to be someplace in Venice that stays open late. It's a restaurant and bar with a huge following for its good casual food and ambience (tel. 041-720-581).

Other places likely to be open after 23:00 include the touristy **American Bar** (under the Clock Tower on St. Mark's Square—see map on page 276). While Irish pubs are popular with locals rather than tourists, **Harry's American Bar** is just the opposite (serving overpriced food and American cocktails to dressy tourists at the San Marco vaporetto stop—see the map on page 276). But be warned: Harry's is, simply put, a rip-off.

Venice doesn't have a good dance scene. The close proximity of apartments means loud music isn't tolerated late at night. The few *discoteche* are overpriced, with expensive drinks and little actual dancing. Still, for a cultural experience and a throbbing techno beat, check out the incredibly soundproofed disco piano bar **Piccolo Mondo el Souk** near the Accademia art museum (daily 23:00–4:00 in the morning, Nov–March closed Mon, €10 cover charge includes one cocktail, drinks after that are all €10, locals won't show up until at least 23:30 or midnight, don't be shy—ring the bell to get in, between Accademia and recommended Pensione Accademia at Calle Corfù 1056a in Dorsoduro—see map on page 282, tel. 041-520-0371).

VENICE CONNECTIONS

This chapter addresses your arrival and departure from Venice—by train, plane, car, and cruise ship.

A two-mile-long causeway (with highway and train lines) connects Venice to the mainland. Mestre, the sprawling mainland transportation hub, has fewer crowds, cheaper hotels, and plenty of inexpensive parking lots, but zero charm. Don't stop in Mestre unless you're parking your car or transferring trains.

By Train

Santa Lucia Train Station

All trains to "Venice" stop at Venezia Mestre (on the mainland). Most continue on to Santa Lucia Station on the island of Venice itself. If your train only stops at Mestre, worry not. Shuttle trains regularly connect Mestre's station with Venice's Santa Lucia Station (6/hour, 10 minutes, €1).

Venice's Santa Lucia train station plops you right into the old town on the Grand Canal, an easy vaporetto ride or fascinating 40-minute walk to St. Mark's Square. Upon arrival, skip the station's crowded TI, because the two TIs at St. Mark's Square are better, and it's not worth a long wait for a minimal map (buy a good one from a newsstand or pick up a free one at your hotel). Confirm your departure plan (stop by train info desk or just study the *partenze*/departures posters on walls).

Consider storing unnecessary heavy bags, although lines for **baggage check** may be very long (at track 1, €4/5 hours, daily 6:00–24:00, no lockers, 45-pound weight limit on bags). **WCs** are at track 1 and in the back of the big bar/cafeteria area inside the station.

Minimize your time in the station—the banks of user-friendly

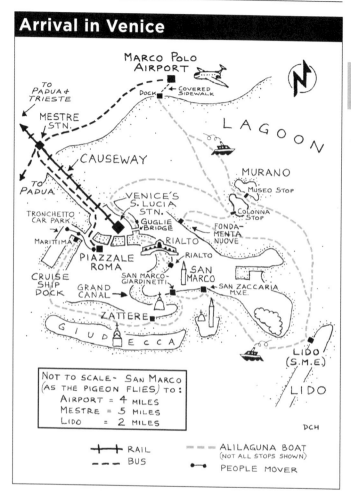

Arrival in Venice

MARCO POLO AIRPORT

TO PADUA & TRIESTE

Dock ← COVERED SIDEWALK

L A G O O N

MESTRE STN.

CAUSEWAY

MURANO

TO PADUA

MUSEO STOP

VENICE'S S. LUCIA STN.

COLONNA STOP

TRONCHETTO CAR PARK

GUGLIE BRIDGE

FONDA-MENTA NUOVE

MARITTIMA

RIALTO

PIAZZALE ROMA

RIALTO

CRUISE SHIP DOCK

SAN MARCO-GIARDINETTI

SAN MARCO

GRAND CANAL →

SAN ZACCARIA M.V.E.

ZATTERE

G I U D E C C A

LIDO (S.M.E.)

LIDO

DCH

NOT TO SCALE - SAN MARCO
(AS THE PIGEON FLIES) TO:
AIRPORT = 4 MILES
MESTRE = 5 MILES
LIDO = 2 MILES

┼─┼─┼ RAIL
─ ─ ─ BUS

─ ─ ─ ALILAGUNA BOAT
(NOT ALL STOPS SHOWN)
●─● PEOPLE MOVER

automated ticket machines (marked *Biglietto Veloce/Fast Ticket*) are handy. They take euros and credit cards, display schedules, issue tickets, and even make reservations for railpass-holders. The gray-only machines are for tickets to nearby destinations such as Padua. Or you could take care of these tasks at downtown travel agencies (see page 28).

For more on train travel in Italy—including your ticket-buying options—see page 377.

To get from the train station to downtown Venice, walk straight out of the station to the canal. On your left is a vaporetto ticket booth and the dock for vaporetto #2 (fast boat down Grand Canal, catch from right side of dock). To your right is the dock for *vaporetti* #1 (slow boat down Grand Canal, catch from far right dock) and #51 (goes counterclockwise around Venice, handy for Dorsoduro hotels). See the hotel listings in the Sleeping in Venice chapter to find out which boat to catch to get to your hotel. See "Getting Around Venice—By Vaporetto," on page 29, for details on vaporetto tickets and passes.

From Venice by Train to: **Padua** (2/hour, 30 minutes), **Vicenza** (2/hour, 1 hour), **Verona** (roughly 2/hour, 1.5 hours), **Ravenna** (hourly, 3–4 hours, transfer in Ferrara or Bologna), **Florence** (hourly, 2-3 hours, may transfer in Bologna; often crowded so make reservations), **Dolomites** (to Bolzano about hourly, 3–4 hours, transfer in Verona; catch bus from Bolzano into mountains), **Milan** (hourly, 2.5 hours), **Cinque Terre/Monterosso** (almost hourly, 6–7 hours, with 1–3 changes), **Cinque Terre/La Spezia** (almost hourly, 5–6 hours, with 1–3 changes), **Rome** (hourly, 3.5 hours, may transfer in Bologna, overnight possible), **Naples** (almost hourly, 5.5–7 hours, with changes in Bologna or Rome), **Brindisi** (7/day, 9–14 hours, most change in Bologna; 1 direct night train, 11 hours), **Bern** (3/day, 6 hours, change in Milan or Brig), **Munich** (4–6/day, 7 hours, change in Verona; 1 direct night train, 8 hours), **Paris** (3/day, 10–16 hours with change in Milan, may also transfer in Basel or Zürich; 1 direct night train, 12.5 hours, important to reserve ahead), **Ljubljana** (3/day, 7.5 hours—take bus from Piazzale Roma to Villach in Austria, then transfer to train; 1 direct night train, 4 hours, but arrives at 2:00 in the morning), and **Vienna** (3/day, 8 hours—take bus from Piazzale Roma to Villach in Austria, then transfer to train; 1 direct night train, 11 hours).

By Plane

Venice has two airports—**Marco Polo** and the smaller **Treviso.** For budget flights within Europe, easyJet uses Marco Polo, while Ryanair, Wizz Air, and Blue use Treviso. (For more on budget carriers, see page 390.)

Marco Polo Airport

Venice's modern airport is on the mainland, six miles north of the city. It's a sleek wood-beam-and-glass terminal, with a TI (daily 9:00–21:00), ATMs, car-rental agencies, a bank, a post office, and a few shops and eateries. For flight information, call tel. 041-260-9260, visit www.veniceairport.com, or ask at your hotel for help.

Transportation between Marco Polo Airport and Venice

There are three ways to get between the airport (which is on the mainland) and downtown Venice (on an island):

• Alilaguna water bus—medium in speed and cost

• water taxis—fastest and most expensive
• buses to Piazzale Roma—slowest and least expensive

Each of these options is explained in detail below. The Alilaguna water buses are the simplest way to reach most of this book's recommended hotels—except those near the train station, which are better served by the bus to Piazzale Roma.

When flying out of Venice, travelers are advised to get to the airport two hours before departure (even for flights within Europe), so allow yourself plenty of time.

Alilaguna Water Bus

These boats make the scenic (if slow) journey across the lagoon, shuttling passengers between the airport and a number of different stops on the island of Venice (€13, 60–90-minute trip depending on your destination; boats leave every 30–60 minutes). There are several lines (blue, red, orange), and it can get confusing. But if you know what stop you want, it's easy to find the line that goes there. Here are some key stops in Venice:

San Marco-Giardinetti—hotels west of St. Mark's Square

San Zaccaria—hotels east of St. Mark's Square

Zattere—Dorsoduro hotels

Guglie—hotels near Santa Lucia train station

Rialto—hotels near the Rialto Bridge

Fondamenta Nuove—hotels on the north side of the city, on the "fish's" back

From the Airport to Venice: The airport's boat dock is an eight-minute walk from the terminal. Exit the arrivals terminal and turn left, following signs along a paved, level, covered sidewalk (easy for wheeled bags). You can buy tickets at the airport's TI or the "Public Transport" window (often crowded), at vending machines inside the airport terminal (cash only), or simply at the ticket booth at the dock. Any ticket-seller can tell you which line to catch to get to your destination. Boats from the airport run from roughly 7:00 to midnight.

From Venice to the Airport: Give yourself plenty of time to make your flight. Ask your hotelier what dock and what line is best. Boats start leaving Venice as early as 3:40 so that passengers can catch early flights.

For a full schedule, see the Alilaguna website (www.alilaguna .it), call 041-523-5775, ask your hotelier, scan the schedules posted at Alilaguna docks, or ask at the TI. Note that the Alilaguna water bus is not part of the ACTV vaporetto system, so it is not covered by city transit passes.

Water Taxi

Luxury taxi speedboats zip directly between the airport and your hotel, getting you within steps of your final destination in about 30 minutes. The official price is €100 for up to four people, though you'll often get a higher quote (around €110)—talk it down. A taxi can be a smart investment for small groups and those with an early departure. From the airport, arrange your ride at the airport's water-taxi desk or at the dock (next to the Alilaguna dock). From Venice, book your taxi trip through your hotel the day before you leave.

Airport Shuttle Buses

Buses take you across the bridge from the mainland to the island, dropping you at the "mouth of the fish," on a square called Piazzale Roma. From there, you can catch a vaporetto down the Grand Canal—convenient for hotels near the Rialto Bridge and St. Mark's Square.

Two companies compete for the airport shuttle business. The ATVO "Venezia Express" and the ACTV bus #5 both connect the airport and Piazzale Roma (€2.50–3, 20–40 minutes, 2/hour, 5:00–24:00, www.atvo.it or www.actv.it). The ATVO is slightly faster and pricier.

From the Airport to Venice: Both buses leave from just outside the arrivals terminal. Buy tickets at the TI, from ticket machines in the terminal or outside next to the buses, or sometimes directly from the driver. Check which ticket you are buying—ATVO tickets are not valid on ACTV buses and vice versa.

When you arrive at Piazzale Roma, you'll find the vaporetto dock by walking to the six-story white building, then taking a right. To go down the Grand Canal, catch either the slow vaporetto #1 or faster #2 toward St. Mark's Square (€6.50 for either boat; for more info, see "Getting Around Venice," page 29). To reach Zattere (and the Dorsoduro hotels), go the other direction on #51. If you're confused, a local commuter or the ticket-seller can help you.

If your hotel is near the train station, you can walk there from Piazzale Roma across the Calatrava Bridge.

From Venice to the Airport: Buses leave Piazzale Roma between 5:00 and 20:40, departing from the northeast corner of the lot near Hotel Santa Chiara.

Other Services

Private Shuttle Bus: Treviso Car Service offers a private minivan service between Marco Polo Airport and Piazzale Roma (€50 per minivan, seats up to 8, tel. 338-204-4390, www.trevisocarservice .com, Andrea).

Connecting to Padua: There's a cheap and easy SITA bus connection from Venice's Marco Polo Airport to Padua's bus station (buy €4.20 ticket from "Public Transport" desk inside airport near TI or pay driver €5, €1/bag in advance, €2/bag on board; 2/hour, 1 hour; as you exit the airport, catch just beyond platform 3 at the far right of the buses, www.sitabus.it).

Treviso Airport

Several budget airlines, such as Ryanair and Blue, use Treviso Airport, 12 miles northwest of Venice (www.trevisoairport.it). Regular ATVO buses take you from the airport to Piazzale Roma (€6, 2–3/hour, 1.25 hours, www.atvo.it). Buy your tickets at the ATVO desk in the airport and stamp them on the bus. The buses also stop at Mestre's train station. Treviso Car Service offers mini-van service to Piazzale Roma (€55 per minivan; see private shuttle bus listing above).

By Car

Parking in Venice

The freeway dead-ends after crossing the causeway at Venice, near several parking lots on the edge of the island. The most central and expensive lot is San Marco, on Piazzale Roma. Tronchetto (across the causeway and on the right) has a bigger and cheaper multistoried garage (€20/day, tel. 041-520-7555). From there, avoid the travel agencies masquerading as TIs, and head directly for the vaporetto docks for the boat connection (#2) to the town center. Don't let water taxi boatmen con you out of the relatively inexpensive €6.50 vaporetto ride.

Venice's new **People Mover** monorail, a shuttle train fixed to a circular cable, opened in 2010 and carries passengers from the parking lot at Tronchetto to Piazzale Roma. It costs €1, departs every few minutes, makes the half-mile trip in three minutes, is completely automated (no crew on board), and drops you a block from the Calatrava Bridge on Piazzale Roma (across the Grand Canal from Santa Lucia train station).

Parking in **Mestre** (on the mainland) is simple and cheap (open-air lots cost €8/day Mon–Fri, €10/day Sat–Sun, across from Mestre train station, easy shuttle-train connections to Venice's Santa Lucia Station—6/hour, 10 minutes, €1). There are also huge and economical lots in Verona, Padua, and Vicenza.

For information on car rental and driving in Italy, see page 386.

By Cruise Ship

Venice Cruise Ship Terminal (Stazione Marittima)

Cruise ships visiting Venice dock at the Stazione Marittima, which is roughly between the Tronchetto parking garage and Santa Lucia train station. The terminal forms "the fish's mouth" of Venice. The San Basilio vaporetto stop is the nearest to the cruise ships, and vaporetto #2 provides regular boat service between the terminal and St. Mark's Square. At night, it is replaced by vaporetto #N. Tickets can be bought from machines or on board (€6.50, buy immediately before you sit down to avoid a fine).

For those moving on from Venice, the new People Mover monorail (€1) links Marittima with Piazzale Roma, which has bus connections to Marco Polo Airport and is also near Santa Lucia train station (both described earlier).

DAY TRIPS
FROM VENICE

Venice is just one of many towns in the Italian region of Veneto (VEN-eh-toh), but few visitors venture off the lagoon. Two important towns and possible side-trips, in addition to the lakes and the Dolomites, make zipping directly from Venice to Milan (or Florence) a route strewn with temptation.

The towns of Padua and Verona are great stops, giving the visitor a low-key slice of Italy that complements the urbanity of Venice, Florence, and Rome. Visiting Padua and Verona couldn't be easier: They are roughly 30–45 minutes apart on the Venice–Milan line. Spending a day town-hopping between Venice and Milan—with stops at Padua and Verona—is exciting and efficient. Trains run frequently enough to allow flexibility and little wasted time. Architecture fans could consider a quick trip to Vicenza, located about halfway between Padua and Verona.

If you're Padua-bound, remember that you need to reserve ahead to see the Scrovegni Chapel. Mondays are not ideal for a trip to Verona, when most sights are closed in the morning, or Vicenza, where the major sights are closed.

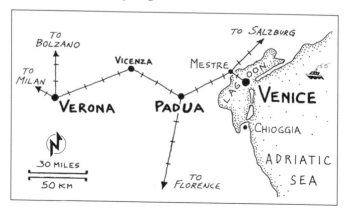

PADUA

Padova

Living under Venetian rule for four centuries seemed only to sharpen Padua's independent spirit. Nicknamed "the brain of Veneto," Padua (Padova in Italian) has a prestigious university (founded in 1222) that hosted Galileo, Copernicus, Dante, and Petrarch. Padua's old town center is elegantly arcaded, filled with students, and sprinkled with surprises. And Padua's museums and churches hold their own in Italy's artistic big league.

Planning Your Time: Padua in Six Hours

Day-trippers can do a quick but enjoyable blitz of Padua—including a visit to the Scrovegni Chapel—in six hours. Trains come and go twice an hour, making for a great day trip from Venice. Once in Padua, everything is a 10-minute walk or quick tram ride apart.

Your Scrovegni Chapel reservation will dictate the order of your sightseeing (see "Reservations" on page 318). When planning your day, also consider these factors: The station has a reliable baggage check desk; the market is vibrant in the morning, dead in the evening; student life is best at the university late in the day; and the Basilica of St. Anthony is open all day, but the reliquary chapel closes from 12:40 to 14:30.

Ideally, I'd do it this way: 9:00—market action and sightseeing in town center, 11:00—Basilica of St. Anthony, 14:00—Scrovegni Chapel tour.

Orientation to Padua

Padua's main tourist sights lie on a north–south axis through the heart of the city, from the train station to Scrovegni Chapel to the market squares (the center of town) to the Basilica of St. Anthony.

It's roughly a 10-minute walk between each of these sights, or about 30 minutes from end to end. I've designed this chapter around Padua's wonderful single tram line, which makes lacing things together quick and easy (see "Getting Around Padua," later).

Tourist Information

Padua has three TIs: at the **train station** (Mon–Sat 9:15–19:00, Sun 9:00–12:30, tel. 049-875-2077), in the **center** (across the street from Caffè Pedrocchi, Mon–Sat 9:00–13:30 & 15:00–19:00, closed Sun, tel. 049-876-7927), and at the **Basilica of St. Anthony** (April–Oct daily 9:00–13:30 & 15:00–18:00, closed Nov–March, tel. 049-875-3087). Pick up a map, a list of sights, and the seasonal Padova Today entertainment listing. The free I-PADova audio tour is creative and works really well. You can download it for free from their website (www.turismopadova.it), or just borrow one of their MP3 players and follow any of the five routes in town.

The **Padova Card** gives you (and one child under 14) unlimited tram travel, free parking, various discounts, and entry to all the recommended sights in this chapter, except the university's Anatomy Theater and the Basilica of St. Anthony's Oratory of St. George. While the card includes the Scrovegni Chapel, you still need to make a reservation to enter. Padova Cards are also sold at all TIs, at included sights, and online at www.padovacard.it (€15/48 hours, €20/72 hours).

Arrival in Padua

By Train: The station is a user-friendly shopping mall with whatever you might need (Despar **supermarket** open daily 7:00–21:00). **WCs** and **baggage deposit** (€4, daily 6:30–18:00, bring your passport) are near track 1.

You can buy train tickets or make seat reservations in the station (at the desk or, to avoid the line, at the gray-and-yellow automatic ticket machines). Leonardi Viaggi-Turismo offers the same services for a small fee a block away (Mon–Fri 9:00–13:00 & 14:30–19:00, Sat 9:00–13:00, closed Sun, up the main drag in front of the station, Corso del Popolo 14, tel. 049-650-455).

The easiest way to get downtown is to simply hop on Padua's handy **tram** (see "Getting Around Padua," later). Leaving the station, the tram stop is 30 yards to the right at the foot of the bridge (avoid the shady characters around here at night). A **taxi** into town (a good option after dark) costs about €8.

By Long-Distance Bus: If you're arriving in Padua by bus (including buses from Venice's Marco Polo Airport), you'll end up at the main bus station at Piazzale Boschetti, several blocks north of the Scrovegni Chapel. From there, Via Gozzi leads into town.

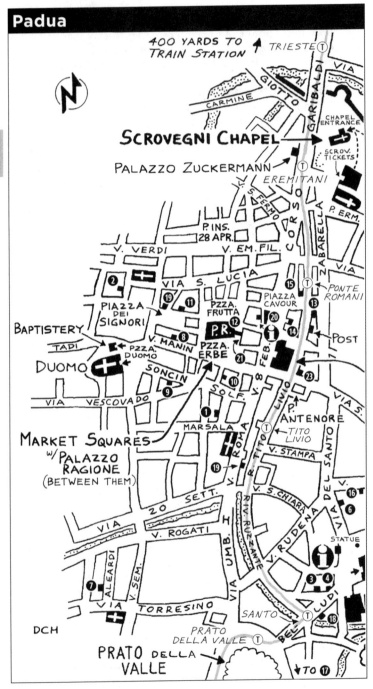

Padua

400 YARDS TO
TRAIN STATION

TRIESTE Ⓣ

CARMINE

VIA
GIOTTO

GARIBALDI

CHAPEL
ENTRANCE

SCROVEGNI CHAPEL →

SCROV.
TICKETS

PALAZZO ZUCKERMANN →

Ⓣ

EREMITANI

P. ERM.

ZABARELLA

S. FERMO

CORSO

P. INS.
28 APR.

V. VERDI

V. EM. FIL.

VIA

❷

VIA S. LUCIA

❶❾

❶❶

**PIAZZA
DEI
SIGNORI**

PZZA.
FRUTTA

❶❺

PIAZZA
CAVOUR

Ⓣ

PONTE
ROMANI

❶❸

❷⓪

BAPTISTERY

❽

V. MANIN

❶❷ P.R.

Ⓘ

❶❹

Post

TADI

PZZA.
DUOMO

PZZA.
ERBE

❷❶

V. 8 FEB.

DUOMO

SONCIN

❾

SOLF.

❶⓪

❷❸

VIA VESCOVADO

V. 8

V. ROMA

MARKET SQUARES
w/ **PALAZZO
RAGIONE**
(BETWEEN THEM)

MARSALA

❶

TITO LIVIO

P.
ANTENORE

Ⓣ

TITO
LIVIO

VIA S.

❶❾

V. STAMPA

VIA 20 SETT.

RIV. RUZZANTE

V. S. CHIARA

VIA DEL SANTO

❶❻

❻

V. ROGATI

VIA
UMB.

STATUE

Ⓘ

❼

V. ALEARDI

V. SEM.

TORRESINO

SANTO Ⓣ

❸ ❹

RUDENA

BELLUDI

❶❽

DCH

PRATO
DELLA VALLE Ⓣ

**PRATO DELLA
VALLE**

↓TO ❶❼

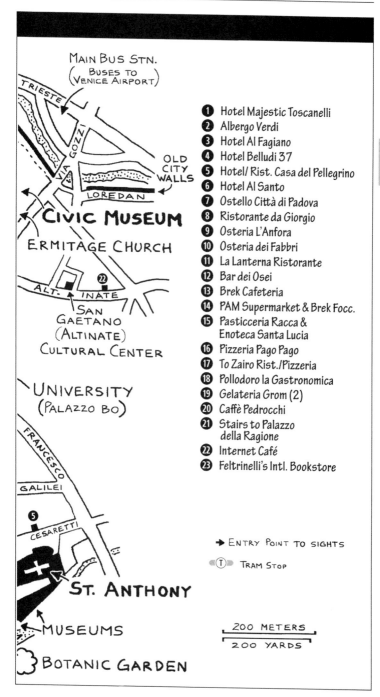

PADUA

MAIN BUS STN.
(BUSES TO VENICE AIRPORT)

TRIESTE

GOZZI

VIA

OLD CITY WALLS

LOREDAN

CIVIC MUSEUM

ERMITAGE CHURCH

ALT. INATE

SAN GAETANO (ALTINATE) CULTURAL CENTER

UNIVERSITY (PALAZZO BO)

FRANCESCO

GALILEI

CESARETTI

ST. ANTHONY

MUSEUMS

BOTANIC GARDEN

1 Hotel Majestic Toscanelli
2 Albergo Verdi
3 Hotel Al Fagiano
4 Hotel Belludi 37
5 Hotel/ Rist. Casa del Pellegrino
6 Hotel Al Santo
7 Ostello Città di Padova
8 Ristorante da Giorgio
9 Osteria L'Anfora
10 Osteria dei Fabbri
11 La Lanterna Ristorante
12 Bar dei Osei
13 Brek Cafeteria
14 PAM Supermarket & Brek Focc.
15 Pasticceria Racca & Enoteca Santa Lucia
16 Pizzeria Pago Pago
17 To Zairo Rist./Pizzeria
18 Pollodoro la Gastronomica
19 Gelateria Grom (2)
20 Caffè Pedrocchi
21 Stairs to Palazzo della Ragione
22 Internet Café
23 Feltrinelli's Intl. Bookstore

➔ ENTRY POINT TO SIGHTS

(T) TRAM STOP

200 METERS
200 YARDS

Helpful Hints

Pronunciation: You say Padua (PAD-joo-wah), they say Padova (PAH-doh-vah).

Internet Access: Oddly, for a college town, Padua has few Internet cafés. The central TI offers free access for 15 minutes (if you fill out a form and show your passport). You can also try **Internet Point** (€2/hour, Mon–Sat 10:00–24:00, Sun 16:00–24:00, Via Altinate 145, 5-minute walk from Porta Altinate, tel. 049-659-292).

Bookstore: Feltrinelli's International Bookstore, with books in English, is near the university (daily 9:00–19:30, Via San Francesco 7, tel. 049-875-4630).

Local Guide: Charming **Cristina Pernechele** is a great teacher (€105/half-day, mobile 338-495-5453, cristina@pernechele.eu).

Best Gelato: Locals line up at *gelateria* **Grom**'s two locations for its fresh ingredients and honest flavors (at Via Roma 101 and on Piazza dei Signoria).

Getting Around Padua

While a tangle of buses serve Padua, visitors should pretend there is only the **tram** and rely on it. There's just one line, which stresslessly and efficiently connects everything you care about (€1.10 ticket good for 75 minutes, departs every 8 minutes, www.trampadova .it). If you see tracks in the street, you know it's the tram.

Before boarding, note the tram direction on posted schedules and above the front window (Pontevigodarzere is northbound, Capolinia Sud is southbound). Stops that matter include the following: Stazione FS (train station), Eremitani (Scrovegni Chapel), Ponti Romani (old town center, market squares, university), Tito Livio (ghetto, old town center, Hotel Majestic Toscanelli), Santo (Basilica of St. Anthony and neighborhood hotels), and Prato della Valle.

You'll see **hop-on, hop-off buses** at the station and around town. While these ubiquitous tourist transporters make sense in some places, they're not worth the time or money in Padua.

Sights in Padua

▲▲▲Basilica of St. Anthony

Friar Anthony of Padua, "Christ's perfect follower and a tireless preacher of the Gospel," is buried here. Construction of this impressive Romanesque/Gothic church (with its Byzantine-style domes) started immediately after St. Anthony's death in 1231. And for nearly 800 years, his remains and this glorious church have attracted pilgrims to Padua.

St. Anthony of Padua
(1195–1231)

One of Christendom's most popular saints, Anthony is known as a powerful speaker, a miracle worker, and the finder of lost articles.

Born in Lisbon to a rich, well-educated family, his life changed at age 25, when he saw the mutilated bodies of some Franciscan martyrs. Their sacrifice inspired him to join the poor Franciscans and dedicate his life to Christ. He moved to Italy and lived in a cave, studying, meditating, and barely speaking to anyone.

One day, he joined his fellow monks for a service. The appointed speaker failed to show up, so Anthony was asked to say a few off-the-cuff words to the crowd. He started slowly, but, filled with the Spirit, he became more confident and amazed the audience with his eloquence. Up in Assisi, St. Francis heard about Anthony and sent him on a whirlwind speaking tour.

Anthony had a strong voice, knew several languages, had encyclopedic knowledge of theology, and could speak spontaneously as the Spirit moved him. It's said he even stood on the shores of the Adriatic Sea in Rimini and enticed a school of fish to listen. Anthony also was known as a prolific miracle worker.

In 1230, Anthony retired to Padua, where he founded a monastery and initiated reforms for the poor. An illness cut his life short at age 36. Anthony said, "Happy is the man whose words issue from the Spirit and not from himself!"

Cost and Hours: The basilica is free and open daily in summer 6:15–19:45, in winter 6:30–18:45. Note that the following sights within the basilica close around lunchtime: Chapel of the Reliquaries (daily 8:00–12:40 & 14:30–19:30, shorter hours in winter), museum (€2.50, daily 9:00–13:00 & 14:30–18:00, shorter hours and closed Mon in winter), and the Oratory of St. George (€2.50, daily 9:00–12:30 & 14:30–19:00).

Information: A modest dress code is enforced inside the basilica. A helpful information desk with Anthony-related pamphlets is in the cloisters, on the right side of the church (daily 8:30–13:00 & 14:00–18:30, shorter hours in winter, public WC nearby, Santo tram stop, tel. 049-878-9722, www.basilicadelsanto.org). If the information desk doesn't have English versions of the pamphlets—one on the saint's life and another about the basilica—head to the Chapel of the Reliquaries and offer a donation. A TI is on the square facing the church.

Basilica Exterior

St. Anthony looks down from the red-brick facade and blesses all. He holds a book, a symbol of all the knowledge he accumulated as a quiet monk before starting his preaching career.

Guarding the church is Donatello's life-size equestrian statue of the Venetian mercenary general, Gattamelata. Though it looks like a thousand other man-on-a-horse statues, it was a landmark in Italy's budding Renaissance—the first life-size, secular, equestrian statue cast from bronze in a thousand years. The church is technically outside of Italy. When you pass the banisters that mark its property line, you're passing into Vatican territory.

Interior

Entering the basilica, grab a pew in the center of the nave. Sit and appreciate the space. Gaze past the crowds and through the incense haze to Donatello's glorious crucifix rising from the altar, and realize that this is one of the most important pilgrimage sites in Christendom.

Along with the crucifix, Donatello's bronze statues—Mary with Padua's six favorite saints—grace the high altar. Late in his career, the great Florentine sculptor spent more than a decade in Padua (1444–1455), creating the altar and Gattamelata.

St. Anthony's Tomb

Head to the left side of the nave to find the gleaming marble masterpiece that is the focus of the visiting pilgrims—the tomb of St. Anthony. Pilgrims file slowly through this side chapel around the tomb, so focused on the saint that they hardly notice the nine fine marble reliefs. These Renaissance masterpieces were carved during the 16th century, and show scenes and miracles from the life of the saint. As you enjoy each scene, notice the Renaissance mastery of realism and 3-D perspective and the intricate frames, which celebrate life with a burst of exuberance.

First Relief: This depicts St. Anthony receiving the Franciscan tunic. The open door illustrates the new ability to show depth by using mathematics. The cityscape above is Padua in about 1500.

Second Relief: A jealous husband has angrily stabbed his wife. Notice the musculature, the emotion, and the determination in the faces of loved ones. Above, Anthony intercedes with God to bring the woman back to life. Notice the etchings of familiar Paduan architecture at the top of the sculptures.

Third Relief: Above this panel, which shows Anthony bringing a young man back to life, is the Palazzo della Ragione looking as it still does today.

Fourth Relief: This scene, by the famous Florentine sculptor Jacopo Sansovino, shows three generations: a dead girl, her distraught mom, and a grandmother who's seen it all. Of course, Anthony will eventually change the mood, but right now it's pretty dire. Above is a relief of this basilica.

Fifth Relief: A fisherman holds a net, sadly having retrieved a drowned boy. The mother looks at Anthony, who blesses and revives the boy. Across from here is the saint's actual tomb. Under thoughtful lighting, it reads *Corpus S. Antonii*. Prayer letters are dropped behind the iron grill.

Sixth Relief: This shows "the miracle of the miser's heart." Anthony's helper dips his hand into a moneylender's side to demonstrate the absence of his heart. At his foot, the square tray with coins and a heart illustrates the scriptural verse "for where your treasure is, there your heart will be also."

Seventh Relief: Anthony holds the foot of a young man who confessed to kicking his mother. Taking a lesson from the saint about respecting your mother a little too literally, the man has cut off his own foot. The hysterical mother implores Anthony's help, and the saint's prayers to God enable him to reattach the foot.

Stand in the corner for a moment, observing the passionate devotion that pilgrims and Paduans alike have for Anthony. Touching his tomb or kneeling in prayer, the faithful believe Anthony is their protector—a confidant and intercessor for the poor. And they believe he works miracles. Believers leave offerings, votives, and written prayers to ask for help or to give thanks for miracles they believe Anthony has performed. By putting their hands on his tomb while saying silent prayers, pilgrims show devotion to Anthony and feel the saint's presence.

Popular Anthony is the patron saint of dozens of things: travelers, amputees, donkeys, pregnant women, infertile women, flight attendants, and pig farmers. Most pilgrims ask for his help in his role as the "finder of things"—from lost car keys to a life companion.

Eighth Relief: This scene makes the point that—unlike St. Francis, who was a rowdy youth—Anthony was holy even as a child. He tosses the glass (representing his faith), which, rather than shattering, breaks the marble floor.

Ninth Relief: An angry husband accuses his wife of cheating. The wife asks Anthony to identify her baby's father. Anthony asks the child, who speaks and says that the husband is his real dad and his mother was not messing around. Everyone is reassured—whew!

Between scenes eight and nine, go into the next room, where you'll enter the oldest part of the church—the original chapel, where Anthony was first buried in 1231. To the left of the altar, note the fine (and impressively realistic for the 14th century) view of medieval Padua, with this church outside the wall (finished by 1300 and looking just like it does today).

Below the cityscape, in a circa-1380 fresco, Anthony on his cloud promises he'll watch over his town. Because people wanted to be buried near a saint, graves lie all around. If you could afford it, this was about the best piece of real estate a dead person could want. (The practice was ended with Napoleonic reforms in 1806.)

Chapel of the Reliquaries

Continue your circuit of the church by going behind the altar into the apse, to the Chapel of the Reliquaries. The most prized relic is in the glass case at center stage—Anthony's tongue. When Anthony's remains were exhumed 32 years after his death (1263), his body had decayed to dust, but his tongue was found miraculously unspoiled and red in color. How appropriate for the great preacher who, full of the Spirit, couldn't stop talking about God.

Work clockwise around the chapel, starting under the dome in front of the staircase at St. Anthony's holy, and holey, tunic *(tonaca)*. His rough-hewn wood coffin is on the left wall. His pillow—a comfy rock—is up the stairs (chest level in first glass case). The center display case contains (top to bottom) the Saint's lower jaw *(il mento)*, his uncorrupted tongue *(lingua)*, and, finally, his vocal chords *(apparato vocale)* discovered intact when his remains were examined in 1981. In the last display case, a fragment of the True Cross *(la croce)* is held in a precious crucifix reliquary.

Above the relics is the *Glorification of St. Anthony*. In this Baroque fantasy, a cloud of angels and giddy *putti* tumble to the left and right in jubilation as they celebrate his presence in heaven.

Cloisters

From the right side of the nave as you face the altar, follow signs to *chiostro;* from outside, find signs on the right side of the church. The main cloister is dominated by an exceptionally bushy magnolia tree, planted in 1810, and by the graves of the most illustrious Padovans, such as Gabriel Fallopius, the scientist who gave his name to his discovery, the Fallopian tube.

Wander around the various cloisters. Picnic tables invite pilgrims and tourists to enjoy meals within the solitude of one of the cloisters (it's covered and suitable even when rainy, also has WCs). The **multimedia exhibit** on the life of St. Anthony is a bit kitschy, as pilgrimage multimedia exhibits tend to be (30 minutes, you move three times as you use headphones to listen to the story of each tableau).

At the far end, a fascinating little **museum** is filled with votives and folk art recounting miracles attributed to Anthony. The abbreviation *PGR* you'll see on many votives stands for *per grazia ricevuta*—for answered prayers.

Oratory of St. George

The small but sumptuous Oratory of St. George faces the little square in front of the basilica. The oratory ("ora" means prayer) is not actually a church, though it's certainly a fine place to pray—it's filled with vivid, circa-1370 frescoes showing scenes not of Anthony, but from the life of St. Catherine. Because many lovers credit St. Anthony with finding them their partners—and this is the closest place to St. Anthony where you can be married—it's popular for weddings. While you can see it all from the door, paying the entry fee lets you sit and enjoy this peaceful spot.

Near the Basilica

Prato della Valle—The square is 150 yards southwest of the basilica (down Via Luca Belludi). Once a Roman theater and later

Anthony's preaching grounds, this square claims to be the largest in Italy. It's a pleasant, 400-yard-long, oval-shaped piazza with fountains, walkways, dozens of statues of Padua's eminent citizens, and grass. It's also a lively **market** scene: fruit and vegetables (Mon–Fri 8:00–13:00), clothing, shoes, and household goods (Sat 8:00–19:00), and antiques (third Sun 8:00–19:00).

Botanic Garden (Orto Botanico di Padova)—Green thumbs appreciate this nearly five-acre botanical garden, which contains the university's vast collection of rare plants. Founded in 1545 to cultivate medicinal plants, it's the world's oldest academic botanical garden still in its original location. A visitors center—in a little cottage to the right of the garden's entrance—houses models of the garden's layout and computer programs that describe the history and composition of the garden in English.

Cost and Hours: Garden—€4; April–Oct daily 9:00–13:00 & 15:00–19:00; Nov–March Mon–Sat 9:00–13:00, closed Sun; entrance 150 yards south of Basilica of St. Anthony—with your back to the facade, take a hard left, Santo tram stop, tel. 049-827-2119, www.ortobotanico.unipd.it.

▲▲▲Scrovegni Chapel (Cappella degli Scrovegni)

You must make reservations in advance to see this glorious, recently renovated chapel (see "Reservations," later). Wallpapered with Giotto's beautifully preserved cycle of nearly 40 frescoes, the chapel holds scenes depicting the lives of Jesus and Mary.

Painted by Giotto and his assistants from 1303 to 1305 and considered by many to be the first piece of modern art, this work makes it clear: Europe was breaking out of the Middle Ages. A sign of the Renaissance to come, Giotto placed real people in real scenes, expressing real human emotions. These frescoes were radical for their 3-D nature, lively colors, light sources, emotion, and humanism.

The chapel was built out of guilt for white-collar crimes. Reginaldo degli Scrovegni (skroh-VEHN-yee) charged sky-high interest rates at a time when the Church forbade the practice. He even caught the attention of Dante, who placed him in one of the levels of hell in his *Inferno*. When Reginaldo died, the Church denied him a Christian burial. His son Enrico tried to buy forgiveness for his father's sins by building this superb chapel. After seeing Giotto's frescoes for the Franciscan monks of St. Anthony, Enrico knew he'd found the right artist to decorate the interior (and, he hoped, to save his father's soul).

Cost and Hours: €13 combo-ticket with Civic Museum (and its worthwhile Pinacoteca and Multimedia Room). The chapel is open Mon 9:00–19:00, Tue–Sun 9:00–22:00 except off-season until 19:00. When the Civic Museum is closed—after 19:00 and on Monday—tickets are €8. The Multimedia Room, adjacent to the Civic Museum, is open daily 9:00–19:00.

Entry Times: Every 15 minutes (on the quarter-hour), the chapel opens for 15-minute visits. After 19:00, the chapel opens every 20 minutes for 20-minute visits (last entry at 21:40).

Reservations: To protect the paintings from excess humidity, only 25 people are allowed in the chapel at a time. Prepaid reservations are required. You can reserve online at www.cappella degliscrovegni.it (also sells Padova Cards—described on page 309). If you reserve by phone, you may need to be persistent and call several times (tel. 049-201-0020; booking office open Mon–Fri 9:00–19:00, Sat 9:00–13:00, closed Sun, provide your credit-card number and hotel telephone number where you can be reached if necessary the day before your visit).

Giotto di Bondone
(c. 1267–1337)

Though details of his life are extremely sketchy, we know that as a 12-year-old shepherd boy, Giotto was discovered painting

pictures of his father's sheep on rock slabs. He became the wealthiest and most famous painter of his day. His achievement is especially remarkable because painters at that time weren't considered anything more than crafts-men and weren't expected to be inno-vators.

After making a name for himself by painting the life of St. Francis fres-coes in Assisi, the Florentine tackled the Scrovegni Chapel (c. 1303–1305). At age 35, he was at the height of his powers. His scenes were more realistic and human than any-thing done for a thousand years. Giotto didn't learn technique by dissecting corpses or studying the mathematics of 3-D perspective. He had innate talent. And his personality shines through in the humanity of his art.

The Scrovegni frescoes break ground by introducing nature—rocks, trees, animals—as a backdrop for religious scenes. Giotto's people, with their voluminous, deeply creased robes, are as sturdy and massive as Greek statues, throw-backs to the Byzantine icon art of the Middle Ages. But these figures exude stage presence. Their gestures are simple but expressive: A head tilted down says dejection, an arm flung out indicates grief, clasped hands indicate hope. Giotto cre-ated his figures not just by drawing outlines and filling them in with single colors; he filled the outlines in with subtle patch-works of lighter and darker shades, and in doing so pioneered modern modeling techniques. Giotto's storytelling style is straightforward, and anyone with knowledge of the episodes of Jesus' life can read the chapel like a comic book.

The Scrovegni represents a turning point in European art and culture—away from scenes of heaven and toward a more down-to-earth, human-centered view.

Book your visit at least 48 hours in advance. It's sometimes possible to buy a ticket for the same day at the ticket office, but don't count on it. (A sign on the desk indicates the next available time.)

Getting There: From the train station, it's a 10–15-minute walk, or a quick tram ride to the Eremitani stop.

Getting In: You'll be instructed to pick up your tickets at the ticket office at least an hour before your visit. In practice,

PADUA

Scrovegni Chapel

BLUE STARRY SKY

J O A C H I M — MARY

S O U T H W A L L

N O R T H W A L L

C H R I S T — LAST JUDGMENT — CHRIST

① ② ③ ④ ⑤ ⑧ ⑨ ⑩ ⑬ ⑥ ⑫ ⑪ ⑦

←WINDOWS

VIRTUES

VICES

TO ALTAR

FROM ANTEROOM (ENTRANCE & EXIT) ←

DCH

❶ Joachim Driven From the Temple
❷ Joachim Returns to the Sheepfold
❸ Mary's Birth Announced to St. Anne
❹ Birth of Jesus
❺ Slaughter of the Innocents
❻ Jesus Astounding the Scholars

❼ Jesus Drives Out the Money Changers
❽ Last Supper
❾ Betrayal of Christ
❿ Jesus Beaten and Humiliated
⓫ Jesus Carrying the Cross
⓬ Lamentation (Deposition)
⓭ Last Judgment

I've found that you can arrive later, but give yourself a minimum of 30 minutes to weather any commotion at the desk. Present your confirmation number, verify your time, and pick up your ticket.

While waiting for your reserved time, blitz the Civic Museum and Multimedia Room (described later). Read the chapel description (below) before you enter, since you'll only have a short time in the chapel itself.

Be at the chapel doors (well-signed, 100 yards to the right of the ticket office as you exit) at least five minutes before your scheduled visit. The chapel doors are automatic, and if you're even a minute late, you'll forfeit your visit and have to rebook and repay to enter.

At your appointed time, you first enter an anteroom to watch a very instructive 15-minute video (with English subtitles) and to establish humidity levels before continuing into the chapel (no photos are allowed). Although you have only a short visit inside the chapel, it is divine. You're inside a Giotto time capsule, looking back at an artist ahead of his time.

Giotto's Frescoes in the Scrovegni Chapel

Giotto painted the entire chapel in 200 working days over two years, but you'll get only 15 minutes to see it.

As you enter the long, narrow chapel, look straight to the far end—the rear wall is covered with Giotto's big *Last Judgment*. Christ in a bubble is flanked by crowds of saints and by scenes of heaven and hell. This is the final, climactic scene of the story told in the chapel's 38 panels—the three-generation history of Jesus, his mother Mary, and Mary's parents.

The story begins with Jesus' grandparents, on the long south wall (with the windows) in the upper-left corner. ❶ In the first frame, a priest scolds the man who will be Mary's father (Joachim, with the halo) and kicks him out of the temple for the sin of being childless. ❷ In the next panel to the right, Joachim returns dejectedly to his sheep farm. ❸ Meanwhile (next panel), his wife is in the bedroom, hearing the miraculous news that their prayers have been answered—she'll give birth to Mary, the mother of Jesus.

From this humble start, the story of Mary and Jesus spirals clockwise around the chapel, from top to bottom. The top row (both south and north walls) covers Mary's birth and life.

Jesus enters the picture in the middle row of the south (windowed) wall. ❹ The first frame shows his birth in a shed-like manger. In the next frame, the Magi arrive and kneel to kiss his little toes. Then the child is presented in the tiny temple. Fearing danger, the family gets on a horse and flees to Egypt. ❺ Meanwhile, back home, all the baby boys are slaughtered in an attempt to prevent the coming of the Messiah *(Slaughter of the Innocents)*.

Spinning clockwise to the opposite (north) wall, you see (in a badly damaged fresco) ❻ the child Jesus astounding scholars with his wisdom. Next, Jesus is baptized by John the Baptist. His first miracle, at a wedding, is turning jars of water into wine. Next, he raises a mummy-like Lazarus from the dead. Riding a donkey, he enters Jerusalem triumphantly. ❼ In the temple, he drives out the wicked money changers.

Turning again to the south wall (bottom row), we see scenes from Jesus' final days. ❽ In the first frame, he and his followers gather at a table for a Last Supper. Next, Jesus kneels humbly to wash their feet. ❾ He is betrayed with a kiss and arrested. Jesus is tried. ❿ Then he is beaten and humiliated.

⓫ Finally (north wall, bottom row), he is forced to carry his own cross, is crucified, and prepared for burial, while his followers mourn (⓬ *Lamentation*). Then he is resurrected and ascends to heaven, leaving his disciples to carry on.

⓭ The whole story concludes on the rear wall, where Jesus reigns at the Last Judgment. The long south wall (ground level) features the Virtues that lead to heaven, while the north wall has the (always more interesting) Vices. And all this unfolds beneath the blue, starry sky overhead on the ceiling.

Some panels deserve a closer look:

Joachim Returns to the Sheepfold (south wall, upper left, second panel): Though difficult to appreciate from ground level, this oft-reproduced scene is groundbreaking. Giotto—a former shepherd himself—uses nature as a stage, setting the scene in front of a backdrop of real-life mountains, and adding down-home details like Joachim's jumping dog, frozen in midair.

Betrayal of Christ, a.k.a. *Il Bacio*, "The Kiss" (south wall, bottom row, center panel): Amid the crowded chaos of Jesus' arrest, Giotto focuses our eyes on the central action, where Judas ensnares Jesus in his yellow robe (the color symbolizing envy), establishes meaningful eye contact, and kisses him.

Lamentation, a.k.a. *Deposition* (north wall, bottom row, middle): Jesus has been crucified, and his followers weep and wail over the lifeless body. John the Evangelist spreads his arms wide and shrieks, his cries echoed by anguished angels above. Each face is a study in grief. Giotto emphasizes these saints' human vulnerability.

Last Judgment (big west wall): Christ in the center is a glorious vision, but the real action is in hell (lower right). Satan is a Minotaur-headed ogre munching on sinners. Around him, demons give sinners their just desserts in a scene right out of Dante...who was Giotto's friend and fellow Florentine. Front and center is Enrico Scrovegni, in a violet robe (the color symbolizing penitence), donating the chapel to the Church in exchange for forgiveness of his father's sins.

Before the guard scoots you out, take a look at the actual altar. Though Enrico's father's tomb is lost, Enrico Scrovegni himself is in the tomb at the altar. The three statues are by Giovanni Pisano—Mary (in the center) supports baby Jesus on her hip with a perfectly natural, maternal, S-shape. She's flanked by anonymous deacons.

Civic Museum (Musei Civici Eremitani)

This museum, next to the Scrovegni Chapel (and covered by the same combo-ticket), was once an Augustinian hermit's monastery. While you can skip the ground-floor Archaeological Museum (with Roman and Etruscan artifacts and no English descriptions), the Pinacoteca and the Multimedia Room are worth visiting.

Cost and Hours: €12 combo-ticket with Scrovegni Chapel, €10 without the chapel. The Civic Museum is open Tue–Sun 9:00–19:00, closed Mon. The Multimedia Room is open daily 9:00–19:00. Another part of the museum, Palazzo Zuckermann (Tue–Sun 9:00–19:00, closed Mon), is across the street. No photos are allowed, and there's a mandatory and free bag check. The museum is on Piazza Eremitani (Eremitani tram stop). Tel. 049-820-4551.

Pinacoteca

The museum's highlight is upstairs, in the Pinacoteca (picture gallery). The collection has 13th- to 18th-century paintings by Titian, Tintoretto, Giorgione, Tiepolo, Veronese, Bellini, Canova, Guariento, and other Veneto artists. But I'd make a beeline for the room with the Giotto crucifix. Ask for it: *"La Croce di Giotto?"*

Originally hung in the Scrovegni Chapel between the Scrovegni family's private zone and the public's worshiping zone, this crucifix is painted on wood by Giotto. If you actually sit on the floor and look up, the body really pops. The adjacent "God as Jesus" piece was the only painting in the otherwise frescoed chapel. (This is hung here because of preservation concerns. Its copy is the only non-original art in the chapel.) Studying these two masterpieces affirms Giotto's greatness.

Behind the crucifix room is a collection of 14th- and 15th-century art. While the works here are exquisite—and came well after Giotto—they're clearly not as modern.

Multimedia Room

The Multimedia Room, dedicated to taking a closer look at the Scrovegni Chapel, is adjacent to the Civic Museum (in the same building). To head straight from the museum entrance to the Multimedia Room, use the entrance to the right of the main entry, step into the courtyard, make a sharp right, and head down the stairs.

Rows of computer screens offer a virtual Scrovegni Chapel visit and provide cultural insights into daily life in the Middle Ages. There are explanations of the individual panels, Giotto's fresco technique, close-ups of the art, and a description of the restoration. They show a 12-minute video (English headphones available) that is similar—but not identical—to the one that precedes your chapel visit. For me, it's worth just taking some time to enjoy a second video that features a mesmerizing, slow montage of close-ups of the Giotto frescoes.

Between the museum and the chapel are the scant remains of Roman Padua. The remnants are from the wall of an arena and nicely fitting pipes that once channeled water so that the arena could be flooded for special spectacles.

Palazzo Zuckermann

This little-visited wing of the Civic Museum, just across a busy street, is included in the same ticket as the Pinacoteca and Multimedia Room. Its first two floors offer a commotion of applied and decorative arts—such as clothes, furniture, and ceramics—from the Venetian Republic (1600s–1700s). On the top floor, the Bottacin collection takes you to the 19th century with coins and delightful (but no-name) pre-Impressionist paintings.

More Sights in the Center

Palazzo della Ragione—This grand 13th-century palazzo, commonly called *il Salone* (great hall), once held the medieval law courts. The first floor consists of a huge hall—265 feet by 90 feet—that was at one time adorned with frescoes by Giotto. A fire in 1312 destroyed those paintings, and the palazzo was redecorated with the 15th-century art you see today: a series of 333 frescoes depicting the signs of the zodiac, labors of the month, symbols representing characteristics of people born under each sign, and, finally, figures of saints to legitimize the power of the courts in the eyes of the Church.

The hall is topped with a hull-shaped roof, which helps to support the structure without the use of columns—quite an architectural feat in its day, considering the building's dimensions. The curious black stone in the corner opposite the big wooden horse is the "Stone of Shame," which was the seat of debtors being punished during the Middle Ages. It was introduced as a compassionate alternative to prison by St. Anthony in 1230. Instead of being executed or doing prison time, debtors sat upon this stone, surrendered their possessions, and denounced themselves publicly before being exiled from the city. The computer kiosks (choose "English") provide excellent information with entertaining videos.

Cost and Hours: €4, Tue–Sun 9:00–19:00, closed Mon. Enter through the east end of Piazza delle Erbe, and go up the long staircase. Tel. 049-820-5006, Ponti Romani tram stop. The WCs are through the glass doors at the opposite end of the hall from the wooden horse.

▲▲Market Squares: Piazza delle Erbe, Piazza della Frutta, and Piazza dei Signori—The stately Palazzo della Ragione (described above) provides a dramatic backdrop for Padua's almost exotic-feeling market that fills the surrounding squares—**Piazza delle Erbe** and **Piazza della Frutta**—each morning and all day

Saturday (Mon–Fri roughly 8:00–13:00, Sat 8:00–19:00, closed Sun). Second only to the produce market in Italy's gastronomic capital of Bologna, this market has been renowned for centuries as having the freshest and greatest selection of herbs, fruits, and vegetables. As you wander, appreciate the local passion for good food: Residents can tell the month by the seasonal selections. Merchants share recipe tips with shoppers. The presentation is an art in itself. And don't miss the ground floor of the Palazzo della Ragione. Wandering through this H-shaped arcade—where you'll find various butchers, *salumerie* (delicatessens), cheese shops, bakeries, and fishmongers at work—is a sensuous experience.

Students gather in the squares after the markets have closed, spilling out of colorful bars and cafés—drinks in hand. Pizza by the slice is dirt cheap. A typical snack stand selling all kinds of fresh, hot, and ready-to-eat seafood appetizers sets up in Piazza della Frutta between 17:00 and 20:30 (daily except Sun). Belly up to the bar with your drink and try whatever's being served.

Piazza dei Signori, just a block away, is a busy clothing market in the morning and the most popular gathering place in the evening for students out for a drink. The circa-1400 clock decorates the former palace of the ruling family. The aggressive lion with unfurled wings on the column was a reminder of the Venetian determination to assert its control. Today that lion can be seen as representing the Veneto region's independence from Rome: Italy's north (Veneto and Lombardy) is tired of subsidizing the south. Grumbling about this issue continues to stir talk of splitting the country.

Drinking a Spritz with the Student Crowd—Each early evening, before dinner, students enliven Padua by enjoying a convivial drink in their favorite places. Piazza dei Signori (described above) is the favorite square. Or you could sit in front of the university, nurse your drink, and watch the graduates get roasted with their crazy gangs of friends (see "Graduation Antics in Padua" sidebar, later). The drink of choice is a *spritz,* an aperitif generally made with Campari (liquor infused with bitter herbs), white wine, and sparkling water, and garnished with a blood-orange wedge. Most Paduan women seem to prefer a lighter *spritz* made with Aperol (orange-flavored liquor, less alcohol content).

Grab a table to be part of the scene, or get your *spritz* to take away *(da portar via),* and join the young people out on the piazza. Either way, this is a classic opportunity to enjoy a real discussion with smart, English-speaking students who see tourists not as pests, but as interesting people from far away. For an instant conversation starter, ask about the current political situation in Italy, the right-wing party's policy on immigrants, or the cultural differences between Italy's north and south. Or ask how President Berlusconi manages to control the media so effectively.

Caffè Pedrocchi—This white-columned Neoclassical café is much more than just a café. A complex of meeting rooms and entertainment venues, it stirs the Italian soul (at least, patriotic Italian souls). Built in 1831 during the period of Austrian rule, the Caffè Pedrocchi was inaugurated for the fourth Italian Congress of Scientists, which convened during the mid-19th century to stir up nationalistic fervor as Italy struggled to become a united nation. As a symbol of patriotic hope, it was the target (no surprise) of a student uprising plot in 1848. You can still see a bullet hole (framed in silver) in the wall of the Sala Bianca, where one of the insurgents was killed. Nowadays, you get more foam than fervor.

Each room is decorated and furnished in a different color: red, white, or green—representing the colors of the Italian flag. In the Sala Verde (Green Room), people are welcome to sit and enjoy the beautiful interior without ordering anything or having to pay. This is where Italian gentlemen read their newspapers and gather with friends to chat about the old days. In the red room, the clock over the bar is flanked by marble reliefs of morning and night, signaling that it was open 24 hours a day (in the 19th century). The maps of the hemispheres with south up top reflect the anti-conventional spirit of the place. The menu offers teahouse fare, including salads, sandwiches, and the writer Stendhal's beloved *zabaglione,* a creamy custard made with *marsala* wine (daily 9:00–24:00, until 21:00 off-season; entrance is at intersection of Oberdan and VIII Febbraio, between Piazza delle Erbe and Piazza Cavour, Ponti Romani tram stop; tel. 049-878-1231).

Piano Nobile: This upper, "noble floor" is more elaborate. The rooms are all in different styles, such as Greek, Etruscan, or Egyptian, with good English descriptions throughout. These rooms were intended to evoke memories of the glory of past epochs, which a united Italy had hopes of reliving.

Museum of the Risorgimento: The Piano Nobile hosts a small museum that traces Padua's role in Italian history, from the downfall of the Venetian Republic (1797) to the founding of the Republic of Italy (1948). Exhibits, a few with English descriptions, include uniforms, medals, weaponry, old artillery, Fascist propaganda posters, and a 30-minute propagandistic video (in Italian, but mostly fascinating footage without narration). The video, played on demand, is a "Luce" production (meaning a Mussolini production) and features great scenes of the town in the 1930s, including clips of Il Duce's visit and later WWII bombardments. The war and propaganda posters in the last room are haunting. An old woman pleads to those who might question the Fascist-driven war effort: "Don't betray my son." Another declares, "The Germans are truly our friends." And another asks, "And you...what are you doing?" (€4, Tue–Sun 9:30–12:30 & 15:30–18:00, closed Mon, tel. 049-820-5007.) Reach Piano Nobile by a stairway to the right of the Caffè's entrance.

▲**Baptistery**—This richly frescoed little building was originally the private chapel of Padua's ruling family. Then, in 1405, Venice took over, killing the family, and making the building a baptistery. Located next to the Duomo, the Baptistery was frescoed (c. 1370) by Giusto de' Menabuoi.

While created 70 years after Giotto, the Baptistery feels older. Because the artist was working for a private family, he needed to be politically correct and not threaten or offend the family's allies, especially the Church. While still mind-blowing, the Baptistery's art seems relatively conservative compared to Giotto's Scrovegni Chapel. Giotto, supported by the powerful Scrovegni family and the Franciscans, could get away with being more progressive and bold.

The Baptistery's complex design must have made perfect and cohesive sense to the faithful in centuries past. Almighty Christ is in majesty on top, while approachable Mary and the multitude of saints provide the devout with access to God. Find the world as it was known in the 14th century (the disk below Mary's feet). It kicks off a cycle of scenes illustrating creation (clockwise from the creation of Adam). The four evangelists (Matthew, Mark, Luke, and John) with their books and symbols fill the corners. A vivid crucifixion scene faces a gorgeous annunciation. And the altar niche features a dim, blue-toned, literal Apocalypse from the book of Revelation (€3, daily 10:00–18:00).

University of Padua—The main building of this prestigious university, known as Palazzo Bo, is adjacent to Caffè Pedrocchi. Founded in 1222, it's one of the first, greatest, and most progressive universities in Europe. Back when the Church controlled university curricula, a group of professors and students broke free from the University of Bologna to create this liberal school, which would be independent of Catholic constraints and accessible to people of alternative faiths.

A haven for free thought, the university attracted intellectuals from all over Europe, including the great astronomer Copernicus, who realized here that the universe didn't revolve around him. And Galileo—notorious for disagreeing with the Church's views on science—called his 18 years on the faculty here the best of his life.

The gawking public is not really welcomed in the university, but you can poke into two courtyards. Enter from the front of the main building (facing city hall on Via VIII Febbraio, 30 yards from Caffè Pedrocchi at #7). You'll pop into a 16th-century courtyard, the school's historic core. It's littered with the coats of arms of important faculty and leaders of the university over the ages. Classrooms, which open onto the square, are still used. Today, students gather here, surrounded by memories of illustrious alumni, including the first woman ever to receive a university degree (in 1678).

A passageway leads from here to an adjacent second courtyard from the Fascist era (c. 1938). The relief celebrates heroic students in World War I. Off of this courtyard, notice the richly decorated stairway, frescoed in the 1930s with themes celebrating art, science, and the pursuit of knowledge.

The big attraction among tourists is Europe's first great **Anatomy Theater** (from 1594), which you can visit only on a guided tour (explained below). Try to get a ticket, but keep in mind that it's not worth any heroics to see. The first two rooms of the tour are underwhelming: One features the supposed "pulpit of Galileo" (c. 1550) and portraits of 40 famous alums. The second is the Aula Magna, a ceremonial room for festivities. The historic Anatomy Theater itself is more impressive. Despite the Church's strict ban on autopsies, more than 300 students would pack this theater to watch  professors dissect human cadavers (the bodies of criminals from another town). This had to be done in a "don't ask, don't tell" kind of way, because the Roman Catholic Church only started allowing the teaching of anatomy through dissection in the late 1800s.

Cost and Hours: While it's free to visit the university, you

PADUA

Graduation Antics in Padua

With 60,000 students, Padua's university always seems to be hosting graduation ceremonies. There's a constant trickle

of happy grads and their friends and families celebrating the big event.

During the school year, every 20 minutes or so, a student steps into a formal room (upstairs, above the university courtyard) to officially meet with the leading professors of his or her faculty. When they're finished, the students are given a green laurel wreath. They pose for ceremonial group photos and family snapshots. It's a sweet scene. Then, craziness takes over.

The new graduates replace their somber clothing with raunchy outfits, as gangs of friends gather around them on Via VIII Febbraio, the street in front of the university. The roast begins. The gang rolls out a giant butcher-paper poster with a generally obscene caricature of the student and a litany of *This Is Your Life* photos and stories. The new grad, subject to various embarrassing pranks, reads the funny statements out loud. The poster is then taped to the university wall for all to see. (Find the plastic panels to the right of the main entry, facing Via VIII Febbraio. Graduation posters are allowed to stay there for 24 hours. The panels are emptied each morning, but by nighttime a new set of posters is affixed to the plastic shields.)

During the roast, the friends sing the catchy but obscene local university anthem, reminding their newly esteemed friend not to get too huffy: *Dottore, dottore, dottore del buso del cul. Vaffancul, vaffancul* (loosely translated: "Doctor, doctor. You're just a doctor of the a-hole...go f-off, go f-off"). After you've heard this song (with its fanfare and oom-pahpah catchiness) and have seen all the good-natured fun, you can't stop singing it.

The crazy show is usually staged late in the afternoon. Outdoor café tables afford great seats to enjoy the spectacle.

must sign up for a 30-minute tour (€5) to see the Anatomy Theater. Only 30 people may enter at a time. Tours run three times a day (March–Oct Mon, Wed, and Fri at 15:15, 16:15, and 17:15; Tue, Thu, and Sat at 9:15, 10:15, and 11:15; no tours on Sun, call for times Nov–Feb—see number below, Ponti Romani tram stop, www.unipd.it). School groups often book the entire visit, and many of the guides speak no English.

Confirm tour times and availability by calling 049-827-3047

or stopping by the ticket window (opens 15 minutes before each tour, located just inside the palace, in the hall reached from the Fascist-era courtyard described above). The bar there is fun for a cheap drink and to see photos of university life.

Sleeping in Padua

Rooms in Padua's hotels are more spacious and a better value than those in Venice. Keep in mind that when large conventions take over the town—several times a year—all hotels raise prices. I've listed two hotels in the center and a group of accommodations near the basilica. All but Albergo Verdi are easily reached from the station by the tram.

In the Center

Tito Livio is the nearest tram stop for these two hotels.

$$$ Hotel Majestic Toscanelli is a central, fancy hotel with 34 pleasant, air-conditioned rooms and a touch of charm, buried in a characteristic ghetto with wonderful cobbled ambience. This area is popular with students at night, and it can be noisy until about 1:00 in the morning; as the hotel's windows are single-paned, request a quiet room on the back side (Sb-€95–110, Db-€150–160, 10 percent Rick Steves discount, superior rooms and suites available at extra cost, check website for special discounts, includes a wonderful breakfast, Wi-Fi, 2 blocks south of Piazza delle Erbe at Via dell'Arco 2, tel. 049-663-244, fax 049-876-0025, www.toscanelli.com, majestic@toscanelli.com). From Piazza delle Erbe, head up Via dei Fabbri and take the first left to Via dell'Arco.

$$ Albergo Verdi, a modern little place, is crammed into an old building on a forgettable street at the edge of the old town, away from the tram. While public spaces are very tight, the 14 rooms are modern and spacious (Db-€90–100, extra person-€30, air-con, elevator, a couple of blocks behind Piazza Duomo at Via Dondi dall'Orologio 7, tel. 049-836-4163, www.albergoverdipadova.it, info@albergoverdipadova.it).

Near Basilica of St. Anthony

Santo is the nearest tram stop for the following hotels. Use the Prato della Valle tram stop for the hostel.

$$ Hotel Al Fagiano feels like an art gallery with crazy, sexy modern art everywhere. The hotel is all about the union of a man and a woman (quite romantic). They rent 30 bright and cheery air-conditioned rooms, each uniquely decorated with Rossella Fagiano's canvases (Sb-€64, Db-€100, Tb-€115, ask for Rick Steves discount, €7 per person less without breakfast, Wi-Fi, 50 yards from the Santo tram stop at Via Locatelli 45, tel. & fax 049-

Sleep Code

(€1 = about $1.25, country code: 39)
S = Single, **D** = Double/Twin, **T** = Triple, **Q** = Quad, **b** = bathroom, **s** = shower only. Unless otherwise noted, credit cards are accepted, breakfast is included, and English is spoken.

To help you easily sort through these listings, I've divided the rooms into three categories based on the price for a standard double room with bath:

$$$ Higher Priced—Most rooms €130 or more.
$$ Moderately Priced—Most rooms between €90–130.
$ Lower Priced—Most rooms €90 or less.

Prices can change without notice; verify the hotel's current rates online or by email. For other updates, see www.ricksteves.com/update.

875-3396, www.alfagiano.com, info@alfagiano.com).

$$ Hotel Belludi 37 is a slick, borderline-pretentious place renting 15 modern rooms shoehorned into an old building. The decor is dark, woody, fresh, and stylish (S-€57, Sb-€80, D-€90, Db-€120, bigger Db-€135, ask for 10 percent Rick Steves discount, €7 less per person without breakfast, air-con, Wi-Fi, free minibar, a block from the Santo tram stop at Via Luca Belludi 37, tel. 049-665-633, fax 049-658-685, www.belludi37.it, info@belludi37.it).

$$ Hotel Casa del Pellegrino, with 150 spotless, cheap, institutional rooms and straight pricing, is home to the pilgrims who come to pay homage to St. Anthony in the basilica next door. But any visitor to Padua is welcome (S-€54, Sb-€71, D-€74, Db-€92, Tb-€109, Qb-€138, air-con, ask for a room off the street, €7 less per person without breakfast, elevator, Via Cesarotti 21, tel. 049-823-9711, fax 049-823-9780, www.casadelpellegrino.com, info@casadelpellegrino.com). For better accommodations, request one of the 24 rooms in the *dipendenza,* the hotel's modern wing (€5 extra/night).

$ Hotel Al Santo, run with charm by Valentina and Antonio, offers 15 spacious rooms with all the comforts a few steps from the basilica (Sb-€65–70, Db-€90, Tb-€120, Qb-€135, double-paned windows, air-con, quieter rooms off street, some rooms have views of basilica, Wi-Fi, Via del Santo 147, tel. 049-875-2131, fax 049-878-8076, www.alsanto.it, alsanto@alsanto.it).

Hostel: **$ Ostello Città di Padova,** near Prato della Valle, is well-run and has 80 beds in 4-, 6-, and 9-bed rooms (beds with sheets and breakfast-€19; 4-person family rooms-€80, with bath-€90; self-service laundry, bike rentals available in summer, lockers, reception open 7:00–9:30 & 16:30–23:30, rooms locked during afternoon but reception staffed if you need to leave bags, 23:30 curfew; Via Aleardi 30—take tram from station to Prato della Valle, then it's a 5-minute walk: walk along Via Cavaletto, turn right on Via Marin, turn left after Torresino church; tel. 049-875-2219, www.ostellopadova.it, ostellopadova@ctgveneto.it).

Eating in Padua

The university population means cheap, good food abounds. For picnic shopping, see "Market Squares," on page 325. My recommended restaurants are all centrally located in the historic core. You'd think there would be fine dining on the charming market squares, but on the piazzas it's a take-out-pizza-and-casual-bar scene (dominated by students after dark). La Lanterna, at the neighboring Piazza dei Signori, is the best on-square option I've found—but it's basically pizza. The dreamily atmospheric ghetto neighborhood (just two blocks off the market squares) thrives after dark with trendy bars and a lively student *spritz* scene.

Fine Dining near the Center

Ristorante da Giorgio is a respected fixture in town for its dressy white-tablecloth dining and good international cuisine. They are passionate about their vegetarian *secondi* and proud of their bean soup, fish soup, cod, and squid. Reservations are smart at night (€12 pastas, €25 *secondi*, meals served from 12:00 and from 19:30, closed Sun, Via Daniele Manin 8, tel. 049-836-0973).

Osteria L'Anfora is a classic place serving classic dishes in a rustic, fun-loving space. Don't be put off by the woody, ruffian decor and the fact that it's a popular hangout for a pre-meal drink. They take food seriously and serve it at good prices, and the energy and commotion add to a great dining experience (€8 pastas, €12 *secondi*, €2 cover, closed Sun, Via dei Soncin 13, tel. 049-656-629, no reservations taken).

Osteria dei Fabbri, with shared rustic tables, offers a good mix of class and accessibility, quality and price. The dining room is spacious, and the dishes are traditional Venetian (€9 pastas, €13 *secondi*, Mon–Sat 12:30–14:30 & 19:30–22:30, closed Sun, Via dei Fabbri 13, tel. 049-650-336).

Cheap Eats near the Center

La Lanterna has a forgettable interior, but a pizza here on Piazza dei Signori includes a rare-in-Padua chance to sit in a grand square under the stars, surrounded by great architecture. Its pizzas are a local favorite, and reservations are recommended (€8 pastas and pizzas, €14 *secondi*, Fri–Wed 12:00–14:30 & 18:00–24:00, closed

Thu, Piazza dei Signori 39, tel. 049-660-770).

Bar dei Osei, on Piazza della Frutta, is a very simple sandwich bar with some of the best seats in town. While Paduans love their delicate *tremazzini* (white bread sandwiches with crusts cut off, €1.80), I'd choose their grilled *porchetta*—pulled pork—sandwiches. The two-foot-long mother lode awaits on the counter for you to say how big a slice you'd like. Wines are listed on the board (Mon–Sat 7:00–21:00, closed Sun, Piazza della Frutta 1, tel. 049-875-9606). With fast, cheap meal and drink in hand, grab a seat and enjoy the market scene.

Brek, tucked into a corner of Piazza Cavour at #20, is an easy self-service chain *ristorante* with healthy and affordable choices. It's big, bright, practical, and family-friendly (daily 11:30–15:00 & 18:30–22:00, tel. 049-875-3788).

Brek Foccacceria, a new branch across from Caffè Pedrocchi and next door to the PAM supermarket, sells big sandwiches that you can eat at outdoor tables (daily 8:00–22:00, Piazzetta della Garzeria 6, tel. 049-876-1651).

If the markets are closed, stock up on picnic items at the **PAM supermarket,** in a tiny *piazzetta* east of Caffè Pedrocchi (Mon–Sat 8:00–21:00, closed Wed evenings and all day Sun, Piazzetta Garzeria 3, tel. 049-657-006).

Pasticceria Racca is a pastry shop/café offering an exquisite selection of chocolates and pastries. Consider a stop here to attend to your sweet tooth, Padua-style (tiny seats, on Piazza Cavour, kitty-corner from Caffè Pedrocchi at Via Pietro Fortunato Calvi 8).

Enoteca Santa Lucia provides a modern alternative for a drink or meal. With a New York jazz-bar sense of style, they serve fine wine by the glass with generous free tapas around the bar or with seating on the square, and modern Mediterranean meals in the cellar with mod decor (€10 pastas, €20 *secondi,* closed Sun, Piazza Cavour at the corner of Via Pietro Fortunato Calvi, tel. 049-655-545).

Near the Basilica of St. Anthony

Pizzeria Pago Pago dishes up wood-fired Neapolitan pizzas (a local favorite) and daily specials depending on what's in season. Get there early for dinner or wait (€5–8.50 pizzas, Wed–Mon 12:00–14:00 & 19:00–23:00, closed Tue; 2 blocks from Basilica of St. Anthony, up Via del Santo and right onto Via Galileo Galilei to #59; tel. 049-665-558, Gaetano and Modesto).

Casa del Pellegrino Ristorante caters to St. Anthony pilgrims with simple, basic, and hearty meals, served in a cheery dining room just north of the basilica. *Baccalà* (cod) is a favorite here (€4.50 pastas, €8 *secondi,* €14 three-course fixed-price meal, daily 12:00–14:00 & 19:30–21:30, Via Cesarotti 21, tel. 049-876-0715).

Zairo is a huge *ristorante*/pizzeria with reasonable prices, delicious homemade pastas, Veneto specialties, snappy service, and a local clientele (Tue–Sun 12:00–14:30 & 19:00–24:00, closed Mon, east side of Prato della Valle at #51, tel. 049-663-803).

Pollodoro la Gastronomica, a take-out deli near the basilica, sells roast chicken, pastas, and veggies, and will make sandwiches (Wed–Mon 8:00–13:30 & 17:00–20:00, closed Tue, 100 yards from basilica at Via Belludi 34; tel. 049-663-718). You can picnic at the nearby cloisters of the basilica.

Padua Connections

From Padua by Train to: Venice (2/hour, 30 min), **Vicenza** (2/hour, fewer on weekends, 20 minutes), **Milan** (1–2/hour, 2.5 hours), **Verona** (2/hour, 1 hour).

By Bus to Venice's Airports: Cheap buses connect Padua and **Marco Polo Airport** (€5 from driver, cheaper if you buy ticket from office, €2/bag, 2/hour from 5:00 to 22:25, 1 hour, departs from Padua's bus station at Piazzale Boschetti, run by SITA, www.sitabus.it).

A **minibus service** runs from Padua to **Marco Polo Airport** (€28/person) or **Treviso Airport** (€39/person, reservations required, tel. 049-870-4425, www.airservicepadova.it).

Near Padua: Vicenza

To many architects, Vicenza (vih-CHEHN-zah) is a pilgrimage site. Entire streets look like the back of a nickel. This is the city of Andrea Palladio (1508–1580), the 16th-century Renaissance architect who gave us the Palladian style that is so influential in countless British country homes. But as grandiose as Vicenza's Palladian facades may feel, there is little marble here. The city lacked the wealth to build with much more than painted wood and plaster. If you're an architecture buff, Vicenza merits a quick stop (on any day but Monday, when major sights are closed). For my expanded coverage of Vicenza, see www.ricksteves.com/vicenza.

Tourist Information: The main TI is at Piazza Matteotti 12 (tel. 0444-320-854, www.vicenzae.org); a smaller office is at Piazza dei Signori 8. Architecture fans appreciate the TI's *Vicenza Città e le Ville del Palladio nel Veneto* booklet (in English). Two websites cover most of the sights in town: www.comune.vicenza.it and www.museicivicivicenza.it.

Arrival in Vicenza: From the train station, it's a five-minute **walk** up wide Viale Roma to the bottom of Corso Palladio. Drivers

Vicenza

can park in one of the cheap parking lots (Parcheggio Bassano and Parcheggio Cricoli), and catch a free shuttle bus to the center.

Helpful Hints: Most of Vicenza's sights are covered by a combo-ticket, **Card Musei** (€8/3 days, sold only at the Olympic Theater), but it doesn't cover the villas outside of town. The only **baggage check** in town is at the hostel, L'Ostello Olimpico, near Piazza Matteotti (long hours, Viale Giuriolo 7/9, tel. 0444-540-222).

Sights in Vicenza

▲▲**Olympic Theater (Teatro Olimpico)**—Palladio's last work is one of his greatest. The theater is a wood-and-stucco festival of classical columns, statues, and an oh-wow stage bursting with perspective tricks (entry only with €8 Card Musei, which covers other Vicenza sights; audioguide available, Tue–Sun 9:00–17:00, closed Mon, occasionally closed when theater is in use, entrance to the left of TI, tel. 0444-222-800). When you step back outside, look up the town's main drag—named after Palladio. It's the same main street you saw in his theater.

▲**Church of Santa Corona**—A block away from the Olympic Theater, this "Church of the Holy Crown" was built in the 13th century to house a thorn from the Crown of Thorns, given to the Bishop of Vicenza by the French King Louis IX. The church has two artistic highlights: the art embellishing its high altar and Giovanni Bellini's fine painting, *Baptism of Christ* (church entry free, small fee to light the Bellini, Tue–Sun 8:30–12:00 & 15:00–17:00, closed Mon).

Archaeological and Natural History Museum—Located next door to the Church of Santa Corona, this museum has a ground floor featuring Roman antiquities (mosaics, statues, and artifacts excavated from Rome's Baths of Caracalla, plus swords) and a barbarian warrior skeleton complete with sword and helmet. Prehistoric scraps are upstairs. Look for English description sheets near exhibit entryways throughout (covered by Card Musei, Tue–Sun 9:00–17:00, closed Mon).

Palazzo Leoni Montanari—Across the street from the Church of Santa Corona, this small museum is a palatial riot of Baroque, with cherub-cluttered ceilings jumbled like a preschool in heaven. A quick stroll shows off Venetian paintings and a floor of Russian icons (small entry fee, Tue–Sun 10:00–18:00, closed Mon, Contrà Santa Corona 25, www.palazzomontanari.com).

Piazza dei Signori—Vicenza's main square has been the center of town ever since it was the site of the ancient Roman forum. The commanding **Basilica Palladiana,** with its 270-foot-tall, 13th-century tower, dominates the square. It was a meeting place for local big shots. It was young Palladio's proposal—to redo Vicenza's dilapidated Gothic palace of justice in the Neo-Greek style—that established him as the city's favorite architect. The rest of Palladio's career was a one-man construction boom. When the basilica is open, it hosts frequent special exhibitions that sometimes involve a fee, but you can often pop in for a free look.

Villas on the Outskirts of Vicenza—Vicenza is surrounded by dreamy Venetian villas. Venice's commercial empire receded in the 1500s when trade began to pick up along the Atlantic seaboard and dwindle in the Mediterranean. Venice redirected its economic agenda to agribusiness, which led to the construction of lavish country villas, such as **Villa la Rotonda** (the inspiration for Thomas Jefferson's Monticello) and **Villa Valmarana ai Nani** (www.villavalmarana.com). Both houses are furnished with period pieces and come with good English descriptions (closed Mon). Pick up the free English brochure on Palladio's villas from the TI if you plan to visit.

Vicenza Connections

From Vicenza by Train to: **Venice** (2/hour, 1 hour), **Padua** (2/ hour, fewer on weekends, 20 minutes), **Verona** (2/hour, 40 minutes), **Milan** (2/hour, 2 hours), **Ravenna** (roughly hourly, 3.5–4 hours, changes in Padua and Ferrara or Bologna).

VERONA

Romeo and Juliet made Verona a household word. Alas, a visit here has nothing to do with those two star-crossed lovers. You can pay to visit the house that falsely claims to be Juliet's (with an almost-believable balcony and a courtyard swarming with tour groups), join in the tradition of rubbing the breast of Juliet's statue to help find a lover (or to pick up the sweat of someone who can't), and even make a pilgrimage to what isn't "La Tomba di Giulietta."

Despite the fiction, Verona—Italy's fourth-most-visited city—has been an important crossroads for 2,000 years and is therefore packed with genuine history. R and J fans will take some solace in the fact that two real feuding families, the Montecchi and the Cappellos, were the models for Shakespeare's Montagues and Capulets. And, if R and J had existed and were alive today, they would still recognize much of their "hometown."

Verona's main attractions are its wealth of Roman ruins; the remnants of its 13th- and 14th-century political and cultural boom; its 21st-century, quiet, pedestrian-only ambience; and its world-class opera festival, held each summer (www.arena.it). After Venice's festival of tourism, Veneto's second city (in population and in artistic importance) is a cool and welcome sip of pure Italy, where dumpsters are painted by schoolchildren as class projects and public spaces are the domain of locals, not tourists. If you like Italy but don't need blockbuster sights, this town is a joy.

Orientation to Verona

The vibrant and enjoyable core of Verona is along Via Mazzini between Piazza Brà (pronounced "bra") and Piazza Erbe, Verona's market square since Roman times. Head straight for Piazza Brà—and stroll. While Via Mazzini attracts mob scenes during the *passeggiata* (evening stroll), don't neglect the parallel Corso Porta Borsari. All sights of importance are located within an easy walk through the old town, which is defined by a bend in the river. For a good day trip to Verona, visit the Roman Arena and take my self-guided walk.

Tourist Information

Verona has two TIs: at the **train station** (Mon–Sat 9:00–19:00, Sun 9:00–15:00, tel. 045-800-0861) and at **Piazza Brà** (Mon–Sat 9:00–19:00, Sun 10:00–16:00, tel. 045-806-8680, www.tourism .verona.it). At either TI, pick up the free city map for a list of sights and opening hours, and confirm the walking-tour schedule. If you're staying the night, ask about concerts or pick up the monthly entertainment guide, *Carnet Verona* (free at TI, €1 at newsstands).

Verona Card: This tourist card covers bus transportation and entrance to all the recommended Verona sights, except the manicured Giardino Giusti garden (€10/day or €15/3 days, sold at TIs and at participating sights). If you arrive at the train station, buy the card at the TI there because it'll cover your bus ride to and from the city center as well as all your sightseeing. Here's the math: €6 (arena) + €6 (tower climb) + €6 (castle) + €5 (two churches) + €2 (two bus rides) = €25. At €10, the card saves a day-tripper intent on blitzing the city 60 percent.

The €5 **Church Card,** sold at all churches that require admission, pays off if you visit at least three.

Arrival in Verona

By Train: Get off at the Verona Porta Nuova Station. You'll emerge into the station from one of two passages. The TI, baggage check (€4/5 hours, daily 7:00–23:00, 45 pounds max), and waiting lounge are together. The main hall includes an efficient collection of all the services you'd hope to find in a station. *Tabacchi* shops sell bus tickets. Buses and taxis are immediately outside.

Avoid the boring 15-minute walk from the station to Piazza Brà by catching a **city bus.** To get to the center, hop on any bus leaving from platform A in front of the station. To cover your trip into town, either get a Verona Card (described earlier) or buy an individual ticket before boarding from a *tabacchi* shop inside the station (€1/1 hour, €3.50 valid until midnight). Confirm the route by asking, *"Per il centro?"* (pehr eel CHEN-troh). If you have an individual ticket, validate it by stamping it in the machine in the bus. If you have a Verona Card, you'll just need to show it if a "controller" asks you for your ticket.

Buses stop on Piazza Brà, the square with the can't-miss-it Roman Arena. The TI is just a few steps beyond the bus stop (located along the medieval walls). You can catch return buses

(#11, #12, or #13) to the station from here or from the bus stop just outside the city wall (on the right), where Corso Porta Nuova hits Piazza Brà.

Taxis pick up only at taxi stands (at Piazza Brà and train station) and cost about €8 for the quick ride between the train station and Piazza Brà.

By Car: The town center is closed to traffic, but if you're staying here, your hotel can get you permission to drive in—ask when you book. Otherwise your license plate could be photographed, and you could have a €100 ticket waiting for you in the mail when you get home.

Drivers will find cheap parking in well-marked lots and garages farther from the center (including two lots in front of the train station). For more central and expensive parking, consider either Garage Arena (off Via Porta Nuova just outside the walls) or Garage Italia (Corso Porta Nuova 91; both guarded, about €2.50/hour, 6:00–24:00, tel. 045-800-6312). Street parking costs €1.50 per hour (buy ticket at *tabacchi* shop to put on dashboard, spaces marked with blue lines, maximum two hours).

By Plane: Efficient shuttle buses connect Verona's airport (Verona-Villafranca, 12 miles southwest of the city) with its train station (€4.50, buy tickets on board or at *tabacchi* shop, daily 6:30–22:30, 3/hour, 15 minutes).

From Brescia Airport, 40 miles west of Verona, a shuttle bus meets Ryanair flights and takes passengers to the Porta Nuova train station (€11, bus schedule is coordinated with Ryanair arrivals and departures).

Helpful Hints

Sightseeing Schedules: Many sights are closed on Monday morning.

Opera: From mid-June through August, Verona's opera festival brings the city to life, with 15,000 music fans filling the Roman Arena for almost nightly performances. The city is packed and festive, as restaurants have pre-scheduled seatings for dinner and hotels jack up their prices (upper-level seats about €26, book tickets either online at www.arena.it or by calling 045-800-5151; box office open Mon–Fri 9:00–12:00 & 15:15–17:45, Sat–Sun 9:00–12:00; during opera season, open daily 10:00–17:45, or until 21:00 on performance days; Via Dietro Anfiteatro 6B).

Internet Access: Try **Verona Web** (Mon–Fri 10:00–22:00, Sat–Sun 14:00–20:00, a couple of blocks off Piazza Brà toward Castelvecchio at Via Roma 17A, tel. 045-801-3394) or **Internet Etc.** (Tue–Sat 9:30–19:45, Sun–Mon 15:30–19:45, off Via Mazzini on Via Quattro Spade 3B, tel. 045-800-0222).

Travel Agency: Welcome Travel is handy if you want to buy a train ticket without going to the station (just outside the gate from Piazza Brà at Corso Porta Nuova 11, tel. 045-806-0126).

Tours in Verona

Walking Tours—The TI organizes 1.5-hour tours daily (often English-only, but sometimes in Italian too) for €10 per person. Tours meet inside the Piazza Brà TI and stroll all the way through the old town (call to find schedule, no reservation necessary, tel. 045-806-8680, mobile 333-219-9645).

Private Guides—Two excellent and enthusiastic Verona guides enjoy giving private tours of the town and region to readers of this book (€105/2 hours and €210/5 hours per group, tours tailored to your interests—villas, wine-tasting, etc.). They are **Marina Menegoi** (tel. 045-801-2174, mobile 328-958-1108, www .venetoguide.it, mmenegoi@gmail.com) and **Valeria Biasi** (mobile 348-9034-238, www.veronatours.com, valeria@veronatours.com). Valeria also offers a Safari Verona tour suitable for families with children (€108/3 hours).

VERONA

Self-Guided Walk

Welcome to Verona Town Walk

This walk covers the essential sights in the town core, starting at Piazza Brà and ending at the cathedral. Allow 1.5 hours (including the tower climb and dawdling, more with the optional detours).

❶ Piazza Brà

If you're wondering about the name, it comes from the local dialect and means "open space." A generation ago this piazza was noisy

with cars. Now it's open and people-friendly—the community family room and natural festival grounds.

Grab a bench near the central fountain called "The Alps." This was a gift from Verona's sister city Munich, which is just over the mountains. You'll see the symbols of the two cities with the peaks carved out of pink marble from this region.

The ancient Arena looming over the piazza is a reminder that the city's history goes back to Roman times. A major East–West trading route once cut across Verona, which fills an easy-to-defend bend in the river. On this walk, we'll meander across what was the

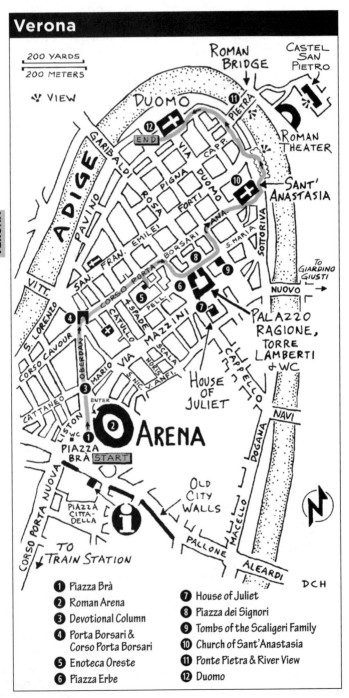

Verona

200 YARDS
200 METERS

↘ VIEW

ADIGE

ROMAN BRIDGE

CASTEL SAN PIETRO

DUOMO

⑪ PIETRA

ROMAN THEATER

⑫ END

VIA GARIBALDI

VIA PIGNA

VIA DUOMO

CAPP.

SANT' ANASTASIA

⑩

ROSA

FORTI

VITT.

S. FRAN.

EMILEI

BORSARI

ANA.

S. MARIA

⑧

SOTTORIVA

To GIARDINO GIUSTI

NUOVO

S. LORENZO

CORSO PORTA BORSARI

④

CORSO CAVOUR

PAVINO

SAN.

⑤

A SPADE

CATULLO

PELL.

⑥

⑨

PALAZZO RAGIONE, TORRE LAMBERTI & WC

③ ENTER

VIA MARIO

NIC.

V. ANFI.

MAZZINI

SCALA

NORIS

⑦

HOUSE OF JULIET

CAPPELLO

CATTANEO

OBERDAN

WC

LISTON

① ② ARENA

PIAZZA BRÀ   START

CORSO PORTA NUOVA

PIAZZA CITTADELLA

ⓘ

OLD CITY WALLS

NAVI

DOGANA

MACELLO

CAPPELLO

N

To TRAIN STATION

PALLONE

ALEARDI

DCH

① Piazza Brà
② Roman Arena
③ Devotional Column
④ Porta Borsari & Corso Porta Borsari
⑤ Enoteca Oreste
⑥ Piazza Erbe
⑦ House of Juliet
⑧ Piazza dei Signori
⑨ Tombs of the Scaligeri Family
⑩ Church of Sant'Anastasia
⑪ Ponte Pietra & River View
⑫ Duomo

VERONA

ancient city, from the Arena on this side to the theater across the river.

With the fall of Rome, Verona became a favored capital of barbarian kings. In the Middle Ages, noble families had to choose sides (Guelphs or Ghibellines) in the civil struggles between emperors and popes. During this time, the town bristled with San Gimignano-type towers, built by different families to symbolize their power. When the Scaligeri family rose to power here in the 14th century, they established stability on their terms and made the other noble families lop off their proud towers—only the Scaligeris were allowed to have a tower. But inter-family feuds made it impossible for the family to maintain a stable government, and in 1405 the town essentially gave itself to Venice, which ruled Verona until Napoleon stopped by in 1796. During the 19th century, a tug-of-war between France and Austria in this area actually divided the city for a time, with the river marking the border of each country's domain. Eventually Verona fell into Austrian hands. The huge Neoclassical city hall facing Piazza Brà (look for the flags) was built by the Austrians to serve as their 19th-century military headquarters. The big statue is of Italy's first king, Victor Emmanuel, and celebrates Italian independence and unity, won in the 1860s.

Apart from all its history, Piazza Brà is about strolling...the *passeggiata* is a national sport in Italy. The broad, shiny sidewalk was named the "Liston" (ribbon) by 17th-century Venetians, who made it big and wide so that promenading socialites could see and be seen in all their finery.

❷ Roman Arena

Just as modern stadiums are usually located outside of downtown districts, the Romans built this stadium outside the town walls. With 72 aisles, this elliptical 466-by-400-foot amphitheater is the

third largest in the Roman world (and it was originally 50 percent taller). Most of the stone you see is original. Dating from the first century A.D., it looks great in its pink marble. Over the centuries, crowds of up to 25,000 spectators have cheered Roman gladiator battles, medieval executions, and modern plays—including the popular opera festival (held every summer), which takes advantage of the Arena's famous acoustics. While there's little to see inside except for the impressive stonework, it is memorable to visit a Roman arena that is still a thriving venue for concerts. If you climb to the top, you'll enjoy great city views (€6, don't bother with the combo-ticket that includes the unimpressive Maffei Museum, Tue–Sun 8:30–19:30, Mon 13:30–19:30, closes at 14:00 during opera season, last entry one hour before closing, WC near entry, tel. 045-800-3204).

• *As you exit the Arena, look to your right. Where the street splits you'll see a column.*

❸ Devotional Column

In the Middle Ages, this column blessed a marketplace held here. Ten yards in front of it, a bronze plaque in the sidewalk shows the Roman city plan—a town of 20,000 placed strategically in the bend of the river, which provided protection on three sides. A wall enclosed the peninsula. The center of the grid was the forum, today's Piazza Erbe. (If you look down Via Mazzini, the busy main pedestrian drag, the bell tower in the distance marks Piazza Erbe.)

• *After viewing the bronze plaque, turn around so your back is to the Arena. Head straight down Via Oberdan and continue a couple of blocks to an ancient gate, the Porta Borsari.*

❹ Porta Borsari and Corso Porta Borsari

You're standing before the main entrance to Roman Verona; back in the day, this functioned as a toll booth (*borsari* means purse, referring to the collection of tolls here). Below the spiral, fluted columns (which parents nickname *"tortiglioni"*—a pasta kids can relate to), you'll see the names of patrons ("this arch was brought to you by the generous support of..."). Outside the café, the stone on the curb is from a tomb—in Roman times, the roads outside the walls were lined with tombstones, as no one could be buried within the town itself. Step into the café. A glass panel on the floor shows the original Roman foundations and pavement stones.

Now cross into the ancient city and walk down Corso Porta Borsari, the ancient main drag, toward what was the forum. Make it a scavenger hunt. As you walk, discover bits of the town's illustrious past—chips of Roman columns, medieval reliefs, fine old facades, fossils in marble—as well as its elegant present of fancy shops, in a setting that prioritizes pedestrians over cars.

• *A block before you reach Piazza Erbe, at Vicolo San Marco in Foro, detour right, following the* Pozzo dell'Amore *sign. Twenty yards off Corso Porta Borsari, you'll find...*

❺ Enoteca Oreste

This funky wine and grappa bar is still run by Oreste (with his Chicagoan wife, Beverly) like a 1970s, old-style *enoteca*. Browse, munch, sample. There's no formal food, but an abundance of fun and hearty bar snacks instead. This historic *enoteca* was once the private chapel of the archbishop of Verona. Traces of the past hide between the bottles—ask Beverly to tell you the story (daily 8:00–20:00, Vicolo San Marco in Foro 7, tel. 045-803-4369).

• *Return to Corso Porta Borsari and continue on until you hit a big square.*

❻ Piazza Erbe

This bustling market square is a photographer's delight. Its pastel buildings corral the fountains, pigeons, and people who have congregated here since Roman times, when this was a forum. Notice the Venetian lion hovering above the square, reminding locals of their conquerors since 1405. During medieval times, the stone canopy in the center held the scales where merchants measured the weight of goods they bought and sold, such as silk, wool, and wood. A fountain has bubbled here for 2,000 years. Its statue, originally Roman, had lost its head and arms. After a sculptor added a new head and arms, the statue became Verona's Madonna. She holds a small banner that reads, "I want justice and I bring peace."

If you were standing here in the Middle Ages, you would have been surrounded by proud noble family towers. Medieval nobles showed off with towers. Renaissance nobles showed off with finely painted facades on their palaces. If you look carefully, you can see remnants of the 16th-century days when Verona was nicknamed "the painted city."

While Piazza Brà is left for the tourists, Pizza Erbe is for the locals, who start their evening with an *aperitivo* here. It's a trendy scene, as young Veronans fill the bars to enjoy their refreshing *spritz* drinks, olives, and chips.

• *At the far end of Piazza Erbe, a market column featuring St. Zeno, the patron of Verona, looks at the crazy crowds flushing into the city's silly claim to touristic fame...the House of Juliet (100 yards down Via Cappello to #23—just follow the crowds). Side-trip there now (but watch your wallet—it's a pickpocket's haven).*

❼ House of Juliet

The tiny, admittedly romantic courtyard is a spectacle in itself, with tourists from all over the world posing on the balcony, Nebraskans polishing Juliet's bronze breast, and amorous graffiti everywhere. Residents marvel that each year, about 1,600 Japanese tour groups break their Venice–Milan ride for an hour-long stop in Verona just to see this courtyard. Hang out and savor the scene. The information boxes (€1 for two people) offer a good history: "While no documentation has been discovered to prove the truth of the legend, no documentation has disproved it either." The "museum," which displays art inspired by the love story, plus costumes and the bed from Franco Zeffirelli's film *Romeo and Juliet,* is certainly not worth the €6 entry fee (Tue–Sun 8:30–19:30, Mon 13:30–19:30, tel. 045-803-4303).

Was there a Juliet Capulet? You just walked down Via Cappello, the street of the cap makers. Above the courtyard entry (looking out) is a coat of arms featuring a hat—representing a family that made hats and which would be named, logically, Capulet.

The world does love Juliet. Upstairs (through the embroidery store on the left as you enter the courtyard) is the home of Verona's Juliet Club (www.julietclub.com). Every day, volunteers respond to countless letters addressed simply to Juliet, Verona, Italy. You can see them at work and read a smattering of love letters (9:00–21:00). There's also a fine view of the courtyard from here.

Watch out: The house may become an even more popular destination thanks to the 2010 movie *Letters to Juliet,* about a young woman (played by Amanda Seyfried) who finds a letter to Juliet and travels through Italy to help the author find her lost love.

• *Return to Piazza Erbe. From the center, head right to Via della Costa—it's marked by a whale's rib suspended under an arch. It was likely a souvenir brought home by a traveling merchant, reminding the townspeople that there was a big world out there. Walk down Via della Costa, into the big square.*

❽ Piazza dei Signori

Literally the "square of the lords," this is Verona's sitting room, more quiet and harmonious than Piazza Erbe. The buildings—which span five centuries—define the square and are all linked by arches. The long portico on the left is inspired by Brunelleschi's Hospital of the Innocents (considered the first Renaissance building) in Florence.

Locals call the square Piazza Dante for the statue of the Italian poet Dante Alighieri that dominates it. Dante—always pensive, never smiling—seems to wonder why the tourists choose Juliet over him. Dante was expelled from Florence for political reasons and was granted asylum in Verona by the Scaligeri family. With the whale's rib behind you, you're facing the brick, crenellated, 14th-century Scaligeri residence. Behind Dante is the yellowish,

15th-century Venetian Renaissance–style Portico of the Counsel. In front of Dante to his right (follow the white *WC* signs) is the 12th-century Romanesque **Palazzo della Ragione.**

Facing the Palazzo della Ragione, a lane on the right leads into its courtyard. Enter the courtyard. The impressive staircase—which goes nowhere—is the only surviving Renaissance staircase in Verona. For a grand city view, you can climb to the top of the 13th-century **Torre dei Lamberti** (€6 for stairs or elevator, daily 8:30–19:30, ticket office just beyond the whalebone on the right). The elevator saves you 245 steps—but you'll still need to climb about 45 more to get to the first viewing platform. It's not worth continuing up the endless spiral stairs to the second viewing platform.

• *Exit the courtyard the way you entered and turn right, continuing downhill. Within a block, you'll find the...*

❾ Tombs of the Scaligeri Family

These exotic and very Gothic 14th-century tombs, with their fine, original, wrought-iron protective cages, evoke the age when one family ruled Verona. The Scaligeri family was to Verona what the Medici family was to Florence. These were powerful people. They changed the law so that they could be buried within the town. They forbade the presence of any towers but their own. And, by building tombs atop pillars, they arranged to be looked up to even in death.

• *Continue 15 yards to the next corner and take a left on Vicolo Cavalletto. At the first corner, turn right and walk to the big, unfinished brick facade of Verona's largest church. For a fragrant and potentially tasty diversion, pop into the recommended **Albertini** and **Gastronomia**, two classic, family-run alimentari, both located on Corso Sant'Anastasia as you approach the Church of Sant'Anastasia. Either can rustle up tasty sandwiches (about €3), and Albertini sells cold beers and juices.*

❿ Church of Sant'Anastasia

This church was built from the late 13th century through the 15th century. Although the facade was never finished (as the builders

ran out of steam), the interior was—and still is—brilliant. Step inside to see the delightful way this region's medieval churches were painted. Note the grimacing hunchbacks holding basins of holy water on their backs (near main entrance at base of columns). And don't miss Pisanello's fresco of *St. George and the Princess* (at the tip of the arch, high above chapel to right of altar). Once colorful, it has oxidized over time to its current monochrome state. For a closer look at its wonderful detail, check out the images on the computer terminal below. Ask for the English brochure, which describes the story of the church (€2.50, March–Oct Mon–Sat 9:00–18:00, Sun 13:00–18:00; Nov–Feb closes daily at 17:00).

• *Leaving the church, make two lefts, and walk along the right side of the church to Via Sottoriva. To the right, the Sottoriva arcade was once busy with colorful wine bars and* osterie, *some of which still exist (see "Eating in Verona," later). But for now, head to the left on Via Sottoriva. In a block, you'll reach a small riverfront area with stone benches that usually have a few modern-day Romeos and Juliets gazing at each other rather than the view. Belly up to the river view.*

⓫ Ponte Pietra and a River View

The white stones of the Ponte Pietra are from the original Roman bridge that stood here. After the bridge was bombed in World War II, the Veronese fished the marble chunks out of the river to rebuild it. From here, you can see the Roman Theater, built into the hillside behind the green hedge (see page 350). Way above the theater (behind the cypress trees) is the fortress, Castello San Pietro.

Continue up the river toward the bridge. You'll pass Gelateria Ponte Pietra (at #23, no sign because of city codes), where Mirko and Stefano dish out fine gelato—try the *riso* flavor (daily 14:30–20:00, until 23:00 in summer). Walk to the high point on the bridge and find the padlocks on the left side. They are locked in place by romantic couples, who then throw the key in the river as proof of the permanence of their love. For some exercise, break away, cross the bridge, and visit the Roman Theater or head up to the Castello for an expansive city view (at the end of the bridge, go up the little road called Scalone Castello San Pietro, or climb the stairs to the left of the theater). Me? I'll just enjoy the view from here.

• *From the bridge, look back 200 yards at the tall spire...that's where you're heading.*

⓬ Duomo

Started in the 12th century, this church was built over a period of several hundred years. Before entering, note the fine Romanesque carvings on its facade. Also notice the elevated tomb (high above on the left)—a donor was buried this way at his request. Step inside, and pick up the leaflet that explains the church's highlights (€2.50, March–Oct Mon–Fri 10:00–17:30, Sat 10:00–16:00, Sun 13:30–17:30, shorter hours off-season, Nov–Feb closed Mon).

Directly ahead is Titian's *Assumption* (Mary calmly rides a cloud—direction up—to the shock and bewilderment of the crowd below). To the right of the Titian (through the last wooden door, left of high altar) are the ruins of an older church. These are the 10th-century foundations of the Church of St. Elena, turned intriguingly into a modern-day chapel featuring exposed fourth-century mosaic floors from the Roman church that originally stood here. Don't miss the adjacent baptistery, with its clean Romanesque lines, hanging 14th-century crucifix, and fine marble font. Try to identify the eight scenes depicted before referring to my answers. (Answers: Annunciation; first Christmas, with animals licking baby Jesus and giving him a barnyard welcome; announcement to shepherds of Jesus' birth; Epiphany, with the Three Kings giving their gifts to baby Jesus; Herod commanding to have firstborn sons killed; Slaughter of the Innocents; flight to Egypt; and finally, facing the entry door, John the Baptist baptizing Christ.) The peaceful Romanesque cloister is to the right as you leave the church, with mosaics from a fifth-century Christian church exposed below the walk.

Sights in Verona

▲▲**Evening *Passeggiata***—For me, the highlight of Verona is the *passeggiata* (stroll)—especially in the evening. Make a big circle from Piazza Brà through the old town on Via Mazzini (one of Europe's many "first pedestrian-only streets") to the colorful Piazza Erbe, and then back down Corso Porta Borsari to Piazza Brà. This is a small town, where people know each other, and they're all out on parade. Like peacocks, the young and nubile spread their wings. The classy shop windows are integral to the *passeggiata* as, for the ladies, shopping is a sport. Their never-finished wardrobes are considered a work in progress, and this is when they gather ideas. If you're going to complement your stroll with a sit in a café or bar, the best plan is to enjoy a *spritz* drink on Piazza Erbe (the oldest and most elegant bars are on the end farthest from Juliet's balcony).

▲**Castelvecchio**—Verona's powerful Scaligeri family built this castle (1343–1356) as both a residence and a fortress. Today, it's a museum showing off Verona's glory days. The extensive collection of Verona's finest art is well-displayed throughout the huge building. The religious statues, once brightly painted, were the city's medieval forte. The paintings were the city's Renaissance forte. There's also armor, and a chance to roam the ramparts with fine views of the city and river. Info sheets with good English descriptions are available throughout, but the audioguide (€3.60, or €5/2 people) is worthwhile (€6, Tue–Sun 8:30–19:30, Mon 13:30–19:30, see map on page 352 for location).

Next to Castelvecchio, the **Fortress Bridge** (Ponte Scaligero) is free, open to the public, and fun to stroll across. Destroyed by the Germans in World War II, it was rebuilt in the 1950s. Today it's understandably a favorite for wedding-day photos.

▲**Basilica of San Zeno Maggiore**—This church is dedicated to the patron saint of Verona, whose remains are buried in the crypt under the main altar. In addition to being a fine example of Italian Romanesque, the basilica features Mantegna's *San Zeno Triptych*, with its marvelous perspective, peaceful double-columned cloisters, and a set of 48 paneled 11th-century bronze doors nicknamed "the poor man's Bible." Pretend you're an illiterate medieval peasant and do some reading. Facing the altar, on the walls of the right-side aisle, you can see frescoes painted on top of other frescoes and graffiti dating from the 1300s. These were done by people who fled into the church in times of war or flooding and scratched prayers into the walls. Druidic-looking runes are actually decorated letters typical of the Gothic period, like those in illuminated manuscripts.

Cost and Hours: €2.50, March–Oct Mon–Sat 8:30–18:00, Sun 13:00–18:00; Nov–Feb Tue–Sat 10:00–13:00 & 13:30–16:00, Sun 13:00–17:00, closed Mon; located on Piazza San Zeno, less than a mile northwest of Castelvecchio.

Roman Theater (Teatro Romano)—Dating from the first century A.D., this ancient theater was discovered in the 19th century and restored. Admission includes the Roman Museum, located high in the building above the theater (reach it via elevator—start at the stage and walk up the middle set of stairs, then continue straight on the path through the bushes).

The museum displays a model of the theater, a small Jesuit chapel, and Roman artifacts, including mosaic floors, busts and other statuary, clay and bronze votive figures, and architectural fragments. You'll find helpful English information sheets throughout.

Cost and Hours: €4.50, Tue–Sun 8:30–19:30, Mon 13:30–19:30, last entry 45 minutes before closing, theater located across the river near Ponte Pietra, tel. 045-800-0360. From mid-June through August, the theater stages Shakespeare plays—only a little more difficult to understand in Italian than in Elizabethan English.

Giardino Giusti—If you'd enjoy a Renaissance garden with manicured box hedges and towering cypress trees, you might find this worth the walk and fee.

Cost and Hours: €6, daily April–Sept 9:00–19:00, Oct–March 9:00–17:00; cross river at Ponte Nuovo, continue up Via Carducci, and turn left on Via Giardino Giusti, or take bus #72 from Piazza Brà and get off at Via Carducci.

Sleeping in Verona

I've listed rates you'll pay in regular season—most of April through May, and September through October. Prices soar above these (about €20–30 more per night) in late June, July, and August (during opera season), early April (during the Vinitaly wine festival— see "The Wines of Verona" sidebar on page 355), and during big trade fairs or major holidays. Prices are lower from November to March. Hotel websites clearly explain their rates.

Near Piazza Erbe

$$$ Hotel Aurora, just off Piazza Erbe, has friendly family management, a terrace overlooking the piazza, and 19 fresh, air-conditioned rooms (S-€70, Sb-€110, Db-€130, Tb-€160, Qb-€200, elevator, Wi-Fi, Piazza Erbe, tel. 045-594-717, fax 045-801-0860, www.hotelaurora.biz, info@hotelaurora.biz, Rita).

Sleep Code

(€1 = about $1.25, country code: 39)
S = Single, **D** = Double/Twin, **T** = Triple, **Q** = Quad, **b** = bathroom, **s** = shower only. Hotels accept credit cards and provide breakfast unless otherwise noted. Everyone speaks English.

To help you easily sort through these listings, I've divided the rooms into three categories, based on the price for a standard double room with bath:

$$$ Higher Priced—Most rooms €130 or more.
$$ Moderately Priced—Most rooms between €100–130.
$ Lower Priced—Most rooms €100 or less.

Prices can change without notice; verify the hotel's current rates online or by email. For other updates, see www.ricksteves.com/update.

Verona Hotels & Restaurants

★ PIAZZA ERBE
↟ VIEW
P PARKING
Ⓑ BUS STOP

1 Hotel Aurora

2 Casa della Giovane

3 To L'Ospite Apartments

4 Hotels Milano & Giulietta e Romeo

5 Hotel Europa

6 Hotel/Rist. Torcolo

7 Hotel Arena

8 To Villa Francescatti

9 Osteria al Duca

10 Bottega del Vin

11 Osteria le Vecete & Pizzeria Du de Cope

12 Osteria Sottoriva

13 Enoteca Can Grande

14 Trattoria al Pompiere

15 Rist. Olivo, Trattoria de Giovanni Rana & Brek Cafeteria

16 PAM Supermarket

17 Albertini & Gastronomia

18 Internet Cafés (2)

19 Welcome Travel

$ Casa della Giovane, run by an association that houses poor women, also rents rooms and dorm beds to female tourists. Buried deep in the old town and up several flights of stairs, the place offers 50 cheap beds in a clean, institutional, and peaceful setting (women only, €22/bed in 11-bed dorm, Sb-€35, Db-€60, Tb-€75, no breakfast, reception open 7:00-23:00, Via Pigna 7, tel. 045-596-880, fax 045-088-5449, www.casadellagiovane.com, info@casa dellagiovane.com).

$ L'Ospite, a 10-minute walk from Piazza Erbe, has six cozy, immaculate, fully equipped apartments and lots of stairs. The rooms, warmly managed by Federica De Rossi, sleep from two to four, include air-conditioning, and—for those who stay longer—free laundry service (Db-€95, Tb/Qb-about €40–55/person, discounts for cash and longer stays, no daily cleaning; cross Ponte Navi bridge and continue straight, hotel is to the left of the San Paolo church at Via XX Settembre 3; tel. 045-803-6994, mobile 329-426-2524, www.lospite.com, info@lospite.com).

Near Piazza Brà

You'll find several options in the quiet streets just off Piazza Brà, within 200 yards of the bus stop. From the square, yellow signs point you to the hotels. The first three are big, business-class places with the service and formality you'd expect. The Torcolo is more homey and friendly.

$$ Hotel Milano, just behind the Arena, is an art hotel with 52 rooms. The lobby and fancier rooms are tricked out in black and chrome (Sb-€75–100, basic Db-€120, fancy Db-€143, air-con, elevator, Wi-Fi, garage-€20/day, Vicolo Tre Marchetti 11, tel. 045-591-692, fax 045-801-1299, www.hotelmilano-vr.it, info @hotelmilano-vr.it).

$$ Hotel Giulietta e Romeo is on a quiet side street just 50 yards behind the Roman Arena. Its 40 well-designed rooms (nine with balconies) are decorated in dark colors (Sb-€95–110, Db-€120, bigger Db-€140, prices vary with season, non-smoking rooms available, air-con, elevator, Wi-Fi, free loaner bikes, laundry, garage-€19/day, Vicolo Tre Marchetti 3, tel. 045-800-3554, fax 045-801-0862, www.giuliettaeromeo.com, info @giuliettaeromeo.com).

$$ Hotel Europa offers sleek, modern comfort in springtime colors. Most of its 46 rooms are non-smoking, and a few rooms have little balconies overlooking the *piazzetta* below (Db-€120–180, 10 percent discount with this book, air-con, elevator, Wi-Fi, Via Roma 8, tel. 045-594-744, fax 045-800-1852, www .veronahoteleuropa.com, hoteleuropavr@tiscali.it).

$ Hotel Torcolo offers 19 comfortable, lovingly maintained, non-smoking rooms with Grandma's furnishings (Sb-€65,

Db-around €100, €8–14 for breakfast—optional except during opera season, air-con, fridge in room, elevator, garage-€20/day; from Piazza Brà promenade, head down the alley to the right of #16 and walk to Vicolo Listone 3; tel. 045-800-7512, fax 045-800-4058, www.hoteltorcolo.it, hoteltorcolo@virgilio.it, well-run by Silvia, Diana, and helpful Caterina).

Near Castelvecchio
$ Hotel Arena, while borderline-dreary, is a good value for those on a tight budget. Located in a peaceful courtyard off a busy street just west of Castelvecchio, it offers 17 very basic, institutional, quiet rooms (S-€45, Sb-€60, D-€75, Db-€85, no air-con, Wi-Fi, 200 yards from Piazza Brà at Stradone Porta Palio #2, tel. & fax 045-803-2440, www.albergoarena.it, info@albergoarena.it, Beatrice).

Hostel
$ Villa Francescatti is a good hostel (€18 beds with breakfast, 6- or 8-bed rooms, one dorm with 35 beds, some family rooms with private bathrooms, €8 dinners, launderette, rooms closed from 9:00 to 17:00 but reception open all day, 24:00 curfew; bus #73 from train station on weekdays or #91 at night and Sun to Piazza Isolo stop, walk over the river beyond Ponte Nuovo at Salita Fontana del Ferro 15; tel. 045-590-360, fax 045-800-9127).

Eating in Verona

Osteria al Duca is a fun, family-run place with a lively atmosphere and good traditional dishes. Locals line up for its affordable, two-course, €15 fixed-price meal. I much prefer their ground floor (*piano terra*—worth requesting). Reservations are advised (closed Sun, half-block from Scaligeri family tombs at Via Arche Scaligere 2, tel. 045-594-474, Alessandro or Daniele).

Ristorante Torcolo is a warm family restaurant, with mom (Paola) running the kitchen and father and son (Roberto and Luca) serving. It's dressy but without pretense, and the service is professional yet fun-loving. There's a happy energy, stoked by carts of boiled meat and desserts rolling temptations through the dining room. They serve all the classic dishes, with an accessible menu and an extensive wine list (€9 pastas, €18 *secondi*, €3 cover, closed Mon, just behind the Piazza Brà scene on a quiet street, Via Carlo Cattaneo 11, tel. 045-803-3730).

Bottega del Vin is pricey, venerable, and proud to have a sister establishment in New York City. Under a high ceiling and walls of wine bottles, brisk black-vested waiters match traditional dishes (polenta, duck, game) with glasses of fine wine. Choose from 100 open bottles—glasses range from €1 to €15. The waitstaff, ambi-

The Wines of Verona

Wine connoisseurs love the high-quality wines of this area. The hills to the east are covered with grapes to make Soave; to the north is Valpolicella country; and Bardolino comes from vineyards to the west.

Valpolicella grapes, which are used to make the fruity, red Valpolicella table wine (found everywhere), are also used to make the full-bodied red Amarone and the sweet dessert wine, Recioto. To produce Amarone, grapes are partially dried *(passito)* before fermentation, then aged for a minimum of four years in oak casks, resulting in a rich, velvety, full-bodied red. Recioto, which in local dialect means "ears," uses only the grapes from the top of the cluster (so they sort of look like the "ears" of the cluster's "head"). Because these grapes get the most sun, they mature the fastest and have the highest concentration of sugar. The grapes are dried for months until all moisture has gone out before pressing, and aged for one to three years.

Bardolino, from the vineyards near Lake Garda, is a light, fruity wine, like a French Beaujolais. It's a perfect picnic wine.

Soave, which might be Italy's best-known white wine, goes well with seafood and risotto dishes. While Soave can vary widely in quality, the best are called "Soave Classico" and come from the heart of the region, near the Soave Castle. Soave is sometimes aged in oak casks, giving it a mellow, rounded flavor.

Sample these and many others at the numerous *enoteche* (wine-tasting bars) or at any restaurant around town. In early April, Verona hosts Vinitaly, the most important international convention of domestic and international wines. Vintners vie for prestigious awards for the past year's vintage. Tourists are welcome to attend at the end of the week, and are shuttled to the convention hall from Piazza Brà. Hotels book up months in advance. Check with the TI and www.vinitaly.com for details.

If you're visiting the area in the fall, consider a day trip to nearby Monteforte d'Alpone, east of Verona. The town hosts a fun, raucous wine festival in September—ask at the TI for more information on this and other regional wine festivals.

ence, and food have deep roots in local culture. I like their front room best (€12 pastas, €21 *secondi,* good daily specials, Wed–Mon 12:00–15:00 & 19:00–24:00, opens at 18:00 for appetizers, closed Tue; take third left off Via Mazzini as you're coming from Piazza Erbe, Via Scudo di Francia 3; tel. 045-800-4535, reservations smart for dinner).

Osteria le Vecete, consisting of just one room under open beams and walls of wine, has an enjoyable, intimate pub ambience. Slide up to the bar for wine and *tartine* (elaborate little open-faced sandwiches), or sit down and order a meal. Choose from daily specials of homemade pastas and Veronese dishes—as well as salads or a selection of *tartine*. The blackboard lists plenty of wines by the glass (€9 pastas, €18 *secondi*, daily 12:30–15:30 & 18:30–23:00, drinks and snacks served between mealtimes and until late; buried in an alley between Via Mazzini and Corso Sant'Anastasia; from Piazza Brà, go down Via Mazzini and turn left onto Via Quattro Spade, then right onto Via Pelliciai to #32A; tel. 045-594-748, Karen).

Pizzeria Du de Cope is a high-energy place that buzzes with smartly attired young waiters and locals who consider the pizza here to be the best in town (big €9 salads, €9 pizzas, Wed–Mon 12:00–14:00 & 19:00–23:00, flamboyant desserts, family-friendly, no reservations, near Osteria le Vecete at Galleria Pelliciai 10, tel. 045-595-562).

VERONA

Osterie *on Via Sottoriva*: Historically, Verona's river served as the motorway. Along the river, a fine old covered arcade (the portico of Via Sottoriva) was the setting for places where business deals could be made over a glass of wine. Several of these survive as rustic, characteristic eateries serving finger food. Browse around and consider the wonderful **Osteria Sottoriva,** with simple soups and pastas, and both indoor and outdoor seating (open from 18:30, behind the Church of Sant'Anastasia in the covered arcade, Via Sottoriva 9).

Enoteca Can Grande enjoys turning people on to great, well-matched food and wine. Their cold plates, designed for wine appreciation, make a fine main dish. I'd trust Giuliano and Corrina to come up with a creative meal that fits your budget. For €35 per person plus wine, they'll blow you away with a *degustatione menu* extravaganza that just keeps on coming. It's a festival of *antipasti* treats, followed by an imaginative pasta. Complementing the food with just the right wines can leave you with a meal you'll never forget. This is a rich and unique gourmet experience that costs no more than dinner at your basic, dressy restaurant (Wed–Mon 12:00–15:30 & 18:00–24:00, closed Tue; a block off Piazza Brà at Via Dietro Liston 19D—if the equestrian statue jogged slightly right, he'd head straight here; tel. 045-595-022).

Trattoria al Pompiere, which has a commitment to regional traditions, is a favorite of foodies and has earned its huge local following. Amid the bustle (contained by walls plastered with photos of local big shots), Stefano and his gang serve gourmet meats and cheeses as *antipasti*, ideal for a mixed plate to complement the huge selection of fine wines. There's not a bad table in this grand, old-style dining room. Reservations are wise (€12 pastas, €15 *secondi*, lunch from 12:30, dinner from 19:30, closed Sun, ladies' menus without prices, Vicolo Regina d'Ungheria 5, tel. 045-803-0537).

Eating on Piazza Brà: A cancan of mainly nondescript restaurants line the *passeggiata* action along Piazza Brà. You may be sacrificing service, value, and quality for the chance to enjoy a view of the floodlit Roman Arena and Verona on parade while you dine. Except for Brek Cafeteria, restaurants on the piazza tend to charge a cover and service fee, making even pizza here a pricey stop. **Ristorante Olivo** and the more upmarket **Trattoria de Giovanni Rana** are fixtures. For the same view at self-service prices, consider the well-run and modern **Brek Cafeteria** (€5 pastas, €6 *secondi*, cheap salad plates, daily, breakfast and sandwiches from 9:30, full menu 11:30–15:00 & 18:30–22:00, indoor/outdoor seating, facing the equestrian statue at Piazza Brà 20, tel. 045-800-4561).

Eating Cheap near Piazza Brà: **PAM supermarket** is just outside the historic gate on Piazza Brà (daily 8:00–21:00, exit Piazza Brà through the gate and take the first right). The *döner kebab* place—just behind Hotel Europa and a few steps off Via Roma—is cheap, fast, and not Italian (great €4 meals).

Eating Cheap near Piazza Erbe: You'll find two family-run *alimentari*—**Albertini** and **Gastronomia** (both Mon–Sat 8:00–20:00, Sun 9:00–13:30)—on Corso Sant'Anastasia, between the end of Vicolo Cavoletto and Church of Sant'Anastasia.

A list of "official" picnicking spots can be picked up at the TI—freelance picnicking in Verona is strongly discouraged. One good spot is along the river by Ponte Pietra.

Verona Connections

From Verona by Train to: Venice (2/hour, 1.5 hours), **Padua** (2/hour, 1 hour), **Vicenza** (2/hour, 40 minutes), **Florence** (about hourly, often with transfer in Bologna, 3 hours, note that all Rome-bound trains stop in Florence—listed as *Firenze* on train schedules), **Bologna** (hourly, 2 hours), **Milan** (2/hour, 1.5–2 hours), **Rome** (hourly, 4–5 hours, often with transfer in Bologna), **Bolzano** (2/hour, 1.5–2 hours, note that Brennero-bound trains stop in Bolzano).

VERONA

VENETIAN HISTORY

In the Middle Ages, the Venetians became Europe's clever middlemen for East–West trade, creating a great trading empire ruled by a series of doges. By smuggling in the bones of St. Mark, Venice gained religious importance as well. But after the discovery of America and new trading routes to the Orient, Venetian power ebbed. Yet as Venice fell, her appetite for decadence grew. Throughout the 17th and 18th centuries, Venice partied on the wealth accumulated in earlier centuries as a trading power.

That's Venetian history in a seashell. Want more? Read on.

500: Rome Falls, Venice Rises

In A.D. 476, the last Roman emperor abdicated, the infrastructure was crumbling, and Italy was crawling with barbarians. Hoping these Visigoths, Huns, and Lombards didn't like water, mainland farmers took refuge on the marshy, uninhabited islands of the lagoon.

The refugees squatted on this wet and miserable land. They sank pilings in the mud to build on, channeled water into canals, and built bridges to lace together the motley collection of about 120 natural islands that would eventually become Venice.

500–1000: Medieval Growth

These former farmers, the first Venetians, now harvested salt and fish for their livelihood, and traded it on the mainland. Though Venice's islands were desolate, the area—known to the Romans as the "Seven Seas"—was strategically important. In 540 A.D., the

Byzantine Emperor Justinian reconquered Italy from the barbarians and briefly reunited the Roman Empire. He established a capital at Ravenna, bringing the Venetian islands under Byzantine influence.

In 726, Venice elected a local ruler, a "doge"—the first of many who would rule for the next 1,100 years. (Though "doge" is linguistically related to our word "duke," Venetian rulers were more like constitutional monarchs, elected by their fellow nobles and expected to govern according to the rule of law.) The first doge established his capital in the town of Rialto, near today's Rialto Bridge.

Under Byzantine protection, Venetians became prosperous seagoing merchants. Acting as middlemen, they bought goods from the sophisticated Byzantine and Islamic lands to the East and sold them to consumers in the West.

Venice's merchant economy boomed while the rest of Europe languished under land-based feudalism. Charlemagne, the Holy Roman Emperor who'd conquered much of Italy (c. 800), eyed the region hungrily. But Venetians, wanting to keep their independence, deposed Charlemagne's bishop and chose one who was loyal to (distant) Byzantium.

To legitimize their new bishop, the Venetians managed to smuggle the holy relics of St. Mark from Egypt in 828, thus becoming a religious power overnight. To seal the city's oriental orientation, Venetian leaders had the grand St. Mark's Basilica built in a distinctly Eastern style. By the 10th century, tiny Venice had effectively established itself as an independent, self-ruling country.

Representative Sights
- Gondolas and the network of canals
- Old crypt under San Zaccaria Church
- San Moisè Church
- Church on Torcello Island

1000–1500: A Seafaring Power

Well-located between northern Europe and the eastern Mediterranean, Venetian sea traders established trading outposts in Byzantine and Muslim territories to the east. At home, a stable, constitutional government ran an efficient, state-operated multinational corporation. The

Venice in the 15th Century

LONDON
BRUGES
PARIS
VIENNA
GENOA
VENICE
RAVENNA
PISA
FLORENCE   ROME
CON-
STAN-
TIN-
OPLE
GIBRALTAR
LEPANTO
DCH
CRETE
TO HOLY LAND
& ALEXANDRIA

BLACK AREA SHOWS VENETIAN
EMPIRE AT ITS PEAK –
THE 15TH CENTURY

shallow lagoon was easily defended against attack. Grand buildings reflected Venice's wealth.

Venetian merchants ran a profitable trading triangle: timber from Venice's mainland to Egypt for gold to Byzantium for luxury goods to Venice. Its merchant fleet was the biggest in the Mediterranean, backed by powerful warships.

By 1104, Venice was running Europe's first industrial complex, the Arsenale. With more than 1,000 workers using an early form of assembly-line production, the Arsenale could produce about one warship a day. This put the "fear of Venice" into visiting rulers. When France's King Henry III dropped by the Arsenale, Venice entertained him with a shipbuilding spectacle: from ribs to finished product in four hours.

When Europe launched its Crusades to the Holy Land (1095–1272), Venice transported soldiers and defended Byzantine and Crusader ports in return for free-trade privileges. This made the eastern Mediterranean a virtual free-trade zone for a very aggressive Venetian trading community to exploit.

Wealthy Venetian nobles built lavish palaces. With a natural lagoon defense, these were not fortified castles like the rest of Europe but luxurious palazzos, complete with loading docks, warehouses, and chandeliered ballrooms. The streets were paved. And by the 12th century, the government provided oil and required that streets be lit—a first in Europe.

Besides sea trade, Venice established strong local industries. Having mastered the art of making glass, Venice was on the cutting edge of the new science of grinding lenses for eyeglasses and telescopes. Understanding medicine as a chemical rather than an herbal pursuit, the city developed Europe's first real pharmaceutical industry. They made Europe's first affordable paper, from rags rather than from sheepskin (parchment). As the city offered the world's first copyright protection, its printing and bookmaking industry boomed, and Venice became a center for new (secular, scientific, democratic) ideas. With mountains of capital and a sophisticated trade system of insurance, joint ventures, and money drafts, Venice's merchants eventually became bankers, loaning money at interest—making them early capitalists.

They were also on the forefront of a budding democracy not seen in feudal Europe. Constitutional limits were placed on the doges, and the Republic was ruled by a voting body of wealthy families.

By the 13th century, Venice was fast becoming a Mediterranean superpower. During the Fourth Crusade (1204), Venetian troops joined other Crusaders in attacking and looting Christian Constantinople. The haul of booty enriched the city, and Venice could now stand up to its former Byzantine protectors. When Venetian ships routed the fleet of their Genoan rivals at Chioggia (on the south end of the lagoon, 1381), Venice became undisputed master of the eastern Mediterranean. Next, they launched attacks on the mainland, conquering much of northern Italy. By 1420, Venice was at the height of its power, with mainland possessions and a powerful overseas trading empire to the east.

VENETIAN HISTORY

Representative Sights
- Doge's Palace
- St. Mark's Basilica
- Frari Church
- Buildings decorated in ornate Venetian Gothic style
- Doge paraphernalia and city history at Correr Museum
- Glass and lace industries
- Arsenale shipbuilding complex

Noteworthy Residents
Enrico Dandolo (r. 1192–1205): Doge during the Fourth Crusade, when Venetian crusaders looted Constantinople, helping to enrich Venice.

Church Architecture

History comes to life when you visit a centuries-old church. Even if you wouldn't know your apse from a hole in the ground, learning a few simple terms will enrich your experience. Note that not every church has every feature, and that a "cathedral" isn't a type of church architecture, but rather a designation for a church that's a governing center for a local bishop.

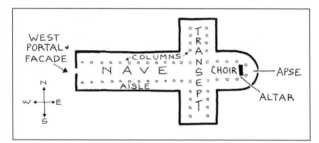

Aisles: The long, generally low-ceilinged arcades that flank the nave.

Altar: The raised area with a ceremonial table (often adorned with candles or a crucifix), where the priest prepares and serves the bread and wine for Communion.

Apse: The space beyond the altar, generally bordered with small chapels.

Choir: A cozy area, often screened off, located within the church nave and near the high altar, where services are sung in a more intimate setting.

Cloister: A square-shaped series of hallways surrounding an open-air courtyard, traditionally where monks and nuns got fresh air.

Facade: The outer wall of the church's main (west) entrance, viewable from outside and generally highly decorated.

Groin Vault: An arched ceiling formed where two equal barrel vaults meet at right angles. Also: a medieval jock strap.

Narthex: The area (portico or foyer) between the main entry and the nave.

Nave: The long, central section of the church (running west to east, from the entrance to the altar) where the congregation stood through the service.

Transept: The north-south part of the church, which crosses (perpendicularly) the east-west nave. In a traditional Latin cross-shaped floor plan, the transept forms the "arms" of the cross.

West Portal: The main entry to the church (on the west end, opposite the main altar).

Marco Polo (1254–1324): Traveler to faraway China whose journal, *The Book of Marvels,* was dismissed by many as fiction.

Paolo Veneziano (1310–1358): Painter who mastered the Byzantine gold-icon style, then added touches of Western realism.

Francesco Foscari (1373–1457): Doge at Venice's peak of power, whose ill-advised wars against Milan and the Ottoman Turks started the Republic's slow fade.

Jacopo Bellini (c. 1400–1470): Father of painting family. His training in Renaissance Florence brought 3-D realism to Venice.

Gentile Bellini (c. 1429–1507): Elder son of painting family, known for straightforward, historical scenes of Venice.

1500–1600:
Renaissance and Seeds of Decline

In 1500, Venice was a commercial powerhouse—among the six biggest cities in Europe. Of its estimated 180,000 citizens, nearly

1,000 were of Rockefeller-esque wealth and power. Europe's richest city-state poured money into the arts. Titian, Tintoretto, Sansovino, the Bellini family, and Palladio called Venice home. St. Mark's Square became the gathering place for merchants and nobles from Venice's vast trading empire. Across Europe, Venice had a reputation as a luxury-loving, exotic, cosmopolitan playground.

But Venice's power was declining. The seeds had been sown in the 15th century. In 1492, Columbus sailed the ocean blue, and established trade in a World that was New. In 1498, Vasco da Gama circled Africa's Cape of Good Hope, finding a new sea-trade route to eastern markets. Venice's sea-trade monopoly was broken.

On the Italian mainland, Venice became locked in draining wars against its economic rivals Milan, Pisa, and Amalfi. Meanwhile, Ottomans were expanding in the East, encroaching on Venice's former monopoly on trade. Venetians and Ottomans became wary trade partners, sometimes dealing peacefully but sometimes battling over strategic ports. In 1453, the Ottomans took Constantinople, and Venice suddenly lost one of its best customers. Venice (and its European allies) scored a temporary victory over the Ottomans at the Battle of Lepanto (1571), but Venice's navy suffered major damage, and the city lost more trading rights. Spain, England, and Holland, with their oceangoing vessels, emerged as superior traders in a more global economy.

Representative Sights
- St. Mark's Square facades and other work by Sansovino
- Palladio's classical facades (San Giorgio Maggiore and Il Redentore churches)
- Masterpiece paintings by Titian, Giovanni Bellini, Giorgione, and Tintoretto (Accademia, Frari Church, Doge's Palace, San Zaccaria Church, Correr Museum, Scuola San Rocco)
- Jewish Ghetto and Jewish Museum

Noteworthy Residents
Giovanni Bellini (c. 1430–1516): The most famous son in the painting family, whose glowing, colorful, 3-D Madonna-and-Childs started the Venetian Renaissance. Teacher of Titian and Giorgione.

Vittore Carpaccio (c. 1460–1525): Painter of realistic, secular scenes and the impressive Scuola Dolmata di San Giorgio.

Giorgione (c. 1477–1511): Innovative painter whose moody realism influenced Bellini (his teacher) and Titian (his friend and fellow painter).

Jacopo Sansovino (1486–1570): Renaissance architect who redid the face of Venice (especially St. Mark's Square), introducing sober, classical columns and arches to a city previously full of ornate Gothic.

Titian (Tiziano Vecellio, 1488–1576): Premier Venetian Renaissance painter. Master of many styles, from teenage Madonnas to sober state portraits to exuberant mythological scenes to centerfold nudes.

Andrea Palladio (1508–1580): Influential architect whose classical style was much imitated around the world, resulting in villas, government buildings, and banks that look like Greek temples.

Tintoretto (Jacopo Robusti, c. 1518–1594): Painter of dramatic religious scenes, using strong 3-D, diagonal compositions, twisting poses, sharp contrast of light and shadow, and bright, "black velvet" colors (late Renaissance/Mannerist style).

Paolo Veronese (1528–1588): Painter of big, colorful canvases, capturing the exuberance and luxury of Renaissance Venice.

1600–1800: Elegant Decline
New trade routes, new European powers, and belligerent Ottomans drained Venice's economy and shrank its trading empire. At home, however, Venice's reputation for luxury—and decadence—still made it a popular tourist destination for Europe's gentry. In some ways, this is the period that most defines Venice: the city of Baroque monuments, masked balls at Carnevale, velvet-dressed nobles at opera debuts, and the roguish debauchery of Casanova.

Venice dwindled economically and politically. In 1669, its last major outpost, Crete, fell to the Ottomans. Several devastating plagues gutted the population at home. The once-enlightened government gained a nasty reputation for corruption and for locking away dissidents in the notorious prisons in the Doges' Palace. In 1797, Napoleon Bonaparte rolled into Venice and toppled the final doge. A thousand-year era of independent rule was over.

Representative Sights

- Ca' Rezzonico (Museum of 18th-Century Venice)
- La Salute Church
- Masks of the Carnevale tradition
- Old cafés (e.g., the Florian and the Quadri, both on St. Mark's Square)
- La Fenice Opera House
- Baroque interiors in many churches
- Canova sculptures (Correr Museum, Frari Church)
- G. B. Tiepolo paintings (Accademia, Doge's Palace, Ca' Rezzonico)
- Paintings of Canaletto, Guardi, and G. D. Tiepolo (Ca' Rezzonico)

Noteworthy Residents

Claudio Monteverdi (1567–1643): The composer and *maestro di capella* at St. Mark's Basilica who wrote in a budding new medium—opera.

Baldassare Longhena (1598–1682): Architect of the Baroque La Salute Church.

Antonio Vivaldi (1678–1741): Composer of *The Four Seasons* ("Dah dunt-dunt-duh dutta dah-ah-ah").

G. B. Tiepolo (Giovanni Battista, 1696–1770): Painter of mythological subjects in colorful Rococo ceilings.

Antonio Canaletto (1697–1768): Painter of photo-realist Venice views.

Carlo Goldoni (1707–1793): Comic playwright who brought refinement to commedia dell'arte buffoonery.

Francesco Guardi (1712–1793): Painter of proto-Impressionist Venice views.

Giacomo Casanova (1725–1798): Gambler, womanizer, and adventurer whose exaggerated memoirs inspired Romantics.

G. D. Tiepolo (Giovanni Domenico, 1727–1804): Painter son of the famous G. B. Tiepolo.

Lorenzo Da Ponte (1749–1838): Mozart's librettist, who popularized Venice's sophisticated and decadent high society.

Antonio Canova (1757–1822): Neoclassical sculptor whose beautiful polished-white statues were especially popular in Napoleon's France.

1800 to the Present: Modern Venice

After Napoleon was defeated at Waterloo, the European allies placed Venice under Austrian rule. Sophisticated Venetians chafed against their bourgeois masters. However, Venice was still a key stop on any traveler's Grand Tour, as Europe's young aristocrats visited the city to complete their education. Venice and Italy became a political backwater as Austrian, French, and British culture dominated.

In 1866, Austria was defeated by Prussia, and rebellious Venetians seized the moment to join Italy's Risorgimento movement, annexing itself to the newly unified, democratic nation of Italy.

Venice joined the Industrial Revolution only reluctantly. The island city became connected to the mainland with a two-mile railroad causeway (1846), which was later paralleled by a highway for cars (1932). On the mainland, unbridled industrialization produced pollution (mainly sulfuric acid) that threatened Venice's stone monuments. In 1966, Venice suffered a disastrous flood, which prompted many plans and projects to control future flooding—some have been enacted, while others are still on the drawing board.

Inside Venice proper, however, there has been little new building for centuries. Today, Venice remains a museum piece for foreigners—one increasingly threatened by mainland pollution, global warming, floods, and hordes of tourists. Venice's leaders face the dilemma of having to pay for essential upkeep by allowing billboard advertising. Local and UNESCO regulations try to preserve Venice as a cultural landmark. When  Venice's venerable Fenice Opera House burned down in 1996, it was rebuilt gloriously in 2003 in the old style. The Punta della Dogana, a museum devoted to contemporary art, opened in 2009, continuing Venice's legacy as a world arts capital. While keeping up with what's new, Venice remains a historic wonderland. Venice is timeless—a place where visitors can easily blink away elements of the modern world and find themselves transported in time.

Representative Sights
- Correr Museum's Risorgimento wing
- Statue of Daniele Manin (between St. Mark's Square and Rialto Bridge)
- Motorized *vaporetti* and taxis
- Train station (1954)
- Peggy Guggenheim Collection
- Biennale International Art Exhibition
- Pollution from the mainland city of Mestre
- Calatrava Bridge (2008)
- Burger King

Noteworthy Residents
Daniele Manin (1804–1857): Rebel who led 1848 Venetian revolt against the city's Austrian rulers, eventually allowing Venice to join a united, democratic, modern Italy.

Peggy Guggenheim (1898–1979): American-born art collector, gallery owner, and friend of modern art and artists.

VENETIAN HISTORY

APPENDIX

Contents

Tourist Information

The Italian national tourist offices **in the US** are a wealth of information. Before your trip, scan their website (www.italiantourism .com) or contact the nearest branch to briefly describe your trip and request information. They'll mail you a general interest brochure, and you can download many other brochures free of charge at their website. If you have a specific problem, they're a good source of sympathy.

In New York: tel. 212/245-5618, brochure hotline tel. 212/245-4822, fax 212/586-9249, newyork@enit.it; 630 Fifth Ave. #1565, New York, NY 10111

In Illinois: tel. 312/644-0996, brochure hotline tel. 312/644-0990, fax 312/644-3019, chicago@enit.it; 500 N. Michigan Ave. #506, Chicago, IL 60611

In California: tel. 310/820-1898, brochure hotline tel. 310/820-0098, fax 310/820-6357, losangeles@enit.it; 12400 Wilshire Blvd. #550, Los Angeles, CA 90025

In Venice, your best first stop is generally the tourist information office (abbreviated **TI** in this book). There are several in Venice (listed on page 23). Useful websites are www.turismo venezia.it (Tourist Board of Venice), www.hellovenezia.com (vaporetto and event schedules), www.museicivicivenezia.it (civic museums in Venice), www.venicexplorer.net (interactive maps), www.veniceforvisitors.com, www.meetingvenice.it, and www.aguestinvenice.com.

Websites on Italy: In addition to the Italian Tourist Board site listed on the previous page, you could check www.musei online.it (museums in Italy) and www.trenitalia.com (train info and schedules).

Communicating

Hurdling the Language Barrier

Many Italians—especially those in the tourist trade and in big cities such as Venice—speak English. Still, you'll get better treatment if you learn and use Italian pleasantries. In smaller, non-touristy towns, Italian is the norm. For a list of survival phrases, see page 403.

Note that Italian is pronounced much like English, with a few exceptions, such as: c followed by e or i is pronounced ch (to ask, *"Per centro?"*—To the center?—you say, pehr CHEHN-troh). In Italian, ch is pronounced like the hard c in Chianti (*chiesa*—church—is pronounced kee-AY-zah). Give it your best shot. Italians appreciate your efforts.

Telephones

Smart travelers use the telephone to reserve or reconfirm rooms, get tourist information, reserve restaurants, confirm tour times, or phone home. Generally the easiest, cheapest way to call home is to use an international phone card purchased in Italy. This section covers dialing instructions, phone cards, and types of phones (for more in-depth information, see www.ricksteves.com/phoning).

How to Dial

Calling from the US to Italy, or vice versa, is simple—once you break the code. The European calling chart later in this chapter will walk you through it.

Dialing Domestically Within Italy

Italy has a direct-dial phone system (no area codes). To call anywhere within Italy, just dial the number. For example, the number of one of my recommended Venice hotels is 041-520-5764. That's the number you dial whether you're calling it from Venice's train station or from Rome.

Land lines start with 0; mobile lines start with 3; toll-free lines start with 80; and expensive toll lines begin with 8 and then any number other than 0. Keep in mind that Italian phone numbers vary in length; a hotel can have, say, an eight-digit phone number and a nine-digit fax number.

Dialing Internationally to or from Italy

If you want to make an international call, follow these steps:

1. Dial the international access code (00 if you're calling from Europe, 011 from the US or Canada).

2. Dial the country code of the country you're calling (39 for Italy, or 1 for the US or Canada).

3. Dial the local number. Note that in most European countries, you have to drop the zero at the beginning of the local number—but in Italy, you dial it. (The European calling chart lists specifics per country.)

Calling from the US to Italy: To call the Venice hotel from the US, dial 011 (the US international access code), 39 (Italy's country code), then 041-520-5764.

Calling from any European country to the US: To call my office in Edmonds, Washington, from anywhere in Europe, I dial 00 (Europe's international access code), 1 (the US country code), 425 (Edmonds' area code), and 771-8303.

Note: You might see a + in front of a European number. When dialing the number, replace the + with the international access code of the country you're calling from (00 from Europe, 011 from the US or Canada).

Public Phones and Hotel-Room Phones

To make calls from public phones, you'll need a prepaid phone card. There are two different kinds of phone cards: international and insertable. (Both types of phone card work only in Italy. If you have a live card at the end of your trip, give it to another traveler to use up.) Coin-op phones are virtually extinct.

Insertable Phone Cards: This type of card can only be used at a pay phone. These Telecom cards, considered "official" since they're sold by Italy's phone company, give you the best deal for calls within Italy and are reasonable for international calls. You can buy Telecom cards in denominations of €5 or €10 at *tabacchi* (tobacco) shops, post offices, and machines near phone booths (many phone booths have signs indicating where the nearest phone-card sales outlet is located).

Rip off the perforated corner to "activate" the card, and then physically insert it into a slot in the pay phone. It displays how much money you have remaining on the card. Then just dial away.

European Calling Chart

Just smile and dial, using this key:
AC = Area Code, LN = Local Number.

European Country	Calling long distance within ...	Calling from the US or Canada to ...	Calling from a European country to ...
Austria	AC + LN	011 + 43 + AC (without the initial zero) + LN	00 + 43 + AC (without the initial zero) + LN
Belgium	LN	011 + 32 + LN (without initial zero)	00 + 32 + LN (without initial zero)
Bosnia-Herzegovina	AC + LN	011 + 387 + AC (without initial zero) + LN	00 + 387 + AC (without initial zero) + LN
Britain	AC + LN	011 + 44 + AC (without initial zero) + LN	00 + 44 + AC (without initial zero) + LN
Croatia	AC + LN	011 + 385 + AC (without initial zero) + LN	00 + 385 + AC (without initial zero) + LN
Czech Republic	LN	011 + 420 + LN	00 + 420 + LN
Denmark	LN	011 + 45 + LN	00 + 45 + LN
Estonia	LN	011 + 372 + LN	00 + 372 + LN
Finland	AC + LN	011 + 358 + AC (without initial zero) + LN	999 (or other 900 number) + 358 + AC (without initial zero) + LN
France	LN	011 + 33 + LN (without initial zero)	00 + 33 + LN (without initial zero)
Germany	AC + LN	011 + 49 + AC (without initial zero) + LN	00 + 49 + AC (without initial zero) + LN
Gibraltar	LN	011 + 350 + LN	00 + 350 + LN
Greece	LN	011 + 30 + LN	00 + 30 + LN
Hungary	06 + AC + LN	011 + 36 + AC + LN	00 + 36 + AC + LN
Ireland	AC + LN	011 + 353 + AC (without initial zero) + LN	00 + 353 + AC (without initial zero) + LN

European Country	Calling long distance within ...	Calling from the US or Canada to ...	Calling from a European country to ...
Italy	LN	011 + 39 + LN	00 + 39 + LN
Montenegro	AC + LN	011 + 382 + AC (without initial zero) + LN	00 + 382 + AC (without initial zero) + LN
Morocco	LN	011 + 212 + LN (without initial zero)	00 + 212 + LN (without initial zero)
Netherlands	AC + LN	011 + 31 + AC (without initial zero) + LN	00 + 31 + AC (without initial zero) + LN
Norway	LN	011 + 47 + LN	00 + 47 + LN
Poland	LN	011 + 48 + LN (without initial zero)	00 + 48 + LN (without initial zero)
Portugal	LN	011 + 351 + LN	00 + 351 + LN
Slovakia	AC + LN	011 + 421 + AC (without initial zero) + LN	00 + 421 + AC (without initial zero) + LN
Slovenia	AC + LN	011 + 386 + AC (without initial zero) + LN	00 + 386 + AC (without initial zero) + LN
Spain	LN	011 + 34 + LN	00 + 34 + LN
Sweden	AC + LN	011 + 46 + AC (without initial zero) + LN	00 + 46 + AC (without initial zero) + LN
Switzerland	LN	011 + 41 + LN (without initial zero)	00 + 41 + LN (without initial zero)
Turkey	AC (if there's no initial zero, add one) + LN	011 + 90 + AC (without initial zero) + LN	00 + 90 + AC (without initial zero) + LN

- The instructions above apply whether you're calling a land line or mobile phone.
- The international access codes (the first numbers you dial when making an international call) are 011 if you're calling from the US or Canada, or 00 if you're calling from virtually anywhere in Europe (except Finland, where it's 999 or another 900 number, depending on the phone service you're using).
- To call the US or Canada from Europe, dial 00, then 1 (the country code for the US and Canada), then the area code and number. In short, 00 + 1 + AC + LN = Hi, Mom!

The price of the call is automatically deducted while you talk.

International Phone Cards: These are the cheapest way to make international calls from Europe—with the best cards, it costs literally pennies a minute. They can also be used to make local calls, and work from any type of phone, including your hotel-room phone. To use the card, you'll dial a toll-free access number, then type in your scratch-to-reveal PIN number. If you're calling from a hotel, be sure to dial the *freephone* number (starts with "80") provided on your card rather than the "local access" number (which would incur a charge).

You can buy the cards at small newsstand kiosks, *tabacchi* shops, Internet cafés, hostels, and hole-in-the-wall long-distance phone shops. Because there are so many brand names, simply ask for an international phone card (*carta telefonica prepagata internazionale,* KAR-tah teh-leh-FOHN-ee-kah pray-pah-GAH-tah in-ter-naht-zee-oh-NAH-lay). Tell the vendor where you'll be making most calls (*"per Stati Uniti"*—to America), and he'll select the brand with the best deal.

Buy a lower denomination in case the card is a dud. I've had good luck with the Europa card, which offers up to 350 minutes from Italy to the US for €5.

Hotel-Room Phones: Calling from your hotel room can be cheap for local calls (ask for the rates at the front desk first), but is often a rip-off for long-distance calls (unless you use an international phone card, explained above). Incoming calls are free, making this a cheap way for friends and family to stay in touch (provided they have a good long-distance plan for calls to Europe—and a list of your hotels' phone numbers).

US Calling Cards: These cards, such as the ones offered by AT&T, Verizon, or Sprint, are the worst option. You'll nearly always save a lot of money by using a locally purchased phone card instead.

Metered Phones: In Italy, some call shops have phones with meters. You can talk all you want, then pay the bill when you leave—but be sure you know the rates before you have a lengthy conversation. Note that charges can be "per unit" rather than per minute; find out the length of a unit.

Mobile Phones

Many travelers enjoy the convenience of traveling with a mobile phone.

Using Your Mobile Phone: Your US mobile phone works in Europe if it's GSM-enabled, tri-band or quad-band, and on a calling plan that includes international calls. Phones from T-Mobile and AT&T, which use the same GSM technology that Europe does, are more likely to work overseas than Verizon or Sprint phones (if you're not sure, ask your service provider). Most US providers charge $1.29 per minute while roaming internationally to make or receive calls, and 20–50 cents to send or receive text messages.

You'll pay cheaper rates if your phone is electronically "unlocked" (ask your provider about this); then in Europe, you can simply buy a tiny **SIM card,** which gives you a European phone number. SIM cards are sold at mobile-phone stores and some newsstand kiosks for about $5–10, and generally include several minutes' worth of prepaid domestic calling time. When you buy a SIM card, you may need to show ID, such as your passport. Insert the SIM card in your phone (usually in a slot behind the battery), and it'll work like a European mobile phone. When buying a SIM card, always ask about fees for domestic and international calls, roaming charges, and how to check your credit balance and buy more time.

Many **smartphones,** such as the iPhone or BlackBerry, work in Europe—but beware of sky-high fees, especially for data downloading (checking email, browsing the Internet, watching videos, and so on). Ask your provider in advance how to avoid unwittingly "roaming" your way to a huge bill. Some applications allow for cheap or free smartphone calls over a Wi-Fi connection.

Using a European Mobile Phone: Mobile-phone shops all over Europe sell basic phones. Phones that are "locked" to work with a single provider start around $20; "unlocked" phones (which allow you to switch out SIM cards to use your choice of provider) start around $60. You'll also need to buy a SIM card and prepaid credit for making calls. (My Italian friends tell me that TIM is a reliable Italian mobile-phone company.) When you're in the phone's home country, domestic calls are reasonable, and incoming calls are free. You'll pay more if you're "roaming" in another country.

Calling over the Internet

Some things that seem too good to be true...actually are true. If you're traveling with a laptop, you can make calls using VoIP (Voice over Internet Protocol). With VoIP, two computers act as the phones, and the Internet-based calls are free (or you can pay a few cents to call from your computer to a telephone). If both computers have webcams, you can even see each other while you chat. The major provider is Skype (www.skype.com), followed by Google Talk (www.google.com/talk).

Useful Phone Numbers

Italy's toll-free numbers start with 80. These numbers—called *free-phone* or *numero verde* (green number)—can be dialed free from any phone without using a phone card. Note that you can't call Italy's toll-free numbers from America, nor can you count on reaching America's toll-free numbers from Italy.

Any Italian phone number that starts with "8" but isn't followed by a "0" is a toll call, generally costing €0.10–0.50 per minute.

Emergencies
English-speaking police help: 113
Ambulance: 118
Road Service: 116

Embassies and Consulates
Nearest US Consulate: tel. 02-290-351 (Via Principe Amedeo 2/10, Milan, http://milan.usconsulate.gov)
US Embassy: 24-hour emergency line—tel. 06-46741, non-emergency—tel. 06-4674-2406 (Via Vittorio Veneto 121, Rome, www.usembassy.it)
Canadian Embassy: tel. 06-854-441 (Via Zara 30, Rome, www.italy.gc.ca)

Travel Advisories
US Department of State: tel. 202/647-5225, www.travel.state.gov
Canadian Department of Foreign Affairs: Canadian tel. 800-267-6788, www.dfait-maeci.gc.ca
US Centers for Disease Control and Prevention: tel. 800-CDC-INFO (800-232-4636), www.cdc.gov/travel

Directory Assistance
Telephone Help (in English; free directory assistance): 170
Directory Assistance (for €0.50, an Italian-speaking robot gives the number twice, very clearly): 12

Internet Access
It's useful to get online periodically as you travel—to confirm trip plans, check train or bus schedules, get weather forecasts, catch up on email, blog or post photos from your trip, or call folks back home (explained earlier, under "Calling over the Internet").

Many hotels offer a computer in the lobby with Internet access for guests. Smaller places may sometimes let you sit at their desk for a few minutes just to check your email, if you ask politely. If your hotel doesn't have access, ask your hotelier to direct you to the nearest place to get online.

Because of an anti-terrorism law in Italy, you may be asked to show your passport (carry it in your money belt) when using a public Internet terminal at an Internet café or in a hotel lobby. The proprietor will likely make a copy of your passport.

Traveling with a Laptop: With a laptop or netbook, it's easy to get online if your hotel has Wi-Fi (wireless Internet access) or a port in your room for plugging in a cable. Most hotels offer Wi-Fi for free; others charge by the minute or hour. A cellular modem—which lets your laptop access the Internet over a mobile phone network—provides more extensive coverage, but is much more expensive than Wi-Fi (in Italy, www.wind.it and www.tim.it offer pay-as-you-go mobile broadband).

Mail

While you can arrange for mail delivery to your hotel (allow 10 days for a letter to arrive), phoning and emailing are so easy that I've dispensed with mail stops altogether. Mail service in Italy has improved over the last few years, but even so, mail nothing precious from an Italian post office. Federal Express makes pricey two-day deliveries.

Transportation

By Car or Train?

If your trip will cover more of Italy than just Venice, you'll need to decide whether to rent a car or take trains. Cars are best for three or more traveling together (especially families with small kids), those packing heavy, and those scouring the countryside. Trains and buses are best for solo travelers, blitz tourists, and city-to-city travelers. While a car gives you the ultimate in mobility and freedom, enables you to search for hotels more easily, and carries your bags for you, the train zips you effortlessly from city to city, usually dropping you in the center and near the tourist office.

Trains

To travel by train cheaply in Italy, you can simply buy tickets as you go. Though train station lines can be long, ticket machines work well and are easy to use (see "Buying Tickets," later). Pay all ticket costs in the station before you board, or you'll pay a penalty on the train.

    Types of Trains: You'll encounter several types of trains in

Italy: pokey *regionali*, slow *diretto* and IR *(interregionali)*, medium-speed *espresso*, fast IC (Intercity) and EC (Eurocity), and super-fast ES (Eurostar Italia, including Alta Velocità and Frecciarossa). If you're traveling with a railpass, note that reservations are optional for IC trains, but required for EC and international trains (€5) and ES trains (€10). Regional trains, such

Italy's Public Transportation

Train Costs in Italy

Map key: Approximate point-to-point one-way second-class rail fares in US dollars. First class costs 50 percent more.

Before deciding to get a railpass, add up the approximate ticket costs for your itinerary. If you'll be making short, inexpensive trips each day, you'll probably find it's cheaper to buy tickets as you go in Italy.

as some Venice-Padua connections, don't require reservations. A new high-speed rail service in Italy—*Nuovo Trasporto Viaggiatori* or NTV—is expected to launch its Italo trains sometime in 2011. For details, see www.ntvspa.it.

For point-to-point tickets, you'll pay more the faster you go, but even the fastest trains are affordable (for example, a second-class ticket on a Venice-Rome express train costs about €70).

Schedules: At the train station, the easiest way to check schedules is at a handy automated ticket machine (described later, under "Buying Tickets"). Enter the desired date, time, and destination to view all your options. Printed schedules are also posted at the station (departure posters are always yellow).

Newsstands sell up-to-date regional and all-Italy timetables (€5, ask for the *orario ferroviario*). On the Web, check http://bahn.hafas.de/bin/query.exe/en (Germany's excellent all-Europe schedule website) or www.trenitalia.it. There is also a single all-Italy telephone number for train information (24 hours daily, toll tel. 892-021, Italian only, consider having your hotelier call for you).

APPENDIX

Railpasses

Prices listed are for 2010 and are subject to change. For the latest prices, details, and train schedules (and easy online ordering), see my comprehensive *Guide to Eurail Passes* at www.ricksteves.com/rail.

"Saver" prices are per person for two or more people traveling together. "Youth" means under age 26. The fare for children 4–11 is half the adult individual fare or Saver fare. Kids under age 4 travel free.

ITALY PASS

	Individual 1st Class	Individual 2nd Class	Saver 1st Class	Saver 2nd Class	Youth 2nd Class
3 days in 2 months	$230	$188	$196	$160	$152
Extra rail days (max 7)	$27-30	$21-24	$22-26	$18-21	$18-20

ITALY RAIL & DRIVE PASS

Any 3 rail days and 2 car days in 2 months.

Car Category	1st Class	2nd Class	Extra Car Day
Economy	$360	$306	$68
Compact	390	336	98
Intermediate	419	365	126
Extra rail days (max 7)	35	26	

Prices are per person, two traveling together. Solo travelers pay about 20 percent more. To order a Rail & Drive pass, call your travel agent or Rail Europe at 800-438-7245. *This pass is not sold by Europe Through the Back Door.*

FRANCE–ITALY PASS

	Individual 1st Class	Individual 2nd Class	Saver 1st Class	Saver 2nd Class	Youth 2nd Class
4 days in 2 months	$338	$288	$288	$245	$220
Extra rail days (max 6)	39-41	33-35	33-35	28-30	25-27

Be aware of your route. Many daytime connections from Paris to Italy pass through Switzerland (an additional $60 2nd class or $90 1st class if not covered by your pass). Routes via Nice, Torino, or Modane will bypass Switzerland. Direct Paris–Italy day or night trains are covered by the pass, regardless of their route.

GREECE–ITALY PASS

	Individual 1st Class	Individual 2nd Class	Saver 1st Class	Saver 2nd Class	Youth 2nd Class
4 days in 2 months	$322	$257	$273	$219	$210
Extra rail days (max 6)	33	27	29	23	21

Covers deck passage on overnight Superfast Ferries between Patras, Greece and Bari or Ancona, Italy (starts use of one travel day). Or 30-50% discount on Hellenic Mediterranean Line ferry with basic cabin Patras-Corfu-Brindisi (does not use a travel day). Does not cover travel to or on Greek islands, except a 30% discount on Blue Star Ferries.

SELECTPASS

This pass covers travel in three adjacent countries. Please visit **www.ricksteves.com/rail** for four- and five-country options.

	Individual 1st Class	Saver 1st Class	Youth 2nd Class
5 days in 2 months	$411	$349	$268
6 days in 2 months	454	387	297
8 days in 2 months	538	460	349
10 days in 2 months	624	528	404

Railpasses

It's usually better to buy point-to-point train tickets than a railpass for traveling in Italy. But if you're taking a multicountry trip, the Eurail Select Pass is worth considering (and mentioned below).

The **Italy Pass** for Italian State Railways saves neither time nor hassle. Use the price map on page 379 to add up your ticket costs. Although the pass covers the full cost of getting you from A to B on many trains in Italy, it doesn't include the price of seat reservations or overnight berths. Reservations are optional for many trains, but are required for the fastest trains between major Italian cities. While the pass does save you from having to buy each train ticket as you go, if you'll be taking a few fast trains, you'll still have to spend time in line or at ticket machines—essentially eliminating the point of buying this pass.

A 21-country **Eurail Global Pass** can work well for an all-Europe trip, but is a bad value for travel exclusively in Italy. A cheaper version, the **Eurail Select Pass,** allows you to tailor a pass to your trip, provided you're traveling in three, four, or five adjacent countries directly connected by rail or ferry. For instance, with a three-country pass allowing 10 days of train travel within a two-month period (about $700 for a single adult in 2010), you could choose France–Italy–Greece or Germany–Austria–Italy. A **France and Italy Pass** combines just those two countries and covers night trains to and from Paris via Switzerland (but if your route crosses Switzerland by day, you'll pay extra—so the Selectpass is a better choice if you want to see the Alps). Before you buy a Selectpass or France and Italy Pass, think carefully how many travel days you'll really need. Use the pass only for travel days that involve long hauls or several trips. Pay out of pocket for tickets on days you're taking only short, cheap rides.

For a summary of railpass deals and the latest prices, check my Guide to Eurail Passes at www.ricksteves.com/rail. If you decide to get a railpass, this guide will help you know you're getting the right one for your trip.

Point-to-Point Tickets

Train tickets are a good value in Italy. Fares are shown on the map on page 379, though fares can vary for the same journey, depending on the time of day, the speed of the train, and more. **First-class** tickets cost 50 percent more than **second-class.** While second-class cars go as fast as their first-class neighbors, Italy is one country where I would consider the splurge of first class. The easiest way to "upgrade" a second-class ticket once on board a crowded train is to nurse a drink in the snack car.

Discounts: Families with young children can get price breaks—kids ages 4 and under travel free; ages 4–11 at half-price.

Anatomy of an Italian Train Ticket

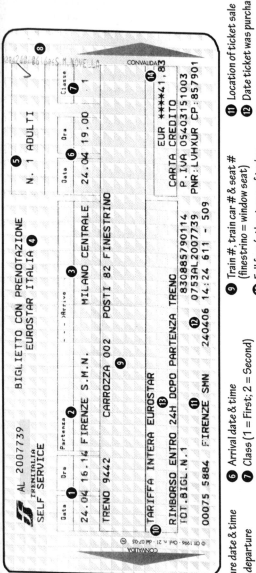

1. Departure date & time
2. Point of departure
3. Destination
4. Ticket with reservation
5. Number of passengers

6. Arrival date & time
7. Class (1 = First; 2 = Second)
8. Validation stamp (once stamped, ticket is good for 1 trip within 24 hours)

9. Train #: train car # & seat # (finestrino = window seat)
10. Full fare (other types of trains can be cheaper and don't require reservations)

11. Location of ticket sale
12. Date ticket was purchased
13. Refundable within 24 hours after train departure
14. Ticket cost

Sometimes the parents get a 20 percent price break. Ask for the "Offerta Familia" deal when buying tickets at a counter (or, at a ticket machine, choose "Yes" at the "Do you want ticket issue?" prompt, then choose "Familia"). The deal doesn't apply to all trains at all times, but it's worth checking out.

Discounts for youths and seniors require purchase of a separate card (Carta Verde for ages 12–26 costs €40; Carta Argento for ages 60 and over is €30), but the discount on tickets is so minor (10–15 percent respectively for domestic travel), it's not worth it for most.

Buying Tickets: Avoid train station ticket lines whenever possible by using automated ticket machines (in train stations) or going to local travel agencies. You'll be able to easily purchase tickets, make seat reservations, and even book a *cuccetta* (koo-CHEHT-tah; overnight berth).

Automated ticket machines (marked *Biglietto Veloce/Fast Ticket*) are user-friendly and found in all but the tiniest stations in Italy. You can pay by cash (they give change) or by debit or credit card. Select English, then wade through a menu of destinations. If you don't see the city you're traveling to, keep keying in the spelling until it's listed. You can choose from first- and second-class seats, request tickets for more than one traveler, and (on the high-speed Eurostar Italia trains) choose an aisle or window seat. When the machine prompts you—"Fidelity Card?"—choose no. Don't select a discount rate without being sure that you meet the criteria (for example, Americans are not eligible for certain EU or resident discounts). Railpass-holders can use the machines to make seat reservations. And you can even validate your ticket in the same machine if you're boarding your train right away.

You can also buy tickets and make reservations at **travel agencies** (see page 28). The cost is only a little more (agencies charge a small fee); it can be more convenient (if you find yourself near a travel agency while sightseeing); and the language barrier can be smaller than at the station's ticket windows (see page 28). But many travelers find it's easiest just to buy them at the ticket machines at the station. You can't buy tickets online on the Italian train website, www.trenitalia.it, because it does not accept US credit cards.

Validating Tickets: Before boarding the train, you must validate (stamp) your train documents in the yellow box near the platform. This includes whatever you need to take a particular trip, which can be as simple as a single ticket, but can also involve a supplement, seat reservation, or *cuccetta* reservation on an overnight train. If you forget to stamp your ticket, go right away to the train conductor—before he comes to you—or you'll pay a fine. Note that you don't need to stamp a railpass or e-ticket.

Train Tips

This section contains information on making seat reservations, storing baggage, avoiding theft, and dealing with strikes.

Seat Reservations: Trains can fill up, even in first class. If you're on a tight schedule, you'll want to reserve a few days ahead for fast trains (see "Types of Trains," earlier). Purchasing required seat reservations onboard a train comes with a nasty penalty. Buying them at the station can be a time-waster unless you use the automatic ticket machines.

If you don't need a reservation, and if your train originates at your departure point (e.g., you're catching the Venice–Florence train in Venice), arriving at least 15 minutes before the departure time will help you snare a seat.

Some major stations have train composition posters on the platforms showing where first- and second-class cars are located when the trains arrive (letters on the poster are supposed to correspond to letters posted over the platform—but they don't always). Since most trains now allow you to make reservations up to the time of departure, conductors are no longer marking reserved seats with a card—instead, they simply post a list of the reservable and non-reservable seat rows (sometimes in English) in each train car's vestibule. This means that if you board a crowded train and get one of the last seats, you may be ousted when the reservation-holder comes along.

Baggage Storage: Many stations have *deposito bagagli* where you can safely leave your bag for about €8 per 12-hour period (payable when you pick up the bag, double-check closing hours). Due to security concerns, no Italian stations have lockers.

Theft Concerns: Italian trains are famous for their thieves. Never leave a bag unattended. I've noticed that police now ride the trains, and things seem more controlled. Still, for an overnight trip, I'd feel safe only in a *cuccetta* (a bunk in a special sleeping car with an attendant who keeps track of who comes and goes while you sleep—approximately €20 in a six-bed compartment, €25 in a less-cramped four-bed compartment).

Strikes: Strikes, which are common, generally last a day. Train employees will simply explain, *"Sciopero"* (strike). But in actuality, sporadic trains, following no particular schedule, lumber down the tracks during most strikes. When a strike is pending, travel agencies (and Web-savvy hoteliers) can check the Internet for you to see when the strike goes into effect and which trains will continue to run. If I need to get somewhere and know a strike is imminent, I leave early (before the strike, which often begins at 9:00), or I just go to the station with extra patience in tow and hop on anything rolling in the direction I want to go.

Deciphering Italian Train Schedules

At the station, look for the big yellow posters labeled
Partenze—Departures (ignore the white posters, which show
arrivals).

Schedules are listed chronologically, hour by hour, showing the trains leaving the station throughout the day. Each
schedule has columns:

- The first column *(Ora)* lists the time of departure.
- The next column *(Treno)* shows the type of train.
- The third column *(Classi Servizi)* lists the services available (first- and second-class cars, dining car, *cuccetta*
  berths, etc.) and, more importantly, whether you need
  reservations (usually denoted by an R in a box). Note
  that all Eurostar Italia (ES) and Alta Velocita (AV) trains,
  many InterCity (IC) and EuroCity (EC) trains, and most
  international trains require reservations.
- The next column lists the destination of the train
  (Principali Fermate Destinazioni), often showing intermediate stops, followed by the final destination, with
  arrival times listed throughout in parentheses. Note that
  your final destination may be listed in fine print as an
  intermediate destination. For example, if you're going
  from Venice to Verona, scan the schedule and you'll
  notice that regional trains that go to Milan usually stop in
  Verona en route. Travelers who read the fine print end up
  with a far greater choice of trains.
- The next column *(Servizi Diretti e Annotazioni)* has perti-
  nent notes about the train, such as "also stops in..." *(ferma
  anche a...)*, "doesn't stop in..." *(non ferma a...)*, "stops in
  every station" *(ferma in tutte le stazioni)*, "delayed..."
  (ritardo...), and so on.
- The last column lists the track *(Binario)* the train departs
  from. Confirm the *binario* with an additional source: a
  ticket-seller, the electronic board that lists immediate
  departures, TV monitors on the platform, or the railway
  officials who are usually standing by the train unless you
  really need them.

For any odd symbols on the poster, look at the key at the
end. Some of the phrasing can be deciphered easily, such as
servizio periodico (periodic service—doesn't always run). For
the trickier ones, ask a local or railway official, try your *Rick
Steves Italian Phrase Book & Dictionary*, or simply take a different train.

You can also check schedules—for trains anywhere in
Italy, not just from the station you're currently in—at the handy
ticket machines. Enter the date and time of your departure (to
or from any Italian station), and you can view all your options.

Renting a Car

If you're renting a car in Italy, bring your driver's license. You're also technically required to have an International Driving Permit—a translation of your driver's license (sold at your local AAA office for $15 plus the cost of two passport-type photos; see www.aaa .com). While that's the letter of the law, I've often rented cars in Italy without having—or being asked to show—this permit.

Rental companies require you to be at least 18 years old and have held your license for one year. Drivers under the age of 25 may incur a young-driver surcharge, and some rental companies do not rent to anyone 75 and over. If you're considered too young or old, look into leasing, which has less-stringent age restrictions.

Research car rentals before you go. It's cheaper to arrange most car rentals from the US. Call several companies and look online to compare rates, or arrange a rental through your home-town travel agent.

Most of the major US rental agencies (such as Alamo/National, Avis, Budget, Dollar, Hertz, and Thrifty) have offices in Italy. It can be cheaper to use a consolidator, such as Auto Europe (www.autoeurope.com) or Europe by Car (www.ebctravel.com), but by using a middleman, you risk trading customer service for lower prices; if you have a problem with the rental company, you can't count on a consolidator to intervene on your behalf.

For the best rental deal, rent by the week with unlimited mileage. I normally rent the smallest, least-expensive model with a stick shift (cheaper than an automatic). Roads and parking spaces are narrow in Italy, so you'll do yourself a favor by renting the smallest car that meets your needs. For a three-week rental, allow $900 per person (based on two people sharing a car), including insurance, tolls, gas, and parking. For trips of this length, consider leasing (see below); you'll save money on insurance and taxes. Compare pick-up costs (downtown can be cheaper than the airport) and explore drop-off options.

You can sometimes get a GPS unit with your rental car or leased vehicle for an additional fee (around $15/day; be sure it's set to English and has all the maps you need before you drive off). Or, if you have a portable GPS device at home, consider taking it with you to Europe (buy and upload European maps before your trip).

When you pick up the rental car, check it thoroughly and make sure any damage is noted on your rental agreement. Find out how your car's lights, turn signals, wipers, and gas cap function, and know what kind of gas the car takes.

Returning a car at a big-city train station can be tricky; get precise details on the car drop-off location and hours. Note that rental offices usually close from midday Saturday until Monday morning. When you return the car, make sure the agent verifies its condition with you.

If you want a car for only a couple of days, a rail-and-drive pass (such as a EurailDrive, Selectpass Drive, or Italy Rail and Drive) can be put to thoughtful use. The basic Italy Rail and Drive Pass, which includes theft insurance and CDW (described below), comes with two days of car rental and three days of rail travel in two months. While rail-and-drive passes are convenient, they're also pricey, particularly for solo travelers.

Car Insurance Options

Accidents can happen anywhere, but when you're on vacation, the last thing you need is stress over car insurance. When you rent a car, you're liable for a very high deductible, sometimes equal to the entire value of the car. Limit your financial risk in case of an accident by choosing one of these two options: Buy Collision Damage Waiver (CDW) coverage from the car-rental company, or get coverage through your credit card (free, but more complicated).

In Italy, most car-rental companies' rates automatically include CDW coverage (which you sometimes can't decline). It's not unusual to decline CDW when you reserve your Italian car, only to find when you show up at the counter that you must buy it after all.

While each rental company has its own variation, the basic **CDW** costs $15–35 a day (figure roughly 25 percent extra) and reduces your liability, but does not eliminate it. When you pick up the car, you'll be offered the chance to "buy down" the basic deductible to zero (for an additional $10–30/day; sometimes called "super CDW").

If you opt for **credit-card coverage,** there's a catch. You'll technically have to decline all coverage offered by the car-rental company, which means they can place a hold on your card (which can be up to the full value of the car). In case of damage, it can be time-consuming to resolve the charges with your credit-card company. Before you decide on this option, quiz your credit-card company about how it works.

Note that **theft insurance** (separate from CDW insurance) is mandatory in Italy. The insurance usually costs about $15–20 a day, payable when you pick up the car.

For more fine print about car-rental insurance, see www.rick steves.com/cdw.

Leasing

For trips of three weeks or more, leasing (which automatically includes zero-deductible collision and theft insurance) is the best way to go. By technically buying and then selling back the car, you save lots of money on tax and insurance. Leasing provides you a

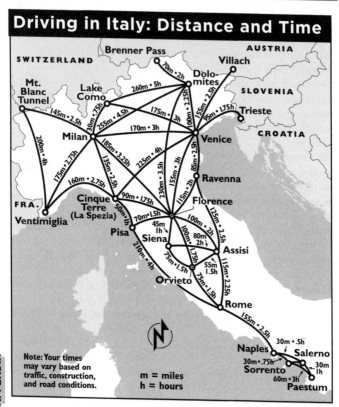

Driving in Italy: Distance and Time

new car with unlimited mileage and a 24-hour emergency assistance program. You can lease for as little as 17 days to as long as six months. Car leases must be arranged from the US. One of many companies offering affordable lease packages is Europe by Car (US tel. 800-223-1516, www.ebctravel.com).

Driving

Driving in Italy can be scary—a video game for keeps, and you only get one quarter. Italian drivers can be aggressive. They drive fast and tailgate as if it were required. They pass where Americans are taught not to—on blind corners and just before tunnels. Roads have narrow shoulders or none at all. Driving in the countryside is less stressful than driving through urban areas, but stay alert. On one-lane roads, larger vehicles have the right-of-way. If you're on a truckers' route, stifle your Good Samaritan impulse when you see provocatively dressed women standing by camper-vans at the side of the road; they're not having car trouble.

   Road Rules: Stay out of restricted traffic zones or you'll risk huge fines. Car traffic is restricted in many city centers. Don't drive or park anywhere with signs reading *Zona Traffico Limitato* (*ZTL*, often shown above a red circle, see image). If you do, your license plate will likely be photographed and a hefty (€100-plus) ticket mailed to your home without your ever having met a cop. Bumbling in and out of these zones can net you multiple

fines. If your hotel is within a restricted area, it's best to ask your hotelier to direct you to parking outside the zone. (Although your hotelier can register your car as an authorized vehicle permitted to enter the zone, this usually isn't worth the hassle.)

As for other road rules, seatbelts are mandatory, and you should keep headlights on at all times outside of urban areas. Ask your car-rental company about additional rules, or check the US State Department website (www.travel.state.gov, click on "International Travel," then specify your country of choice and click "Traffic Safety and Road Conditions").

Tolls: Italy's freeway system, the autostrada, is as good as our interstate system, but you'll pay about a dollar for every 10 minutes of use. While I favor the freeways because I feel they're safer, cheaper (saving time and gas), and less nerve-racking than smaller roads, savvy local drivers know which toll-free *superstradas* are actually faster and more direct than the autostrada. For more information, visit www.autostrade.it.

APPENDIX

Fuel: Gas is expensive—often about $6 per gallon. Diesel cars are more common in Europe than back home, so be sure you know what type of gas your car takes before you fill up. Gas pumps are color-coded for unleaded (*senza piombo*) or diesel (*gasolio*). Autostrada rest stops are self-service stations open daily without a siesta break. Many 24-hour-a-day stations are entirely automated. Small-town stations are usually cheaper and offer full service but shorter hours.

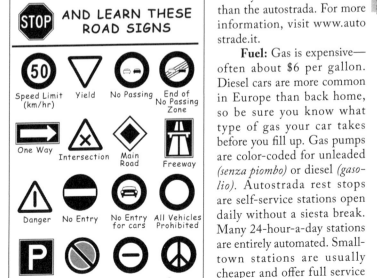

Maps and Signage: A good map is essential. Learn the universal road signs (explained in charts in most road atlases and at service stations). Although roads are numbered on maps, actual road signs don't list route numbers. Instead, roads are indicated by blue signs with a city name on them (for example, if you want to take a road heading east out of Venice—marked route S-11 on your map—you'd follow signs to Padua, the next town along this road). The signs are inconsistent: They may direct you to the nearest big city or simply the next town along the route.

Theft: Cars are routinely vandalized and stolen. Thieves easily recognize rental cars and assume they are filled with a tourist's gear. Try to make your car look locally owned by hiding the "tourist-owned" rental-company decals and putting an Italian newspaper in your back window. Be sure all of your valuables are out of sight and locked in the trunk, or even better, with you or in your room.

Parking: White lines generally mean parking is free. Blue lines mean you'll have to pay—usually €1 per hour (use machine, leave time-stamped receipt on dashboard). If there's no meter, there's probably a roving attendant who will take your money. Study the signs. Often the free zones have a 30- or 60-minute time limit. Signs showing a street cleaner and a day of the week indicate which day the street is cleaned; there's a €100 tow-fee incentive to learn the days of the week in Italian.

Zona disco has nothing to do with dancing. Italian cars come equipped with a time disk (a cardboard clock), which you set at your arrival time and lay on the dashboard so the attendant knows how long you've been parked. This is a fine system that all drivers should take advantage of. (If your rental car doesn't come with a *zona disco,* pick one up at a tobacco shop or just write your arrival time on a piece of paper and place it on the dashboard.)

Garages are safe, save time, and help you avoid the stress of parking tickets. Take the parking voucher with you to pay the cashier before you leave.

Cheap Flights

If you're traveling beyond Venice, you might want to look into flying one of the affordable intra-European airlines. While trains are still the best way to connect places that are close together, a flight can save both time and money on long journeys.

One of the best websites for comparing inexpensive flights is www.skyscanner.com. Other comparison search engines include www.wegolo.com and www.whichbudget.com. Many budget airlines—such as easyJet, Ryanair, and Blue—serve Venice.

Be aware of the potential drawbacks of flying on the cheap: nonrefundable and nonchangeable tickets, minimal or nonexistent customer service, treks to airports far outside of town, and pricey baggage fees. Especially if you're traveling with lots of luggage, a cheap flight can quickly become a bad deal. To avoid unpleasant surprises, read the small print before you book.

Resources

Resources from Rick Steves

Books: *Rick Steves' Venice 2011* is one of many books in my series on European travel, which includes country guidebooks, city guidebooks (Rome, Florence, Paris, London, etc.), Snapshot guides (excerpted chapters from my country guides), Pocket guides (full-color little books on big cities), and my budget-travel skills handbook, *Rick Steves' Europe Through the Back Door*. My phrase books—for Italian, French, German, Spanish, and Portuguese—are practical and budget-oriented. My other books include *Europe 101* (a crash course on art and history) and *Travel as a Political Act* (a travelogue sprinkled with tips for bringing home a global perspective). For a list of my books, see the inside of the last page of this book.

Video: My public television series, *Rick Steves' Europe*, covers European destinations in 100 shows, with 14 episodes on Italy, including two on Venice. To watch episodes, visit www.hulu.com /rick-steves-europe; for scripts and other details, see www.rick steves.com/tv.

Audio: My weekly public radio show, *Travel with Rick Steves*, features interviews with travel experts from around the world. I've also produced free self-guided audio tours of the top sights and neighborhoods in Venice, Rome, Florence, and more. I've combined all of my audio content into Rick Steves Audio Europe, an extensive online library organized by destination. Choose whatever interests you, and download it for free to your iPod, smartphone, or computer at www .ricksteves.com or iTunes.

Maps

The black-and-white maps in this book, designed by my well-traveled staff, are concise and simple. The maps are intended to help you locate recommended places and get to local TIs, where

At our travel website, you'll find a wealth of free information on European destinations, including fresh monthly news and helpful tips from thousands of fellow travelers. You'll also find my latest guidebook updates (www.ricksteves.com/update) and my travel blog.

Our **online Travel Store** offers travel bags and accessories specially designed by me and my staff to help you travel smarter and lighter. These include my popular carry-on bags (roll-aboard and rucksack versions), money belts, totes, toiletries kits, adapters, other accessories, and a wide selection of guidebooks, planning maps, and DVDs.

Choosing the right **railpass** for your trip—amid hundreds of options—can drive you nutty. We'll help you choose the best pass for your needs, plus give you a bunch of free extras.

Rick Steves' Europe Through the Back Door travel company offers **tours** with more than three dozen itineraries and about 400 departures reaching the best destinations in this book...and beyond. Our Italy tours include "the best of" in 17 days, Village Italy in 14 days, South Italy in 13 days, Venice–Florence–Rome in 10 days, the Heart of Italy in 9 days, Sicily in 9 days, and a week-long Rome tour. You'll enjoy great guides, a fun bunch of travel partners (with small groups of generally around 28), and plenty of room to spread out in a big, comfy bus. You'll find European adventures to fit every vacation length. For all the details, and to get our Tour Catalog and a free Rick Steves Tour Experience DVD (filmed on location during an actual tour), visit www.ricksteves.com or call us at 425/608-4217.

you can pick up more in-depth maps of towns or regions (usually free). Better maps are sold at newsstands and bookstores. Before you buy a map, look at it to be sure it has the level of detail you want. Drivers will want to pick up a good, detailed map in Europe (I'd recommend a 1:200,000- or 1:300,000-scale map).

Other Guidebooks

For most travelers, this book has more than enough information. But if you're heading beyond my recommended neighborhoods and destinations, $40 for extra maps and books can be money well spent.

The following books are worthwhile, though are not updated annually; check the publication date before you buy. The Access guide (which combines Venice and Florence) is well researched, organized by neighborhood, and color-coded for sights, hotels, and restaurants. Focusing mainly on sights, the colorful Eyewitness guide (on Venice and Veneto) is fun for its great graphics and photos, but it's relatively skimpy on content and weighs a ton. (Their *Top 10 Venice* book, which features top-10 lists, is lighter.) You can buy these in Venice (no more expensive than in the US) or simply borrow them for a minute from other travelers at certain sights to make sure you're aware of that place's highlights. In Venice, local guidebooks (sold at kiosks) are cheap and give you a map and a decent commentary on the sights.

If you'll be traveling elsewhere in Italy, consider these books in the Rick Steves series: *Italy, Rome,* and *Florence & Tuscany.*

Recommended Books and Movies

To learn more about Venice past and present, check out a few of these books or films.

Non-Fiction

A History of Venice (Norwich) covers the city from its beginnings until Napoleon ended the Republic's independence. *Venice: A Maritime Republic* (Lane) explains how dominance on the high seas brought in piles of riches. *Venice: Lion City* (Wills), another city history, has a more academic tone. *Francesco's Venice* (da Mosto), based on a BBC series, balances history with coffee table–book illustrations.

Filled with stories of a woman abroad, *Venice Observed* rings with Mary McCarthy's engaging voice. *The City of Falling Angels,* by best-selling author John Berendt, hinges on a devastating fire at La Fenice Opera House. Based on once-hidden letters found in a palazzo, *A Venetian Affair* (di Robilant) tells a true love story. *Venice: A Cultural and Literary Companion* (Garrett) also covers the nearby islands, while *A Literary Companion to Venice* (Littlewood) includes walking tours of the city, as does *Strolling Through Venice* (Freely). For a traveler's insight into Venice, consider picking up Barrie Kerper's *Venice: The Collected Traveler*. Kids of all ages enjoy the whimsical and colorful impressions of the city in Miroslav Sasek's classic picture-book *This is Venice*.

Fiction

Henry James set many of his best books in Venice, including *The Wings of the Dove, Italian Hours,* and *The Aspern Papers and Other Stories*. Thomas Mann also chose this city for his doomed tale *Death in Venice*.

Invisible Cities (Calvino) takes place during the era of Genghis Khan and Marco Polo, while *The Palace: A Novel* (St. Aubin de Terán) has the Italian Risorgimento as its backdrop. Set in the Napoleonic era, *The Passion* (Winterson) is both a complex love story and a work of literary fiction. *In the Company of the Courtesan* (Dunant) novelizes the drama and romances of Renaissance Venice.

Venice's murky waters make a perfect setting for intrigue. Mystery fans will enjoy *Dead Lagoon* (Dibdin), *Dirge for a Doge* (Eyre), *Stone Virgin* (Unsworth), and *The Haunted Hotel* (Collins). In *Death at La Fenice*, one of a dozen of her novels set in Venice, Donna Leon chronicles the adventures of detective Guido Brunetti and his wife Paola. Fans of the series will enjoy *Brunetti's Venice* (Sepeda) that leads visitors on intimate walks through the city, highlighting Brunetti's haunts and settings from Leon's novels.

Films

Summertime (1955) sends melancholy Katherine Hepburn to Venice for romance. *Death in Venice* (1971), based on the book (see above), shows the devastating impact of a troubling infatuation. *Don't Look Now* (1973), based on a novel by Daphne du Maurier, uses Venice as a mysterious backdrop for a haunting tale.

Only You (1994) is a cute (and even sappy) love story, while *Bread and Tulips* (2000)—equally romantic, but firmly grounded in reality—shows the power of Venice in reviving a wounded soul. *Dangerous Beauty* (1998), meanwhile, keeps love out of the picture in the story of a 16th-century prostitute. *Wings of the Dove* (1997), based on the Henry James novel, is a tale of desire that takes full advantage of its Venetian locale.

The 2003 version of *The Italian Job* begins its fluffy, fun crime caper in Venice. Shakespeare fans will appreciate *The Merchant of Venice* (2004), which won raves for Al Pacino. The Woody Allen musical *Everyone Says I Love You* (1997) is partially set in Venice. Another Hollywood flick filmed here is *Casanova* (2005), starring Heath Ledger as the master of *amore*. And the climax of the

2011

JANUARY						
S	M	T	W	T	F	S
						1
2	3	4	5	6	7	8
9	10	11	12	13	14	15
16	17	18	19	20	21	22
23/30	24/31	25	26	27	28	29

FEBRUARY						
S	M	T	W	T	F	S
		1	2	3	4	5
6	7	8	9	10	11	12
13	14	15	16	17	18	19
20	21	22	23	24	25	26
27	28					

MARCH						
S	M	T	W	T	F	S
		1	2	3	4	5
6	7	8	9	10	11	12
13	14	15	16	17	18	19
20	21	22	23	24	25	26
27	28	29	30	31		

APRIL						
S	M	T	W	T	F	S
					1	2
3	4	5	6	7	8	9
10	11	12	13	14	15	16
17	18	19	20	21	22	23
24	25	26	27	28	29	30

MAY						
S	M	T	W	T	F	S
1	2	3	4	5	6	7
8	9	10	11	12	13	14
15	16	17	18	19	20	21
22	23	24	25	26	27	28
29	30	31				

JUNE						
S	M	T	W	T	F	S
			1	2	3	4
5	6	7	8	9	10	11
12	13	14	15	16	17	18
19	20	21	22	23	24	25
26	27	28	29	30		

JULY						
S	M	T	W	T	F	S
					1	2
3	4	5	6	7	8	9
10	11	12	13	14	15	16
17	18	19	20	21	22	23
24/31	25	26	27	28	29	30

AUGUST						
S	M	T	W	T	F	S
	1	2	3	4	5	6
7	8	9	10	11	12	13
14	15	16	17	18	19	20
21	22	23	24	25	26	27
28	29	30	31			

SEPTEMBER						
S	M	T	W	T	F	S
				1	2	3
4	5	6	7	8	9	10
11	12	13	14	15	16	17
18	19	20	21	22	23	24
25	26	27	28	29	30	

OCTOBER						
S	M	T	W	T	F	S
						1
2	3	4	5	6	7	8
9	10	11	12	13	14	15
16	17	18	19	20	21	22
23/30	24/31	25	26	27	28	29

NOVEMBER						
S	M	T	W	T	F	S
		1	2	3	4	5
6	7	8	9	10	11	12
13	14	15	16	17	18	19
20	21	22	23	24	25	26
27	28	29	30			

DECEMBER						
S	M	T	W	T	F	S
				1	2	3
4	5	6	7	8	9	10
11	12	13	14	15	16	17
18	19	20	21	22	23	24
25	26	27	28	29	30	31

James Bond thriller *Casino Royale* (2006) takes place along—and under—the canals of Venice.

Holidays and Festivals

Italy celebrates many holidays, which close sights and bring crowds. Holidays seem to strike without warning. For instance, every town has a festival honoring its patron saint. Your best source for information on holidays and festivals is the Venice tourist information office (www.turismovenezia.it). You could also check with Italy's national tourist offices (www.italiantourism.com), listed at the beginning of this chapter.

Venice is always busy with special musical and artistic events. The free monthly *Un Ospite di Venezia* lists all the latest in English (free at fancy hotels, or check www.aguestinvenice.com).

Here are some of the major holidays in 2011:

Jan 1	New Year's Day
Jan 6	Epiphany
Feb 26–March 8	Carnevale
April 24	Easter Sunday
April 25	Easter Monday
April 25	Italian Liberation Day, St. Mark's Day (Venetian patron saint)
May 1	Labor Day
Late May–Early June	Vogalonga Regatta
June 2	Anniversary of the Republic, Feast of the Ascension
June 23	Feast of Corpus Christi
July 16–17	Feast and Regatta of the Redeemer
Aug 15	Assumption of Mary (Ferragosto)
Sept 3–4	Historical Regatta
Nov 1	All Saints' Day
Nov 21	Feast of Our Lady of Good Health
Dec 8	Feast of the Immaculate Conception
Dec 25	Christmas
Dec 26	St. Stephen's Day

Festivals in Venice

Venice's most famous festival is **Carnevale,** the celebration Americans call Mardi Gras (Feb 26–March 8 in 2011, www .carnevale.venezia.it). Carnevale, which means "farewell to meat," originated centuries ago as a wild two-month–long party leading up to the austerity of Lent. In Carnevale's heyday—the 1600s and 1700s—you could do pretty much anything with anybody from any social class if you were wearing a mask. These days it's a tamer 10-day celebration, culminating in a huge dance lit with fireworks on St. Mark's Square. Sporting masks and costumes, Venetians from kids to businessmen join in the fun. Drawing the biggest crowds of the year, Carnevale has nearly been a victim of its own success, driving away many Venetians (who skip out on the craziness to go skiing in the Dolomites).

Every odd year (including 2011), the city hosts the **Venice Biennale International Art Exhibition,** a world-class contemporary art fair spread over the Arsenale and sprawling Castello Gardens. Artists representing 70 nations from around the world offer the latest in contemporary art forms: video, computer art, performance art, and digital photography, along with painting and sculpture (take vaporetto #1 or #2 to Giardini-Biennale; for details and an events calendar, see www.labiennale.org). The actual exhibition usually runs from June through November, but other events—film, dance, theater—loosely connected with the Biennale are held throughout the year (starting as early as Feb) in various venues on the island.

Other typically Venetian festival days filling the city's hotels with visitors and its canals with decked-out boats are **Feast of the Ascension Day** (June 2 in 2011), **Feast and Regatta of the Redeemer** (third Sun in July and the preceding evening), and the **Historical Regatta** (old-time boats and pageantry, first Sat and Sun in Sept). **Vogalonga** is a colorful regatta that attracts more than 1,500 human-powered watercraft; teams of often costumed participants follow a 20-mile course through the canals and lagoon (late May–early June, www.vogalonga.it). Smaller regattas include the **Murano Regatta** (early July) and the **Burano Regatta** (mid-Sept).

Venice's patron saint, **St. Mark,** is commemorated every April 25. Venetian men celebrate the day by presenting roses to the women in their lives (mothers, wives, and lovers).

Every November 21 is the **Feast of Our Lady of Good Health.** On this local "Thanksgiving," a bridge is built over the Grand Canal so that the city can pile into La Salute Church and remember how Venice survived the gruesome plague of 1630. On this day, Venetians eat smoked lamb from Dalmatia (which was the cargo of the first ship admitted when the plague lifted).

Conversions and Climate

Numbers and Stumblers

- Europeans write a few of their numbers differently than we do. 1 = 1, 4 = 4, 7 = 7.
- In Europe, dates appear as day/month/year, so Christmas is 25/12/11.
- Commas are decimal points and decimals commas. A dollar and a half is 1,50, and there are 5.280 feet in a mile.
- When pointing, use your whole hand, palm down.
- When counting with fingers, start with your thumb. If you hold up your first finger to request one item, you'll probably get two.
- What Americans call the second floor of a building is the first floor in Europe.
- On escalators and moving sidewalks, Europeans keep the left "lane" open for passing. Keep to the right.

Metric Conversions (approximate)

A kilogram is 2.2 pounds, and 1 liter is about a quart, or almost four to a gallon. A kilometer is six-tenths of a mile. I figure kilometers to miles by cutting them in half and adding back 10 percent of the original (120 km: 60 + 12 = 72 miles, 300 km: 150 + 30 = 180 miles).

1 foot = 0.3 meter	1 square yard = 0.8 square meter
1 yard = 0.9 meter	1 square mile = 2.6 square kilometers
1 mile = 1.6 kilometers	1 ounce = 28 grams
1 centimeter = 0.4 inch	1 quart = 0.95 liter
1 meter = 39.4 inches	1 kilogram = 2.2 pounds
1 kilometer = 0.62 mile	32°F = 0°C

Roman Numerals

In the US, you'll see Roman numerals—which originated in ancient Rome—used for copyright dates, clocks, and the Super Bowl. In Italy, you're likely to observe these numbers chiseled on statues and buildings. If you want to do some numeric detective work, here's how: In Roman numerals, as in ours, the highest numbers (thousands, hundreds) come first, followed by smaller numbers. Many numbers are made by combining numerals into sets: V = 5, so VIII = 8 (5 plus 3). Roman numerals follow a subtraction principle for multiples of fours (4, 40, 400, etc.) and nines (9, 90, 900, etc.); the number four, for example, is written as IV (1 subtracted from 5), rather than IIII. The number nine is IX (1 subtracted from 10).

Rick Steves' Venice 2011—written in Roman numerals—would translate as *Rick Steves' Venice MMXI*. Big numbers such as dates can look daunting at first. The easiest way to handle them is to read the numbers in discrete chunks. For example, Michelangelo was born in MCDLXXV. Break it down: M (1,000) + CD (100 subtracted from 500, or 400) + LXX (50 + 10 + 10, or 70) + V (5) = 1475. It was a very good year.

M = 1000	XL = 40
CM = 900	X = 10
D = 500	IX = 9
CD = 400	V = 5
C = 100	IV = 4
XC = 90	I = duh
L = 50	

Clothing Sizes

When shopping for clothing, use these US-to-European comparisons as general guidelines (but note that no conversion is perfect).
- Women's dresses and blouses: Add 30
  (US size 10 = European size 40)
- Men's suits and jackets: Add 10
  (US size 40 regular = European size 50)
- Men's shirts: Multiply by 2 and add about 8
  (US size 15 collar = European size 38)
- Women's shoes: Add about 30
  (US size 8 = European size 38½)
- Men's shoes: Add 32–34
  (US size 9 = European size 41; US size 11 = European size 45)

Venice's Climate

First line, average daily high; second line, average daily low; third line, days of no rain. For more detailed weather statistics for destinations in this book (as well as the rest of the world), check www.worldclimate.com.

J	F	M	A	M	J	J	A	S	O	N	D
42°	46°	53°	62°	70°	76°	81°	80°	75°	65°	53°	46°
33°	35°	41°	49°	56°	63°	66°	65°	61°	53°	44°	37°
25	21	24	21	23	22	24	24	25	24	21	23

APPENDIX

Temperature Conversion:
Fahrenheit and Celsius

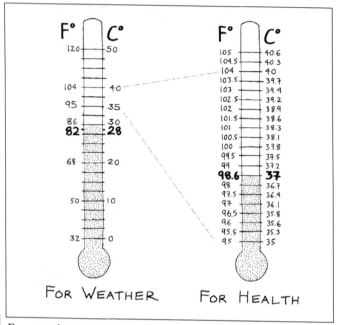

FOR WEATHER   FOR HEALTH

Europe takes its temperature using the Celsius scale, while we opt for Fahrenheit. For a rough conversion from Celsius to Fahrenheit, double the number and add 30. For weather, remember that 28°C is 82°F—perfect. For health, 37°C is just right.

Essential Packing Checklist

Whether you're traveling for five days or five weeks, here's what you'll need to bring. Remember to pack light to enjoy the sweet freedom of true mobility. Happy travels!

- ❑ 5 shirts
- ❑ 1 sweater or lightweight fleece jacket
- ❑ 2 pairs pants
- ❑ 1 pair shorts
- ❑ 1 swimsuit (women only—men can use shorts)
- ❑ 5 pairs underwear and socks
- ❑ 1 pair shoes
- ❑ 1 rain-proof jacket
- ❑ Tie or scarf
- ❑ Money belt
- ❑ Money—your mix of:
  - ❑ Debit card for ATM withdrawals
  - ❑ Credit card
  - ❑ Hard cash in US dollars ($20 bills)
- ❑ Documents (and back-up photocopies):
  - ❑ Passport
  - ❑ Printout of airline e-ticket
  - ❑ Driver's license
  - ❑ Student ID and hostel card
  - ❑ Railpass/car rental voucher
  - ❑ Insurance details
- ❑ Daypack
- ❑ Sealable plastic baggies
- ❑ Camera and related gear
- ❑ Empty water bottle
- ❑ Wristwatch and alarm clock
- ❑ Earplugs
- ❑ First-aid kit
- ❑ Medicine (labeled)
- ❑ Extra glasses/contacts and prescriptions
- ❑ Sunscreen and sunglasses
- ❑ Toiletries kit
- ❑ Soap
- ❑ Laundry soap
- ❑ Clothesline
- ❑ Small towel
- ❑ Sewing kit
- ❑ Travel information
- ❑ Necessary map(s)
- ❑ Address list (email and mailing addresses)
- ❑ Postcards and photos from home
- ❑ Notepad and pen
- ❑ Journal

If you plan to carry on your luggage, note that all liquids must be in three-ounce or smaller containers and fit within a single quart-size baggie. For details, see www.tsa.gov/travelers.

Hotel Reservation

To: _____   _____
　　　　　　　hotel　　　　　　　　　　　　　　　*email or fax*

From: _____   _____
　　　　　　　name　　　　　　　　　　　　　　　*email or fax*

Today's date: _____ /_____ /_____
　　　　　　　　day　*month*　*year*

Dear Hotel _____ ,
Please make this reservation for me:

Name: _____

Total # of people: _____   # of rooms: _____   # of nights: _____

Arriving: _____ /_____/ _____   My time of arrival (24-hr clock): _____
　　　　　　day　*month*　*year*　　　　(I will telephone if I will be late)

Departing: ____ /____ /____
　　　　　　　day　*month*　*year*

Room(s): Single___   Double ___   Twin ___   Triple ___   Quad___

With: Toilet _____   Shower _____   Bath _____   Sink only ___

Special needs: View___   Quiet___   Cheapest ___   Ground Floor___

Please email or fax confirmation of my reservation, along with the type of room reserved and the price. Please also inform me of your cancellation policy. After I hear from you, I will quickly send my credit-card information as a deposit to hold the room. Thank you.

_____
Name

_____
Address

_____
City　　　　　　　　　　**State**　　　**Zip Code**　　**Country**

Before hoteliers can make your reservation, they want to know the information listed above. You can use this form as the basis for your email, or you can photocopy this page, fill in the information, and send it as a fax (also available online at www.ricksteves.com/reservation).

Italian Survival Phrases

Good day.	**Buon giorno.**	bwohn JOR-noh
Do you speak English?	**Parla inglese?**	PAR-lah een-GLAY-zay
Yes. / No.	**Sì. / No.**	see / noh
I (don't) understand.	**(Non) capisco.**	(nohn) kah-PEES-koh
Please.	**Per favore.**	pehr fah-VOH-ray
Thank you.	**Grazie.**	GRAHT-seeay
You're welcome.	**Prego.**	PRAY-go
I'm sorry.	**Mi dispiace.**	mee dee-speeAH-chay
Excuse me.	**Mi scusi.**	mee SKOO-zee
(No) problem.	**(Non) c'è un problema.**	(nohn) cheh oon proh-BLAY-mah
Good.	**Va bene.**	vah BEHN-ay
Goodbye.	**Arrivederci.**	ah-ree-vay-DEHR-chee
one / two	**uno / due**	OO-noh / DOO-ay
three / four	**tre / quattro**	tray / KWAH-troh
five / six	**cinque / sei**	CHEENG-kway / SEHee
seven / eight	**sette / otto**	SEHT-tay / OT-toh
nine / ten	**nove / dieci**	NOV-ay / deeAY-chee
How much is it?	**Quanto costa?**	KWAHN-toh KOS-tah
Write it?	**Me lo scrive?**	may loh SKREE-vay
Is it free?	**È gratis?**	eh GRAH-tees
Is it included?	**È incluso?**	eh een-KLOO-zoh
Where can I buy / find...?	**Dove posso comprare / trovare...?**	DOH-vay POS-soh kohm-PRAH-ray / troh-VAH-ray
I'd like / We'd like...	**Vorrei / Vorremmo...**	vor-REHee / vor-RAY-moh
...a room.	**...una camera.**	OO-nah KAH-meh-rah
...a ticket to ___.	**...un biglietto per ___.**	oon beel-YEHT-toh pehr
Is it possible?	**È possibile?**	eh poh-SEE-bee-lay
Where is...?	**Dov'è...?**	DOH-veh
...the train station	**...la stazione**	lah staht-seeOH-nay
...the bus station	**...la stazione degli autobus**	lah staht-seeOH-nay DAYL-yee OW-toh-boos
...tourist information	**...informazioni per turisti**	een-for-maht-seeOH-nee pehr too-REE-stee
...the toilet	**...la toilette**	lah twah-LEHT-tay
men	**uomini, signori**	WOH-mee-nee, seen-YOH-ree
women	**donne, signore**	DON-nay, seen-YOH-ray
left / right	**sinistra / destra**	see-NEE-strah / DEHS-trah
straight	**sempre diritto**	SEHM-pray dee-REE-toh
When do you open / close?	**A che ora aprite / chiudete?**	ah kay OH-rah ah-PREE-tay / keeoo-DAY-tay
At what time?	**A che ora?**	ah kay OH-rah
Just a moment.	**Un momento.**	oon moh-MAYN-toh
now / soon / later	**adesso / presto / tardi**	ah-DEHS-soh / PREHS-toh / TAR-dee
today / tomorrow	**oggi / domani**	OH-jee / doh-MAH-nee

In the Restaurant

I'd like...	Vorrei...	vor-REHee
We'd like...	Vorremmo...	vor-RAY-moh
...to reserve...	...prenotare...	pray-noh-TAH-ray
...a table for one / two.	...un tavolo per uno / due.	oon TAH-voh-loh pehr OO-noh / DOO-ay
Non-smoking.	Non fumare.	nohn foo-MAH-ray
Is this seat free?	È libero questo posto?	eh LEE-bay-roh KWEHS-toh POH-stoh
The menu (in English), please.	Il menù (in inglese), per favore.	eel may-NOO (een een-GLAY-zay) pehr fah-VOH-ray
service (not) included	servizio (non) incluso	sehr-VEET-seeoh (nohn) een-KLOO-zoh
cover charge	pane e coperto	PAH-nay ay koh-PEHR-toh
to go	da portar via	dah POR-tar VEE-ah
with / without	con / senza	kohn / SEHN-sah
and / or	e / o	ay / oh
menu (of the day)	menù (del giorno)	may-NOO (dayl JOR-noh)
specialty of the house	specialità della casa	spay-chah-lee-TAH DEHL-lah KAH-zah
first course (pasta, soup)	primo piatto	PREE-moh peeAH-toh
main course (meat, fish)	secondo piatto	say-KOHN-doh peeAH-toh
side dishes	contorni	kohn-TOR-nee
bread	pane	PAH-nay
cheese	formaggio	for-MAH-joh
sandwich	panino	pah-NEE-noh
soup	minestra, zuppa	mee-NEHS-trah, TSOO-pah
salad	insalata	een-sah-LAH-tah
meat	carne	KAR-nay
chicken	pollo	POH-loh
fish	pesce	PEH-shay
seafood	frutti di mare	FROO-tee dee MAH-ray
fruit / vegetables	frutta / legumi	FROO-tah / lay-GOO-mee
dessert	dolci	DOHL-chee
tap water	acqua del rubinetto	AH-kwah dayl roo-bee-NAY-toh
mineral water	acqua minerale	AH-kwah mee-nay-RAH-lay
milk	latte	LAH-tay
(orange) juice	succo (d'arancia)	SOO-koh (dah-RAHN-chah)
coffee / tea	caffè / tè	kah-FEH / teh
wine	vino	VEE-noh
red / white	rosso / bianco	ROH-soh / beeAHN-koh
glass / bottle	bicchiere / bottiglia	bee-keeAY-ray / boh-TEEL-yah
beer	birra	BEE-rah
Cheers!	Cin cin!	cheen cheen
More. / Another.	Ancora un po.' / Un altro.	ahn-KOH-rah oon poh / oon AHL-troh
The same.	Lo stesso.	loh STEHS-soh
The bill, please.	Il conto, per favore.	eel KOHN-toh pehr fah-VOH-ray
tip	mancia	MAHN-chah
Delicious!	Delizioso!	day-leet-seeOH-zoh

For more user-friendly Italian phrases, check out *Rick Steves' Italian Phrase Book & Dictionary* or *Rick Steves' French, Italian, and German Phrase Book.*

INDEX

INDEX

Music: 296–297, 340

MAP INDEX

Free mobile app (and podcast)

With the **Rick Steves Audio Europe** app, your iPhone or smartphone becomes a powerful travel tool.

This exciting app organizes Rick's entire audio library by country—giving you a playlist of all his audio walking tours, radio interviews, and travel tips for wherever you're going in Europe.

Let the experts Rick interviews enrich your understanding. Let Rick's self-guided tours amplify your guidebook. With Rick in your ear, Europe gets even better.

Thanks Facebook fans for submitting photos while on location! From top: John Kuijper in Florence, Brenda Mamer with her mother in Rome, Angel Capobianco in London, and Alyssa Passey with her friend in Paris.

Find out more at ricksteves.com/audioeurope

Join a Rick Steves tour

Enjoy Europe's warmest welcome...

with the flexibility and friendship of a small group

getting to know Rick's favorite places and people.

It all starts with our free tour catalog and DVD.

Great guides, small groups, no grumps.

Free information and great gear to

▶ Plan Your Trip

Browse thousands of articles and a wealth of money-saving tips for planning your dream trip. You'll find up-to-date information on Europe's best destinations, packing smart, getting around, finding rooms, staying healthy, avoiding scams and more.

▶ Eurail Passes

Find out, step-by-step, if a railpass makes sense for your trip—and how to avoid buying more than you need. Get a bunch of free extras!

▶ Graffiti Wall & Travelers' Helpline

Learn, ask, share—our online community of savvy travelers is a great resource for first-time travelers to Europe, as well as seasoned pros.

Rick Steves' Europe Through the Back Door, Inc.

turn your travel dreams into affordable reality

▸ Free Audio Tours & Travel Newsletter

Get your nose out of this guide book and focus on what you'll be seeing with Rick's free audio tours of the greatest sights in Paris, London, Rome, Florence and Venice.

Subscribe to our free Travel News e-newsletter, and get monthly articles from Rick on what's happening in Europe.

▸ Great Gear from Rick's Travel Store

Pack light and right—on a budget—with Rick's custom-designed carry-on bags, roll-aboards, day packs, travel accessories, guidebooks, journals, maps and DVDs of his TV shows.

130 Fourth Avenue North, PO Box 2009 • Edmonds, WA 98020 USA
Phone: (425) 771-8303 • Fax: (425) 771-0833 • www.ricksteves.com

NOW AVAILABLE: eBOOKS, APPS, DVDS, & BLU-RAY

eBOOKS

Most guides available as eBooks from Amazon, Barnes & Noble, Borders, Apple iBook and Sony eReader, beginning January 2011

RICK STEVES' EUROPE DVDs

Austria & the Alps
Eastern Europe, Israel & Egypt
England & Wales
European Travel Skills & Specials
France
Germany, Benelux & More
Greece & Turkey
Iran
Ireland & Scotland
Italy's Cities
Italy's Countryside
Rick Steves' European Christmas
Scandinavia
Spain & Portugal

BLU-RAY

Celtic Charms
Eastern Europe Favorites
European Christmas
Italy Through the Back Door
Surprising Cities of Europe

PHRASE BOOKS & DICTIONARIES

French
French, Italian & German
German
Italian
Portuguese
Spanish

JOURNALS

Rick Steves' Pocket Travel Journal
Rick Steves' Travel Journal

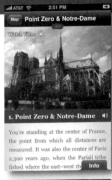

APPS

Rick Steves' Ancient Rome Tour
Rick Steves' Historic Paris Walk
Rick Steves' Louvre Tour
Rick Steves' Orsay Museum Tour
Rick Steves' St. Peter's Basilica Tour
Rick Steves' Versailles

PLANNING MAPS

Britain, Ireland & London
Europe
France & Paris
Germany, Austria & Switzerland
Ireland
Italy
Spain & Portugal

Rick Steves' Guidebook Series

Country Guides

Rick Steves' Best of Europe
Rick Steves' Croatia &
    Slovenia
Rick Steves' Eastern Europe
Rick Steves' England
Rick Steves' France
Rick Steves' Germany

Rick Steves' Great Britain
Rick Steves' Ireland
Rick Steves' Italy
Rick Steves' Portugal
Rick Steves' Scandinavia
Rick Steves' Spain
Rick Steves' Switzerland

City and Regional Guides

Rick Steves' Amsterdam,
    Bruges & Brussels
Rick Steves' Athens &
    the Peloponnese
Rick Steves' Budapest
Rick Steves' Florence &
    Tuscany
Rick Steves' Istanbul
Rick Steves' London

Rick Steves' Paris
Rick Steves' Prague &
    the Czech Republic
Rick Steves' Provence &
    the French Riviera
Rick Steves' Rome
Rick Steves' Venice
Rick Steves' Vienna,
    Salzburg & Tirol

Rick Steves' Phrase Books

French
French/Italian/German
German
Italian
Portuguese
Spanish

Snapshot Guides

Excerpted chapters from country guides, such as *Rick Steves'
Snapshot Barcelona, Rick Steves' Snapshot Scotland,* and
Rick Steves' Snapshot Hill Towns of Central Italy.

Pocket Guides (new in 2011)

Condensed, pocket-size, full-color guides to Europe's top
cities: Paris, London, and Rome.

Other Books

Rick Steves' Europe 101: History and Art for the Traveler
Rick Steves' Europe Through the Back Door
Rick Steves' European Christmas
Rick Steves' Postcards from Europe
Rick Steves' Travel as a Political Act

Avalon Travel
a member of the Perseus Books Group
1700 Fourth Street
Berkeley, CA 94710

Text © 2010 by Rick Steves
Maps © 2010 by Europe Through the Back Door
Printed in the United States of America by Worzalla
First printing August 2010

Portions of this book were originally published in *Rick Steves' Mona Winks* © 2001, 1998, 1996, 1993, 1988 by Rick Steves and Gene Openshaw, and in *Rick Steves' Italy* © 2010, 2009, 2008, 2007, 2006, 2005, 2004, 2003, 2002, 2001, 2000 by Rick Steves.

ISBN: 978-1-59880-659-5
ISSN: 1538-1595

For the latest on Rick's lectures, guidebooks, tours, public radio show, and public television series, contact Europe Through the Back Door, Box 2009, Edmonds, WA 98020, tel. 425/771-8303, fax 425/771-0833, www.ricksteves.com, rick@ricksteves.com.

Europe Through the Back Door Reviewing Editor: Cameron Hewitt
ETBD Editors: Sarah McCormic, Jennifer Madison Davis, Gretchen Strauch, Tom Griffin, Cathy Lu
ETBD Managing Editor: Risa Laib
Avalon Travel Senior Editor and Series Manager: Madhu Prasher
Avalon Travel Project Editor: Kelly Lydick
Copy Editor: Patrick Collins
Proofreader: Jamie Andrade
Indexer: Claire Splan
Cover Design: Kimberly Glyder Design
Graphic Content Director: Laura VanDeventer
Maps & Graphics: David C. Hoerlein, Laura VanDeventer, Lauren Mills, Barb Geisler, Mike Morgenfeld, Brice Ticen
Production & Typesetting: McGuire Barber Design
Photography: Rick Steves, David C. Hoerlein, Laura VanDeventer, Dominic Bonuccelli, Bruce VanDeventer, Michael Potter, Gene Openshaw, Jennifer Hauseman, p. 87, St. Mark's Basilica interior golden mosaic of Jesus Christ, Venice © Peter Barritt/Alamy
Front Cover Photo: Grand Canal © Cameron Hewitt
Front Matter Color Photos: p. i, St. Mark's Basilica, Venice, Italy © Rick Steves